When Norms Collide

WHEN NORMS COLLIDE

Local Responses to Activism against Female
Genital Mutilation and Early Marriage

Karisa Cloward

OXFORD
UNIVERSITY PRESS

OXFORD
UNIVERSITY PRESS

Oxford University Press is a department of the University of Oxford. It furthers
the University's objective of excellence in research, scholarship, and education
by publishing worldwide. Oxford is a registered trade mark of Oxford University
Press in the UK and certain other countries.

Published in the United States of America by Oxford University Press
198 Madison Avenue, New York, NY 10016, United States of America.

Library of Congress Cataloging-in-Publication Data
Cloward, Karisa, author.
When norms collide : local responses to activism against female genital mutilation and early
marriage / Karisa Cloward.
  pages cm
Includes bibliographical references and index.
ISBN 978-0-19-027491-7 (hardcover : alk. paper) — ISBN 978-0-19-027492-4 (pbk. : alk. paper)
1. Female circumcision—Kenya—Case studies.   2. Child marriage—Kenya—Case studies.
3. Teenage marriage—Kenya—Case studies.   4. Maasai (African people)—Kenya—Social life
and customs.   5. Samburu (African people)—Kenya—Social life and customs.
6. Social influence.   7. Social norms—Kenya.   8. Human rights advocacy—Kenya.   I. Title.
GN484C65 2016
392.1096762—dc23
2015028720

9 8 7 6 5 4 3 2 1
Printed by Sheridan, USA

For my parents

CONTENTS

FIGURES AND TABLES

FIGURES

TABLES

ACKNOWLEDGMENTS

I have been thinking about this research project, in one form or another, for 15 years. Motivated by a deep interest in women's human rights issues, I first started writing papers about female genital mutilation (FGM) as an undergraduate, where my senior thesis investigated variation in the spread of national anti-FGM laws. In graduate school I clarified my focus and began to identify theoretical frames that would help me evaluate practices like FGM and early marriage as political and social phenomena. Completing my dissertation involved a rich field experience and an opportunity to engage at length with the people and practices I had long been reading about, introducing nuance into my thinking about traditional practices. In the years since, I have worked to build a finished text that does justice to the issues I care about, the theoretical debates with which I've engaged, and the communities I've studied. This book has been a labor of love, and one that would not have been possible without the advice, assistance, and support of many incredible people.

Because the book began its life as a doctoral dissertation, particular thanks are owed to the members of my advising committee at Yale University. The chair of the committee, Frances Rosenbluth, helped me to think about this project from different perspectives, introduced me to new literatures, and provided a steady stream of encouragement throughout the process. Susan Hyde always made herself available to me as a sounding board and armchair psychiatrist, and never failed to provide thoughtful comments on draft chapters. She also imparted advice at a critical stage of the project's formulation, helping me to crystallize the theoretical contribution I wanted to make, and she has continued to be a source of support and advice in the years since. Elisabeth Wood taught me the value of good qualitative skills and responsible fieldwork, provided detailed and helpful feedback on my work, and generally pushed me to be better. Don Green shared with me his passion for experiments and helped me to think carefully about causal processes and empirical evidence.

Along the way, many others have provided ideas, feedback, and moral support. At Yale, Ryan Sheely was an invaluable source of information and contacts in advance of my first field trip to Kenya, and helped me to conceptualize my methodological approach in the field. Robert Person, Mario Chacon, and Pierre Landry each helped me extensively with the task of managing and analyzing the survey data I collected. Chris Blattman served as an external reviewer of my dissertation, and helped me to focus on methodological rigor and transparency. Additionally, participants of the Jackson Institute / MacMillan Center International Relations Workshop at the Department of Political Science provided very useful feedback on early drafts of several chapters, and I received additional feedback from participants at several panels in which I participated at American Political Science Association and International Studies Association annual meetings.

At Southern Methodist University, the John G. Tower Center for Political Studies sponsored a "book-in-progress" workshop that substantially shaped the book's final form. I am especially indebted to Aili Mari Tripp and Catherine Weaver for traveling to Dallas, reading the manuscript in full, and providing uniquely incisive and constructive comments. I am also grateful for the feedback I received from SMU colleagues who attended the workshop, including Jim Hollifield (also the Director of the Tower Center), Chelsea Brown, Shubha Ghosh, Jill Kelly, Joe Kobylka, Dayna Oscherwitz, Harold Stanley, Hiroki Takeuchi, and Sandy Thatcher. In general, I am thankful for the support and collegiality of my colleagues and the staff in the SMU Department of Political Science. I must particularly thank Melissa Emmert for her indispensable assistance in creating the maps found in the book. In addition, Pam Corley, Sheri Kunovich, Chelsea Brown, and Hiroki Takeuchi gave feedback and guidance as part of a small research productivity group. Beyond SMU, Heidi Hardt provided ongoing encouragement and navigational assistance through the vagaries of the book-publishing process, and Alexander Betts supplied notes on the manuscript's framing.

I would like to thank Angela Chnapko, my editor at Oxford University Press, who has been an enthusiastic booster for this book and who patiently guided me through the editorial process. I must especially thank Gerry Mackie for reviewing the manuscript and for drawing on his deep knowledge of social norms, FGM, and early marriage to provide incredibly thoughtful and detailed comments. My thanks also go to the other, anonymous reviewer, who helped me in particular to think about how I could frame the book for cross-disciplinary audiences.

My research was made possible through generous institutional financial support. Yale University provided research funds through the Institute for Social and Policy Studies, the Whitney and Betty MacMillan Center for International and Area Studies, and the Georg Walter Leitner Program in International and Comparative Political Economy. SMU supported the book's revision and publication through the University Research Council and the Tower Center for Political Studies.

In the course of my fieldwork in Kenya I came to count on the assistance of a large number of people. Richard Legei was my go-to source for insight into the Maasai community. He introduced me to many valuable contacts, recruited survey enumerators, and served as an 11th-hour translator. He was also a good friend who helped me adjust to a new place. Francis Merinyi at ILAMAIYO, Lotte Lund at Pastoralist Women for Health and Education, and Agnes Pareiyo at Tasaru Ntomonok Initiative were each gracious enough to partner with me in the administration of my original survey. Josephine Kulea was a great source of contacts, information, and insight into the Samburu community, and Oriatta Lemungasi helped me to recruit survey enumerators. Reverend Peter Nkamasiai, Elizabeth Ndilai, and Chief Nicholas Nkunkuu in Duka Moja; Pastor Sam Letapi and Father Angello Guchu in Oldonyiro; Francis Merinyi in Dol Dol; and Morten Kattenhøj, James Koinare, and Wenslaus Musindayi in Nanyuki each took it upon themselves to help me locate and interview countless other people. Yiaku People's Association in Mukogodo and World Vision Kenya in Mau invited me to witness and participate in alternative rites of passage that they conducted as part of their activities against FGM. And Catherine Ndungo in the Department of Gender and Development at Kenyatta University provided me with a local university affiliation and assisted me in securing a research permit.

Along the way, a number of people selflessly took me into their homes and treated me like family. Margaret Sankei in Nairege Enkare, Francis and Jacline Merinyi in Dol Dol, Ruth Kesuwna and Ann in Narok, and Maria von Weissenberg in Nairobi each opened their lives to a near stranger. Resian, Sharon, and Gloryannah Sankei and Francah Naserian became my sisters. Megan and Joshua Hershey allowed me to share their apartment for several months and served me delicious meals that reminded me of home. As a fellow political scientist, Megan's hospitality also gave me the opportunity to have meaningful discussions about the direction of my research while still in the field. Andrew Dinsmore, Jennifer Douthwaite, Graham Stirling, Gayle Kothari, Naftali Honig, Njeri Macheru, Annalise Blum, and Siva Sundaresan supplied a much-needed social life. John Mureithi, Simon, and Shawnee at Boulangerie plied me with coffee and made me feel at home.

Finally, this book would not be what it is without the love and support of my friends and family, and especially of my parents, Renate Tritz and Kell Cloward. Throughout this long process, they have anchored me to reality, buoyed my confidence, and lent a sympathetic ear when necessary. Writing a book comes with many emotional ups and downs, and they have been my constant cheerleaders and support system from beginning to end.

Some of the text in this book has been drawn from two previously published articles, and has been reprinted with permission from Cambridge University Press and Springer, respectively:

"False Commitments: Local Misrepresentation and the International Norms against Female Genital Mutilation and Early Marriage." *International Organization* 68.3 (2014): 495–526.

"Elites, Exit Options, and Social Barriers to Norm Change: The Complex Case of Female Genital Mutilation." *Studies in Comparative International Development* 50.3 (2015): 378–407.

When Norms Collide

CHAPTER 1

Introduction

I n February 1979, the World Health Organization held a seminar called "Traditional Practices Affecting the Health of Women and Children" in Khartoum, Sudan. Participants from nine African and Middle Eastern countries discussed the health consequences of several "traditional practices," including female "circumcision" and early and child marriage, and shared details about the status of these practices in their own countries. The seminar concluded by making a series of recommendations, including recommending the creation of national policies, national commissions, and education programs to abolish female circumcision, and recommending the creation of education programs and legislation to discourage childhood marriage (World Health Organization 1979). That same year, the United Nations Children's Fund issued its first statement opposing female circumcision, and the UN General Assembly adopted the Convention on the Elimination of All Forms of Discrimination Against Women (CEDAW), which recognized harmful customary practices and child marriages as violations of women's human rights (United Nations Children's Fund 2013a, 10).

Coming in the middle of the 1975–1985 UN Decade for Women, these events helped kick off a wave of international interest in harmful traditional practices and violence against women. In 1980, female circumcision was a major topic of discussion at the Non-Governmental Organizations Forum of the Second World Conference on Women in Copenhagen, where it sparked significant debate among the African and Western delegates (Dorkenoo 1994, 62). This was followed by the adoption of the Convention on the Rights of the Child in 1989 and the African Charter on the Rights and Welfare of the Child in 1990, both of which called for the protection of children from harmful traditional practices. Violence against women was declared to be a human rights violation at the World Conference on Human Rights in Vienna in 1993, and the Beijing Declaration and Platform for Action (which came out of the Fourth World Conference on Women in Beijing in 1995) called for the abandonment of both female circumcision—renamed "female genital mutilation," or FGM, by activists—and early marriage. Since the mid-1990s, the United Nations and other international and regional organizations have reinforced their opposition to these practices through additional treaties and consensus documents such as the 2002 UN General Assembly resolution on traditional or customary practices affecting the health of women and girls and the 2005 Protocol to the African Charter on Human and People's Rights on the Rights of Women in Africa (also known as the Maputo Protocol), through a number of UN agency resolutions and interagency statements, and through awareness-raising activities such as the International Day of Zero Tolerance to Female Genital Mutilation and the Day of the African Child. The UN also appointed a Special Rapporteur on Violence Against Women, Radhika Coomaraswamy, in 1994, a Donors Working Group on Female Genital Mutilation/Cutting (FGM/C) was founded in 2001, and the United Nations Population Fund and United Nations Children's Fund undertook a Joint Programme on FGM/C beginning in 2007. The efforts of these international governmental organizations have been buoyed by and have occurred partly in response to increasing pressure from many international and domestic nongovernmental organizations (NGOs), which have built transnational coalitions on violence against women with the rallying cry, "Women's rights are human rights" (A. M. Clark, Friedman, and Hochstetler 1998, 15–16).

Yet practices like FGM and early marriage persist, performed by diverse groups for a wide range of reasons. An estimated 125 million women and girls alive today have undergone FGM, with as many as three million African girls at risk annually (United Nations Children's Fund 2013a, 114). FGM is practiced in 29 countries in Africa and the Middle East, as well as among isolated groups in Southeast Asia and among some immigrant communities in North America and Europe.[1] Early marriages occur in all regions of the world, but survey data suggest that at least 58 million girls

1. There is also evidence that genital surgeries, including removal of the clitoris, were performed in Europe and North America from the early part of the 19th century through the first half of the 20th century as a medical treatment for a variety of perceived psychological and behavioral conditions, including hysteria, excessive masturbation, and nymphomania (Gruenbaum 2001, 9–12). In this context the practice did not constitute a social norm.

were married before age 18 in just the first decade of the 21st century, and that 15 million of those girls were married before age 15 (Hervish and Feldman-Jacobs 2011, 1). All told, more than one in three women between the ages of 20 and 24 in the developing world were married by the time they turned 18, including 46 percent in South Asia and 39 percent in sub-Saharan Africa (United Nations Children's Fund 2009, 10).

The larger transnational campaign on violence against women has created and now promotes international norms against both FGM and early marriage, sometimes linking the two norms together. At the same time, however, many communities subscribe to local norms supporting these practices. What happens when the conflicting international and local norms collide? When does transnational activism lead individuals and communities to abandon local norms and embrace international ones?

These broader theoretical questions can frame the challenges that activists attempting to tackle gender violence have encountered on the ground. In Kenya, one of the first efforts to address FGM was organized by Maendeleo Ya Wanawake (MYWO), a national women's organization. MYWO began FGM sensitization activities in 1993, and in 1996 it partnered with the Program for Appropriate Technologies in Health (PATH), an American NGO, to implement the first "alternative rite of passage" program, essentially attempting to mirror the symbolic transition to adulthood that female circumcision provides for girls in some communities. By 2001, some 3,000 girls in five districts had participated in the "Circumcision Through Words," and the program gained substantial recognition for its efforts, both in Kenya and abroad (Chege, Askew, and Liku 2001; Mohamud, Radeny, and Ringheim 2006).

But though the program was popular, was sustained over time, and endeavored to tailor activities to particular local contexts, the actual results were mixed. An external evaluation of the program showed that, among the Maasai population of Narok District, participants and their families did increasingly embrace the activists' normative messages about the health and human rights consequences of FGM (Chege, Askew, and Liku 2001, 28–30). There was also evidence that the program reduced participant families' intention to circumcise their daughters in the future, and increased support for discontinuing female circumcision in the community generally (Chege, Askew, and Liku 2001, 32). Yet there were significant complications. Girls' parents showed a "notable lack of enthusiasm" for participating in and contributing to the public ceremony that concluded the alternative rite, and in some cases it appeared that neither the participating girls nor their parents fully understood what they had signed up for, leading in certain instances to the girls being circumcised at a later date (Chege,

Askew, and Liku 2001, 21–22). More generally, the evaluation showed that the local norm supporting female circumcision continued to carry a lot of weight (Chege, Askew, and Liku 2001, 32–33). Many families persisted in seeing real value in the practice, or worried about what others in the community would think or do if they were to reject circumcision (Chege, Askew, and Liku 2001, 28). Though program staff were themselves quite optimistic about the long-term prospects for change, they too recognized a number of potential hurdles, including increasing medicalization of circumcision and a tendency for the practice to go underground (Mohamud, Radeny, and Ringheim 2006, 101). In all, the evidence suggests that though many families accepted parts of the normative message against FGM, they did not always adapt their behavior in the way that activists desired. Other families continued to demonstrate significant resistance to any type of change.

In the 20 years since the MYWO program was first introduced, many additional efforts have been undertaken to try to stop FGM (and early marriage), in Kenya and elsewhere. While some of these efforts have been more successful than others, all have faced the significant challenge of trying to promote a set of ideas in the face of built-in resistance on the ground. But though the obstacles activists face in attempting to change traditional practices are unavoidable, that doesn't mean they are necessarily insurmountable.

In this book I present a theory of individual and community-level norm change in the presence of a direct conflict between international and local norms. I argue that, conditional on exposure to an international normative message, individuals can decide to change their attitudes, their actual behavior, and the public image they present. That is, once people *know* about the international norm, they can alter what they *think*, what they *do*, and what they *say*. Through extensive field research employing an innovative mixed-methodological strategy, I find that the impact of transnational activism on individual decision-making substantially depends on the salience of the international and local norms to their respective proponents. I further find that where there are significant barriers to defecting from local norms, meaningful norm change becomes quite complex and exhibits both social and temporal dimensions.

THEORETICAL PERSPECTIVES ON NORMS AND TRANSNATIONAL ACTIVISM

Many international relations scholars have investigated the role and importance of norms in shaping behavior in the international arena. Following

Finnemore and Sikkink (1998, 891), I define a norm as a shared "standard of appropriate behavior for actors with a given identity." The key characteristic of a norm is that it carries a "prescriptive ... quality of 'oughtness'" (Finnemore and Sikkink 1998, 891).[2] Norms often have a moral component—people should comply with a norm because it is the right thing to do—but they always have a social component—people should comply with a norm because others expect them to. The set of actors who share and potentially enforce the norm can be described as the reference group (Mackie et al. 2014). Norms may emerge within a given reference group through incremental adaptation or a more deliberate process, but ultimately a norm can be said to exist when there is collective, although not necessarily universal, agreement on the proper way for group members to behave, and all members are aware of the consensus—the expectation of compliance is common knowledge. Once such a consensus is reached, those who violate the norm will be subject to the judgment of the group and may feel pressure to hide, minimize, or justify their actions (Finnemore and Sikkink 1998, 891–92).

However, a group's collective internalization of a particular norm does not necessarily mean that adherence to the norm is performed in an unconscious or completely reflexive way. While some norms may be so deeply internalized that violations are in fact unthinkable (in the most literal sense of the word—the norm is so fundamentally embedded within a reference group that the possibility of violating it simply doesn't occur to anyone, making compliance automatic), this is not a necessary characteristic of a norm. Indeed, in many cases people are acutely aware of a particular norm and actively choose whether to comply with it.

In such a conscious decision-making process, there is room for both morality and rationality. Thus, the paradigmatic division between constructivist and rational choice approaches in international relations is unhelpful when applied to norms (Klotz 1995, 166). Though the study of norms has traditionally been the purview of constructivists, arguing that "ideas matter," there is nothing fundamentally irrational about the notion that people will often choose to act so as to maximize positive social sanctions and minimize negative ones. Norm-compliant behavior can certainly involve sincere adherence to moral and social precepts, but it can also be strategic and self-interested (Checkel 2005, 818; Nadelmann 1990, 480). Indeed, Finnemore and Sikkink (1998, 912) identify two branches of norm analysis—one that is predicated on a logic of appropriateness, in

---

2. Thus, I am excluding the common usage of the term to describe pure behavioral regularities that lack prescriptive or injunctive content.

which actors conform to norms "because they understand the behavior to be good, desirable, and appropriate," and one that is predicated on a logic of utility maximization,[3] in which "actors ... conform to norms because norms help them get what they want."[4] They usefully point out that while a lot of debate has centered on the question of which of these two logics is correct, the fact of the matter is that they are not mutually exclusive. Thus, the more relevant question is "Which logic applies to what kinds of actors under what circumstances?" (Finnemore and Sikkink 1998, 913). Following that advice, this book remains agnostic about the essential bases of norm compliance and consequently observes a good deal of variation in whether people respond reflexively or deliberately to norms, and whether they are motivated by material, reputational, or ideational considerations.

Beyond definitional and conceptual questions about the functioning of norms, the international norms literature has been primarily occupied with questions about how and why particular norms emerge and about the conditions under which norms diffuse and influence behavior. While some norms scholarship focuses on the instrumental creation of norms that facilitate interstate cooperation, primarily within the context of international institutions (Keohane 1984; Krasner 1985), a significant branch of the norms literature addresses the development and promotion of "principled" international norms by transnational activists, or "norm entrepreneurs" (Finnemore and Sikkink 1998; Florini 2000; Keck and Sikkink 1998; Klotz 1995; Nadelmann 1990; Price 1998; Risse, Ropp, and Sikkink 1999, 2013; Schmitz 2001; Sikkink 1993; Smith, Chatfield, and Pagnucco 1997; Tarrow 2005; Thomas 2001).[5] For example, in a relatively early work Ethan Nadelmann (1990, 484–85) outlines a "common evolutionary pattern" for what he terms "global prohibition regimes," in which transnational moral entrepreneurs problematize previously acceptable behaviors and then employ strategies such as coercion, material incentives, and persuasion in order to promote prohibitionary international conventions and domestic laws. The common feature in the principled-norm scholarship is the existence of networks of morally motivated state and nonstate actors, who deploy various tools at their disposal in an attempt to leverage international norm-compliant behavior from the otherwise recalcitrant targets of their activism. The principled norms under

3. March and Olsen (1998, 949) describe this as a "logic of consequences."
4. Peyton Young (2008) notes that norms can serve a pure coordination function, and thus can be held in place solely in the interest of reducing transaction costs. Such norms are likely to be self-enforcing, but can still be considered to fall under the label of utility maximization—conforming to the norm makes social life easier.
5. Price (1998, 615) uses "the term 'transnational' to refer to interactions across national boundaries where at least one actor is a nonstate agent."

investigation have included a wide range of human rights issues—torture, apartheid, and land mine usage are but three examples—as well as various issues of environmental protection, political rights, and democratization.

Within this literature, Keck and Sikkink's (1998) "boomerang" model has been particularly influential. The basic premise of the model is that, in a given country, domestic groups may oppose some policy or action being pursued by their own government and yet have limited ability to directly influence the government's decisions. When this occurs, the domestic activists may try to bolster their position by seeking out more powerful international allies who can apply pressure to the state on the domestic activists' behalf (1998, 12). Through their efforts they form what Keck and Sikkink call transnational advocacy networks (TANs)— groups consisting primarily of NGOs, international governmental organizations, and states "who are bound together by shared values, a common discourse, and dense exchanges of information and services" around a particular issue (1998, 2). TANs employ a range of strategies, including monitoring states' behavior and framing and disseminating relevant information, in order to persuade, shame, or negatively sanction noncompliant states (1998, 16).

While the basic boomerang model is fairly simple, the processes by which TANs exert their influence are neither static nor uniform. Indeed, a number of scholars have conceptualized these processes in terms of "stages" of change. Keck and Sikkink themselves describe five stages of network influence: an initial period in which TANs work to generate international attention and engage in agenda setting, a second period in which TANs elicit discursive commitments from their targets, a third period in which the targets make procedural changes, a fourth period in which they make policy changes, and a final period in which they make meaningful behavior changes (1998, 25). Thus, the accomplishments of each stage serve as the foundation for subsequent stages.

Risse and Sikkink (1999) build on these insights to generate a more detailed and dynamic "spiral" model focused on transnational human rights advocacy, in which the causal mechanisms underlying norm socialization change as the socialization process progresses. In early phases of socialization, target states are likely to engage in instrumentally motivated adaptation to external pressure, attempting to deny the validity of international norms or making small tactical concessions. In subsequent phases, states can become trapped by their own instrumental rhetoric, and TANs are able to use tactics such as argumentation, dialogue, and shaming to pressure states into conforming with their prior rhetorical commitments to international norms. If these prior phases succeed and international norms gain "prescriptive status" in the target state, then over time—and with continued pressure from TANs—norm compliance may become institutionalized and habitual.

In addition to looking at the processes by which norms influence individual target states, scholarship has focused on the processes by which norms diffuse across states. For example, Finnemore and Sikkink (1998) describe a "norm life cycle" with three stages and emphasize that the causal logic underlying states' commitment to international norms varies according to the stage of the life cycle. The international norm emerges slowly in the first stage, as norm entrepreneurs work to persuade a critical mass of relevant states to adopt the norm and become "norm leaders." The recruitment of such a critical mass generates a tipping point, which triggers a second stage of broad and rapid norm acceptance by most remaining states—what Finnemore and Sikkink call a "norm cascade." In this second stage, the previously noncompliant states, or "norm followers," are motivated to imitate the norm leaders based on pressure to conform and on a desire for international legitimation and esteem. The active socialization of the second stage then ultimately gives way to habituation in the third stage, as both norm leaders and norm followers fully internalize the norm. Price (1998, 640) makes a similar point in discussing international efforts to ban land mines, arguing that while the early stages of a transnational campaign tend to be characterized by moral proselytism, emulation becomes the more important dynamic in later stages, as instrumental motives push states to adopt international norms in order to avoid being labeled "rogue."

One thing that binds the various "stage" models together is a primary focus on the international level and on the actions of *norm makers*—central questions relate to the nature of the relationships between actors in transnational networks and to the strategies these norm entrepreneurs use to leverage desired change. But a second wave of the norms literature has placed increasing emphasis on sources of variation in the effectiveness of international norm promotion efforts, particularly in terms of the role of domestic politics (e.g., Betts and Orchard 2014a).[6] Some of this literature has focused on institutional constraints and on domestic actor interests: Risse-Kappen (1995, 22), for instance, argues that transnational actors' influence on state policymakers is conditioned on domestic political institutions, policy networks, and social structure, and Betts (2013, 43) highlights the role of domestic elites' interests in shaping international

---

6. The earlier norm entrepreneurship literature does not completely overlook domestic factors. Finnemore and Sikkink (1998, 893), for example, acknowledge that "international norms must always work their influence through the filter of domestic structures and domestic norms."

norm implementation. But a significant chunk of the "domestic fit" literature has focused on aspects of domestic culture.

For example, Legro (1997, 37) emphasizes the importance of organizational culture within the relevant domestic decision-making group, arguing that culture "shapes organizational identity, priorities, perception, and capabilities," and thus significantly affects the domestic reception of international norms. He recognizes that "principles and beliefs that characterize . . . subsystemic communities may be found to be as or more important than those of international society" (Legro 1997, 58). Looking specifically at warfare decisions by military bureaucracies, Legro finds that militaries' existing beliefs about "the appropriate ways to fight wars" largely determine whether these organizations embrace international norms prohibiting the use of specific types of force.

Checkel (1999, 87) makes a somewhat broader point about domestic culture in introducing the concept of cultural match, which he defines as "a situation where the prescriptions embodied in an international norm are convergent with domestic norms." Checkel argues that the extent of cultural match—viewed as a spectrum ranging from complete congruence to complete incongruence—significantly affects the speed with which international norms diffuse in specific domestic contexts. He makes the additional observation that because it is generally easier for norms to become institutionalized in the domestic arena than in the international one, state agents who encounter norm incongruence are likely to feel the pull of the domestic norm more strongly (Checkel 1999, 108).

Cortell and Davis (2000, 73) take things a step further, identifying four domestic factors that contribute to the "domestic salience of international norms." In addition to borrowing Checkel's concept of cultural match, they highlight the importance of political rhetoric by national elites, the material interests of various domestic groups, and domestic political institutions. Significantly, they note that the domestic fit of international norms is dynamic. Both international and local norms can evolve, which "implies that the match between the two sets of normative structures may change over time—both greater consonance and dissonance are possible" (Cortell and Davis 2000, 75).

While the dynamism Cortell and Davis describe entails essentially independent changes in international and local norms, Amitav Acharya (2011) proposes a theory of "constitutive localization" that involves an interactive process of contestation between international and local norms. He explicitly stresses the agency of *norm takers*, arguing that domestic actors can in fact reconstitute international norms to suit local realities. Acharya appreciates the fact that existing local norms can be deeply institutionalized, such that it may not be possible to adopt international norms without first actively adapting them through various discursive strategies.[7] Thus, congruence between international and local norms is something that, under the right conditions, can be *created* by strategic local actors.

These authors make an important contribution in recognizing that new international norms do not enter a normative vacuum at the domestic level (Acharya 2011, 5). But both the domestic fit literature and the earlier wave of transnational advocacy literature have tended to focus mainly on the ways in which international norms influence *state* behavior, with more limited attention to the mechanisms by which international norms might diffuse at the subnational level or among nonstate actors, challenging local norms (Simmons 2010, 292).[8]

Part of the explanation for this state-centrism hinges on implicit assumptions about the identities and interests of the various actors involved in norm entrepreneurship. In Keck and Sikkink's (1998) boomerang model, for example, transnational activists are essentially representing the interests of the domestic population against the state. That is, actors both "above" and "below" the state—at the international and domestic level—are largely united in their support for some "progressive" international norm. The state is the relevant target for activism, and thus the appropriate object of study, because the state is the only actor holding out against this norm.

Such an assumption makes sense given the types of international norms being examined in much of the existing literature. For transnational campaigns related to such topics as chemical weapons, land mines, apartheid, forced "disappearances," suffrage, and large dam construction, the state is the natural referent (Keck and Sikkink 1998; Khagram 2004; Klotz 1995; Legro 1997; Price 1998; Ropp and Sikkink 1999). In all of these cases, the state is the actor violating international norms, and so it is the state that must be persuaded to change. But not all international norms fit this mold, and states are not always the (only) bad guys.

To begin with, sometimes state conformity with an international norm actually precedes widespread domestic demand for norm compliance, and

7. A number of other authors have recognized the potential legitimacy and persuasiveness of competing normative frames and meanings (see Jetschke and Liese 2013, 35; Jetschke 2011, 4; Payne 2001, 42; Wiener 2009, 177).

8. Though Acharya (2011, 16) discusses contestation between international and local norms, this language is a bit misleading. What he refers to as "local" norms are actually Asian regional norms and can be construed as local only insofar as the regional level is local relative to the international level. His attention remains focused on the behavior and preferences of state elites.

norm-compliant state policies may even encounter outright resistance in some domestic arenas (Cortell and Davis 2000, 74–75; Simmons 2009, 200). For instance, state elites have introduced legislative gender quotas or reserved seats for women in several dozen countries worldwide since the 1980s, which is consistent with an emergent international norm about the importance of women's political representation (Dahlerup 2006). However, in some countries this policy move has occurred despite the absence of any significant domestic mobilization on behalf of quotas (Krook 2006, 313).

This outcome runs counter to the expectations of the boomerang and spiral models, both of which argue that sustained domestic pressure is critical to states' decisions to change their behavior (Keck and Sikkink 1998; Risse and Sikkink 1999).[9] But at least in the case of gender quotas, the state remains the primary target for transnational activism. Quota policy is generally made at the national level, and the state has full authority over its implementation, such that any domestic groups that oppose the policy are unable to opt out. When, however, states attempt to implement laws and policies governing the behavior of *nonstate actors*, one has to ask not just about the state's commitment but also about its *capabilities* (Chayes and Chayes 1993, 194; Chayes and Chayes 1995, 14). In particular, where the activity in question can be concealed to some degree, states are likely to have limited enforcement capacity (Nadelmann 1990, 486). For example, laws prohibiting recreational drug use and prostitution are routinely flouted. And the enforcement problem is likely to be exacerbated where the individuals or groups that are subject to the law fundamentally disagree with its underlying norm—just as the international community is rarely able to force states to comply with norms with which they don't agree, states are rarely able to force their citizens to comply with norms with which *they* don't agree. The Prohibition era in the United States is a prime example of state failure to impose new norms of behavior from above—many people simply found creative ways to evade the law while maintaining the local norm that said alcohol consumption was acceptable behavior (Miron and Zwiebel 1991).

Enforcement challenges are further compounded in weak or failed states, where the central state bureaucracy simply lacks the power apparatus and resources to control its entire territory and routinely enforce many of its laws (Herbst 2000; Jackson and Rosberg 1982; Migdal 1988;

---

9. However, the diffusion of gender quotas *is* consistent with earlier work by Finnemore (1993) on international actors as "teachers" of norms, in which she suggests that states can be genuinely persuaded of the validity of international norms even in the absence of significant pressure.

Risse 2011). Under such conditions of limited statehood, individuals and groups will have significantly greater freedom to pick and choose which laws to obey and which to ignore, guided by their own interests and beliefs. Thus, to the extent that local norms conflict with national policy, one should expect low levels of compliance with the latter (Börzel 2002). A number of African countries, for example, have fought a losing battle against poaching of endangered and threatened species. In addition to commercial hunting of large game such as elephants and rhinoceroses for their tusks and horns, respectively, many communities engage in culturally sanctioned "bushmeat" hunting, including hunting of a number of vulnerable primate species. Such behavior has proved relatively immune to national laws attempting to protect specific species or territories (Leader-Williams and Albon 1988; Rowcliffe, Merode, and Cowlishaw 2004; Wilkie and Carpenter 1999).

Some more recent research has recognized that limited state capacity and nonstate norm violators pose problems for prominent theories of transnational activism. Lutz and Sikkink (2000, 639), for example, find that efforts to achieve international norm compliance can slow or stall when decision-making about a given action is decentralized. In particular, they point to the fact that local political actors can make decisions about the use of torture without the direct consent of the central state. Morrow (2007, 561) makes a similar point about limitations to states' control of their own soldiers' behavior during warfare, as does Simmons (2009, 200) with respect to fair trials. Börzel et al. (2010) and VanDeveer and Dabelko (2001) argue that state administrative capacity significantly impacts the degree of compliance with European law and with international environmental agreements, respectively, while Betts and Orchard (2014b) note that capacity issues can vary subnationally. In addition, a number of researchers have begun to analyze the extent to which nonstate actors such as corporations and insurgent groups are susceptible to international norms and transnational activism (Börzel et al. 2011; DeSombre 2006; Flohr et al. 2010; Greenhill, Mosley, and Prakash 2009; Jo and Thomson 2014; Prakash and Potoski 2007). And in an edited volume that seeks to update and extend their original spiral model, Risse, Ropp, and Sikkink (2013) acknowledge both that limited statehood inhibits norm compliance and that norm socialization becomes substantially more complex where states assume legal responsibility for compliance but the norm in question actually pertains to the behavior of private actors. Several contributors to the volume then take up these issues in greater detail (Börzel and Risse 2013; Brysk 2013; Deitelhoff and Wolf 2013; Jo and Bryant 2013; Mwangi, Rieth, and Schmitz 2013).

This increased recognition of nonstate actors as potential norm violators is promising, particularly where the researchers have taken the additional step of actually evaluating the conditions under which nonstate actors might choose to comply with international norms. But at least thus far, these more ambitious projects have concentrated on the behavior of large, structured, relatively hierarchical nonstate *organizations* such as corporations, industry groups, and rebel movements; there has not been commensurate attention paid to how individuals, families, and loosely bound communities might respond to international norms and transnational activism. Instead, in cases for which private citizens are the primary violators of a particular international norm, most authors have persisted in focusing almost exclusively on how that norm influences *state* behavior (Nadelmann 1990, 485). Indeed, even where the authors explicitly recognize the mismatch between the object of their analysis and the actual norm violators, this observation serves mainly as a caveat to the state-focused theory—rather than shifting the unit of analysis from states to individuals, the degree of centralized state control over a particular behavior simply becomes an additional variable in the model, complicating the process of state compliance (Risse and Ropp 2013, 19).

A similar pattern of state-centrism is observable in the subset of the transnational activism literature that addresses violence against women, despite the fact that such violence is almost universally carried out in private homes. Thus, even if a government were to make all of the appropriate international pledges and enact corresponding national laws in good faith, these state actions would be insufficient to protect women from abuse because the primary perpetrators are individuals—husbands, fathers, brothers, mothers—rather than the government. This is not to say that the state bears no responsibility for protecting women from violence—on the contrary, the state's responsibility to protect vulnerable individuals even within the private sphere is clearly codified in international law—but rather to highlight the limitations on states' powers to control individual activities and private interactions, even if one were to impute to them the very best of intentions. Under such conditions, the primary path to domestic conformity with the international norm will be through the general population, not through the state.[10]

Despite this fact, individual and community-level norm change has received scant attention. Keck and Sikkink (1998, 180, 192), for example,

---

10. Simmons (2009) finds that states' ratification of CEDAW does contribute to improved outcomes for women in several issue areas. However, the issues she considers—access to education, family-planning services, and public sector employment—involve some degree of control by the central state. Also, she finds that the positive effect of treaty ratification disappears when the state has a weak judicial system.

investigate the transnational advocacy network on violence against women as one of their cases, and though they acknowledge that such violence is carried out in the household, they ask only whether the network has effectively targeted states and international organizations. And where the literature on violence against women *has* considered the role of the general public in inhibiting norm change, the actions of the state and of activists themselves continue to dominate the discourse. Johnson (2009, 11–13), in her study of gender violence in Russia, considers whether foreign intervention aids the work of local feminist activists and promotes broader public awareness of violence against women, but when it comes to actual substantive change, the focus is primarily on state policies. Sundstrom (2005, 422, 442), also looking at the Russian case, recognizes that a hostile public may be more of a barrier to change than the state itself. However, while she does briefly consider whether the Russian women's movement, backed by international donors, has influenced some nonstate behavior—specifically, women reporting cases of domestic violence to authorities—this is secondary to the effects of activism on state conduct. And Merry (2006, 215–16) investigates how local activists appropriate and adapt the language of the international human rights regime on gender violence, but concentrates on when and how women use these reinterpreted international norms to place claims on the state, not on the men in their communities. Alison Brysk (2013, 268) goes the farthest, emphasizing in her analysis of the transnational anti-FGM campaign the necessity of working toward "multi-level change in [both] state policy and local behavior by private actors." This is a critically important point, and she takes the additional step of discussing how transnational activists' framing of FGM contributes to observed variation in the extent of local abandonment of the practice (Baer and Brysk 2009, 102–4; Brysk 2013, 271–73). But in part because her conclusions are based on anecdotal evidence from secondary sources, what's missing is a detailed exploration of the causal mechanisms driving individual and community-level behavior change.

Thus, throughout the literature (with the partial exception of Brysk), individuals and local groups appear as activists, spoilers, or secondary characters, but not as the primary targets of activism (Betts and Orchard 2014b). This is unfortunate, because there are good reasons to think that private individuals and other loosely defined groups may behave differently in response to international norm pressure than either states or more corporate nonstate actors do. In particular, transnational corporations and insurgent groups are similar to states in a couple of important respects—they are large enough and cohesive enough that their compliance with international norms can be monitored by activists, which then allows the activists to deploy a range of tools to try to hold these groups individually accountable for their behavior (Brysk 2005, 26). Private individuals and other leaderless groups, on the other hand, are generally either too small or too loosely defined to be targeted with the kinds of "naming and shaming" tactics or individualized sanctions that characterize the boomerang and spiral models, in which states' instrumental tactical concessions are later leveraged to elicit meaningful behavior change (Keck and Sikkink 1998; Risse, Ropp, and Sikkink 1999).

In the absence of systematic monitoring capability by either transnational activists or the state, significant local-level behavior change is likely to occur only where activists actually manage to convince individuals to reject existing local norms and embrace international ones—imposing a top-down legal regime will be far less effective than employing a bottom-up strategy of *persuasion*. Of course, persuading people to relinquish long-held values and beliefs is not a simple matter. The purpose of this book is thus to investigate the micro-level processes through which such persuasion occurs. Faced with an explicit conflict between international and local norms,[11] how do individuals negotiate the competing demands placed on them by their own communities and by transnational activists? Under what conditions are individuals most likely to comply with international norms? How does compliance spread through communities? And why are some communities more susceptible to transnational activism than others?

ARGUMENT OVERVIEW

Elements of Norm Change

This book attempts to explain both the processes by which activists convince individuals to embrace international norms, and the processes by which international norms diffuse across individuals and through communities.[12] Understanding these processes requires a close look at the micromechanisms

11. As opposed to a latent norm conflict in which groups hold rival norms but do not attempt to impose their respective norms on one another.
12. I define a community in geographic terms. In this way a community is distinct from, though related to, the reference group that holds a particular norm. Many but not all reference groups are geographically concentrated—group members may well range beyond a single geographic community—and some are not geographically isolated—group members may live among members of normative out-groups. I focus on geographically delimited communities largely as a practical consideration, because reference group members are likely to be most influential where they have the opportunity to interact directly with one another and potentially engage in concrete sanctioning rather than provide only abstract approval or disapproval. In effect, a community is likely to contain the "core" of a reference group.

of *norm change*, where norm change refers to the set of beliefs and behaviors that denote at least partial recognition of the legitimacy of an international norm or its underlying logic.[13] If the status quo ante is complete adherence to the local norm, then norm change involves some form of movement away from the existing local norm and toward the international norm. Specifically, I identify three discrete types of individual-level changes that contribute to the overall process of norm change.

First, individuals can change their attitudes about the logics underlying the international and local norms. All norms contain some informational content or reasoning that attempts to justify why complying with the norm constitutes appropriate behavior. This logic may be strong or weak, simple or complicated, but norms always emerge for a reason, even if that reason shifts over time.[14] Given this, attitude change involves recognition by the individual that the logic of the international norm is at least partly valid. However, it does not require complete rejection of the logic of the local norm—it is possible to be persuaded by aspects of the reasoning underpinning each norm. In the case of FGM, for example, the international norm's content is about health, gender equality, and human rights, while the local norm's content may be about any of a number of factors including tradition, cultural preservation, control of women's sexual activity, religious obligation, and transition to adulthood. Yet one can simultaneously believe that FGM has potentially significant health consequences *and* that it is an important rite of passage. Thus, attitude change is not strictly dichotomous; it can be viewed as a continuum ranging from no attitude change (complete attitudinal agreement with the local norm) to full attitude change (complete attitudinal agreement with the international norm). However, an important threshold along the continuum is the point at which the individual finds the balance of evidence to be in favor of the international norm and against the local norm.

Second, individuals can change the primary behavior covered by the international and local norms. All norms apply to the way in which people

---

13. Norm change does not, however, require that an individual recognize the international norm as an "international norm" (e.g., know that it is codified in international law or that people in many other countries support and adhere to it).

14. When norms are mature and have been broadly internalized, people may not give much thought to the logic of the norm, and may instead comply with it purely out of habit or convenience because doing otherwise would require significant mental effort (whether or not they are aware that people in other reference groups subscribe to alternative norms). The introduction of a competing norm may be what forces people to actually think carefully about the content of their existing norm. On close inspection, they may find this content compelling, or they may not. The logic of the competing norm is, of course, also open to scrutiny.

behave—norms govern actions, not beliefs. Thus, to say that an international and local norm directly conflict with one another is to say that they demand incompatible behaviors. For instance, behavioral compliance with the international norms against FGM and early marriage requires that families do not allow their daughters to be cut or to be married underage, respectively, while the local norms supporting these practices ask families to take the opposing actions. In these cases at least, behavior change is an all-or-nothing proposition; parents either do or do not subject their daughters to FGM and early marriage.[15] Thus, I use the terms "primary behavior change," "international norm compliance," and "local norm defection" interchangeably.[16] Producing such change is transnational activists' central objective.

Third, individuals can change the way they talk about their attitudes and behavior or change secondary aspects of how they conduct the behavior covered by the international and local norms. Such peripheral actions may be taken in part to shape the image they project to transnational activists (though they may also reflect indigenous changes in the absence of transnational intervention—cultural "traditions" are rarely static for long, but rather are constantly being reinterpreted and adapted from within). In the case of FGM, for example, individuals can make a rhetorical commitment to the international norm against the practice. They can also attempt to minimize public exposure by making changes to the way FGM is performed so that it is less visible. While these are not the kinds of actions international norm entrepreneurs desire, they should nonetheless be categorized as aspects of norm change because they signal recognition that the international norm has some degree of legitimacy or power within the community (even if the individuals in question do not think the norm is legitimate). Absent this recognition, one would not expect any significant deviation from the customary performance of the practice.

It is important to disaggregate these various elements of norm change because they do not always occur together. As described above, the defining characteristic of a norm is the social expectation of compliance. Thus, irrespective of whether someone personally values the specific behavior a norm promotes, she may perform that behavior because other members of the group expect her to do so. Indeed, violation of the norm may provoke

15. Some transnational activists have advocated for less severe forms of FGM, or for delaying the age of marriage a little, even if not until after age 18. However, they represent a distinct minority.

16. The term "defection" is drawn from game theory and refers here to the abandonment of a previous (implicit) agreement or commitment. It should not be considered strictly pejorative.

some form of punishment by the group. When an individual faces conflicting international and local norms, she is likely to find herself in a particularly difficult position, being pulled in two different directions at once. Even if she changes her attitudes and comes to agree with the international norm, this does not guarantee primary behavior change because local social pressure may overwhelm her personal preferences. She may want to comply with the international norm, but feel unable to do so. Alternatively, if most of a given group has already defected from a local norm in favor of an international one, any remaining local norm adherents may feel pressure to defect as well, even if they have not truly embraced the logic of the international norm—primary behavior change is possible in the absence of attitude change.

Secondary behavioral and rhetorical changes can also be disconnected from attitude change and primary behavior change. Indeed, secondary changes can be a strategic response to competing sets of normative expectations held by alternative reference groups, particularly where an individual identifies with both groups. Individuals often possess multiple identities simultaneously (based on ethnicity, religion, educational attainment, country of origin, occupation, etc.) that become relevant under different conditions, but this can create problems if the associated groups demand conflicting behaviors. In the case of a conflict between an international and local norm, it may be that an individual continues to identify with the group upholding the local norm and seeks to be perceived favorably by that group, but also wishes to identify, for example, as a "modern" or "cosmopolitan" citizen of the world, and thus seeks to be perceived favorably by transnational activists. While the individual cannot actually comply with both the international and local norms, she *can* try to convince each group that she is complying with that group's norms. A number of scenarios are possible here—in addition to openly complying with the international norm or openly complying with the local norm, an individual could attempt to hide her local norm compliance (with or without attitudinal agreement) from transnational activists or, more rarely, attempt to hide her international norm compliance from the local community.

There is thus a range of possible local-level responses to transnational activism. The purpose of this book is to identify the conditions under which each of the elements of norm change is most likely to occur, and to trace out the pathways by which individuals and communities reach these outcomes. Though achieving primary behavior change is generally the main goal of transnational activists, the particular challenge of a norm conflict is that individuals and communities must navigate a complex, incompatible set of demands placed on their loyalties and commitments. Thus, attitude change and secondary behavioral and rhetorical change become an important part of the overarching story of norm change, in some cases aiding and in others impeding primary behavior change.

Sources of Norm Change

The likelihood of observing each of the elements of norm change is fundamentally shaped by the *salience* of the international and local norms to their respective proponents, where salience refers to the prominence of the norm and to the depth of adherents' commitment. In this respect, all norms are not created equal.

International norm salience and local norm salience each affect the probability of norm change through several mechanisms. First, norm salience influences the level of local exposure to and awareness of the international normative message. The salience of the international norm at the international level affects norm awareness through its impact on international aid allocation. When an international norm is highly salient to the international community and to major international donors, aid is made available to NGOs willing to address the issue, thus driving up the level of activism. In addition, the salience of the local norm at the local level affects norm awareness through its impact on NGOs' motivation. When a local norm is highly salient to a local group, locally based NGOs will avoid promoting the conflicting international norm for fear of vexing fellow group members, thus driving down the level of activism. Though outside activists may persist in promoting the international norm, most transnational campaigns depend on local activist groups to provide access and insight into a target community, so resistance on the part of these groups can undermine the strength of the overall campaign.

Second, norm salience influences the quality of the international normative message. When an international norm is highly salient, it will lead some NGOs to take up the cause *only* because of the availability of funding and not because of any deeper commitment to the norm. As a result, these organizations will be unmotivated to seek out and pursue the most effective strategies in their promotion of the norm, thus driving down the average quality of activism. If the corresponding local norm is also highly salient, any local NGOs that do engage in activism to promote the international norm will face incentives to shirk in the performance of that activism since an aggressive approach might upset the community, thus also driving down the average quality of activism.

Third, norm salience influences individuals' susceptibility to changing their behavioral beliefs—beliefs about the outcomes associated with a particular behavior (Fishbein and Ajzen 2010, 18). When a local norm is highly salient, the general psychological tendency to discount new information that challenges one's existing beliefs is likely to be particularly pronounced. Thus, false behavioral beliefs about salient local norms are especially likely to persevere, even in the face of disconfirming evidence presented through a high-quality international normative message.

Fourth, norm salience influences the barriers to defecting from the local norm. When a local norm is highly salient, local social punishment for violating the norm will be significant. This punishment may include reputational costs, tangible material or physical costs, or both. As a result, those individuals who would like to defect from the local norm and embrace the international norm may be quite reluctant to actually do so, and will require some ability to mitigate social costs if they are to take the leap.

Norm salience thus affects each of the elements of norm change. It impacts the probability of attitude change through its contribution to both the level of activism and the quality of activism promoting the international norm, as well as through its contribution to belief perseverance. Without awareness of a conflicting external norm, few people will independently question the validity of a long-established local norm—high-quality, persistent transnational activism may well be necessary to jolt people into reconsidering their existing beliefs and behaviors. Norm salience affects the probability of primary behavior change indirectly through its impact on attitude change and directly through its impact on the barriers to defection from the local norm. Where barriers to defection are low, individual attitude change will be closely followed by primary behavior change. However, where barriers to defection are high, primary behavior change is likely to lag substantially behind attitude change. Finally, norm salience affects the probability of secondary behavioral and rhetorical change through its impact on the level of activism promoting the international norm, since people will have no incentive to try to conceal their continued adherence to the local norm in the absence of some exposure to the competing international norm. All in all, the salience of the competing international and local norms affects both the message people receive and how they respond to it.[17]

In addition to the sources of variation in the probability of norm change that can be derived from properties of the international and local norms

17. Cialdini, Reno, and Kallgren (1990) have also emphasized the importance of salience in driving norm compliance, although their work focuses on the idea that individual norms can be more or less salient in particular situations. I agree that salience is variable across different conditions, but suggest that some norms are more salient than others on average.

themselves, there are also community-level and individual-level sources of variation to consider. That is, for any given norm conflict, some communities and some individuals within communities will be more susceptible to norm change than others. At the community level, the density of NGOs operating in the area contributes substantially to the level of activism around any particular international norm—though high international norm salience may drive up the level of international aid available to tackle a particular issue, there must be NGOs on the ground capable of taking advantage of this increased funding and distributing the international normative message. Besides NGO density, a second important community-level variable is the availability of an exit option from the local norm. Particularly where the local norm is highly salient and average barriers to defection are high, primary behavior change is most likely to occur in communities where many people have the opportunity to exit from the local norm in some way, possibly through access to normative out-groups. If people who subscribe to a particular local norm happen to live in a heterogeneous community, they may be able to mitigate social punishment for defection by joining one of these out-groups, effectively switching their reference group. Of course, in addition to varying at the level of the community, both of these factors may also vary at the level of the individual—within any given community, some individuals will be more likely than others to be exposed to activism and to have good exit options. There will likely be other individual-level characteristics that influence the likelihood of norm change as well, although the relevant characteristics (e.g., age, sex, wealth, and education) will certainly vary according to the particular norm conflict.

Pathways of Communal Norm Change

While the sources of norm change described above affect individuals' decisions, these decisions do not occur in isolation. Because norms are social, the decisions of some individuals will affect the decisions of other individuals, meaning that, particularly in the case of a highly salient local norm, there is a strong temporal dimension to norm change. Each additional person who defects from a local norm in favor of an international one lowers the average social costs of defection for others in the community, making it easier for those others to defect in turn.

The pattern of international norm diffusion through any given community depends on the distribution of preferences and interests across individuals within that community. That is, for any given norm different individuals will have different thresholds for primary behavior change. These thresholds are determined by the social costs and benefits they anticipate as a result of changing their behavior, weighed against the strength of their true feelings and the internal cost to their personal sense of integrity of failing to act in accordance with those feelings (Kuran 1991, 17–18).

For simplicity's sake, we can divide people into two basic groups, borrowing from Finnemore and Sikkink's (1998, 895) terminology—norm leaders and norm followers. *Norm leaders* are the first movers in any process of communal norm change. They are those individuals who are willing to defect from a local norm, even at the risk of potentially significant negative social sanctioning by members of their local reference group, because the transnational norm entrepreneurs have truly persuaded them of the validity of the conflicting international norm and they feel this new commitment very deeply. Though norm leaders will be relatively less sensitive to local social pressures, they will certainly not be immune, and thus norm leaders may well have faced lower than average barriers to defection. *Norm followers* are those individuals who defect from the local norm only when many other people have already defected and thus local negative sanctions for further defections are substantially reduced. Norm followers make their behavioral decisions based on the way the wind is currently blowing, and so their commitment to the international norm is conditional—they will imitate the norm leaders only if it appears that the community is headed in the direction of mass defection.

Thus, the supply of potential norm leaders and norm followers determines the extent and speed of norm change in a particular community, and this supply is in turn shaped by the systemic and community-level factors described above. A group of norm leaders is most likely to emerge in communities that have received a high-quality international normative message and that provide widespread opportunities for exit from the local norm. And while good exit options lower social costs for the norm leaders, the presence of "influentials" within the leader group can further reduce social costs for the norm followers. That is, norm followers are most likely to emerge if transnational activists manage to recruit particularly influential locals to the group of norm leaders, since their public stance will send a fairly strong signal that the local norm is weakening. If there are few potential norm leaders and followers, norm change will be slow and uneven, or perhaps nonexistent. But if potential norm leaders and followers exist in sufficient numbers, the introduction of transnational activism has the potential to kick off an iterated process of widespread behavior change, or a norm cascade, in which a few individuals' actions trigger many others to follow suit.

Overall, the theory describes a complex process of norm change. Multiple factors at the international, community, and individual levels intervene to shape the incentives and pressures people face in deciding how they will resolve a norm conflict, and their individual decisions interact dynamically with the broader pattern of norm change in the community. Transnational norm entrepreneurs thus face significant challenges in their efforts to influence what people know, think, do, and say with respect to competing international and local norms.

FGM AND EARLY MARRIAGE: CAMPAIGN AND PRACTICE

In this book I focus on the norm conflicts surrounding FGM and early marriage. As will become clear, gaining a better understanding of these conflicts is substantively valuable both because of the scope of the two practices and because there is still significant scholarly debate about the conditions under which each practice is likely to decline. However, it is important to note that the theory can be applied to any conflict between international and local norms for which legal or policy actions consistent with the international norm are not fully enforceable.[18] Indeed, as discussed in greater detail in chapter 8, much of the theory is applicable to any case of norm promotion that depends heavily on persuasion as a tactic, whether or not the norm being promoted is international in its scope. It is also important to emphasize in advance that the theory applies globally—it is not limited only to cases in which activists from the global North target local communities in the global South—and that it does not assume that northerners are morally superior or that Africans in particular or southerners in general are uniquely reluctant to abandon their local norms.

Definitions and Terminology

The World Health Organization (WHO) (2008b) provides a widely accepted definition of FGM as a practice comprising "all procedures that involve partial or total removal of the external female genitalia, or other injury to the female genital organs for non-medical reasons." The three main types of FGM are clitoridectomy, which involves the removal of part or all of the clitoris; excision, which involves the removal of the clitoris and part or all of the labia minora; and infibulation, which involves the removal of the clitoris, labia minora, and labia majora, as well as the subsequent stitching

18. Note that many, but not all, international norms are legally codified in international treaties.

or narrowing of the vaginal opening. The WHO also identifies a fourth residual category of FGM that includes all other medically unnecessary procedures on the female genitalia, including pricking, piercing, incising, scraping, and cauterization of the genital area.

Early marriage is defined simply as marriage of children and adolescents under the age of 18. While boys are occasionally subjected to this practice, the overwhelming majority of early marriages involve girls married to older men. A girl may be actually forced into marriage, or she may simply be too young to make an informed decision about marriage and thereby give consent (United Nations Children's Fund 2001, 2).

The appropriate terminology to describe these two practices has been the subject of extensive debate, particularly in the case of FGM. The term "female circumcision" was widely used by both observers and activists during the early period of campaigning against the practice, and is an accurate English translation of the terminology used by some, though by no means all, practicing groups (United Nations Children's Fund 2013a, 6–7). However, the word "circumcision" suggests an equivalence with male circumcision that many activists came to view as deeply problematic, since all three major forms of the procedure are substantially more invasive than the circumcision that is performed on males. As a result, the term "female genital mutilation" gained in popularity starting in the late 1970s and was officially adopted by several international bodies during the 1990s (World Health Organization 2008a, 22). Yet some researchers and activists ultimately came to view "FGM" as too judgmental, concluding that use of the term by activists might alienate target communities and also that the word "mutilation" suggests an *intention* to harm girls that is unfair to the practicing communities (Gruenbaum 2001, 3). Parents have their daughters undergo the cut because they believe it is in the girls' best interest, not because they want to hurt them. Consequently, some commentators have adopted the term "female genital cutting," or "FGC," as a more objective description of the practice. Acknowledging the competing legitimacies of the words "mutilation" and "cutting," some UN agencies have in recent years adopted the hybrid term "female genital mutilation/cutting," or "FGM/C" (United Nations Children's Fund 2013a, 7).[19]

I agree that "FGC" is the most neutral term, but while it has recently gained popularity, particularly among academics, it is still not widely used by activists. And "FGM/C" is simply unwieldy to use in everyday speech. Thus, I have elected to use the terms "FGM" and "female circumcision."

19. Other, less common terms include "female genital surgeries" and "female genital operations" (Gruenbaum 2001, 4). In addition, some commentators have chosen to use the more specific terms "clitoridectomy," "excision," and "infibulation."

Specifically, I will refer to the practice as "FGM" when I am writing about the transnational campaign, since the activists and NGO workers I spoke with almost universally used this terminology. I will, however, refer to the practice as "female circumcision" when I am writing about the cultural tradition and the practicing communities, since (at least in the research context in which I operated) this is how they genuinely perceive the practice. For them, "circumcision" is not a euphemism. In both cases, I am attempting to respect the terminological preferences of my research subjects rather than to impose my own preferences. I will also occasionally use the word "cut" as both a noun and a verb, since it is relatively neutral and is in use among both activists and practicing communities.

The terminological debate has not been as emotionally charged in the case of early marriage, but there are nonetheless several different terms in use. In addition to "early marriage," some commentators and activists have employed the terms "child marriage" and "forced marriage." However, the way in which the latter two terms are defined has varied across different contexts, causing some confusion. While some have used "child marriage" to refer to all marriages before the age of 18, others have used the term to refer only to marriages of young children, distinguishing "child marriage" from marriage of (older) adolescents (S. Clark, Bruce, and Dude 2006). Similarly, the term "forced marriage" is sometimes used narrowly to refer only to marriages in which one or both partners are truly unwilling to enter into the marriage, but is sometimes used more broadly to also include marriages in which one or both partners cannot give legal consent, regardless of their willingness to marry (United Nations Children's Fund 2001, 8). Thus, the three terms—"early marriage," "child marriage," and "forced marriage"—are sometimes used interchangeably and sometimes used to refer to overlapping but distinct phenomena. To complicate matters further, some organizations have recently embraced the compound term "child, early, and forced marriage," or CEFM, but the acronym is not yet in widespread use. To avoid conceptual confusion, I will use the term "early marriage," which is consistently defined as marriage before age 18 and which applies regardless of the stated or private preferences of the parties to the marriage. "Early marriage" also has the benefit of being reasonably value-neutral and acceptable to both activists and practitioners.

Global Prevalence

The most reliable data on the practice of FGM come from two sets of nationally representative household surveys conducted across dozens of countries—the Demographic and Health Surveys (DHS) and the Multiple Indicator Cluster Surveys (MICS). In some countries, these surveys have even been conducted in multiple rounds, thus generating time series as well as cross-sectional data. The surveys provide details on broad patterns and sources of variation in the performance of FGM, though there are some differences in the questions asked across countries and rounds.

The surveys demonstrate that FGM prevalence varies significantly, both cross-nationally and subnationally (United Nations Children's Fund 2013a). Figure 1.1 shows that among girls and women aged 15 to 49, FGM prevalence exceeds 90 percent in Djibouti, Egypt, Guinea, and Somalia, but is less than 10 percent in Cameroon, Ghana, Iraq, Niger, Togo, and Uganda. However, prevalence is not distributed evenly within these countries; instead, the national figures reflect the high prevalence of FGM among some ethnic groups and the low prevalence or absence of FGM among others. Indeed, FGM as a practice is strongly associated with ethnicity and ethnic identity, even when controlling for other variables (Wagner 2015, 13), though this relationship is generally descriptive rather than causal. In addition, the practice is usually, although not always, more common in rural areas, in poor households, and among the

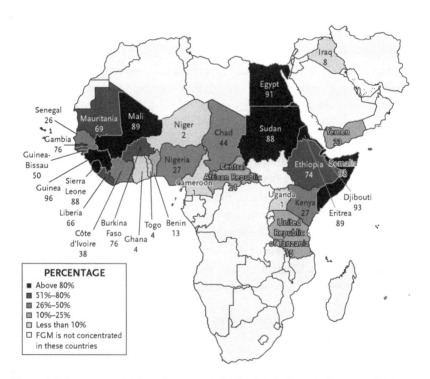

Figure 1.1: Percentage of girls and women aged 15 to 49 who have undergone FGM
Source: United Nations Children's Fund 2013a.

daughters of uneducated mothers (United Nations Children's Fund 2013a). Thus, one should not read national-level figures, including those presented below, as describing an "average" family or community; it is possible that no subnational group exhibits the mean characteristics of the country as a whole.

Among the countries for which data are available on the type of FGM performed, the evidence suggests that clitoridectomy and excision are the most common (United Nations Children's Fund 2013a).[20] However, there are several countries in which the most invasive form of FGM—infibulation—is widely practiced, including Somalia (63 percent of girls), Eritrea (38 percent), Niger (35 percent), and Djibouti (30 percent). There is also substantial cross-national variation in the age at which girls undergo FGM. In Nigeria, Mali, Eritrea, Ghana, and Mauritania, more than 80 percent of girls were cut before the age of 5, while in Somalia, Egypt, Chad, and the Central African Republic, more than 80 percent were cut between the ages of 5 and 14. Though the practice is less common, some girls are also cut after age 15, including more than 10 percent of girls in Guinea-Bissau, Kenya, and the Central African Republic. Occasionally the practice is carried out on adult women. The practice also varies according to the practitioner, the location of the procedure, and the cutting instrument used. All of these details of the performance of FGM vary across ethnic groups in addition to varying cross-nationally.

DHS and MICS data also provide a picture of early marriage around the world (see figure 1.2). Among women aged 20 to 49, more than 50 percent were married by age 18 in Bangladesh, Burkina Faso, Central African Republic, Chad, Ethiopia, Guinea, India, Malawi, Mali, Nepal, Niger, Sierra Leone, and Yemen, and more than 20 percent were married by age 15 in Bangladesh, Central African Republic, Chad, Ethiopia, Guinea, Mali, and Niger (Measure DHS 2014; United Nations Children's Fund 2013b).[21] Though at lower levels, the surveys track and show evidence of early marriage in more than 90 additional countries worldwide. There is also evidence in some countries of a positive relationship between living in rural areas and early marriage, and a negative relationship between household wealth and early marriage and between girls' educational attainment and early marriage (National Research Council 2005, 426; United Nations Children's Fund 2005b, 2009). Education in particular appears to be a strong predictor of early marriage, with girls who attended primary school generally less likely to marry before age 18 than girls with no formal education, and girls who attended secondary school less likely to marry

20. Clitoridectomy and excision grade into one another and are thus often difficult to separate in practice.
21. These figures come from the most recent DHS or MICS survey round (conducted between 2005 and 2011) for each country.

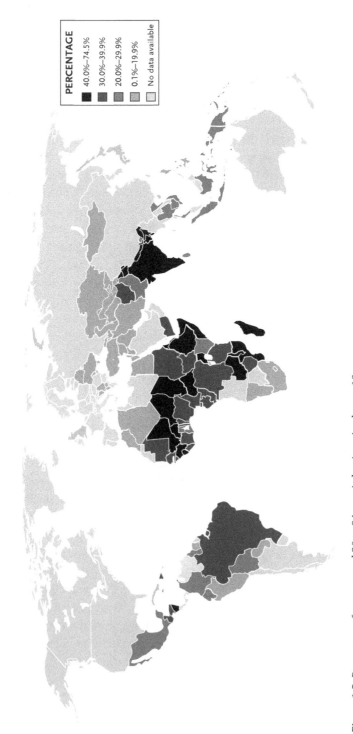

Figure 1.2: Percentage of women aged 20 to 24 married or in union by age 18
Source: United Nations Population Fund 2012.

before age 18 than girls who only attended primary school (International Center for Research on Women 2007, 22; United Nations Children's Fund 2005b, 6). Among all countries for which DHS data are available, early marriage is most prevalent among the poorest 20 percent of the population, and there is also a negative correlation between a country's gross domestic product per capita and its early-marriage prevalence rate (International Center for Research on Women 2006; National Research Council 2005, 422; United Nations Children's Fund 2005b, 6). However, multivariate analysis suggests that the descriptive correlation both between household wealth and early marriage and between living in rural areas and early marriage may in fact be proxying for the effect of girls' education or other variables (International Center for Research on Women 2007, 25–26; United Nations Children's Fund 2005b, 26). The relationship between education and early marriage may itself reflect a selection effect—those parents inclined to marry off their daughters early are likely to be disinclined to send them to school.

A number of studies utilizing the DHS and MICS data identify some common characteristics of early marriages. A United Nations Children's Fund (UNICEF) (2005b, 26) study found that in the vast majority of countries, women who were five or more years younger than their husbands were significantly more likely to have married early than women who were less than five years younger than their husbands. This age gap appears to occur not only because girls who marry early are by definition younger than girls who don't, but because, on average, the husbands of girls who marry before age 18 are older than the husbands of women who marry after age 18 (National Research Council 2005, 445). The median age gap is also larger in countries with higher prevalence rates of early marriage—10 or more years in Guinea, Niger, Mali, and Nigeria (International Center for Research on Women 2007, 23–24). In addition, there appears to be a structural relationship between early marriage and polygyny—that is, marriages in which one man has two or more wives. The UNICEF study found that in all but five countries for which data were available, women in polygynous marriages were more likely to have married underage than women in monogamous marriages (2005b, 7), and evidence from a separate multivariate analysis suggests that the younger a girl is when she marries, the more likely it is that her husband has multiple wives (International Center for Research on Women 2007, 26).

Local Norms

Groups, families, and individuals practice female circumcision and early marriage for a variety of reasons. The local norm supporting female circumcision varies descriptively across countries and groups, and may be based on a logic related to control of women's sexual behavior, cultural tradition, religion, or some combination of the three. Cross-nationally, female circumcision is commonly justified as a method for preserving a girl's premarital virginity (United Nations Children's Fund 2013a, 68), on the thinking that a girl will experience less sexual desire if her clitoris has been removed.[22] A similar logic underlies the justification of female circumcision as a means to ensure marital fidelity (Gruenbaum 2001, 78). In addition, female circumcision is sometimes justified as part of a rite of passage to adulthood that grants girls fertility, age status, or entry into secret societies, assigns gender identity, or legitimates future reproduction (Ahmadu 2000; Boddy 1982; Gruenbaum 2001), and the practice may further serve as a means of promoting femininity, modesty, honor, beauty, cleanliness, and even health (Dorkenoo 1994; United Nations Children's Fund 2005a, 11; World Health Organization 2008b).[23]

Female circumcision is also sometimes viewed as a religious requirement, particularly among Muslim communities that practice the cut (Boddy 1991, 15; United Nations Children's Fund 2013a, 69). However, it is important to note that many Muslims do not practice female circumcision (it is extremely rare in Muslim communities outside of Africa, and is not universally practiced among Muslim communities on the continent), while many non-Muslims do (Shell-Duncan and Hernlund 2000, 23). Furthermore, the belief that Islam requires female circumcision is textually suspect, as the Koran does not prescribe or even mention the practice (Gruenbaum 2001, 64).[24] Indeed, many Muslim religious leaders are opposed to FGM and have issued religious edicts prohibiting the practice. Still, the DHS and MICS data suggest that, in Africa, FGM is more common among Muslims than among Christians, Jews, or followers of traditional religions (United Nations Children's Fund 2013a, 73; Wagner 2015, 13). Though the specific believed religious function of the cut varies across groups, one common

22. In the case of infibulation, the sealing of the vaginal opening is also believed to provide a physical barrier to sexual intercourse (Gruenbaum 2001, 78).

23. The reasons for maintaining an existing norm may be quite different from the reasons for initiating a new norm. Mackie (2000, 267–68) hypothesizes that female circumcision emerged first in the Sudan as a method for promoting sexual fidelity and minimizing "paternity uncertainty" under conditions of extreme polygyny or concubinage within the imperial court of Meroe, and that the practice diffused across the African continent over several thousand years through status and resource hierarchies within Sudanic empires and across ethnic groups, and through the movement of pastoralist elites.

24. However, there is some debate among Islamic scholars about whether the Hadith—reports of the sayings of the Prophet Mohammed during his lifetime—require, promote, or simply condone a mild form of FGM that is sometimes referred to as *sunna* (Gruenbaum 2001, 64–65). There is also debate about the reliability of the specific

justification is that female circumcision serves as a cleansing or purification ritual that allows women to participate fully in religious practice (M. C. Johnson 2000, 219; United Nations Children's Fund 2010c, 8).

But for individuals and families, the primary reason to circumcise a daughter is often simply to gain social acceptance—that is, once a local norm is in place, the specific justifications for the norm at the group level take a backseat to social conformity (United Nations Children's Fund 2013a, 66). Parents want their daughters to be accepted by other members of the group, both for the general advantages of inclusion and for specific functional goals such as the ability of daughters to marry within the group. Indeed, among practicing groups FGM is often a requirement for marriage—in multivariate analysis of DHS data, Wagner (2015, 14) finds evidence that FGM does in fact improve marriageability—so that parents who value their daughters' marriageability face strong incentives to have those daughters cut (Mackie and LeJeune 2009, 7).

Like the local norm supporting female circumcision, the logic of the local norm supporting early marriage also varies both cross-nationally and subnationally, and may be based in some combination of economic need, culture, and religion. In impoverished areas, girls are often viewed as an economic burden, and so early marriage is perceived as a mechanism for reducing financial strain on the family (International Center for Research on Women 2007, 9; United Nations Children's Fund 2001, 6). And the material incentives for early marriage are even stronger among groups for which the payment of bridewealth, or "bride price," is customary. In such settings, the transfer of money, livestock, or other goods from the bridegroom to the bride's family may significantly improve the latter's financial circumstances. Counterintuitively, early marriages are also common among groups that practice dowry—payments in cash or in kind from the bride's family to the bridegroom's family—rather than bridewealth, since dowry demands often increase with the bride's age and education (International Planned Parenthood Federation and Forum on Marriage and the Rights of Women and Girls 2006, 19). Early marriage may also serve the purpose of settling an outstanding debt between the bride's family and the bridegroom or his family.

In addition to economic motivations, early marriage may also be justified as facilitating cultural or religious beliefs governing the appropriate behavior of wives and of women in general (United Nations Children's Fund 2001, 6). In particular, a young wife may be viewed as more likely to

Hadith relaying the Prophet's views on female circumcision, since initially Hadith were transmitted orally and were therefore subject to the trustworthiness of the tellers. More generally, Islamic theology is not exclusively bound to written texts.

be easily controlled and submissive to the will of her husband and his family, and a young wife will likely bear more children over the course of her life (Mathur, Greene, and Malhotra 2003, 4). In contexts in which premarital virginity is highly valued, either for intrinsic or instrumental reasons, parents may also be motivated to arrange their daughters' marriages at a young age so as to reduce the likelihood that they will engage in sexual activity before marriage or become pregnant out of wedlock. In addition, the marriage and engagement of children may serve as a tool for cementing alliances between families or for settling interfamilial disputes (including offering a girl in marriage as compensation for a crime committed by a member of the girl's family) (International Planned Parenthood Federation and Forum on Marriage and the Rights of Women and Girls 2006, 17).

The HIV/AIDS epidemic has created a further justification for early marriage, particularly in sub-Saharan Africa, with men seeking younger brides in the hope that they will be virgins and therefore uninfected with the virus (United Nations Children's Fund 2001, 6). Some parents of girls also appear to believe that their daughters will be at lower risk of HIV infection if they marry early and have only one sexual partner, and caregivers of AIDS orphans may view early marriage as a solution to unexpected financial stress.

However, it is important to note that one of the most common justifications for both FGM and early marriage "is simply that 'such is the custom or tradition here'" (Mackie 1996, 1004). While an explanation like this may appear reductive, it is nonetheless valid—when a local norm is mature and has been widely internalized, members of the group may well comply with it on the basis of tradition and not expend a lot of effort thinking about any deeper meaning behind the practice. The value placed on adhering to tradition in and of itself should not be underestimated (Shell-Duncan and Hernlund 2000, 20).

International Norms and Transnational Activism

The international norms against FGM and early marriage are based on logics of their own, which compete with the logics of the local norms supporting these practices. Much of the international discourse around both FGM and early marriage centers on issues of health, gender equality, and human rights.

A major focus of transnational activism against FGM has been the potential health consequences of the practice, including short-term complications, long-term complications, and obstetrical complications (Shell-Duncan and Hernlund 2000, 14). The WHO (2008a, 33–35) reports that immediate health risks associated with the various forms of FGM include severe pain, shock, excessive bleeding, septic shock, urine and feces retention, infections (including tetanus and HIV) from the use of contaminated instruments, unintended labia fusion, and death as a result of hemorrhage or infection. Over the long term, women and girls who have undergone FGM may be at greater risk of chronic pain from exposed or trapped nerve endings, recurrent pelvic and urinary tract infections, dermoid cysts, abscesses, genital ulcers, reproductive tract infections, genital herpes, and HIV infection due to increased risk of bleeding during intercourse. In addition, cut women and girls appear to face higher risk of certain childbirth complications, including prolonged and obstructed labor, postpartum hemorrhage, and vaginal tearing, and there is some evidence of higher newborn death rates.

Beyond medical complications, FGM can result in decreased sexual sensitivity and pain during sexual intercourse, and there is also some suggestion that FGM may produce psychological consequences including post-traumatic stress disorder, anxiety, depression, memory loss, and fear of sexual intercourse. The health risks associated with FGM appear to increase with the severity of the procedure and are especially pronounced among women who have been infibulated. Not only is significantly more tissue removed in the case of infibulation, but infibulated women may require later surgeries in order to reopen the vagina to allow sexual intercourse and childbirth, and they may be reinfibulated afterward. These repeated surgeries compound their risk. However, it is important to note that the public health studies establishing the health consequences of FGM vary in quality, and many face both internal and external validity problems due to nonrandom sampling procedures and nonexperimental evidence (Shell-Duncan and Hernlund 2000, 15; Wagner 2015, 5). Some have argued that the probability of cut women experiencing serious health complications has been significantly overstated by activists (Shell-Duncan 2008, 226).

The health approach to FGM eradication efforts is complemented by, and to some extent has been supplanted by, a human rights approach (Shell-Duncan and Hernlund 2000; United Nations Children's Fund 2013a, 8).[25] FGM can be construed as violating a wide range of rights and therefore falling under the purview of international human rights law.

---

25. Despite the increasing popularity of the human rights frame over the health frame, Boyle and Carbone-Lopez (2006) find that the latter has been more fully embraced by women from circumcising groups who ultimately come to oppose the practice. They theorize that women who must justify their opposition to FGM to their own communities embrace a medical discourse because of its perceived neutrality—they selectively adopt international normative language in a way that best fits their own local context.

Activists and various international bodies have argued that FGM violates the right to health and bodily integrity, and the right to freedom from violence, torture, and cruel, inhuman, or degrading treatment. The rights approach has also involved arguments that the practice violates the rights of women, the rights of the child when it is performed on minors, and the right to life when it results in death.

The content of the international norm against early marriage touches on similar themes, and the rights-based approach has focused on the rights of the child, the rights of women, the right to freedom from slavery, the right to consensual marriage, the right to health, the right to education, and the right to freedom from physical and sexual abuse (Somerset 2000, 15; United Nations Children's Fund 2001, 3; United Nations Children's Fund 2005b, 1).

Activists and international bodies have identified a range of negative consequences of early marriage that underlie such rights-based claims. In terms of health consequences, girls who enter into early marriage appear to be at greater risk of early pregnancy (International Center for Research on Women 2007, 7–8). Particularly in developing countries where access to medical care may be limited, early pregnancy puts both mother and child at risk because the mother's body may not be sufficiently physically developed to allow for unobstructed natural labor. The result is higher rates of maternal mortality and obstetric fistula, as well as stillbirth, premature birth, and low birth weights. Young mothers' poor feeding behavior also leads to increased risk of infant malnutrition and death.

Beyond the problems associated with early pregnancy, girls who marry early may also have limited access to healthcare and health information, and appear to be at greater risk than their sexually active unmarried counterparts of contracting HIV (Bruce and Clark 2004). This latter finding is particularly noteworthy because it directly contradicts the expectations of parents who arrange for their daughters to marry early in the hope of protecting them from HIV. In fact, HIV risk appears to be higher, not lower, in part because married girls have less control over their sexual activity (including frequency of sexual intercourse and condom use) than unmarried girls (Bruce 2007). Moreover, sexually active unmarried girls tend to have sex with boys and men who are close to their own age and thus who have had few past sexual partners from whom they might have contracted HIV. Married girls, on the other hand, often have significantly older spouses who have had more past sexual partners (S. Clark 2004).

Additional potential negative consequences of early marriage relate to power and decision-making within the marriage and household (Jensen and Thornton 2003, 14; National Research Council 2005, 444–45). When a girl marries early, and particularly when there is a large age differential between the husband and wife, she is likely to have less control over a variety of decisions related to her health, sexual activity, freedom of movement, and ability to work (International Center for Research on Women 2007, 8). Underage brides' low status also puts them at significantly greater risk of domestic violence and marital rape (Jensen and Thornton 2003, 16). Moreover, there is some suggestion that underage brides in polygynous unions are likely to be junior rather than senior wives, further reducing their power within the household (National Research Council 2005, 445).

Finally, many activists have emphasized the detrimental effects of early marriage on girls' education. While it is certainly the case that a girl's marriage generally precludes her from continuing her education, there is only limited evidence that girls are actually withdrawn from school in order to marry (National Research Council 2005, 436). In countries where early marriage is common, the average age at leaving school is several years younger than the average age at marriage.

Many different types of actors are engaged in promoting the international norms against FGM and early marriage, including UN agencies such as UNICEF, the United Nations Population Fund (UNFPA), and the WHO; multilateral and bilateral aid agencies such as the World Bank and the US Agency for International Development; other international, national, and local government agencies; major international development NGOs such as World Vision, Save the Children, and CARE; women's rights advocacy groups such as the International Center for Research on Women (ICRW) and the Foundation for Women's Health Research and Development; a wide range of national- and local-level NGOs based in the global South; foundations; churches; and media. Organizational actors have also built various networks, including the Donors Working Group on FGM/C, the Inter-African Committee on Traditional Practices Affecting the Health of Women and Children, the Working Group on Girls, the Forum on Marriage and the Rights of Women and Girls, and Girls Not Brides.

Among these diverse actors, attention to FGM has been particularly marked. The Donors Working Group on FGM/C assists in coordinating the anti-FGM efforts of 25 institutional donors, including nine bilateral development agencies and 12 UN organizations. As far back as 1990, the UN Committee on the Elimination of Discrimination Against Women singled out FGM among other harmful traditional practices in its General Recommendation No. 14 (United Nations 1990). In 2008, 10 UN agencies produced a joint statement on eliminating FGM that called for increased resource mobilization and greater interagency cooperation. This was followed by two reports on eliminating FGM from the UN secretary-general to the Commission on the Status of Women in 2010 and 2012, and by a UN

General Assembly Resolution explicitly addressing FGM in 2012 (United Nations Commission on the Status of Women 2009, 2011; United Nations General Assembly resolution 2012). Beginning in 2008, UNICEF and UNFPA coordinated on a large-scale joint program to promote the abandonment of FGM in 15 countries, mobilizing almost $37 million for its activities between 2008 and 2013 and seeking to raise $54 million for the program's second phase (United Nations Population Fund and United Nations Children's Fund 2013, 4; United Nations Population Fund and United Nations Children's Fund 2014, 1). Indeed, international scrutiny is such that countries may be penalized for failing to take at least some rudimentary steps to combat the practice. Starting in 1999, the United States began instructing its representatives at the World Bank and other financial institutions to oppose loans to countries that did not run educational programs against FGM.

In contrast, international attention to early marriage has been more limited and is often subsumed within broader efforts to promote women's rights. A UNICEF (2001, 2–3) report on the practice states bluntly that "early marriage has received scant attention from the modern women's rights and children's rights movements," and that "there has been virtually no attempt to examine the practice as a human rights violation *in itself*." Another report finds that only Bangladesh, India, and Nepal have seen significant interventions directed specifically at early marriage (National Research Council 2005, 472–73), while a third report conducted an Internet-based program scan and was able to identify only 66 programs worldwide that were addressing early marriage either directly or indirectly (International Center for Research on Women 2007, 33–34). The level of attention has begun to expand only in the last several years, with the formation of the civil society network Girls Not Brides.

Though the overall level of international interest in FGM and early marriage clearly varies, the mobilization that has occurred has shaped the evolution of the international norms against both practices, and at the same time contributed to a broader transnational discourse on violence against women and women's human rights. This discourse has taken place in the context of the various UN-sponsored world conferences described at the beginning of this chapter, as well as through both formal and informal activist networks and through academic and feminist debates spanning the global North and South.

Especially as international attention to FGM began to take off during the 1980s and 1990s, activists and scholars from the North and South exhibited remarkably different views on the issue (Boyle and Corl 2010, 198). North American and European women's rights activists like Fran Hosken and Mary Daly took an absolutist anti-FGM stance that emphasized the most horrific aspects of the practice and attributed its perpetuation to patriarchy and the intentional subjugation of women (Daly 1978; Hosken 1982). Early accounts of the practice such as the *Hosken Report* concluded that girls and women were cut against their will and that any and all steps should be taken to save them from this fate. While many African feminists and activists also opposed FGM, and indeed played an early and major role in raising the practice's profile at the international level, they tended to take a more nuanced view that acknowledged the agency of African women and did not dismiss the importance of culture and tradition (Abusharaf 1998; El Saadawi 1980). Some other African activists and scholars, however, questioned why FGM was receiving so much international attention at the expense of what they perceived as more pressing problems (Dorkenoo 1994, 63). Still others defended the practice and disputed the argument that it was disempowering or particularly harmful to women, rejecting claims that female practitioners and supporters were suffering from false consciousness (Ahmadu 2000).

These debates have fed into larger debates in the human rights arena and in academic discourse over the appropriate stance toward "traditional" practices, pitting proponents of a "universalist" position against proponents of a "cultural relativist" position (Hernlund and Shell-Duncan 2007). The universalist perspective, championed by human rights activists and some Western feminists and academics, argues that there are some fundamental human rights that apply to all people across cultural contexts (Donnelly 1989). Harmful practices can be determined objectively according to universal standards, and practices like female genital mutilation clearly meet these standards (Konner 1990). By contrast, the cultural relativist perspective, often associated with academic anthropologists, contends that determinations of right and wrong are subjective to some degree and that practices cannot be judged independently of their cultural context (Renteln 1988).[26] Those inclined toward universalism have suggested that hardline cultural relativists are essentially excusing a range of human

26. Debates about morality and relativism have also cropped up in the international norms literature. Acharya (2011, 10–11) observes a tendency toward what he terms "moral cosmopolitanism" in works on transnational activism, in which authors unproblematically assume that international norms are good or progressive while contested national and local norms are bad or retrogressive. Checkel (1999, 88) makes a similar point about the risks of assuming a dichotomy between good transnational activists and bad states, while Nadelmann (1990, 484) suggests that the power of the West has allowed it to define what is considered moral in international law and norms. Finnemore and Sikkink (1998, 892) note that perspectives on right and wrong are situational: "There are no bad norms from the vantage point of those who promote the norm."

rights abuses (Gordon 1991, 13) and question why groups' cultural rights should trump women's individual rights (Okin 1997). Cultural relativists have responded that universalists are engaging in a form of paternalism by assuming they know what is best for the peoples of the global South, treating southern women as victimized objects rather than subjects able to make their own choices (Mohanty 1988, 66; Morsy 1991, 21; Obiora 1996, 303). Literature in African studies has advanced a related critique, pointing out that Western activism in the present cannot be divorced from a long history of cultural imperialism, facilitated by highly unequal power relations, in which Africans in general and African women in particular were perpetually defined as primitive and as "other" in a relational sense—as such, universalism smacks of neocolonialism (Ferguson 1999; Mbembe 2001). Yet common ground exists and enables a way forward. One can accept that some universal principles exist while continuing to value cultural difference and to appreciate that having a culture is in itself valuable to people (Appiah 2006). Many Western activists have become less judgmental and ethnocentric and have recognized the importance of partnering closely with activists from the global South—indeed it is these latter activists who have frequently led the way (Dorkenoo 1994, 63). Many anthropologists and other social scientists support change in practices like FGM and early marriage even as they call for greater cross-cultural understanding and respect for the experiences and knowledge of local women (Gruenbaum 2001, 23; Gunning 1991, 191; Tripp 2006, 303).

This discursive evolution has paralleled and contributed to the evolution of direct activism and advocacy against FGM and early marriage over the last several decades.[27] At one level, the sustained transnational interest in issues of violence against women and women's human rights has put increased pressure on international and regional governmental bodies like the UN and the African Union to address such practices in conventions and other consensus documents, and activists have also lobbied national governments to change domestic laws. Other groups have focused on reporting and documenting the practices, and on generally raising awareness internationally. But beyond advocacy and research activities, much of the activism surrounding FGM and early marriage involves programs aimed directly at practicing groups with the goal of persuading them to abandon

27. Though the modern campaign on violence against women began in the 1970s and gained steam in the 1980s and 1990s, there was some early activism against female circumcision in Kenya (discussed in chapter 3), Egypt, and Sudan during the colonial era (United Nations Children's Fund 2010c), as well as against early marriage in India (Nair 1995). There are even reports that the Roman Catholic Church took a short-lived stand against female circumcision in 16th-century Ethiopia (Slack 1988, 479).

these practices. In this context, there is an emerging consensus that recognizing and working to understand the local meanings of circumcision and marriage may be the only effective way to actually change them (Abusharaf 1998, 23; Boddy 1991, 16; Gruenbaum 2001, 28).

All of this international attention has in fact helped to produce a number of changes at the domestic level. Of the 29 African and Middle Eastern countries in which FGM is practiced, 24 have enacted some form of legislation or decree against the practice, though the scope of the legislation and associated penalties vary (United Nations Children's Fund 2013a, 8). While the Central African Republic and Guinea passed legislation in the mid-1960s, the laws in the other 22 countries were all enacted in the 1990s or 2000s, suggesting that the passage of such laws is a direct response to international pressure (Boyle 2002, 95; Boyle and Preves 2000). Thirty-five other countries have also passed laws against FGM, generally to protect girls in immigrant communities. There has been a similar expansion of legal protections with respect to early marriage. Between 1990 and 2000, at least 25 countries in the global South raised the legal minimum age of marriage for women or introduced a legal minimum for the first time (International Planned Parenthood Federation and International Women's Rights Action Watch 2000, as cited in National Research Council 2005). As of 2010, 158 countries had set the legal minimum age of marriage for women without parental consent at 18 (though 146 allowed marriage before age 18 with parental consent or the approval of a pertinent authority), compared to 180 countries with the same minimum for men (United Nations Population Division, Department of Economic and Social Affairs 2011, 1).[28] Legal commitments can also be observed in ratifications of and accessions to relevant international treaties. All but seven UN member states are parties to CEDAW, and all but three are states' parties to the Convention on the Rights of the Child. In Africa, 47 of 54 countries are parties to the African Charter on the Rights and Welfare of the Child, and 36 are parties to the Maputo Protocol. To varying degrees, countries have also implemented a range of policy instruments such as national action and strategic plans and national committees to complement legal prohibitions against FGM

28. However, this is complicated by the fact that many countries also have systems of customary and religious laws governing marriage that may contradict national laws (United Nations Children's Fund 2001, 7). It is sometimes unclear whether national laws have legal precedence over customary laws, and in practice the latter often trumps the former. Thus, the true legal status of early marriage within a particular country can be quite murky.

and early marriage (United Nations Population Fund and United Nations Children's Fund 2012, 11).

Beyond legal and policy changes, there have been real changes in the prevalence of FGM and early marriage. The incidence of FGM has begun to decline in more than half of the 29 countries in which it is practiced: the most recent DHS and MICS data show that women and girls aged 15 to 19 (the surveys' youngest age cohort) are significantly less likely to report having undergone FGM than women aged 45 to 49 (the surveys' oldest age cohort) (United Nations Children's Fund 2013a, 99). The pace of change has varied both across countries and subnationally, but has been particularly marked in Benin, the Central African Republic, Iraq, Kenya, Liberia, Nigeria, and Tanzania, where prevalence rates are in the low to moderate range. Early marriage has also become somewhat less common, though rates of decline have leveled off in the 21st century (United Nations Population Fund 2012, 26). For a sample of 92 developing countries, DHS and MICS data collected between 2000 and 2008 reveal that 48 percent of women aged 45 to 49 reported being married by age 18, compared to 35 percent of women aged 20 to 24 (United Nations Children's Fund 2010a).[29] Analysis of post-2000 DHS data from 65 countries shows that early-marriage prevalence was more than 50 percent lower in the youngest age cohort relative to the oldest cohort in Egypt, Indonesia, Jordan, the Maldives, Morocco, Pakistan, Rwanda, and Swaziland. As with FGM, these are countries with low to moderate early-marriage prevalence rates (Measure DHS 2014).

Thus, there are clear norm conflicts over both FGM and early marriage (Boyle 2002, 119). There is also clear variation in the scope of transnational activism against the practices and in the degree to which meaningful norm change has occurred, both across norms and across national and subnational contexts. These sources of variation require empirical exploration.

RESEARCH DESIGN AND METHODS

Case Selection

In the empirical portion of this book I look at the norm change paths followed by three Maa-speaking Kenyan communities—Oldonyiro, Mukogodo, and Mau. Kenya is an ideal setting in which to evaluate norm change because it

29. It is important to recognize that some of the decline in prevalence may be due to underreporting of circumcision and early marriage among younger women—they may be more aware of or particularly sensitive to legislation and activism against FGM and early marriage, and thus disinclined to admit they underwent the practices (National Research Council 2005, 418; United Nations Children's Fund 2013a, 88).

exhibits significant subnational variation in the prevalence of FGM and early marriage, both across and within individual ethnic groups. Within-group variation is valuable because it allows me to focus on a single language family and thus to "hold culture constant," making it easier to isolate political and social processes that may contribute to individual and community responses to international norm promotion. Cross-group variation is valuable because it means variation in normative in-groups' exposure to out-groups, and thus enables evaluation of the impact of an exit option on primary behavior change. In addition, Kenya is one of only a few countries to have experienced declines over time in the prevalence of both FGM and early marriage, which is a necessary prerequisite in order to observe the conditions under which norm change actually occurs.

The decision to focus on Maa-speaking peoples—including the Maasai and the Samburu, among others—was driven by the need to identify a group that has historically practiced both female circumcision and early marriage, since the two practices do not always go together. Furthermore, though different communities of Maa-speakers share a larger cultural tradition, they are engaging in norm change to varying degrees and at varying rates, and this variation can be exploited empirically. Maa-speakers such as the Maasai and Samburu also commonly self-identify as being particularly committed to maintaining their traditional cultural ways and practices (Hodgson 2001, 250), which makes them something of a hard case for norm change. To the extent that norm change is nonetheless observed within this group, the conditions that produced the change can be expected to produce change elsewhere.

The three specific case study communities were selected in order to leverage variation on the outcomes of interest—awareness, attitudes, primary behavior, and secondary behavior and rhetoric—and thereby enable the identification of causal processes. As the empirical chapters will show, Oldonyiro has experienced minimal norm change, with low levels of awareness about the international norms against FGM and early marriage corresponding to very low levels of attitude change, primary behavior change, secondary behavior change, and misrepresentation. Mukogodo holds the middle ground, with high levels of awareness, moderate levels of attitude change, and modest levels of primary behavior change. The people of Mukogodo also have the highest tendency to make false commitments to the international norms, which suggests a conflicted community in transition. Mau has experienced the greatest degree of norm change, though defection from the local norms is far from universal. The community exhibits the highest levels of awareness, attitude change, and primary behavior change, but its people are still quite likely to misrepresent their normative commitments to international actors.

Looking at norms around two different issue areas was beneficial because the theory makes predictions about how and to what extent norm change will occur given the properties of the competing norms—specifically, the salience of the international norm at the international level and the salience of the local norm at the local level. As such, it was important to introduce variation in norm salience across the issues selected, and FGM and early marriage fit this requirement, with the additional advantage of being comparable practices in a number of other respects. More broadly, evaluating the theory against two issues gives greater credence to the theory's generalizability to other norm conflicts, suggesting that the processes of norm change identified here are not unique to a specific case.

Methods

I employed a mixed-method empirical strategy to evaluate the theoretical framework, collecting data over 14 months of intensive fieldwork between 2007 and 2011.[30] The first element of this strategy was a series of approximately 150 semistructured in-depth interviews. I spoke with workers at NGOs and community-based organizations (CBOs),[31] local politicians, teachers, school officials, nurses, public health workers, government employees, church leaders, elders, traditional circumcisers, and traditional birth attendants in the three study areas. Interviewees were selected on the basis of their knowledge and experience—each was sufficiently involved with the practices of FGM and early marriage, and activism against them, that they were able to speak in a thoughtful manner to the broader causal processes underlying resistance to and support for norm change. I identified most interviewees through a snowball sample, asking initial interviewees if they could recommend other individuals to whom I should speak. Because each case study area is a relatively small community, the snowball strategy enabled me to identify all relevant stakeholders within each area. In particular, I was able to speak with at least one person (usually the director or chairperson) from every active NGO or CBO in the three

30. The methodological appendix contains additional details about the design and implementation of the empirical strategy.
31. In Kenya, the distinction between an NGO and a CBO is a legal one. While CBOs are meant to be tied to a specific geographic area, NGOs have more freedom to expand their operations to new areas of the country. The distinction does not relate to the size of the organization—some CBOs are larger than some NGOs—or to the organization's funding sources—many registered CBOs are directly funded by international organizations. Also, in practice, many registered NGOs operate in circumscribed geographic areas no larger than CBOs' areas of operation.

communities. Outside of the snowball sample, I also attempted to speak to people holding specific government job titles in each study area—chiefs, district commissioners, district officers, gender officers, children's officers, development officers, social development officers, education officers, and public health officers. In general, potential interviewees were quite willing, and often enthusiastic, to participate in interviews.

All interviews consisted of open-ended questions, most of which were drawn from a protocol designed in advance of the interviews, but some of which were constructed on the spot in order to probe interviewees' responses. The vast majority of interviews were conducted in English, which is one of Kenya's two national languages. On the rare occasions when an interviewee did not speak English, the interview was conducted in Maa with the aid of an interpreter.

Interviewees were asked to provide their insights into the larger trends in their communities. Questions focused on interviewees' perceptions of community attitudes and practices with respect to FGM and early marriage, and on the extent to which they believed these attitudes and practices had changed over time. Questions also sought to explore any variation in openness to norm change across different groups within the community, and to interrogate possible sources of change. Different groups of interviewees were uniquely situated to provide particular kinds of insights in response to these questions. NGO and CBO workers could address the motivations of their peers and the challenges they faced in attempting to deliver the normative message. Government workers, politicians, teachers, and church leaders could speak openly about the successes and shortcomings of the campaign. And traditional leaders and circumcisers could explain why they and others in the community were reluctant to abandon their traditional practices.

The second element of the empirical strategy was an original representative survey about FGM and early marriage, carried out in November 2008 among 600 members of the general population in the three case study areas. Each study area had a sample size of 200, and respondents were drawn from across all 20 administrative sublocations of the study areas using a random walk procedure. Respondents were male and female Maa-speakers aged 15 to 85. Though women have more direct experience with FGM and early marriage, it was important to also include male respondents in the survey given their centrality to family decision-making. For similar reasons, there was no upper age limit on survey participation because of the significant role elders play in community norm-setting. The lower age limit of 15 was selected in order to capture girls who had been recently circumcised or married, providing insight into the current incidence of FGM and early marriage.

Setting the participation age any younger would have risked including girls who had not yet been circumcised but would be in the future (as discussed in chapter 3, Maasai and Samburu girls are generally circumcised during puberty), producing a potentially misleading picture of the incidence rate. It was also helpful for analysis purposes to be able to break up respondents into five-year age cohorts, and thus 15 was a convenient starting point.[32] Each questionnaire was completed verbally and entirely in Maa, which was necessary because some Maasai and Samburu speak neither English nor Kiswahili, but which also served as a practical way to limit the survey to Maasai and Samburu residents of the study communities without having to ask potential interviewees about their ethnicity up front. Questionnaire enumerators were recruited from within each study area and matched with respondents according to sex.

Respondents were asked a series of questions designed to assess their knowledge, beliefs, attitudes, experiences, and behaviors with respect to both practices. Gathering this data allowed for estimation of the magnitude of the relationships and trends identified by the qualitative interviewees, including the extent to which exposure to high-quality activism and normative out-groups, and beliefs about influential locals' attitudes, shape individuals' own attitudes and behavior, and the extent to which this varies across the two practices and the three communities.

The third element was a randomized experiment, which was embedded in the larger survey to gauge respondents' willingness to rhetorically commit to the international norms against FGM and early marriage while simultaneously maintaining their compliance to local norms. In the survey,

32. Setting an age-based minimum for survey participation did have potential drawbacks, as Maasai and Samburu do not always know their exact ages (Coast 2001, 68). However, recording of birth dates has become more common over time (Cronk 2004, 15), such that younger potential respondents were very likely to know their age. Indeed, the survey itself asked respondents to report their exact age, but if they were unable to do this enumerators prompted them to estimate their age. Among those reporting their age as below 18 years old, 43 respondents reported their age exactly while only 5 estimated their age. Estimation was more common among respondents who reported that they were older, especially among those reporting that they were over 35. "Heaping"—the tendency to estimate numbers that end in "0" or "5" (Shryock and Siegel 1976, 116)—was also more common among older respondents. There is the additional possibility that potential respondents misreported their ages, since questions about age can be viewed as personal (Cronk 2004, 8). However, one would expect this view to be less common among the young given their generally greater interaction with ethnic out-groups who do not view age in this way. In any case, the absence of heaping among younger respondents suggests that any misreporting was not systematic in one direction or the other. Overall, the drawbacks to employing an age-based selection strategy were outweighed by the value of being able to ultimately sort respondents into roughly accurate age cohorts, as a means to assess trends over time.

half of the participants—the treatment group—were randomly assigned to be told that their answers would reach an international audience, while the other half—the control group—were told that their answers would reach a local audience. The experiment assessed whether the treatment group was more likely to declare opposition to the two practices. Including the survey experiment presented a unique opportunity to actually measure individuals' strategic engagement with the international community. More broadly, the experiment is able to provide direct evidence of social desirability bias in survey response.

Methodological Contribution and Field Challenges

My own experience in the field directly informed the design and implementation of each of the elements of the empirical strategy. Because of the extended period of time I spent in and around the three field sites, I was able to build relationships with a range of activists and other community stakeholders that ultimately shaped the questions I asked, my understanding of the answers I received, and my access to relevant local players and events. In particular, in each case study area I relied on two or three key informants who served as information resources and access points. These informants were generally individuals who had engaged in public activism against FGM or early marriage but who also had strong roots in their communities—individuals who had a foot in each world and could reflect critically and thoughtfully on both. In addition to formal interviews, I had extended informal conversations with my informants over many months and sometimes years, and in some cases stayed in their homes during field visits. The informants helped me piece together starter lists of potential interviewees and filled me in on the local social, cultural, and political context so that I could be an informed conversational partner in interviews. At times they also directly introduced me to interviewees who would otherwise have been difficult to track down on my own, including circumcisers, traditional birth attendants, and certain elders. In addition, they helped me secure access to trainings, workshops, and public events around FGM, early marriage, and child rights, including two alternative rites of passage, a public celebration of the Day of the African Child, an FGM symposium, and the marriage ceremony of an underage girl.

The extended nature of my fieldwork and the relationships I formed with my interviewees helped me to overcome some of the challenges I faced due to my positioning as a foreign researcher and due to the potentially fraught subject matter of the research. Though by no means taboo, FGM and early marriage are complicated issues to discuss under any conditions, encompassing actions that take place within families and that involve the female body. In the context of this research, they are also politicized issues as a result of activist efforts against them, placing them in the sphere of ongoing public debate. In addition, as will be discussed in greater detail in chapter 3, both FGM and early marriage have been criminalized in Kenya. This general context might make some individuals reluctant to talk about the practices at all, or to talk about them freely and openly. Indeed, the theory itself predicts a degree of misrepresentation and other evasive behavior. In particular, it predicts that some individuals who continue to comply with the local norms supporting FGM and early marriage will nonetheless present themselves as complying with the international norms opposing these practices when faced with an international audience. This makes my own status as a foreigner highly relevant—I couldn't expect to be treated as simply a neutral interlocutor to whom people would automatically be willing to reveal their "true" actions and opinions.[33]

In the face of these challenges, I made specific efforts to minimize potential distortions in the data I gathered and the conclusions I reached. In the context of the interviews, I attempted to limit the risk that interviewees might feel uncomfortable, and the incentive for interviewees to misrepresent themselves, by remaining as neutral as possible with my own language and by not asking them directly about their own experiences or behavior, instead asking them to describe the community at large. Asking interviewees about other people gave them room to share their thoughts without necessarily directly implicating themselves, a strategy that has been successfully deployed to reduce response bias in surveys (see, e.g., Fisher 1993). I also provided for the confidentiality of interviewees' responses, lest they be concerned that their comments would be revealed to others in the community. Furthermore, I came to believe that my status as a young woman facilitated both access to interviewees and relatively open conversation, because I was generally perceived as nonthreatening.[34] Most critically, the substantial

33. However, my outsider positioning did provide certain benefits. People's general curiosity about me tended to open doors, and the widespread perception of Westerners as holding high status afforded me relatively easy access in particular to government officials and government data.

34. Other field researchers have also found that being a (Western) woman often improves access to research subjects, even in ostensibly conservative settings (Schwedler 2006; Cammett 2013, note 6).

amount of time I spent with many of the interviewees—interviews generally lasted from one to two hours, and were sometimes repeated on separate occasions—allowed me in many cases to build relationships of trust that produced surprisingly honest and insightful commentary. And because of the large number of interviews I conducted, I was not obligated to accept any individual interviewee's (self-)assessment as fact. Interviewees were more than happy to report on one another (demonstrated in the qualitative interview data presented in chapter 7), and I was thus able to triangulate the different perspectives to get a comprehensive picture of the reality on the ground. Ultimately, while it is undoubtedly true that, given my outsider status and the nature of the issues themselves, some portion of the interviewees sought to portray themselves as more adamantly opposed to the practices of FGM and early marriage than they actually were, I have confidence in my interpretation of the data. Indeed, my overall experience was that interviewees were generally willing to be quite candid—the very fact that I was able to interview several traditional circumcisers, each of whom knew FGM was both illegal and the subject of significant activism, and who nonetheless agreed to speak with me, supports this conclusion.

In the context of the survey, care was also taken to make respondents comfortable and allow them to speak freely. Surveys were conducted in private with only the enumerator present, and respondents were informed that the information they provided would be kept confidential. Enumerators were also recruited and matched with respondents with an eye toward minimizing response bias. Identified with the assistance of my key informants, enumerators were uniformly young secondary school graduates and native Maa-speakers who lived within the case study areas. Enumerators were recruited locally on the expectation that Maasai and Samburu interviewees would be more willing to reveal personal information to "insiders" (see Coast 2001, 61). The advantage of such access was viewed as outweighing the risk that any existing relationships between enumerators and interviewees could complicate data collection. Enumerators' insider status in the survey context also helped balance my outsider status in the qualitative interviews.[35] Moreover, enumerators' youth likely served to put respondents at ease. Among the Maasai and Samburu, elders must be accorded respect (*enkanyit*) (Talle

---

35. There is a long-standing debate about the advantages and disadvantages of both insider and outsider status in field research, as well as a more recent recognition that insider/outsider positionality might more profitably be thought of as a continuum rather than a dichotomy (Merriam et al. 2001).

1988, 92; Spencer 1965, 135). This has the potential to constrain conversation, but respondents would not feel such pressure when speaking to a young man or woman (Hodgson 2001, 18). In addition, because the practices of FGM and early marriage have traditionally not been discussed across gender lines, female enumerators interviewed female respondents and male enumerators interviewed male respondents. This was considered especially important because respondents were being asked to describe their own experiences—it seemed unlikely that a woman would feel comfortable discussing the details of her own circumcision with a man.[36]

My own status and positioning was less relevant for the survey because I was not a visible part of its administration. This was done intentionally to avoid the risk that my presence would contaminate the survey experiment—it was important that the control group not be exposed to an international audience, and thus to me as an international observer. Instead, a local partner NGO or CBO in each study area served as the public face of the survey. In this way, the positioning of the partner organizations within their respective communities comes into play. The three groups were Pastoralist Women for Health and Education in Oldonyiro, the Indigenous Laikipiak Maasai Integrated Youth Organization (ILAMAIYO) in Mukogodo, and Tasaru Ntomonok Initiative in Mau. These organizations were selected for their significant presence in each of the three communities and their generally good reputations, such that potential respondents were likely to recognize the names and react favorably to them. Each group was staffed predominantly by locals from in or around the case study areas, and had some track record of addressing FGM and early marriage, along with other issues. Nonetheless, it remains possible that variation in the way respondents perceived the three groups might have shaped survey responses to some degree. Encouragingly, any such effect should have been the same for both the treatment and control groups, and thus should not have interfered with the experimental design.

36. Though some studies have found evidence of interviewer effects on survey response as a result of the interaction between interviewer and respondent gender, the existence of such effects appears to be highly contingent on the broader survey context and on the nature of specific questions. Studies on interviewer age effects have also been inconclusive (Davis et al. 2010, 22). Moreover, very few studies have evaluated interviewer effects in surveys conducted outside of the United States (Flores-Macias and Lawson 2008). In the absence of clear guidance from the literature, I based my decision to use younger enumerators and to match enumerators and respondents according to gender on my own understanding of the local context in the case study communities.

Overall, the mixed-method approach itself provides additional insurance against the possibility that the contested nature of the subject matter or the positioning of my partners, my enumerators, and myself significantly swayed the findings. Because the individual sets of data were collected under different conditions, the interview data serve as a check on the validity and reliability of the survey and experimental data, and vice versa. Moreover, mixed methods enjoy a number of additional advantages over single-method research, particularly when studying something as complex as norm change, with its multiple levels of analysis and many moving parts. Where statistical analysis is good for identifying patterns and establishing the relative significance of various correlations, qualitative interviews are good for teasing out causal processes. Qualitative data can illuminate diverse individual motivations, while quantitative data can more clearly show the social and political structures within which individual decisions are made.

In evaluating my theory, the qualitative and quantitative approaches have proved complementary. The general population survey and experiment provide a representative picture of each case study community at a particular moment in time, while the qualitative interviews of key community stakeholders allow me to drill down into the actual mechanisms of norm change and also to gain insight into historical trends in the three communities. The design of the survey questionnaire and experimental instrument was also informed by some of the discussions I had during early interviews, thus improving the quantitative data collection. Thus, the methods employed enable a holistic view of the object of inquiry that is greater than the sum of its qualitative and quantitative parts. Though the empirics are focused on three small cases within a single country, this is justified by the fact that the processes described in the theory cannot really be observed without close study, and such close study is best accomplished using an intensive mixed-methodological strategy.

On the whole, the empirical evidence provides strong support for the theoretical framework outlined above. I find that increased exposure to international normative messages, contact with normative out-groups, and the presence of influential locals among the group of norm leaders are indeed strongly associated with positive individual responses to activism against FGM and early marriage. I also find that respondents who received the experimental treatment do misrepresent their behavior and intentions, supporting the argument that individuals face both strategic and psychological motivations for deception in the context of conflict between international and local norms. And at each level,

I identify important variation between the two practices and across the three case study communities.

OUTLINE OF THE BOOK

The next chapter presents the central theoretical framework for understanding local-level norm change in response to a conflict between international and local norms. It disaggregates individual norm change into three discrete activities—attitude change, primary behavioral change, and secondary behavioral and rhetorical change—and establishes the conditions under which each of these changes is most likely to occur. It also identifies factors that influence the extent of exposure to the international normative message. The theory highlights systemic, local, and individual-level sources of variation in both exposure and norm change. It then considers the processes by which international norms diffuse across individuals and through communities, emphasizing both social and temporal dimensions of change.

Chapter 3 outlines the practice of and campaign against FGM and early marriage in Kenya, among the Maasai and Samburu, and in the three case study communities (which are introduced in greater detail in this chapter). It discusses the scope of the two practices and the nature of the local norms supporting them, as well as observed changes. It also considers the history and range of activism against the practices, and the activities of the Kenyan government. The chapter draws on quantitative data from Kenya's Demographic and Health Surveys and from my own original survey, as well as qualitative data from a range of primary and secondary sources.

Chapters 4 through 7 present the major empirical support for the theory, drawing on both the qualitative interview data and the original survey data. In chapter 4, I focus on exposure to and awareness of international norms. I show that there have been comparable levels of transnational activism against FGM and early marriage in the study communities. While the high salience of the international norm against FGM drives up activism by aid-dependent NGOs, the high salience of the local norm supporting the practice drives down activism by other community organizations. The low salience of both the international and local norms surrounding early marriage drives down activism by aid-dependent NGOs but creates space for activism by actors that are financially independent. However, the level of activism against both practices varies by community—awareness of the international norms against FGM and early marriage is most likely when communities, and individuals within communities, are accessible to NGOs and other activists.

In chapter 5 I address attitude change in response to transnational activism against FGM and early marriage. I find that individual attitude change is most likely to occur when the international normative message people receive is not only frequent but also of high quality, and that aid-dependent NGOs are less likely to provide such a high-quality message. While message quality is difficult to operationalize, I am able to show that individuals with a strong grasp of the content of the international norms—that is, knowledge of the health and human rights consequences of FGM and early marriage—are more likely to express opposition to the two practices. I also show that, for any given level of activism, individuals are less likely to change their attitudes about FGM than about early marriage, because of FGM's higher local salience.

Chapter 6 considers the barriers to individual primary behavior change and the diffusion of behavior change through communities. I show that because of the relatively low salience of the local norm supporting early marriage, individual behavior change closely tracks attitude change. However, the high salience of the local norm supporting FGM means that individual behavior change lags significantly behind attitude change. Due to FGM's high local salience, behavior change is most likely to occur where individuals are able to somehow mitigate the high barriers to defection—I find that exposure to noncircumcising ethnic groups is associated with individual behavior change in communities that have experienced minimal norm change, and that local elites' opposition to FGM is associated with individual behavior change in communities that are at both early and advanced stages of transition.

In chapter 7 I focus on rhetorical and secondary behavioral change. I find that many individuals take steps to misrepresent or hide their true attitudes and behavior with respect to FGM and early marriage, and that they are motivated to do this by both reputational and material considerations. The survey experiment shows that individuals are willing to make false rhetorical commitments to international norms when they encounter an international audience, and the qualitative interviews show a propensity both for rhetorical misrepresentation to international activists and for actively hiding local norm compliance from local activists and authorities. However, these types of activities occur primarily in communities that have experienced significant exposure to the relevant international norms.

Chapter 8 concludes by summarizing the theory and central findings. It also places the theory in a broader context by applying it to FGM and early marriage cross-nationally and by applying it to two additional issues—girl-child education and dowry. Finally, it discusses a number of theoretical and policy implications, enumerates the book's contributions to diverse literatures and areas of inquiry, and explores avenues for further research.

CHAPTER 2

A Theory of Local-Level Responses to International Norm Promotion

In this chapter, I lay out a theoretical framework of micro-level norm change in the context of competing international and local norms. Within this framework, I focus on two sets of related processes. First, I consider how individuals negotiate the competing demands placed on them by transnational activists and by their own local reference groups. To do this, I establish the conditions under which each of three elements of norm change—attitude change, primary behavioral change, and secondary behavioral and rhetorical change—is most likely to occur. I also identify factors that influence the extent of individual and community exposure to the international normative message. Second, I consider how international norms diffuse across individuals and through communities, emphasizing the dynamic interplay between individual and group behavior. Both sets of processes are heavily shaped by the social aspect of norms, and depend on ideational as well as instrumental considerations.

I apply this theoretical framework to the specific issues of FGM and early marriage. Here it is important to note that, as discussed in general terms in chapter 1 and with respect to the Maasai and Samburu in chapter 3, the practices of FGM and early marriage are closely linked to each other in many communities, as is activism against the practices, raising the possibility that any individual- and community-level change in one of these practices will be dependent on or interdependently related to change in the other. However, there are reasons to doubt the extent of such dependence or interdependence. It is true that in places where both FGM and early marriage occur, declines in one practice have tended to correlate with declines in the other. Moreover, a number of the qualitative interviewees made an explicit connection between the two practices, suggesting that FGM eradication would precipitate early-marriage eradication. But this argument seems primarily to reflect a desire to justify the fact that some NGOs are not engaging in much direct activism against early marriage, instead tacking a vague commitment to end early marriage onto their more concerted activism against FGM (as demonstrated in chapter 4). If bringing an end to FGM would solve the early-marriage issue too, then failure to directly address early marriage could not be perceived as a shortcoming of the organization. However, as described in chapter 1, the underlying causes of each practice are generally distinct. While FGM may be associated with lower marriage age at the individual level (Wagner 2015, 14), and while FGM may in some cases be a requirement for marriage and occur directly before marriage, girls are not married early *because* they have been circumcised, but instead because of a range of cultural, religious, and economic incentives. Ending FGM will not eliminate those incentives, and thus will not eliminate early marriage. Similarly, there is no reason to think that ending early marriage would somehow eliminate FGM, though it might perhaps delay the age at which girls are cut in communities where FGM and marriage are temporally linked. The fact that one frequently observes the two practices declining in tandem likely has more to do with the fact that activists themselves are engaging in activism against both practices simultaneously, producing largely independent but correlated declines. At most, it might be fair to say that successful activism against one practice could "soften up" a community and make them more willing to consider abandoning other traditional practices. In any event, for the purposes of theoretical parsimony, I will keep the two practices conceptually distinct.

INDIVIDUAL DECISION-MAKING PROCESSES

Explaining International Norm Exposure

Though a conflict may exist between international and local norms, this conflict is only meaningful to individual decision-making if the individual is aware of the international norm. I define international norm awareness as knowledge of the fact that international actors have a common preference with respect to a particular behavior, irrespective of whether the individual has complete information about the logic underlying the international norm.

To emphasize the importance of international norm awareness is not to deny that local norms can evolve on their own, in the absence of a competing international norm.[1] Certainly, norms of appropriate behavior are rarely perfectly static over long periods of time. However, in the absence of an outright norm conflict, most local norms will change only gradually; rapid norm shifts are likely to be the product of concerted action on the part of motivated activists. Indeed, even where the behavior promoted by the local norm is actually harmful, independent local recognition of this fact may be quite slow to emerge. This is because public opinion around a well-established norm is likely to be completely unanimous, such that individuals are rarely forced to think about the content of the norm. In the absence of any obvious alternatives, there is little impetus for individuals to devote much energy to either mentally justifying the status quo or to considering a nonexistent debate about it. "Because of their cognitive limitations, [people] must think selectively, relying extensively on social proof. They will thus treat as settled most matters on which they have inherited no public disagreement, reserving their mental powers primarily for ones that appear controversial" (Kuran 1995, 185).

The difficulty of contesting an otherwise uncontested belief and drawing causal conclusions about harm certainly applies to FGM and early marriage, since both are traditional practices that date back at least a few generations, if not hundreds or thousands of years. Under such conditions, it is unsurprising to see practitioners justify the practices mechanically, saying simply that "it is tradition." Indeed, unless prompted, many people may not even think about the reasons that they are performing these practices, because failing to perform them is not an option that enters into their minds. Thus, they are less likely to internalize or even notice information—including personal experience—that suggests the practices may cause harm. And especially because the health consequences associated with the two practices are often delayed—many of the side effects associated with both FGM and early marriage appear during or after childbirth—it can be relatively easy for women and men alike to convince themselves that the practice itself is not responsible.[2] Where the consequences are immediate—as when

1. Chapter 3 includes a description of some such changes in the practices of female circumcision and early marriage among the Maasai and Samburu.
2. Lest one think that the failure to make a causal connection between a dangerous behavior and future health consequences is unlikely, consider the case of cigarettes. Despite the fact that people were inhaling smoke directly into their lungs and subsequently developing lung cancer and emphysema, few smokers perceived a causal relationship between cigarette smoking and lung disease until they were presented with overwhelming scientific evidence in the 1960s. Even then, not everyone was receptive to the message.

a girl suffers severe blood loss from circumcision—it may still be easier to believe that the girl has been cursed or that some other supernatural force is at work (Koso-Thomas 1987, 36). And women may not recognize the loss of sexual pleasure due to circumcision if they were not sexually active prior to the cut. Mackie (1996, 1009) points to two studies that seem to confirm the obstacles to independently recognizing harm, at least in the case of FGM: a study by Koso-Thomas (1987) in which Sierra Leonean women who were sexually active both before and after clitoridectomy reported decreased sexual satisfaction and yet were unable to identify clitoridectomy as the cause; and a study by Lightfoot-Klein (1989, 22) in which infibulated Sudanese women simultaneously described their urination as "normal" and as taking up to 15 minutes.

These examples illustrate why independent, rapid abandonment of FGM and early marriage is unlikely. Some isolated individuals within practicing groups may overcome these hurdles and decide on their own that the local norms are problematic (and these individuals may go on to join the ranks of transnational activists opposing the practices), but they are likely to be the exception rather than the rule. When local norms are long-standing and universally applied, some significant external action may be the only way to jolt large numbers of adherents into reconsidering their stance. It is this external action that produces the outright norm conflict with which individual group members must contend.

So, given that all decisions in response to a norm conflict are predicated on exposure to the international normative message, what conditions influence the extent of this exposure? I focus on three main causal factors: international norm salience, local norm salience, and NGO density.

A norm's *salience* to its proponents matters. At the international level, some issues are able to capture and hold the attention of the international community better than others, and there has been some speculation about the criteria that are most likely to produce high international norm salience and an associated transnational campaign. Keck and Sikkink (1998, 27), for example, have suggested that two issue characteristics are good predictors of international salience—whether or not the issue constitutes bodily harm to vulnerable populations, and whether or not legal equality of rights is being violated. They argue that the ability to frame a campaign around one of these two problems and the ability to establish a short causal chain of responsibility go a long way toward explaining the existence of most international campaigns around principled issues. Price (1998, 623) similarly emphasizes the power of graphic images of human tragedy, and both he and Finnemore and Sikkink (1998, 908) suggest that norms gain prominence if they can be effectively linked to existing salient norms. Carpenter (2007) further proposes that individual agents and power relationships within and between activist networks may play important mediating roles in issue emergence.

Whatever the reason, when an international norm is highly salient and becomes the subject of a dedicated transnational campaign, it will drive up activism around that issue, and thus drive up local exposure to the international normative message. Recall that a transnational campaign is dependent on a variety of supporters playing a variety of roles. Some actors operate internationally, including bilateral and multilateral aid agencies, international governmental organizations, and international NGOs, while others operate domestically, including national and local NGOs and other nonstate actors such as religious institutions. Maintaining a transnational campaign depends not just on the commitment of these actors but also on the continuing availability of funding to support the campaign's activities. Though not exclusively, much of this funding comes from the transnational campaign's international supporters, while much of the boots-on-the-ground activism is performed by domestic organizations. Thus, we should expect local activism to increase as more and more funding becomes available from international donors, and we should expect this donor support to increase as a particular international norm gains salience.

However, the salience of the international norm to transnational activists is not the only factor driving activism; the salience of the local norm to the target group matters as well. When a local norm is highly salient, transnational activists may find it difficult to recruit many local organizations willing to join the cause and speak out openly against it, for fear of alienating their fellow group members. This reluctance on the part of local organizations doesn't necessarily preclude all activism against the norm—the task can still be performed by other domestic and international organizations—but it does undermine the overall strength of the effort.

In basic terms, the higher the salience of an international norm to transnational activists, the higher the level of activism should be. And the higher the salience of the local norm to the target group, the lower the level of activism should be. The interaction of these two forces will thus strongly influence the overall level of activism observed. Figure 2.1 presents a simple two-dimensional picture of norm salience that provides expectations about the level of activism around a particular issue. Four basic interactions are possible. First, if the local population cares a lot about maintaining the local norm (local norm salience is high), and transnational activists aren't highly committed to the international norm (international norm salience is low), then the overall level of activism should be quite low, as shown in the upper-left cell. Conversely, if the local population doesn't care very deeply about maintaining the local norm, and transnational activists care a

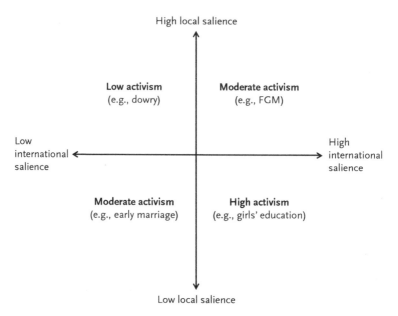

Figure 2.1: Dimensions of norm salience and expected levels of activism

lot about spreading the international norm, then the level of activism should be quite high, as shown in the lower-right cell. However, if both groups either have a low level of commitment to their respective norms (the lower-left cell) or a high level of commitment to those norms (the upper-right cell), the level of activism should be moderate. In the former case, relatively low interest on the part of transnational actors meets very little resistance to the international norm at the local level—while limited funding is available, it is not difficult to recruit local activists. In the latter case, there is a real tension between the interests of the two groups, with international actors' commitment to the international norm (and corresponding funding provision) driving activism up and local actors' resistance simultaneously driving activism down.

Where do the issues of FGM and early marriage fall within this rubric? As described in chapter 1, the international norm against FGM is highly salient and has produced a sustained transnational campaign. This fits Keck and Sikkink's expectations about campaign emergence, since FGM clearly falls into the category of bodily harm to vulnerable populations. By contrast, the international norm against early marriage is significantly less prominent and has not had a dedicated transnational campaign of its own (at least until very recently).[3] While one could certainly argue that

3. On a personal note, when I tell people that I do research on FGM and early marriage, they almost universally pepper me with questions about the former and ignore the latter.

early marriage also constitutes bodily harm, the causal chain is not quite as short; early marriage does not so much cause bodily harm directly as it puts girls at much higher risk of other, more proximate causes of harm such as marital rape, early pregnancy, and domestic violence. Moreover, the image of FGM as a single, agonizing event is far more dramatic than the image of early marriage, where the cutoff age of 18 may seem fairly arbitrary—why is an 18-year-old mature enough to marry but not a 17-year-old? The fact that the international norm against FGM is more salient than the international norm against early marriage does not, however, mean that FGM is necessarily a more pressing problem than early marriage. Indeed, if one were to trace out all of the harmful consequences girls might face as a result of the two practices, early marriage tends to have the more negative long-term repercussions. This is not to downplay the harm associated with FGM or the legitimacy of the campaign around it, but rather to emphasize that international norms gain salience for reasons that extend beyond harm.

At the local level, on the other hand, the norm supporting female circumcision tends to be highly salient for most practicing groups, while the local norm supporting early marriage tends to be more peripheral. These tendencies are not universal—as already discussed, different groups practice FGM and early marriage for different reasons, and thus their commitment to the practices also varies—but there are some common patterns. In particular, for many groups that practice FGM, undergoing the cut is a requirement for marriage, which essentially makes the practice compulsory and which also means that individual families will be highly committed to it. The practice also tends to be fairly prominent among a group's cultural traditions because of its supposed connection to valued female characteristics such as virginity, chastity, and docility. By contrast, the cultural value of early marriage is generally not as clear. Indeed, even where early marriage is in fact universally practiced within a given group, it tends to be a product of tradition or financial imperative rather than of a deep cultural commitment.[4] Moreover, the numerous variables involved in arranging a marriage mean that there will always be some variation in the age of marriage; it would be difficult to imagine a scenario in which all girls within a group were required to marry by the same specific age. As a result, slight increases in the average age of marriage might even go unnoticed by the

4. There are exceptions to this. Among the Xhosa of South Africa, for example, underage girls are ritually abducted for marriage in a practice known as *ukuthwalwa*. The practice is "condoned as a necessary part of a woman's life," and according to a Xhosa prince, "*Ukuthwalwa* like all our other customs was and remains an important part of who we are as people" (Fihlani 2009).

group. Early marriage as a local norm simply doesn't provide the same focal point for most practicing groups that FGM does.

The respective salience of the international and local norms around FGM and early marriage combine to create expectations about the overall level of activism against the two practices. Because international donors are highly committed to the international norm against FGM, they have consistently provided funding to support anti-FGM activities by NGOs and other state and nonstate actors. The availability of this funding should create strong incentives for these recipient organizations to at least nominally adopt FGM as a priority. However, the financial incentives should be partly offset by the high salience of the local norm supporting female circumcision, which should make local organizations reluctant to tackle the issue. In this situation, the interests of donors do not align well with the interests of many local NGOs. The end result is that while the level of anti-FGM activism is likely to be higher than it would be if the local organizations had full control over their own agendas, it is likely to be lower than the international donors would prefer. Essentially, the mobilizing effect that the high international salience of FGM has on activism balances out the dampening effect that the high local salience of female circumcision has on activism. Conversely, international donors have not been seriously committed to eradicating early marriage, such that funding tied specifically to supporting anti-early-marriage activities has been fairly limited. However, if activists *are* able to find funding support, there are rarely significant local barriers to speaking out against early marriage. Therefore, as with FGM, one should expect moderate levels of activism against the practice, though this activism will be achieved via a different process.

International and local norm salience thus helps to explain variation in the level of activism targeted at specific issues, but it can't do much to explain variation in the level of activism that actually reaches specific communities. I argue that the *density* of NGOs in a particular place is a critical factor affecting the spread of an international normative message, where NGO density refers to the sheer number and size of NGOs operating within a specified geographical area (and not to the number of NGOs actually headquartered in that area).

While international norm salience affects the demand for activism around a particular issue and local norm salience affects the supply of NGOs willing to address that issue, NGO density affects the supply of NGOs capable of addressing any issue at all in a particular location. There are two prior propositions underpinning this statement. The first is that many NGOs and their workers are not issue-specific. It is certainly the case that some people become NGO workers only because they are deeply motivated to address a particular problem, but most people who work for NGOs are in fact professionals, which is to say NGO work is their livelihood. Since the appeal of being a professional NGO worker is unlikely to change dramatically just because the issues on the international agenda change, one should not expect a tidal wave of new entrants onto this career path just because a particular norm gains international prominence—the total stock of NGOs and NGO workers in the world should be largely unaffected by changes in international norm salience. In the case of FGM, the rise of the transnational campaign did not generate a lot of brand-new NGO workers whose only commitment was to eradicating FGM and who would cease to be NGO workers if the campaign succeeded. Instead, it mostly reordered the priorities of existing NGOs, who either came to legitimately care about FGM or else shifted their activities strategically in order to take advantage of increased funding availability.

The second proposition is that NGOs and their workers do not simply materialize wherever they are needed—it is not the case, for example, that anti-FGM activists show up in every community where people practice FGM. Instead, there can be significant variation in NGO density for reasons unrelated to actual need (although need may certainly play a role) (Fruttero and Gauri 2005). One factor to consider is the state's willingness to tolerate NGOs. A major source of variation here is regime type, with democracies generally much more willing to embrace NGO mobilization than dictatorships are (Bratton 1989, 575). Authoritarian leaders are likely to fear that NGOs will challenge state control, and accordingly clamp down on NGO operations. In addition to regime type, another source of potential variation is the extent to which the political system runs on patronage—politicians who need to distribute private or club goods to their constituencies in order to ensure their political survival may attempt to funnel service-providing NGOs into their home regions.

There is also a temporal component to NGO density. While change over time in international interest in particular issues is unlikely to change the total stock of NGOs, change over time in international donors' willingness to directly fund NGOs *has* had a major impact on the total stock of these organizations. Since the 1980s, more and more international aid has been granted to NGOs rather than to governments, reaching approximately $20 billion annually by 2011 (Organization for Economic Cooperation and Development 2013). This shift toward NGOs occurred for a number of reasons, including a desire to avoid giving money to corrupt national governments as well as the hope that NGOs would be more nimble and efficient

(Bratton 1989, 572; Edwards and Hulme 1996, 2–3). The result is that, particularly in developing countries, the increased availability of aid for NGOs has spurred on many new entrants into the NGO sector (Ottaway and Carothers 2000, 299). While the reality is that many NGOs in fact struggle to consistently win grants, the common perception is that grant funding is easy to attract, and it is this *perception* that has driven the formation of new NGOs (Bob 2005, 14).

A final factor to think about is practical constraints on NGOs' willingness and ability to work in certain areas. In particular, a community's physical location and accessibility is likely to contribute to the density of NGOs operating there. Remote communities may not attract large national and international organizations, which make decisions about where to intervene based in part on ease of access and other convenience factors (Brass 2012). Long distance from the capital and poor road conditions can both be deterrents, especially if there is a similarly needy community that is more accessible. Certain community characteristics can also stifle the development of homegrown local NGOs, particularly issues such as low educational provision and rurality. In developing countries, NGOs tend to be started by individuals with secondary school or more advanced degrees, but some areas have a larger pool of such people than others. In communities where few people receive secondary or higher education, there may simply not be enough human capital on the ground to serve as a foundation for an active civil society. Moreover, local NGOs that do form in these areas may be less likely to have knowledge about how to access international aid (e.g., how to write grant proposals), which may circumscribe their reach and their lifespan. These problems are likely to be compounded by a process of subnational brain drain, in which the best-educated individuals flee rural areas for more cosmopolitan urban centers.

In general, NGO density can vary both nationally and subnationally for a variety of political, strategic, and practical reasons. NGO density and international and local norm salience then jointly influence the level of activism around a particular issue in a particular community. High international norm salience creates funding opportunities for NGOs to mobilize around a given issue. If in fact there is a strong NGO base operating in a given community, that base should be able to take advantage of the increased resource availability and tailor projects accordingly, although local NGOs may be reluctant to do so if the contradictory local norm is highly salient. However, the relative salience of international and local norms will be largely irrelevant to a community if there are few or no NGOs operating there.

Explaining Individual Norm Change

Though exposure to an international normative message through transnational activism is a necessary condition for local-level norm change, it is by no means sufficient. A number of additional factors contribute to whether individuals exposed to activism will ultimately change their attitudes, their primary behavior, and their secondary behavior and rhetoric. Specifically, I focus on the impact of activism quality, local social sanctions, exit options, and time effects.

Attitude Change

Attitude change is a critical hurdle to overcome for transnational activists seeking to promote an international norm at the local level. While the state-centric transnational advocacy literature has found that states sometimes behaviorally comply with international norms for instrumental rather than ideational reasons, this is much less likely to be the case among private individuals. The primary reason for this is the difficulty of monitoring individual behavior relative to monitoring state behavior. An important mechanism for eliciting desired behavior change from states is the so-called "naming and shaming" strategy (see, e.g., Risse, Ropp, and Sikkink 1999). In this approach, transnational activists monitor the behavior of states that have rhetorically committed to a particular international norm, and then publicly call those states out if their behavior fails to match their commitment. This can ultimately push states to behaviorally comply with the international norm even if they are not truly persuaded of the validity of that norm, because behavioral compliance is simply an instrumental response to international pressure. But it can be difficult, if not impossible, for transnational activists to consistently monitor the actual behavior of private citizens. If activists can't observe whether individuals are behaviorally complying with an international norm and leverage those observations to elicit desired behavior change, then one should expect primary behavior change only if individuals have actually been persuaded of the validity of the international norm. The only exception to this expectation would be in communities that are already in a relatively advanced stage of norm change—it is possible to imagine some individuals engaging in primary behavior change in the absence of attitude change if most other people in their original local reference group have already changed their behavior and are pressuring the remaining holdouts to follow suit. Here strategic behavior change might make sense because although transnational activists may have a hard time monitoring individual behavior at the local level, one's fellow community members should be in a better position to do so.

The main point is that persuasion will be the dominant mechanism by which transnational activists elicit behavior change at the local level. If activists must persuade individuals of the validity of the international norm, then it is important to think seriously about the conditions under which they are most likely to provide a high-quality message. This is especially important because simple exposure to the international normative message is unlikely to provoke attitude change on its own, given that activists are attempting to displace an existing local norm. To get people to switch their attitudinal commitment from the local to the international norm, activists must really work hard to justify the logic of the international norm.

Activism quality is a broad term that cannot be easily boiled down to a single all-encompassing definition. However, there is increasing scholarly and practical agreement about the kinds of general NGO behaviors that improve the overall quality of their work (see, e.g., Banerjee 2007). Commonly identified elements include whether programs are tailored to specific local contexts, whether programs are sustained over time, whether NGOs coordinate their programs with other NGOs, and whether NGOs rigorously evaluate program effectiveness. Adhering to these guidelines is not a guarantee of program effectiveness, but it is a strong indicator of quality.

With respect to the issues of FGM and early marriage, more and more evidence is becoming available about specific strategies that work well (see, e.g., Berg and Denison 2013; Boyle and Corl 2010, 204–6; Malhotra et al. 2011; Toubia and Sharief 2003). For instance, Winterbottom, Koomen, and Burford (2009) found that framing FGM as a cultural problem made Maasai communities in Tanzania resistant to educational campaigns, while a field experiment in northern Ghana showed that community-based education about FGM was more effective than livelihood skills training for girls and women in reducing the incidence of the practice (Feldman-Jacobs and Ryniak 2006, 15). Chege, Askew, and Liku (2001) concluded that the alternative-rite-of-passage approach was more effective where it was preceded by intensive sensitization of the whole community, but that it varied in effectiveness across ethnic groups according to the traditional performance method and function of female circumcision within those groups. Though there have not been as many evaluations of early-marriage programs, the available evidence is suggestive. Arends-Kuenning and Amin (2000, 13) found that secondary school scholarships for girls, combined with parental pledges that daughters would not marry early, contributed to a significant reduction in rates of marriage among adolescent girls in

Bangladesh. Mathur, Mehta, and Malhotra (2004, 51) found that a multi-dimensional approach combining social and economic components led to a reduction in early marriage in urban but not rural areas of Nepal. And a meta-analysis by the ICRW of 23 programs worldwide showed that programs that directly targeted girls with information, life skills, and other resources provided the strongest and most consistent results (Malhotra et al. 2011, 23).

A few notable NGOs have pursued winning strategies. In particular, the Tostan Village Empowerment Program, operating in Senegal since 1996, is widely recognized as a leader in activism against both FGM and early marriage. Tostan's approach has been in-depth, multidimensional, and sensitive to local contexts. Working at the village level, Tostan recruits local facilitators who are approved by the participants, and then implements an 18-month-long basic education program targeting women (and some men). Over the course of more than 400 hours of training, participants are given information on a variety of topics that is intended to improve their health, education, and welfare (Mackie 2000). Because discussion of FGM and early marriage is part of this larger whole, and because participants feel that they are gaining something valuable in return for listening to the messages about FGM and early marriage, the approach has resulted in a major success. Between 1997 and 2003, 1,271 separate Senegalese villages held public ceremonies in which they declared their abandonment of FGM and early marriage (Diop et al. 2003). By the end of 2011, that number had increased to 5,315 (United Nations Children's Fund 2013, 13). Pre- and postintervention surveys in southern Senegal also showed a decline in the prevalence of FGM among daughters of women exposed to the human-rights-based program (Diop and Askew 2009, 313; Diop et al. 2004, 23), as well as a decline in the prevalence of marriages before age 15 in intervention villages (United Nations Children's Fund 2008b, 51). The program has since been exported to a number of other West African countries.

Other highly regarded anti-FGM interventions include the integrated community empowerment and human-rights-based approaches of KMG in the Kembatta Tembaro Zone of Ethiopia and of the Coptic Evangelical Organization for Social Services in Minya, Egypt (Dagne 2009; United Nations Children's Fund 2010, 19, 30). On early marriage, the Population Council's Berhane Hewane program has experienced success by addressing the economic incentives of marrying early and providing social support for girls in the Amhara region of Ethiopia, while the Maharashtra Life Skills Program in India has had an impact by providing skills training for adolescent girls (Erulkar and Muthengi 2009; International Center for Research on Women 2007, 39; Pande et al. 2006, 10–11).

But undertaking these kinds of programs requires commitment, persistence, and sensitivity, and unfortunately, not all NGOs demonstrate these characteristics. Why might this be? I argue that the increased availability of international aid to NGOs has had consequences not just for the proliferation of NGOs, but also for the incentives those NGOs face in pursuing various activities.

To begin with, not all NGOs are motivated by altruism. While it would be nice if this were true, the reality is that the widespread availability of international aid has produced countless "briefcase NGOs"—organizations that exist only on paper, for the express purpose of cheating donors out of their money (Barr, Fafchamps, and Owens 2005; Fowler 1997; Holloway 2001). But even among NGOs that are operational and staffed by genuinely well-intentioned workers, there are a number of structural challenges that can work against the adoption of effective programming (Brass 2012, 389–90; Prakash and Gugerty 2010). To think more concretely about what these challenges might look like, we should consider the conditions under which many NGOs get started and why many NGO workers become NGO workers in a world where international aid for NGOs is widely available.

Particularly in developing countries, individuals with a secondary school or university education frequently find themselves unemployed or underemployed. In such circumstances, starting an NGO becomes an attractive option because it is a perceived mechanism for local job creation. Without strong alternative job prospects, NGO leaders may sincerely want to help their communities, but their other goal—to remain employed—often takes precedence. Moreover, their desire to help their community can be fairly abstract. If the primary impetus for the formation of the organization is employment, then the specific activities the NGO pursues may not be of central concern to its members.

Thus, in order to remain employed in the NGO sector, many NGO leaders are likely to make strategic choices about which issues they address, allowing donors' interests to set or reorder their priorities (Hulme and Edwards 1997; Morfit 2011; Smillie 1995). Rather than a system in which NGOs identify the most significant issues facing their community and then work to persuade donors to fund projects that address those issues, it is instead a system in which donors decide which issues matter (including, as discussed above, FGM) and then fund organizations that work on those issues.

Because donors generally have multiple priorities and because those priorities change over time, individual NGOs can end up working on a wide range of issue areas (Bob 2005, 41–42). They may begin by addressing one or two main issues, but over the years they broaden their focus in order to continue to take advantage of available funding sources (Watkins,

Swidler, and Hannan 2012, 293). They add new projects without ever quite abandoning the projects that came before, so that eventually their mission embraces 6, 8, 10, or more discrete issue areas. This phenomenon is known as "mission creep."

While donor-driven issue selection and mission creep can be particularly problematic for the many relatively new national and local NGOs based in developing countries, they can also plague both established developing-country NGOs and international NGOs. International NGO workers, many of whom come from the global North, are likely to have somewhat higher levels of human capital and thus better alternative job prospects than NGO workers from the global South, which suggests that they may have initially chosen their profession for somewhat more consistently altruistic reasons. The same can be said of NGO workers in developing countries who entered the NGO sector before the glut in availability of international aid. Yet that doesn't mean that these workers are actually indifferent to their organizations' continued existence. The oft-repeated mantra in development circles is that NGOs should be working toward their own extinction, but this is rarely pursued in practice. Organizations of all kinds, including NGOs, tend to develop bureaucratic systems that seek their own reproduction, however noble their other goals (Bob 2005, 26; Cooley and Ron 2002; Henderson 2002, 147; Prakash and Gugerty 2010, 11).[5] One reason is that individuals working in a given job build up specific human capital that is suited to that particular industry and to that particular job; it may not be easily transferable to a different job or career. Also, job hunting is time consuming and entails a fair amount of uncertainty, which often makes one's current job more attractive than a hypothetical alternative. Thus, long-established international and national NGOs and their workers are not immune to the financial incentives that donors create, and can similarly fall prey to mission creep and the reordering of priorities if these things help keep the organization afloat. Moreover, these organizations may be further disadvantaged by a lack of contextual knowledge about the communities in which they're working, and by a lack of credibility among the targets of their activism due to their outsider status.

What are the consequences of donor-driven issue selection and of mission creep? First, if NGOs aren't working on issues about which they are passionate, they may not be as motivated to seek out the most effective

5. An example of the survival imperative outside of the NGO sector comes from Weaver (2008), who discusses the incentives created by resource dependency at the World Bank. Though the Bank is a donor in its own right, it is also dependent on its own member states for continued funding.

strategies or to develop the necessary human capital to effectively tackle these issues—a classic principal–agent problem. When designing a project to address a particular issue, an organization would ideally conduct a wide-reaching assessment of projects that have been implemented by other organizations in the past, identify which projects have been most effective, and then carefully tailor their own project so that it incorporates the best aspects of those past projects while taking into account any particular challenges that might arise in adapting them to a different setting. Following initial implementation, the organization would regularly and rigorously evaluate the project, making changes as needed. However, this path is both time consuming and labor intensive. It also may require specific skills, such as language or statistical fluency.

Thus, if one is not deeply motivated to solve the particular problem the project will address, it might be more appealing to take a path of least (or lesser) resistance. This path might mean reflexively copying any relevant project the organization happens to learn about, without considering whether it was effective in its original setting or how well it will translate to a new setting (Watkins, Swidler, and Hannan 2012, 297). It might also mean simply choosing projects that are easier to implement, or failing to conduct a project evaluation (especially since direct evidence that a project isn't working might actually jeopardize future funding) (Fyvie and Ager 1999, 1391; Mendelson and Glenn 2002, 4). Furthermore, it might mean that NGO workers simply do not invest in learning any specific skills they don't already have, while at the same time the organization does not make the effort to recruit outside assistance to compensate for the lack of in-house expertise.

Second, even if NGO leaders and workers are motivated, mission creep can limit capacity. When an organization's mission expands to 8 or 10 sectors but its staff numbers don't increase accordingly, any given project will suffer. This type of overextension is particularly common among local NGOs, some of which have only one or two full-time staff members who are nonetheless tasked with running large numbers of distinct projects.

Third, working on a wide range of issues lowers the average effectiveness of an NGO's projects. Even a large, motivated, highly skilled staff will not be equally good at all things—they will have particular skill sets that give them a comparative advantage at tackling some issues relative to others. By spreading its activities across multiple sectors, an organization loses gains from specialization (Barr, Fafchamps, and Owens 2005, 664).

Of course, organizational resistance to pursuing high-quality programs and projects would not be as much of a problem if donors consistently held their grantees to account. Yet historically, donors haven't shown much interest in ensuring effective use of their funds or in demanding rigorous evaluation (Watkins, Swidler, and Hannan 2012, 301–3). In fact, governmental donors can actually face penalties for failing to disburse all allocated funding, which creates incentives to push the money out the door and not look too carefully at how it is being spent (Birdsall 2004, 8).

The end result of this set of perverse incentives is that many NGOs are pursuing the same narrow set of issues, duplicating and in some cases interfering with each other's efforts while failing to learn from their own or others' past mistakes. But some NGOs and some NGO programs are more susceptible to these pathologies than others. Once again, the salience of specific international and local norms matters.

As already discussed, when an international norm is highly salient, international donors become more willing to fund activities that promote the norm, thus driving up the overall level of activism around the issue. However, because many NGOs will be less motivated by their own commitment to the issue and more by donors' commitment to the issue, these organizations are more likely to shirk in the performance of their activism. This problem of shirking may well be compounded if the conflicting local norm is also highly salient, as local NGOs try to avoid being too aggressive in challenging a norm that the targets of their activism hold dear. Thus, where both the international and the local norm are highly salient, the local agents' interests will not align well with the international principals' preferences, and the result is that, on average, the quality of activism will be lower. Conversely, where the international norm is less salient, one should expect any NGOs that do take up the cause to be fairly sincere in their commitment, and where the local norm is less salient, there will be few local constraints on NGOs pursuing bold action. In these cases, the average quality of activism should be higher.

Looking more closely at the cases of FGM and early marriage can help illustrate how norm salience and the incentives of the international aid regime might affect activism quality in the real world. FGM's high international salience creates incentives for NGOs to take up the campaign, even if they are not strongly motivated to address FGM and even though the highly salient local norm in favor of female circumcision means that there is often significant local resistance to anti-FGM activism. In fact, many NGOs, at least nominally, work on FGM regardless of what other issues they pursue—it is not uncommon for an NGO to claim to address both land reform and FGM, or peace building and FGM.

Yet the existence of so many NGOs that are ostensibly trying to tackle FGM has not necessarily translated into an abundance of effective activism against the practice (Shell-Duncan et al. 2011, 1275). Indeed, though researchers have made significant progress in recent years in identifying successful strategies to address FGM, as described above, on-the-ground activities have often not kept pace with these advances. In particular, despite the near-universal recognition in the literature that FGM interventions must be tailored to specific local contexts, many NGOs run generic, cookie-cutter programs: for instance, in a study in northern Tanzania, the authors found that many of the materials and frames used by activists were inappropriate for the local Maasai audience (Winterbottom, Koomen, and Burford 2009).

This kind of uncritical program adoption can be seen clearly in the overuse of the alternative rite of passage (ARP) approach. The idea behind this approach is that, among groups for which the performance of FGM is part of a larger transition to adulthood, people may be reluctant to abandon the practice if they conclude that doing so would also lead to the abandonment of the broader ceremonial transition. The goal of the ARP, then, is to keep the ceremony and any other important associated activities while eliminating the circumcision aspect of the rite of passage. While there is evidence that this approach can be effective, the problem is that it is sometimes used among groups for which the function of female circumcision is unrelated to a transition to adulthood (Chege, Askew, and Liku 2001, 44). And even for groups in which circumcision does serve as part of a rite of passage, particular components of an ARP can be inappropriate, such as replacing a traditionally private circumcision ceremony with a public ARP celebration. Beyond problems of cultural relevance, another problem arises when the ARP is deployed in isolation. That is, the ARP should be the culmination of a much longer, intensive process of community sensitization and persuasion—it is most likely to work if the families of the participating girls and relevant traditional elites have already been convinced of the harmful consequences of FGM (Chege, Askew, and Liku 2001, 45). When shortcuts are taken, parents may still let their daughters participate in the ARP, but such participation is unlikely to signal genuine acceptance of the international norm, and many of the participating girls will still undergo FGM at a later date (Prazak 2007, 24–25).

More generally, issues arise when NGOs fail to target the appropriate audiences. Many NGOs focus their efforts on raising the awareness of school-age girls since they are an easy-to-reach, captive audience as well as the group that is directly at risk, but neglect to engage in similar activities with parents and local traditional elites who are more geographically dispersed and whose views are likely to be more entrenched. Yet parents and traditional elites are the main decision-makers regarding circumcision, not the girls themselves, and thus, engaging with the former groups is essential

(Berg and Denison 2013, 92). Talking only to girls will only succeed in making the girls fearful of a procedure they cannot avoid. And when NGOs do hold FGM workshops for the broader community, these workshops often take place in major towns rather than in the villages. Though holding trainings in town is more convenient for the NGO, it is also less likely to draw a truly at-risk crowd. In fact, the proliferation of such trainings has led to the emergence of "professional" workshop attendees who repeatedly attend various NGOs' trainings, often on the same subject, because the NGOs typically provide them with free meals and travel per diems.[6]

Conversely, though the low international salience of early marriage has limited funding for large-scale programs designed to directly address the practice, the evidence suggests that smaller-scale programs, and programs in which early marriage is one target among several, are becoming more common (Malhotra et al. 2011). Because such activities are often driven by the legitimate concerns of activists on the ground, they have tended to be somewhat more effective on average (but are by no means perfect): though the small scale of most programs has limited rigorous evaluation, it appears that many unevaluated programs are following strategies similar to those successfully employed by the handful of evaluated programs.

The overall point is that there is some systematic variation in the quality of activism, and that international norm promoters could often be doing a better job of providing a high-quality normative message, thinking more critically about the local context and about how their time and money could be most effectively spent. Moreover, the quality of activism has significant consequences for the likelihood of any substantial attitude change at the local level. But in addition to activism quality, it is important to consider how receptive people will be to hearing even a high-quality normative message. There are a couple of reasons that simply receiving "the facts" in support of an international norm might not be sufficient to produce attitude change.

First, research in psychology indicates that cognitive and motivated biases may cause people to discount new information that is inconsistent with their existing beliefs and understanding of the world, thereby contributing to a phenomenon known as belief perseverance. That is, "Data that

---

6. Workshops and trainings have become an increasingly popular tool among NGOs tackling a wide range of development issues (Barr, Fafchamps, and Owens 2005, 667). They appeal to donors because they produce concrete, easily quantifiable outcomes—the number of people trained—even if such outcome measures do not capture meaningful real-world changes (Thörn 2011, 243). Training local volunteers is also meant to foster the donor goals of participation and sustainability (Watkins, Swidler, and Hannan 2012, 299).

might have had an impact before their beliefs took shape have no immediate influence when they arrive afterward" (Kuran 1995, 173). I have already suggested that practitioners of female circumcision and early marriage may not recognize any consequences they themselves experience as a result of these practices—that the long-standing absence of any debate about the local norms makes it unlikely that individuals will independently question their validity. But even once an open debate is introduced via transnational activism, beliefs may be quite resistant to change. So long as an individual has already decided that one side of the debate is right, he or she will have a tendency to dismiss or even completely overlook information that supports the other side, even if that information is presented directly and persuasively.

Human beings are not perfect, neutral evaluators of data who constantly update their beliefs in response to each new credible piece of information they receive. Instead, there are a number of mechanisms by which people manage to ignore evidence that disconfirms their existing beliefs. All of these mechanisms can be grouped under the broad heading of motivated confirmation bias, in which individuals unwittingly "treat evidence in a biased way when they are motivated by the desire to defend beliefs that they wish to maintain" (Nickerson 1998, 176). One such mechanism—biased search for information—essentially involves placing oneself in an echo chamber. That is, one chooses to seek out people and information sources that one expects in advance to agree with, and to avoid people and information sources that one expects to disagree with (Festinger 1957; Hart et al. 2009). For example, many Americans who identify as Republicans choose to watch the right-leaning Fox News and avoid the left-leaning MSNBC, and many Democrats make the opposite choice. While these choices may seem commonsensical, they artificially circumscribe the universe of information to which individuals are exposed.

A second mechanism is biased interpretation or assimilation, in which a person presented with mixed evidence will focus on the confirming evidence and de-emphasize or set a higher burden of proof for the disconfirming evidence, and a person presented with neutral or ambiguous evidence will perceive the evidence as supporting his or her existing beliefs (Lord, Ross, and Lepper 1979; Slowiaczek et al. 1992). For example, consider an individual who believes that school voucher programs are a bad idea. If that person reads about a study that finds that school voucher programs undermine public schools, she is likely to take this as confirmatory evidence that she is right, and feel even more secure in her beliefs. But if the study also finds that school voucher programs lead to improved educational outcomes among children from socioeconomically disadvantaged groups, she is likely to question the validity of that finding or otherwise find a way to diminish its importance.

A third mechanism is biased memory, or selective recall, in which people are more likely to forget evidence that contradicts their beliefs, and to remember evidence that confirms their beliefs (Hastie and Park 1986; Taylor and Crocker 1981). Using the same school voucher example, the reader may not even remember, several months later, that the study had a finding about educational outcomes for disadvantaged children.

All of these mechanisms of confirmation bias can contribute to belief perseverance (Lord, Ross, and Lepper 1979; Nisbett and Ross 1980; Ross, Lepper, and Hubbard 1975). In the cases of FGM and early marriage, biased interpretation and biased memory of the content of the international normative message are particularly likely to hinder attitude change. Biased search for information may also play a role to the extent that some individuals are able to choose to avoid transnational activists. And one should expect belief perseverance to be a particularly thorny problem if the local norm is highly salient, as is generally the case with FGM. When people are deeply committed to a local norm, they should be more skeptical about the validity of any countervailing evidence—and thus less likely to change their attitudes—than when a local norm has low salience (Nickerson 1998, 176).

Second, even a full appreciation of the harms associated with practices like FGM and early marriage might not be sufficient to offset the legitimate benefits people associate with these practices or the harm they believe will occur in the absence of the practices. With respect to FGM, some groups hold erroneous beliefs about uncircumcised women that they are unable to evaluate because, in fact, they encounter no uncircumcised women. This is what Mackie (1996, 1009) calls a self-enforcing belief—"a belief that cannot be revised because the believed costs of testing the belief are too high." He notes that "the Bambara of Mali believe that the clitoris will kill a man if it comes in contact with the penis during intercourse," and that "in Nigeria, some groups believe that a baby will die if its head touches the clitoris during delivery." My own qualitative research shows that some Somali believe that if the clitoris is not cut in childhood, it will grow until it touches the ground,[7] a belief similar to one held by the Kono of Sierra Leone and by some groups in Ethiopia (Ahmadu 2000, 297; Dorkenoo 1994, 34). In the case of early marriage, parents may "believe marriage will protect girls from sexual assault and pregnancy before marriage, extend girls' child-bearing years or ensure obedience to their husband's household" (United Nations

---

7. Author's interview with traditional circumcisers, July 8, 2007, Garissa, Kenya.

Children's Fund 2006, 4). Moreover, they may be convinced that the immediate economic advantages of marrying a daughter early outweigh the long-term economic benefits of keeping a daughter in school so that she can go on to hold a good job and help support her family. These kinds of beliefs will be particularly hard to overcome because the counterfactual situation is not observed.

Thus, it is reasonable to anticipate significant attitude stability even in the face of a high-quality normative message—attitude change does not necessarily follow naturally from knowledge of the content of the international norm. But though confirmation bias and belief perseverance are part of the human condition, some types of individuals may be more susceptible to particular international normative messages than others. The evidence in chapter 5 suggests that young people and women will be the most receptive to the international norms against FGM and early marriage. Some individuals also likely have greater baseline openness to new ideas than others.

Primary Behavior Change

The story I have told to this point suggests that there may be some significant hurdles to overcome for transnational activists pursuing norm change. Not only is exposure to the international normative message often limited by a variety of social and structural constraints, but there are a number of reasons why NGOs may do a poor job of delivering the normative message to the people they do reach, and also why, even if the message is good, people may nonetheless be quite reluctant to embrace it. Yet the challenges don't stop there—even if an individual has been persuaded of the superiority of an international norm to a conflicting local norm, this will not necessarily produce the primary behavior change activists desire. Because of the social aspect of the local norm, individuals who are thinking about changing their behavior must consider not only their own preferences but also the preferences of fellow group members in the local community.[8] Not being able to think of individuals as purely autonomous decision-makers certainly complicates matters, but I will draw on Timur Kuran's (1995) useful framework of multiple utilities to help clarify some of the processes at work and enable a more social view of primary behavior change.

8. In the interest of parsimony, I will model decision-making about behavior at the individual level—the decision-maker is a generic parent. However, across families, the specific people involved in the family's decision-making process, and the relative impact each person has on the ultimate decision, will likely vary. In many families,

Thus far I have talked about a norm's social expectation of compliance in fairly abstract terms, but now I will endeavor to specify its content and potential consequences more concretely. Within a group that holds a given norm, group members may reward other members who comply and punish members who defect. These *social costs and benefits* are distinct from the perceived intrinsic costs and benefits of the behavior itself—that is, one's personal (nonsocial) attitude toward the behavior—and may well exert significant influence over individuals' actions.[9] Indeed, social psychologists including Solomon Asch (1963) and Stanley Milgram (1974) have convincingly demonstrated that social expectations and directives are frequently met with high levels of conformity, even when the costs of defection are minor.

Of course, some norms impose higher costs than others (Kuran 1995, 29). Once again, the salience of a norm matters. Among many groups that practice female circumcision, individuals can reasonably expect that others in the group will pursue fairly severe negative sanctions for defection, in large part because the practice is usually quite highly valued. A girl who is not circumcised often will not be able to participate in the group's marriage market (Mackie 1996), and in traditional societies an unmarried woman may well be financially dependent on her family for life. In addition, if an uncircumcised woman becomes pregnant she may, among some groups, be subject to a forced abortion, and a child born to an uncircumcised woman may become an outcast or even be killed (Shell-Duncan, Obiero, and Muruli 2000, 117). Beyond these tangible (that is, material or physical) costs, there are also reputational costs associated with a failure to circumcise. Uncircumcised girls and women risk social stigma and potentially social ostracism (Hernlund 2000, 239; Rajadurai and Igras 2005, 10). Uncircumcised women may be regarded as and treated like children for the rest of their lives, and uncircumcised girls are frequently ridiculed by their peer group or by circumcised co-wives (Ahmadu 2000, 301; Hernlund and Shell-Duncan 2007, 53; Shell-Duncan et al. 2011, 1278). The social judgment may extend to the girl's family as well, leading to a loss of social standing or a challenge to family honor (Mackie and LeJeune 2009, 20).

fathers will have total decision-making authority—especially in Maasai and Samburu communities, as described in chapter 3—but in some other families, mothers, other family members, and perhaps girls themselves may exert a measure of influence. Nonetheless, I treat any internal negotiations within a family as a black box, since their existence does not fundamentally alter the theory's expectations: girls, especially if they are older, may be able to influence their parents' decisions, but they generally cannot disregard those decisions once made, short of running away from home.

9. I assume that the family decision-maker (or decision-makers) is considering the social and intrinsic costs and benefits for the family as a whole.

Uncircumcised women may also be excluded from various communal events and from communal and family decision-making (Shell-Duncan et al. 2011, 1279). These various costs combine to form a high barrier to defection from the norm. In comparison, most groups that practice early marriage do not directly punish defectors. Even if universally practiced within the group, it is rarely seen as a practice that is critical to the group's understanding of itself. Thus, any social sanctions are likely to be more minor and purely reputational—a girl who delays marriage may, for example, be the subject of ridicule, including comments about her undesirability to potential husbands and questions about her virginity (Caldwell, Reddy, and Caldwell 1983, 351; International Planned Parenthood Federation and Forum on Marriage and the Rights of Women and Girls 2006, 19). The family of an older, unmarried girl may also be criticized and socially excluded to some degree, and this may harm the marriage prospects of her siblings (Maertens 2013, 7).

Yet for any given norm, different individuals may experience these costs and benefits to a different degree. First, in terms of reputational costs, local elites may be less open to criticism than the average group member. Particularly if elites are respected as norm-setters, they may be given more latitude as norm-breakers, and people will privately judge them less. Or they may incur just as much private criticism, but they may be sufficiently powerful that other group members are not willing to challenge them openly. Second, some people may simply care more about their reputation than others—across all behaviors they tend toward conformism and susceptibility to peer pressure. Third, people may value their reputation within some groups more than they value their reputation within others. An individual who identifies with multiple groups is unlikely to be equally invested in all of these group identities, and an individual who moves among many groups may be less likely to internalize the negative opinion of any one group.

Fourth, some individuals may have a greater ability to avoid or mitigate any tangible costs of defection. The major pathway by which such costs could be minimized is if individuals have the *opportunity to exit* from the norm. This could involve a literal physical exit—such as actually moving away from the area in which the normative reference group resides—or a more limited exit—such as ceasing to participate in some or all of the group's activities. In the case of FGM, this would be the difference, for example, between moving to a different part of the country versus simply having a daughter marry somebody from a different ethnic group and thereby escaping the original group's marriage market. In the former case, well-educated, wealthier individuals will be in a better position to physically exit the group,[10] while in the latter case, individuals living in relatively urban areas with access to normative out-groups will be in a better position to facilitate exit from participation in their own group's marriage market.[11]

This last point serves as a challenge to a theory proposed by Gerry Mackie (1996), who has argued that FGM usually acts as a convention, much like driving on the right-hand side of the road. An individual can't deviate unilaterally from a convention without incurring extreme negative consequences, meaning that even if the entire group of adherents were convinced of the inferiority of the status quo to some alternative, substantive behavior change would still not occur unless a sufficient proportion of the group were able to reach a coordinated consensus in favor of change.[12] In the case of FGM, he contends that the cost of being forced out of the group's marriage market is so great that families would only be able to abandon the practice through a process of "organized" diffusion, in which a critical mass of first movers coordinates with one another, conditionally agrees to abandon the practice, and then recruits additional members of the intramarrying group to conditionally commit, up to a tipping point past which the group would publicly commit to changing their actual behavior (Mackie and LeJeune 2009, 11–12). This public commitment would change individual families' expectations about other families' intentions, giving them confidence that uncut daughters would be able to find marriage partners and thereby allowing them to abandon the practice en masse. Mackie concludes that abandoning the FGM convention is essentially an all-or-nothing proposition—either nobody defects or, over a relatively short period of time, everybody defects. Because Mackie does not account for an exit option, he perceives the barrier associated with unilateral defection to be not just high, but in fact insurmountable. By contrast, I argue that some individuals with access to an exit

10. Alternatively, such individuals could have the resources to marry coethnics in other regions who have already engaged in norm change.

11. Living near normative out-groups may also be beneficial because it can provide information about alternative local norms. If other domestic groups have divergent norms, this can serve as a foil for charges that transnational activists are engaging in some form of Western imperialism and trying to impose new norms from above. Domestic normative out-groups may be viewed as more relatable than international activists, and any disdain or disapproval that these out-groups express for practices like female circumcision and early marriage may resonate more strongly with practicing groups. However, this does not mean that the presence of normative out-groups is necessarily "causing" norm change in a direct sense. Though normative out-groups may lower average barriers to defection, transnational activism is valuable because it focuses people's attention on the issue and makes the contrast between different local group norms relevant.

12. In later work, Mackie and LeJeune (2009, 21–23) acknowledge that FGM can be maintained by a marriageability convention, a social norm, or both, but this does not change their expectations about the required process for abandoning the practice.

option will see their costs of defection fall sufficiently that they may be willing to defect unilaterally.[13] They don't even necessarily need to use the exit option for its existence to have an effect on behavior; as Hirschman (1970) has argued, simply knowing the exit option exists can encourage the use of voice against the status quo.

The availability of an exit option is not merely a theoretical proposition. Of the 29 countries in which FGM is practiced, only 4—Egypt, Somalia, Djibouti, and Guinea—have reported prevalence rates exceeding 90 percent of the female population. Moreover, 15 of the 29 countries have prevalence rates below 50 percent (United Nations Children's Fund 2013, 26). While some of the subnational groups that practice FGM in these lower-prevalence countries may live in complete geographical isolation from the nonpracticing groups, this should not always be the case. This suggests that many FGM practitioners live near or among normative out-groups. Moreover, the empirical evidence presented in chapter 6 shows that at least some communities are able to make a gradual change away from FGM; Mackie's all-or-nothing predictions don't always hold.

Fifth, there is a *temporal* component to both the reputational and tangible costs associated with defection. The individuals who move first to defect from a local norm are more likely to face social sanctions than individuals who defect in successive periods. In the case of FGM, later defectors are less likely to experience social ostracism or to be excluded from the group's marriage market, since their children can marry the children of the first movers, or norm leaders. In addition, early defectors may actually overestimate the costs of defection because of incomplete information. For example, as discussed above, the logic of local norms underlying female circumcision tends to predict fairly severe consequences for women who don't undergo the cut, and yet these predictions may have never been tested because violating the norm is off-the-path behavior. Accordingly, the first defectors may incorrectly expect a range of bad things to happen to their daughters, while later defectors will be able to directly observe what happens to the daughters of the norm leaders and see that these negative consequences do not obtain. Essentially, the daughters of the norm leaders can end up providing a kind of demonstration effect by showing that uncut women can lead successful lives—that they can do things like have families, get

---

13. This is not to downplay the very real social costs of early unilateral defection. As discussed above, uncircumcised girls and their families may be subject to a range of local negative social sanctions separate from the inability to marry within the normative in-group. In the scenario I describe, defection becomes possible, but it is not suddenly attractive.

education, and hold jobs. These women can serve as flesh-and-blood role models for future families thinking about abandoning the local norm, and their existence is likely to be more reassuring than transnational activists' promises. However, it is important to note that the nearby presence of a normative out-group can provide a similar demonstration effect, thus mitigating the incomplete information problem for norm leaders.[14] The broader point, though, is that as more people defect from the status quo—the local norm—the cost of further defections declines because the norm leaders alter the average public behavior of the group as a whole.

Overall, then, a given norm produces average social costs associated with defection, but these costs can change over time, and different people will occupy different positions within the distribution of costs across the group. I will call the net social costs and benefits experienced by a given individual for a given action at a given moment in time that individual's *social utility*.[15] This social utility must be balanced against an individual's true attitudes, which, in Kuran's terminology, determine the *intrinsic utility* the individual receives from taking a given action (1995, 25). Intrinsic utility will be highest where an individual's public action aligns perfectly with his or her private attitudes.

So if an individual actually holds views that are contrary to a local norm, the individual must decide whether to act in accordance with those views and risk social punishment, or to suppress his or her true preferences—engage in preference falsification—and continue to comply with the status quo (Kuran 1995, 3). For any given level of intrinsic utility associated with local norm defection, a reduction in the social costs of defection will increase the probability that an individual actually defects. But since overall social utility is itself the product of multiple variable costs (social costs can vary across norms, across individuals, and across time), high costs on one front need to be offset by lowered costs on the others. In the case of female circumcision, because the initial cost of defection is so high, those wanting to abandon the practice will need to have lower-than-average individual costs (such as elite status or personal opportunities for exit) or else they'll need to see evidence of temporal shifts in public opinion (such as the presence of highly visible previous defectors). In more general terms, the higher the initial barrier

14. Mackie and LeJeune (2009, 16) recognize the value of an out-group demonstration effect, but conclude only that this makes coordinated defection easier to facilitate, and not that it might enable unilateral defection.

15. Kuran (1995, 27) has called this same concept *reputational utility*, but this term isn't sufficiently descriptive because the concept actually encompasses both reputational and tangible costs and benefits imposed by society.

to defection, the greater an individual's need for signals about either exit opportunities or changing expectations of compliance. In the presence of these signals, the individual will be more likely to reject preference falsification and cease "living a lie."

Still, intrinsic and social utility are not the only determinants of individuals' behavior. In Kuran's framework, one must also consider the extent to which an individual derives benefits from truthful self-expression—what Kuran calls *expressive utility* (1995, 31). Essentially, people vary in how willing they are to falsify their preferences about any issue. For most individuals, acting inconsistently with one's true attitudes brings a level of discomfort, but some individuals have a lower tolerance for this discomfort than others. While expressive utility varies naturally across individuals (and may also vary systematically across groups—one could imagine that it is more important in "individualistic" societies than in "collective" societies), one can think of it as exogenous and fixed for any one individual.

The sum of an individual's intrinsic, social, and expressive utility is then the *total utility* the individual derives from a given public action (Kuran 1995, 35). If considering two possible public actions, the point at which the total utilities associated with each action are equal is the point at which the individual is indifferent between the two actions, and the distribution of public behavior that corresponds to this indifference point is the individual's *political threshold* (Kuran 1995, 64). It is the individual's threshold relative to actual public behavior that determines the individual's action. For example, if an individual is indifferent between circumcising a daughter and not circumcising a daughter when 70 percent of the group circumcises daughters, then he will circumcise his own daughter if in fact 80 percent of the group is actually circumcising their daughters, and he will not circumcise his daughter if only 60 percent of the group is actually circumcising their daughters. His choice depends on other people's choices.

The bottom line here is that, because norms entail a social expectation of compliance, individuals who are considering defecting from a local norm must consult both their own attitudes and preferences and the attitudes and preferences of the local group to which they belong. The more salient the local norm, the greater the potential social sanctions and the higher the barrier to defection. Under such conditions, behavior change is likely to lag substantially behind attitude change, and is likely to be pursued by individuals who have both strong attitudinal agreement with the international norm and some ability to mitigate the social costs of defection.

Clearly there are some significant challenges associated with achieving actual primary behavior change. The more that people believe an international norm is fundamentally at odds with their local norm, the less likely it is that a campaign will produce rapid behavioral change at the grassroots level. Yet transnational activism may still have an impact on individuals' actions, even if that impact is unanticipated or unintended.

In particular, individuals who are not complying with the international norm may nonetheless decide to try to project an image of compliance to certain parties. There are a number of ways to attempt to hide continued local norm compliance, but the simplest strategy is to rhetorically commit to the international norm while in the presence of international activists. For practices like FGM and early marriage, the act itself is only performed at a single discrete moment in time—outside of the circumcision day or wedding day itself, there is only an individual's word about his or her current beliefs and intentions.

The international norms literature, despite its general state-centrism, can shed some light on the reasoning behind decisions to falsely commit to international norms, since it has long recognized that rhetorical norm allegiance is not equivalent to compliance (Hafner-Burton and Tsutsui 2005, 1374; Hathaway 2002, 1940). The promise of foreign aid, international trade and investment, and membership benefits in international organizations; fear of punishment or sanction; and reputational and status concerns can encourage states to attempt to signal compliance with international norms—especially if those signals are relatively costless—despite contradictory behavior.

For example, Hathaway (2003, 1838–39; 2007, 590) and Vreeland (2008, 70) each point to authoritarian states that have willingly signed human rights treaties such as the Convention Against Torture, a step that serves as a very public signal of commitment to norms promoting human rights. However, because treaties like the CAT are essentially unenforceable, states risk very little by disingenuously signing them, and may gain various international benefits. Furthermore, rhetorical commitments to international norms may have the additional advantage (for noncompliant states) of redirecting attention elsewhere and thereby allowing the state to continue its previous behavior with impunity. Hathaway (2002, 1942) suggests that "state expressions of commitment to human rights through treaty ratification may sometimes relieve pressure on states to pursue real changes in their policies and thereby undermine the instrumental aims of those very same treaties." And even when the signal is somewhat more costly—as in the case of election observation—states may still find it in their interest to attempt to mask their true type to the international community (Hyde 2011, 3).

This disjuncture between states' rhetoric and behavior has a natural corollary in the actions of individuals. Indeed, much of the theoretical underpinning of arguments about states' desire for legitimacy is derived from psychological literature on individuals' reactions to peer pressure and other aspects of group dynamics (Finnemore and Sikkink 1998, 903–4). These findings have often been aggregated up to the state level, with corresponding assumptions about states as unitary actors. Refocusing on the individual level allows one to dispense with such assumptions.

Research in social psychology provides a basis for understanding how both material and reputational concerns might lead to the projection of an international-norm-compliant image. A relevant strain of the literature on attitudes focuses on a concept called self-presentation, sometimes referred to as image management (Goffman 1973, 259). Self-presentation concerns "the seminal idea that people attempt to regulate and control, sometimes consciously and sometimes without awareness, information they present to audiences, particularly information about themselves" (Schlenker and Weigold 1992, 134). While image management may be motivated by a range of goals, one important motivation is that "conveying the right impression increases the likelihood that one will obtain desired outcomes and avoid undesired outcomes. Some such outcomes are interpersonal in nature, such as approval, friendship, assistance, power, and so on . . . [while] other such outcomes are material" (Leary and Kowalski 1990, 37).

Different audiences, and the norms and expectations they endorse, can elicit different versions of the self and "alter the norms and roles that seem relevant" (Schlenker and Weigold 1992, 154). And individuals are more likely to present a version of the self that is in line with the preferences of the audience when that audience is significant in some way, whether because of power, high status, expertise, or some other valued characteristic (Nowak, Szamrej, and Latané 1990, 365). Ingratiating oneself to an audience through, for example, "opinion agreement" is particularly desirable when the individual is somehow dependent on the audience (Jones 1990, 178–79). These kinds of dynamics are certainly present in the unequal relationship between local and international actors. International actors can be viewed as possessing prestige and authority, and they also have control over aid distribution. It is thus no surprise that some individuals will seek to be perceived favorably by international actors, and that one way to accomplish this is to appear compliant with these actors' favored norms.

Self-presentation can involve an essentially honest, if selective, portrayal of oneself, but it can also involve deception when reality does not mirror the image one wishes to project (Schlenker and Weigold 1989, 253; Tetlock and Manstead 1985, 62). DePaulo et al. (1996, 991) find that outright lying in regular social interactions is quite common, is generally self-serving (as opposed to benefiting others), and is most often motivated by a desire for psychic, rather than material, benefits. Individuals in their study lied in order to "make themselves appear kinder or smarter or more honest than they believe themselves to be and to protect themselves from embarrassment or disapproval or conflict." Essentially, people lied in order to be perceived as more agreeable by the person to whom they were telling the lie. This may be easier to achieve when the relationship between presenter and audience is fairly superficial, as is the case with rural residents and international actors (Buss and Briggs 1984, 1313). That is, there is a high probability that international actors will believe those who present themselves as opponents of FGM or early marriage, since these actors are unlikely to have recurring interactions with the same individual, and are similarly unlikely to be able to investigate any one individual's claims.

Though the psychology literature points to reputational motives (whether reputation is valued intrinsically or instrumentally) dominating material motives for misrepresentation, there may still be financial incentives to dissimulate.[16] Individual communities in developing countries are unlikely to be the direct recipients of large-scale foreign aid in the same way that states are, but they can still benefit indirectly, as the final link in an "aid chain" running from donors to international NGOs to national and local NGOs operating on the ground (Bebbington 2005; Wallace, Bornstein, and Chapman 2007). As already discussed, donors' interests tend to shape the stated priorities of NGOs. Through the sheer volume of talk by donors and their local proxies, individuals even in rural areas are likely to discover what the international community wants to hear, and some may ultimately conclude that expressing agreement with donor preferences is a good way to access donor support. Such material incentives for misrepresentation may well be present for the community at large, but they are likely to be

16. However, it is worth noting that the effects of material incentives may not be unidirectional. Goodman and Jinks (2013, 108, 112) argue that material incentives have the potential to *reduce* international norm commitments through a variety of psychological mechanisms. In variations of what they term the "overjustification" effect, individuals may avoid commitments to international norms when material incentives are in place precisely because they do not want to be perceived as being motivated by financial considerations (a "social signaling" effect), or because they do not want to see themselves or be perceived by others as susceptible to external pressures (a "self-determination" effect).

particularly relevant for local NGO workers. Though some of these workers may actually continue to comply with local norms, they may well try to
project an international-norm-compliant image to donors and other international audiences in order to gain access to international funding; their
new official priorities may not be genuine (Sundstrom 2006, 104).

Regardless of motivation, deceptive self-presentations allow one to create a desired identity that is not mirrored by reality. This desired identity
may reflect pure strategy, but it can also be aspirational—the identity is
one that the presenter wishes were true (Schlenker and Weigold 1992).
Either of these motivations is possible in the context of competing norms.
That is, one may for strategic reasons want to be perceived by an international audience as complying with the international norm, while simultaneously holding contradictory opinions. However, it is also possible for
an individual to wish to comply with the international norm, and present
him- or herself accordingly to international actors, but feel too bound by
the local norm to actually fulfill that wish in reality.

Beyond rhetorical commitment, individuals may also change various
aspects of the way in which they perform the behavior associated with the
local norm, in order to better conceal it from external observation. While
rhetorical commitment is likely to be effective primarily when directed at
an international audience, secondary behavioral changes tend to be performed for the purpose of hiding local-norm-compliant behavior from
local activists or local authorities. Locally based activists and authorities
are more likely than international actors to be in a position to observe
actual local behavior, and thus individuals who continue to comply with
challenged local norms may find that they need to do more to hide their
actions than simply stating their commitment to the international norm.[17]
Of course, the specific strategies used will naturally vary according to the
norm in question. In the case of female circumcision, one trend has been
to move away from public celebrations of the event (Hernlund 2000, 242).
There is also evidence that the age at circumcision is dropping in some
places (United Nations Children's Fund 2013, 112), which may reflect a
recognition on the part of parents that younger girls will have less ability
to resist the cut. There is further, though limited, evidence that some parents are choosing to perform less severe versions of the procedure (United
Nations Children's Fund 2013, 111), which would limit the likelihood of

---

17. The empirical evidence in chapter 7 suggests that while local NGOs and local
authorities do have some ability to monitor norm compliance, their enforcement
capabilities are sufficiently limited that they have been unable to induce individuals to
instrumentally change their primary behavior.

complications that might result in a hospital visit that could be observed by authorities.[18] While early marriages are more difficult to conceal, some degree of hiding may still be possible, such as by bribing authorities to look the other way.

As described to this point, local norm compliers (whether or not they actually agree with the local norm) use rhetorical and secondary behavior change to try to project a false image of international norm compliance to the international norm's proponents. But another possibility is that some individuals who are actually complying with the international norm may try to project a false image of local norm compliance to the local norm's proponents. The availability and potential effectiveness of such a strategy is likely to depend on the nature of the particular local norm and on the ability of the local reference group to monitor individual behavior. For example, parents who have chosen not to subject their daughters to FGM may nonetheless wish to convince other members of their local reference group that their daughters are cut and that they are still adhering to "tradition." The only real option for these individuals would be to "fake" a circumcision, such as by holding a celebration to mark a circumcision that didn't actually take place. However, this is a risky strategy, since it hinges on the girl's future husband, and possibly his family, not being able to tell whether the girl has been cut. It's possible that the husband may be sufficiently unfamiliar with the actual procedure involved in circumcision that he wouldn't be able to distinguish between cut and uncut genitalia, but the likelihood of such an outcome surely declines with the severity of the form of FGM practiced in that location. With a practice like early marriage, it is difficult to imagine a scenario in which parents whose daughters were not married early would be able to convince their local community that they actually had been married early.

But regardless of the specific manifestation of secondary behavioral or rhetorical change, the takeaway point is that an incentive for misrepresentation exists whenever individuals' loyalties and commitments are being pulled in diametrically opposite directions. When faced with norm conflicts like those surrounding FGM and early marriage, one can try to please everyone, but cannot do so honestly. Individuals must ultimately choose whether to present themselves accurately to all audiences and risk alienating one side or the other, or to try to have the best of both worlds through some form of image management.

---

18. In addition to making concealment easier, this can also be a reflection of increased awareness among parents that more severe forms of the cut are more dangerous—a positive outcome of international norm promotion.

The preceding discussion suggests that individuals must consider a complex set of factors when deciding whether to engage in any form of norm change, and that their choices may well be influenced by both ideational and instrumental motivations. But in addition to understanding how individuals make decisions about norm change at any given point in time, it is also important to consider how norm change spreads across individuals over time.

I've already introduced the concepts of multiple utilities—intrinsic, social, and expressive—and political thresholds to help explain the conditions under which primary behavior change is most likely to occur, and argued that public behavior (the behavior of other members of one's normative reference group within one's community) affects individuals' thresholds and therefore actions through its impact on social utility. As more people defect from a local norm, individual thresholds drop and additional defections become easier. Yet the overall distribution of individual thresholds across the local reference group determines the group's collective public behavior, meaning that public behavior and individual actions coexist in a dynamic relationship.

This dynamism would make it difficult to draw out the causal processes behind any broader norm change, except that individual actions and public behavior can, and frequently do, settle into an equilibrium, a historical status quo that can serve as the starting point for making sense of any future changes. Public behavior reaches an equilibrium when it is in nobody's interest to defect—no one is able to reach his or her threshold for change (Kuran 1995, 18). The status quo will remain stable so long as the distribution of thresholds remains the same. Thus, if one wants to understand how an entire community can move away from a local norm and toward an international norm, one must consider the distribution of individual thresholds across local reference group members and the kinds of catalysts that can lead to a shift in that distribution.

A successful catalyst is likely to be an event, a shock to the system that causes individuals to reevaluate their preferences. Events can change public behavior by altering just a few individuals' thresholds for change, creating a group of norm leaders who, through their actions, shift public behavior enough so that others' thresholds are also crossed. Such an event need not be large—even a marginal change in a few thresholds can set off a bandwagon effect that leads to dramatic changes in overall public behavior (Kuran 1995, 20). Conversely, a major event and a large change in thresholds may not be sufficient to spur any change whatsoever if all individuals' thresholds begin by being very far from the status quo. There are no guarantees—small events can have a big impact on behavior, and big events can have a negligible impact.

If, for example, the universal practice of female circumcision or early marriage is the historical status quo in a given group, then the introduction of transnational activism against these practices is the potentially catalytic event, with the power to alter the status quo under certain circumstances.[19] As individuals become more aware of the harms associated with FGM and early marriage, and private opposition to the practices increases (attitude change occurs), the intrinsic utility of defecting from the local norms also increases. An increase in the intrinsic utility of defection means that individuals will require a lower level of social utility in order to maintain the same level of total utility. And since the distribution of public behavior is the main source of variation in social utility over time, these individuals now require a lower level of existing public support for the international norm, and their thresholds shift accordingly. Whether or not these shifts are sufficient to produce a change in actual public behavior is a different question. For a group to begin to abandon female circumcision or early marriage, some individuals' thresholds have to change enough that they are willing to be the norm leaders.

Who might these norm leaders be? Most likely, they will be people who, prior to the change in intrinsic utility, already had high expressive needs and lower-than-average social costs for defecting from the status quo. This is particularly true when public opinion is strongly in favor of the status quo, as is the case with female circumcision; to overcome this barrier, one would need to have a very strong attitudinal commitment to abandoning FGM, great expressive needs, and possibly some ability to mitigate the social punishment—through good exit options or low reputational costs—that would come from being an early defector.

The interaction of intrinsic and expressive utility is critical. According to Kuran (1995, 50), "A complete theory of collective action requires

19. While transnational activism is not the only possible catalytic event, it is the most likely one, because it creates a focal point for anti-FGM or anti-early-marriage sentiment. As already discussed, an independently generated, broad local opposition is unlikely, in part because of the difficulties of recognizing the harmful consequences of these practices in the absence of any open debate (though of course debate itself does not guarantee receptivity). In addition, any individuals who do harbor reservations about the practices will be unlikely to share these thoughts openly, since they would have no reason to believe that anybody else would agree with them. The introduction of transnational activism provides an opportunity for people to realize that their private opposition might be shared by others, and, moreover, it creates a public discourse that allows potential norm leaders to actually identify like-minded others.

recognition that some people have unusually intense wants on particular matters, coupled with extraordinarily great expressive needs. Relative to most people, such individuals are insensitive to the prevailing reputational incentive, because they obtain unusually high satisfaction from truthful self-expression." Recognizing the role of expressive utility thus changes the playing field, because it creates an opening for principled action where one might not otherwise exist. Mackie (1996), for instance, weighs only private preferences against social sanctions in his discussion of FGM, and thus concludes that where negative social sanctions are severe, private preferences cannot overcome them. He does not account for the possibility that a small minority of individuals could feel the weight of their opposition to the status quo so strongly that they would be willing to accept severe social sanctions.[20] Such individuals may be rare, but they can still play a critical role in explaining the presence or absence of larger changes in public behavior. Their willingness to unilaterally defect from the status quo has the potential to lower the average social costs that the far more numerous norm followers face for subsequent defections.

Though potential norm leaders may be insensitive to social costs relative to others in their normative reference group, they will nonetheless be more likely to defect from the status quo if the social costs they do experience are lower than average. As already discussed, the social costs associated with a given action at a given point in time can vary across individuals, and so if an individual is considering defecting from the local norm, it helps to be on the lower end of that distribution. The individual can face lower tangible costs, lower reputational costs, or both. Elites and other authority figures may experience lower reputational costs, while individuals with good exit options will likely experience lower tangible costs. Of course, not all exit options are the same. Those who only escape the social consequences of defection by exiting the system entirely cannot be fairly categorized as norm leaders, because their very absence means that they cannot activate anyone else in the community.[21] If exit from the system is the dominant form of defection from the local norm, then the process of behavior change within the system itself is likely to be much slower (Kuran 1995, 105). If, on

20. More generally, Mackie, following Schelling, assumes a homogenous population (United Nations Children's Fund 2008a, 49). Because I assume that thresholds are heterogeneous across a population (this is in line with many threshold models; see, e.g., Granovetter and Soong 1983), my model allows for greater variability in the extent and speed of norm change, as described below.

21. This is consistent with the "Positive Deviance" approach to producing behavior change within communities, which emphasizes the importance of change agents being close at hand (Pascale, Sternin, and Sternin 2013).

the other hand, individuals can defect from the local norm by exiting from just one aspect of the system—such as the local marriage market—they can begin to shift the distribution of public behavior that other group members witness.

So even in the face of an initially strong local commitment to the status quo, a shock to the system such as the introduction of transnational activism against FGM can potentially cause a shift in the distribution of thresholds for change through its impact on intrinsic utility. If this shift is sufficient to create a set of norm leaders, their unilateral defections from the local norm may in turn be sufficient to set off a bandwagon effect in the larger group by activating a set of norm followers. This is what Finnemore and Sikkink (1998, 895) have called a "norm cascade."[22] While norm leaders are likely responding to lower-than-average social costs for defecting from the local norm, in conjunction with their high intrinsic and expressive utility, norm followers are likely responding to a decrease in the *average* social costs facing the entire original reference group within the community. Through the norm leaders' initial behavior change, the norm followers now have options for mitigating social punishment that didn't exist before. In the case of FGM, the norm followers' daughters can suddenly participate in a small marriage market with the original norm leaders' sons, thus facing lower tangible costs, as well as gain the approbation of those leaders, thus reducing reputational costs.

To see how this might actually play out, it is helpful to consider an illustrative example. Imagine a group of 10 families. Following an awareness-raising campaign by transnational activists, seven of these families privately change their attitudes and wish circumcision would stop, while three privately wish circumcision would continue. According to Mackie's convention account, all 10 will continue to practice FGM unless a substantial subset of the seven FGM-opposing families coordinates to abandon FGM simultaneously. While the families may have different private preferences, nobody's private preference against FGM is sufficiently strong that they would be willing to incur the costs of abandoning FGM unilaterally.

If, however, the group of 10 families lives near a normative out-group rather than living in isolation, the FGM opponents' utility calculations are

---

22. A norm cascade can occur even if there are no further changes in the intrinsic utility for defection of the norm followers; they can be induced to change their own behavior without a change in their own thresholds, but instead solely through the change in social costs that results from the previous shift in public behavior. Of course, norm followers' intrinsic utility for defection *may* increase over time as a response to the transnational campaign, but it is not necessary.

likely to change slightly, which may in turn produce a significantly different outcome for the group as a whole. Though having a daughter exit one's own group in order to marry into an out-group is often not a particularly attractive option, it is certainly superior to the option of nonmarriage (especially if the out-group is of a status equal to or higher than that of the practicing group), which may well be the only option available to an uncircumcised girl in an isolated group.[23] In such a context, the social costs of defection are lower—the nonmarriageability cost is replaced by the somewhat lower cost of exiting from the norm through intermarriage. Yet for each of the seven FGM-opposing families, the cost–benefit calculation will be different. Some families will feel more strongly the harmfulness of the consequences associated with circumcision, and some will feel less strongly the costs of intermarriage and of negative social sanctions by others in the local reference group.

Let us say that in the first round of calculations, only one of the seven families views the benefits of defection as outweighing the costs. Their daughter is not circumcised, and she marries somebody from the noncircumcising out-group. This initial defection acts as a signal about the social expectation of compliance, especially if the first family includes an influential person within the group. The second family's daughter will also likely need to marry somebody from the out-group, but there is a chance that she will be able to marry a son from the first family. For the second family, this signal decreases the costs sufficiently that they subsequently defect. These first two defections send an even stronger signal about a changing social expectation of compliance to the third family, which also defects. By now the remaining FGM-opposing families, in considering their options, have access to a sizable pool of in-group potential husbands for their daughters, as well as a sense that the local norm cannot be all that compulsory if three families have already defected. Thus, with each additional defection, both the tangible and reputational costs of future defections continue to drop,

23. Mackie acknowledges that overlapping marriage markets exist, but in his account these markets are class-based, such that the richest individuals introduce FGM to control multiple wives, and the next richest take up the practice in order to have a chance at marrying into the richest group (1996, 1008). This pattern of class-based diffusion continues down to the poorest groups. In this story, the group engaging in FGM is always the dominant group, so the normative out-group always has an incentive to take up the practice. (The exception to this is in Mackie's discussion of public community commitments not to circumcise—should such community-level coordination occur, he provides for the possibility of a norm cascade across interlinked communities [Mackie 2000].) But not all intergroup interactions conform to this dynamic; sometimes the group engaging in FGM is of a status lower than or equal to that of nonpracticing groups. This leaves open the possibility that intermarriage will produce more nonpractitioners rather than more practitioners.

and the result is a norm cascade. Ultimately, even the three families who privately supported female circumcision may feel pressure to abandon the practice.[24]

So from an initial status quo of total local norm compliance, an external shock may thus produce a norm cascade of changing public behavior across an entire community. But it may also produce only a small change among a few committed individuals, or it may produce no change at all. The outcome depends both on the extent to which individual thresholds shift and on the distribution of thresholds across the normative reference group.

What is the likelihood that a group of norm leaders will actually emerge and that the norm leaders will trigger a group of norm followers? This likelihood is bound to vary substantially according to the characteristics of the community. First, norm leaders will be more likely to emerge in communities that have experienced high-quality activism—the better the activism, the greater the expected attitudinal change and thus the greater the change in intrinsic utility and in individual thresholds.

Second, norm leaders will be more likely to emerge in communities in which many people have access to an exit option from the local norm—the more available and attractive the exit option, the higher the average person's social utility for defection and thus the closer the distribution of thresholds to the status quo. In the case of FGM, substantial ethnic heterogeneity within a given geographic area can end up being an important driver of change because it provides most people in the circumcising group with access to out-group marriage markets, and also provides a demonstration effect. While the social costs of defection would still be high for the norm leaders, they would not be quite so high as Mackie imagines them to be. If the circumcising group is instead isolated and noncircumcising groups live at a distance, then high-resource families may still be able to

---

24. While the eventual outcome of a norm cascade against female circumcision will almost certainly be complete group-wide abandonment, rapid change is not a given. In Mackie's account, FGM's status as a convention means that there are only two possible equilibria—one at full compliance, and one at full defection (1996, 1012). If we relax the convention assumption, however, we can recognize a number of avenues by which those who are truly committed to circumcision can hold out against the tide of norm change. First, they can exit through intermarriage with other circumcising groups. Second, they can coordinate to form a subgroup of circumcision supporters. And third, they can continue to marry their circumcised daughters to the sons of noncircumcising families. While uncircumcised girls in circumcising groups may not be able to marry, the reverse is unlikely to be true, at least initially. Noncircumcising families may embrace a norm stating that they will not circumcise their own daughters, but there is no reason to assume that they will also adhere to a norm stating that their sons cannot marry circumcised women. Given these options, it may take a generation or two before the entire group moves to a zero-FGM equilibrium.

arrange for their daughters to marry into these groups, but doing so would require the daughters to physically move away from the local community and thus prevent the women from serving as future norm leaders and exercising their voice locally to oppose FGM. Accordingly, they would not send the kind of positive signal to others that might trigger a norm cascade. And for low-resource families, the absence of a local normative out-group would mean that potential norm leaders would need to have extraordinarily high intrinsic and expressive utility for defection—they would have to be so intensely committed to abandoning FGM that they would be willing to incur very high social costs as the price of being true to their beliefs. The demonstration effect would also be absent, except perhaps obliquely through media messages about uncut girls.

Norm leaders are particularly likely to emerge where high-quality activism meets good exit options, and where the same set of people within the community benefit from both. With respect to FGM, educated people and those living in more urban areas are generally among the first to embrace the international normative message against the practice, and these are also likely to be the people with the greatest ability to access alternative marriage markets. Furthermore, they may be less susceptible to reputational costs to the extent that their educational attainment leads them to be authority figures in the community and to the extent that they embrace alternative identities and reference groups (occupational or socioeconomic, for example) that are unrelated to the local community or ethnicity. For these reasons, those individuals who are most likely to have high intrinsic utility for defecting from the local norm may very well overlap quite a bit with those individuals who are most likely to have high social utility (low social costs) for defection.

Yet even if norm leaders do emerge, there is no guarantee that their existence will produce a set of norm followers. Again, this depends on the distribution of thresholds across the local reference group. It is possible that a handful of families will defect from a local norm and yet trigger no broader norm cascade if there is a significant gap between the thresholds of the norm leaders and the thresholds of the potential norm followers. Two factors in particular are likely to matter here—the raw number of norm leaders and the composition of the group of norm leaders. As the number of norm leaders increases, public behavior moves toward the thresholds of the remaining local norm compliers, and a norm cascade becomes more likely. And if influential locals are among the group of norm leaders, this will reduce the social costs of defection for potential norm followers because the choices of socially powerful individuals generally carry more weight than the choices of those who are socially marginalized. As the social costs of defection fall, thresholds also fall, again making a norm cascade more likely.

So having an exit option and seeing that influential locals are among the set of norm leaders can be powerful motivators of communal change when the local norm in question is highly salient within the reference group, as is usually the case with female circumcision. But if the costs of defection are much lower, as with early marriage, then one should expect to see that public behavior much more closely resembles private attitudes, and individual decision-makers are much less in need of exit options or signals about changing norm strength. Early marriage may be a local norm, but it is rarely a local norm for which compliance is enforced by direct social sanctioning (though other incentives to comply may remain). This means that unilateral defections from such a norm should be much easier, although it also means that a community is less likely to experience a tipping point past which no families engage in the practice. That is, unilateral retention of the local norm will also be easier, such that where community-wide change occurs, it is likely to be fairly idiosyncratic rather than following a smooth bandwagon pattern.

Once again, imagine a group of 10 families. Following a modest awareness-raising campaign by transnational activists, five of these families begin to privately oppose early marriage, while the remaining five families continue to see nothing wrong with the practice. But unlike with FGM, each of the five progressive families can reasonably assume that they will not face significant social costs if they choose to delay the marriages of their daughters. Thus, without consulting the communal trend on early marriage or even necessarily informing other community members about their changing views, they each wait until their daughters are older. The five traditionalist families can continue to marry their daughters off at an early age except insofar as they seek to marry those daughters into one of the progressive families.

Overall, then, one can envision multiple paths to communal normative change. With weaker local norms, like the one supporting early marriage, a shock to the system that increases the intrinsic utility of defecting from the status quo is likely to be mirrored by changes in actual public behavior. With highly salient local norms, like the one supporting female circumcision, the social costs of defection are likely to create a gap between private preferences and public behavior.

Whether this gap can be overcome will depend on individuals' tolerance for preference falsification, the strength of their views, and the extent to which social costs can be mitigated. If everybody has a high tolerance for preference falsification or weak attachment to their controversial views, then nobody will move first and the community will be stuck in the status quo. Societal change demands that some individuals are willing to risk alienating public opinion or actual punitive measures in order to live consistently with their beliefs. Similarly, if exit options are restricted, as in Mackie's theory, then the likelihood of a set of norm leaders emerging also falls, since individuals must have heroic commitment to the cause in order to risk the punitive measures associated with defection, or else they must have the ability to identify other potential first movers and coordinate. Facing lowered social costs, such as the option to exit the local marriage market, will be a critical motivating factor for potential norm leaders. If norm leaders can overcome these hurdles, the prospects for wider community norm change improve. Norm followers will have an easier time changing their public behavior because, in addition to the exit option, they can also take advantage of changing signals about expectations of local norm compliance, particularly if the group of first movers includes influential locals.

CONCLUSIONS

The collision between an international and local norm puts people in a difficult position, caught between the demands of the international community and transnational activists on the one side, and the demands of their own local normative reference group on the other. I have argued here that different people will negotiate these competing demands in different ways, and that a range of systemic, local, and individual-level factors help explain the variation. The way in which these factors are distributed within particular communities also helps explain broader patterns of norm change.

Conditional on exposure to an international normative message, individuals can decide to change their attitudes, the primary behavior covered by the norm, and the public image they present to international and local audiences. Each of these changes signals some recognition of the legitimacy of the international norm, and thus they constitute elements of norm change. However, though interdependent, they do not always occur together.

Attitude change is most likely to come about where transnational activism is not only present but also of high quality. This, in turn, depends substantially on the salience of the international and local norms to their respective proponents. When an international norm is highly salient, it drives up local exposure to the international norm as international aid is made available to NGOs willing to address the issue. However, it may drive down the average quality of the normative message if some NGOs are only taking up the cause because of the funding availability and are therefore unmotivated to identify and implement effective programs. When a local norm is highly salient, it drives down local exposure to the international norm and the quality of the normative message, as local NGOs avoid promoting the international norm for fear of alienating their group members. The interaction of international and local norm salience thus contributes to the overall quantity and quality of transnational activism around any particular issue, and combines with NGO density to explain the quantity and quality of activism that reaches any particular community. However, it is important to keep in mind that attitudes about local norms may be fairly resistant to change because of a number of cognitive and motivated biases, as well as legitimate benefits associated with the norms.

Primary behavior change is most likely to occur where attitude change is widespread and where social sanctions for defecting from the local norm are low. Where the social barrier to defection is low, individual attitude change will be closely followed by behavior change, with individuals making their behavioral choices more or less independently of one another. However, where the barrier to defection is high, behavior change is likely to lag substantially behind attitude change, and any individuals who do change their behavior will likely do so because they have some ability to mitigate the costs of defection through some form of exit option from the local norm, or because they have received signals that the local norm is weakening over time.

Finally, secondary behavior and rhetorical change is most likely to occur where individuals have been exposed to the international norm but are not behaviorally complying with that norm. For both reputational and material reasons, individuals may try to "manage" the image they present to different audiences in an attempt to convince both sides that they are acting in compliance with that side's preferred norm.

Because of the social component of norms, however, individuals' choices are not discrete. Instead, they exist in a dynamic relationship with the choices being made by other people in their community, and as a result, international norms can diffuse through communities in a number of different ways. Where the local norm is not particularly salient, international norms are likely to diffuse relatively idiosyncratically. But where the local norm is highly salient, the international norm's impact at the community level will depend on the distribution of potential norm leaders and norm followers within that community. Norm leaders are most likely to emerge in communities that have been exposed to high-quality activism and that provide a widely available exit option. The existence of such norm leaders then lowers the barriers to defection for the norm followers, particularly if influential locals are among the leader group. This has the potential to kick off a bandwagon of broader norm change, or norm cascade.

Overall, then, I have a presented a theoretical framework for understanding mechanisms of norm change at the individual and community level. In the remainder of the book, I empirically evaluate the specific propositions within this overarching framework by investigating the practices of FGM and early marriage in three Maa-speaking Kenyan communities. The next chapter provides background on the practice of and transnational activism against FGM and early marriage in Kenya as a whole, among the Maasai and Samburu, and within the three specific case study communities.

CHAPTER 3

FGM and Early Marriage in Kenya

Before testing my theory against the evidence, it is important to understand the context in which that evidence was collected. This chapter discusses how and why FGM and early marriage are practiced in Kenya, with specific reference to the Maasai and Samburu and to the three case study communities of Oldonyiro, Mukogodo, and Mau. It also describes early and modern-day efforts by transnational activists, the Kenyan government, and others to eliminate the two practices. Table 3.1 provides data on the prevalence, practice, and correlates of FGM for Kenya as a whole, for the Maasai, and for the case study communities. Table 3.2 presents similar data on early marriage.

KENYA

Prevalence and Characteristics of FGM and Early Marriage

Kenya has a moderate FGM prevalence rate that places it near the median of the distribution of countries in which the practice occurs (United Nations Children's Fund 2013, 26). In the 2008–2009 Kenya Demographic and Health Survey, 27 percent of women aged 15 to 49 and 30 percent of women aged 20 to 49 reported having undergone FGM. But the national prevalence rate masks significant subnational variation in prevalence by religion, ethnicity, and various socioeconomic characteristics. Across religious groups, 51 percent of Muslim women aged 15 to 49 reported having undergone FGM, compared with 29 percent of Roman Catholics, 24 percent of Protestants and other Christians, and 38 percent of respondents with no

Table 3.1: FGM CHARACTERISTICS

Variable	2008–2009 Demographic and Health Survey			2008 Original survey		
	Kenya	Maasai	All areas	Oldonyiro	Mukogodo	Mau
Percentage of women aged 20 to 49 who have undergone FGM						
By age group						
20–29	0.230	0.776	0.943	1.000	0.967[a]	0.880
	(0.01)	(0.06)	(0.03)	(0.00)	(0.03)	(0.06)
30–39	0.321	0.845	0.955	0.941	1.000	0.929
	(0.01)	(0.08)	(0.03)	(0.06)	(0.00)	(0.07)
40–49	0.439	0.862[a]	0.945	1.000[a]	0.953[a]	0.896[a]
	(0.01)	(0.09)	(0.04)	(0.00)	(0.05)	(0.10)
By education level						
No formal education	0.530	0.942	0.993	1.000	0.972	1.000
	(0.02)	(0.04)	(0.01)	(0.00)	(0.03)	(0.00)
Primary school	0.320	0.879	0.976	0.809[a]	1.000[a]	1.000[a]
	(0.01)	(0.07)	(0.02)	(0.17)	(0.00)	(0.00)
Secondary school +	0.211	0.509[a]	0.832	1.000[a]	0.957[a]	0.734[a]
	(0.01)	(0.11)	(0.06)	(0.00)	(0.04)	(0.10)
Total	0.303	0.809	0.948	0.983	0.977	0.904
	(0.01)	(0.04)	(0.02)	(0.02)	(0.02)	(0.04)
Age at circumcision						
0–4	0.023	0.000	0.000	0.000	0.000	0.000
	(0.00)					
5–9	0.211	0.045	0.029	0.000	0.113	0.000
	(0.01)	(0.03)	(0.02)		(0.06)	
10–14	0.419	0.462	0.410	0.346	0.531	0.385
	(0.01)	(0.06)	(0.05)	(0.07)	(0.09)	(0.08)
15+	0.312	0.433	0.561	0.654	0.356	0.615
	(0.01)	(0.06)	(0.05)	(0.07)	(0.08)	(0.08)
Circumciser						
Traditional circumciser	0.770	0.824	0.953	0.997	1.000	0.883
	(0.01)	(0.05)	(0.02)	(0.00)	(0.00)	(0.05)
Traditional birth attendant	0.035	0.014	0.000	0.000	0.000	0.000
	(0.00)	(0.01)				
Doctor	0.060	0.034	0.027	0.000	0.000	0.068
	(0.01)	(0.02)	(0.02)			(0.01)
Trained nurse/midwife	0.109	0.128	0.016	0.000	0.000	0.039
	(0.01)	(0.04)	(0.01)			(0.03)

Note: Figures weighted by inverse sampling probabilities. Standard errors in parentheses.
[a] Fewer than 25 observations.

Table 3.2: EARLY-MARRIAGE CHARACTERISTICS

Variable	2008–2009 Demographic and Health Survey		2008 Original survey			
	Kenya	Maasai	All areas	Oldonyiro	Mukogodo	Mau
	Percentage of women aged 20 to 49 married by age 15					
Total	0.080	0.196	0.084	0.249	0.092	0.000
	(0.00)	(0.04)	(0.02)	(0.07)	(0.06)	
	Percentage of women aged 20 to 49 married by age 18					
By age group						
20–29	0.276	0.418	0.379	0.610[a]	0.148[a]	0.240[a]
	(0.01)	(0.07)	(0.08)	(0.12)	(0.14)	(0.11)
30–39	0.314	0.416	0.399	0.920[a]	0.472[a]	0.304[a]
	(0.01)	(0.11)	(0.08)	(0.08)	(0.14)	(0.11)
40–49	0.358	0.692[a]	0.643[a]	0.534[a]	0.674[a]	0.696[a]
	(0.01)	(0.12)	(0.11)	(0.17)	(0.21)	(0.17)
By education level						
No formal education	0.570	0.728	0.699	0.755	0.917[a]	0.587[a]
	(0.02)	(0.07)	(0.07)	(0.08)	(0.08)	(0.13)
Primary school	0.388	0.467	0.351	0.307[a]	0.282[a]	0.420[a]
	(0.01)	(0.10)	(0.09)	(0.21)	(0.14)	(0.14)
Secondary school +	0.098	0.037[a]	0.013	0.133[a]	0.000[a]	0.000[a]
	(0.01)	(0.04)	(0.01)	(0.13)		
Total	0.305	0.470	0.452	0.653	0.428	0.364
	(0.01)	(0.05)	(0.05)	(0.08)	(0.11)	(0.08)
	Age difference in years between husband and wife					
Wife married by age 18	8.688	9.764	17.471	19.045	16.252[a]	16.622
	(0.16)	(1.56)	(2.05)	(4.11)	(2.85)	(2.55)
Wife married after age 18	6.391	6.171	9.513	10.769	7.308[a]	9.907
	(0.11)	(1.11)	(0.89)	(1.93)	(1.69)	(1.14)

Note: Figures weighted by inverse sampling probabilities. Standard errors in parentheses.
[a] Fewer than 25 observations.

religious affiliation (Kenya National Bureau of Statistics and ICF Macro 2010, 265). By ethnic group, the highest reported prevalence rates were among the Somali (98 percent) and Kisii (96 percent). Groups such as the Kalenjin and Embu exhibited moderate prevalence rates of 40 and 51 percent respectively, while FGM was almost nonexistent among the Luo and Luhya. FGM was more common in rural areas (31 percent of women aged 15 to 49) than in urban areas (17 percent), and among less educated and poorer women. Only 21 percent of women aged 20 to 49 who had attended at least some secondary school reported having undergone FGM, compared to 53 percent of women with no formal education. Similarly, only 15 percent of women aged 15 to 49 in the highest wealth quintile reported having undergone the procedure, compared to 40 percent of women in the lowest quintile (Kenya National Bureau of Statistics and ICF Macro 2010, 265).

Respondents also reported on various aspects of the performance of FGM (keeping in mind the caveat that the following national-level figures can mask significant variation across subnational reference groups as well as homogeneity *within* groups). The vast majority of circumcised women aged 15 to 49—83 percent—reported having undergone a cut that involved the removal of some flesh (corresponding loosely to clitoridectomy or excision). Thirteen percent of respondents reported that their genitalia were sewn closed (corresponding to infibulation), while 2 percent reported that they were cut or nicked but that no flesh was removed, and a further 2 percent were unable to identify the type of cut they had undergone. However, infibulation was the most commonly reported form of FGM among ethnic Somalis, accounting for 75 percent of cases within that group. Among respondents who had undergone FGM, the most commonly cited benefit of the practice was gaining social acceptance, followed by the preservation of virginity (Kenya National Bureau of Statistics and ICF Macro 2010, 267).

Women in Kenya undergo FGM at a wide range of ages. A plurality (42 percent) of circumcised women aged 20 to 49 reported being cut between the ages of 10 and 14, but 2 percent were cut before age five, 21 percent were cut between the ages of five and nine, and 31 percent were cut at age 15 or above. Respondents reported that traditional practitioners carried out the procedure in 81 percent of cases, while health professionals (doctors, nurses, and midwives) performed the procedure in 17 percent of cases.

The 2008–2009 DHS also reports on the practice of early marriage in Kenya. It found that among women aged 20 to 49, 8 percent had been married by age 15, and 31 percent had been married by age 18 (Kenya National Bureau of Statistics and ICF Macro 2010, 83).[1] This

---

1. Early marriage is much less common among men, with less than 4 percent of men aged 20 to 49 having been married by age 18.

puts Kenya in the middle quintile for early-marriage prevalence among countries for which DHS data are available. By ethnic group, the highest rates of early marriage were among the Somali (22 percent married by age 15 and 50 percent by age 18), Mijikenda (18 percent married by age 15 and 48 percent by age 18), and Maasai (20 percent married by age 15 and 47 percent by age 18). As with FGM, early-marriage prevalence decreases with education and wealth. Among women aged 20 to 49, fully 57 percent of those with no formal education were married by age 18, compared to just 10 percent of those with a secondary school education or higher. Additionally, 52 percent of women aged 20 to 24 in the lowest wealth quintile were married by age 18, relative to 14 percent of those in the highest wealth quintile (United Nations Population Fund 2012, 73). Early-marriage prevalence also varied according to location of residence—31 percent of female respondents aged 20 to 24 who lived in rural areas reported being married underage, versus 17 percent of those who lived in urban areas.

Additionally, the DHS data reveal some information about the context in which early marriages occur. In the 2008–2009 round of the survey, 20 percent of female respondents aged 20 to 49 who married before age 18 reported that they were in a polygynous marriage, compared to only 10 percent of respondents who married after age 18. And among married female respondents aged 20 to 49, those who married before age 18 were, on average, 8.7 years younger than their husbands, while those who married after age 18 were, on average, only 6.4 years younger. This reflects not only the fact that the women who married early were by definition younger than those who married later, but also that their husbands were actually older than the husbands of women who married later.

Activism and Government Efforts

Kenya experienced some of the earliest international activism against female circumcision. Beginning as early as 1906 and escalating in the 1920s, a number of Protestant missions, led by Dr. John Arthur and the Church of Scotland Mission, began to take a strong stand against female circumcision, pushing for the reform or eradication of the practice among their converts in the Kikuyu, Meru, and Embu ethnic groups (Murray 1976, 92–93). They argued both that circumcision was brutal and dangerous to women's health and that the various practices that constituted the broader initiation ritual were pagan (Leakey 1931, 279; Tignor 1976, 236). In 1926, partly in response to missionary pressure, the governors of the East African dependencies circulated new guidelines to reduce the severity of the procedure, and these guidelines were subsequently adopted (though apparently not enforced) by some local native councils (Pedersen 1991, 647; J. Spencer 1985, 73–74).

The situation escalated significantly in 1929, when a number of missions began to demand repudiation of circumcision by church members, and to punish those who failed to do so by denying them baptism, confirmation, and communion and by barring their children from mission schools (Murray 1976, 99; Pedersen 1991, 648). In some cases, the missionaries pursued excommunication (Rosberg and Nottingham 1966, 117). This led to a significant backlash, particularly among the Kikuyu. The Kikuyu Central Association (KCA), a nascent Kikuyu nationalist organization, actively took up the defense of female circumcision and linked it to the anticolonial cause, a move that bolstered both the KCA's own popularity and the practice of female circumcision itself (Pedersen 1991, 651–52). The KCA argued that the campaign against circumcision represented wider efforts by the colonial administration to impose foreign values and strip local peoples of their culture, traditions, and land (Clough 1990, 144). As Jomo Kenyatta, the general secretary of the KCA and the future president of Kenya, wrote in *Facing Mount Kenya* (1965 [1938], 130):

> The overwhelming majority of [Gikuyu] believe that it is the secret aim of those who attack this centuries-old custom to disintegrate their social order and thereby hasten their Europeanisation. The abolition of *irua* [circumcision] will destroy the tribal symbol which identifies the age-groups, and prevent the Gikuyu from perpetuating that spirit of collectivism and national solidarity which they have been able to maintain from time immemorial.

Reverend Arthur retaliated against the KCA's position by requiring that teachers in mission schools formally declare both that they would not circumcise their daughters and that they were not members of the KCA (Robertson 1996, 623). Though a segment of local church elders embraced Arthur's position, the Church of Scotland's Kikuyu Mission lost some nine-tenths of its members in just one month (Rosberg and Nottingham 1966, 124). Over time and in many areas, new independent schools and churches emerged (Tignor 1976, 235).

Thus, the controversy created a norm conflict, with Kikuyu nationalists on one side and missionaries (and to a lesser extent the colonial administration) on the other. Ultimately, the colonial government backed off its anticircumcision policy out of concern that it was in fact contributing to the rise of the nationalist movement (J. Spencer 1985, 77). The controversy around female circumcision, and the practice itself, do appear to have subsided somewhat in the 1930s and 1940s, but they were revived during the Mau Mau Uprising in the 1950s, as circumcision became a test of loyalty to the Land and Freedom Army and government efforts to ban the practice once again increased (Davison 1989, 43–44; Robertson 1996, 628). For example, when the local Njuri Ncheke Council of Meru, urged on by the Meru African District Council, passed a ban on female circumcision in 1956, many Meru girls chose to defy the prohibition and circumcise one another (Thomas 2000). In response to local political opposition, the colonial government rescinded all resolutions governing female circumcision in 1958 (Chege, Askew, and Liku 2001, 2).

By comparison, attention to early marriage during the colonial period was minimal, which is perhaps not surprising given that the legal age of marriage for girls in Britain was only raised to 16 under the Age of Marriage Act of 1929, and girls as young as 12 had been legally able to marry under common law prior to that time. In Kenya, no law regulated the minimum age of marriage until after independence—the Marriage Ordinance of 1964 set the minimum age at 16—though the age of consent outside of marriage was set at 16 under the Kenyan Penal Code.[2] In fact, colonial law did not even make provision for the recognition of marriages according to customary practice (Christian marriages were conducted under the Native Christian Marriage Ordinance of 1904) (Hetherington 2001, 159).

What limited efforts did take place to address early marriage were primarily focused on marriage of prepubescent girls. At the urging of Reverend Douglas Hooper of the Church Missionary Society, the commissioner of the East African Protectorate convened a committee of investigation on child marriages among the Giriama of Kenya's coastal region in 1899, though the committee's legislative recommendations were never implemented on the grounds that they would be disruptive to social order (Shadle 2006, 44–45). However, the issue resurfaced with respect to the Giriama in the 1940s and 1950s. The Giriama African Native Council passed a resolution in 1942 prohibiting marriages of girls who had not gone through puberty, though it appears not to have been approved.[3] Following the marriage of a 12-year-old

2. L. 167/10/10 Acting Crown Counsel for Attorney General, to the Acting Colonial Secretary, August 28, 1933.
3. L & O. 19/9/5/35 Sgd. M. G. Power, representative for District Commissioner, Kilifi, to Provincial Commissioner, Coast Province, February 15, 1950.

Giriama girl in 1949, the native courts officer stated that "the Government does not favour the practice of child marriage" and that "the practice of child marriages of girls under 16 is repugnant to morality and should cease."[4] Though the provincial commissioner of Coast Province resisted the idea of trying to force a resolution against child marriage through the council,[5] such a resolution was ultimately passed in 1950.[6] In the subsequent six months, eight cases of child marriage were taken to the native courts, involving the prosecution of both the husband and father of the girls in question.[7] However, such regulation and activity appears to have been limited to the case of the Giriama, despite the widespread existence of early marriage elsewhere in the colony. The only other notable effort to address child marriages came in the 1930s in the context of a campaign against forced marriages by a Church Missionary Society archdeacon based in western Kenya and by the Britain-based feminist organization St. Joan's Social and Political Alliance (Shadle 2006, 62–63). Yet their efforts met resistance from the Colonial Office and from Kenya's colonial administrators, ultimately fizzling out without producing any meaningful change on the ground.

With respect to female circumcision, activist and government efforts in Kenya were revived in the 1970s and 1980s, as the transnational campaign against the practice was taking off. Indeed, both Kenyan government officials and Kenyan NGOs participated in the world conferences on women that took place during the UN Decade for Women and that highlighted the issue of FGM (United Nations Children's Fund 2010b, 35). The bishop of Mount Kenya East Diocese made a plea to Christians to stop the practice in 1977 (United Nations Children's Fund 2013, 10), and in 1982 President Daniel arap Moi publicly condemned FGM, partly in response to the deaths of 14 girls from medical complications stemming from the operation (*Nairobi Times* 1982). Yet while Moi called for the prosecution of circumcisers, the ban was not in fact legally enforceable (Shell-Duncan and Olungah 2009). Subsequent presidential decrees were issued in 1989, 1998, and 2001 (along with a series of policy directives from the director of medical services and the Ministry of Health prohibiting the performance of FGM in healthcare facilities and by medical personnel), but they faced

4. ADM. 40/8/1.II/35 Native Courts Officer to Chief Native Commissioner, January 27, 1950.
5. MDS. 2/2/104 Provincial Commissioner, Coast Province, to Native Courts Officer, January 12, 1950.
6. L & O. 17/9/5/39 District Commissioner, Kilifi, to Chief Secretary, Nairobi, April 13, 1950.
7. L & O. 17/9/5/52 District Commissioner, Kilifi, to Chief Secretary, Nairobi, November 30, 1950.

similar legal limitations (Evelia et al. 2007, 8; United Nations Children's Fund 2013, 10–12). Kenya also made international commitments during this period, acceding to CEDAW in 1984 and ratifying the Convention on the Rights of the Child in 1995.

Though several attempts in the 1990s to pass anti-FGM legislation failed, in 2001 the Kenyan parliament passed the Children's Act (Shell-Duncan and Olungah 2009; Rahman and Toubia 2000, 176). The act outlawed FGM before the age of 18, as well as early marriage. Section 14 of the act stated that "no person shall subject a child to female circumcision, early marriage or other customs or traditional practices that are likely to negatively affect the child's life, health, social welfare or physical or psychological development," and Section 20 provided for a penalty of up to 12 months in prison, a fine of up to 50,000 Kenya shillings (approximately $600), or both. Following a broad-based campaign, the Kenyan government further institutionalized its position against FGM with the 2011 Prohibition of Female Genital Mutilation Act, thereby resolving several perceived problems with the Children's Act. In particular, where the Children's Act only regulated the performance of FGM on children, the Prohibition of FGM Act expanded the prohibition to include adult women. The Prohibition of FGM Act also criminalized the act of bringing a girl or woman either into or out of Kenya for the purpose of having her undergo FGM, and increased minimum penalties to three years in prison or 200,000 Kenya shillings (approximately $2,400) or both.

However, enforcement of the Children's Act and the Prohibition of FGM Act has been limited.[8] Arrests under the acts have been rare—one report noted three arrests in two counties under the Prohibition of FGM Act in the year following its passage—and actual prosecutions have been even less common (United Nations Population Fund and United Nations Children's Fund 2012, 11).[9] A number of FGM and early-marriage cases that have gone to

8. Kenya does not appear to be an isolated case in this regard. Boyle and Corl (2010, 199–201) argue that enforcement of anti-FGM laws is generally low, and moreover that criminalization of the practice is not associated with declines in prevalence. Mackie (2012) suggests that a likely culprit is the absence of social norms of generalized legal obedience, a point to which I will briefly return in chapter 8.

9. Kenya's penal code has also been construed to apply to FGM. Articles 250 and 251 cover acts of bodily harm and have been used as the basis for prosecution of several circumcisers (United Nations Children's Fund 2010a, 28). In addition, there have been a number of cases in which girls brought civil suits against members of their own families, winning injunctions to prohibit those family members from forcing them to undergo FGM (United Nations Children's Fund 2010a, 33). The most prominent of these cases involved the Kandie sisters, who successfully sued their father in 2000, thereby preventing their excision and forced early marriage (Shell-Duncan and Olungah 2009).

court have resulted in light sentences such as probation or community service (Equality Now 2014, 25; National Stakeholders Forum on Female Genital Mutilation 2007).[10] In part this is because many people are not aware of the laws, as the Children's Act in particular was not well publicized (United Nations Population Fund 2013). Moreover, many of those who do know about the laws object to their provisions, and are thus unwilling to report violations. The police may also fail to pursue cases that are brought to their attention, since the officers themselves sometimes do not support the laws or are reluctant to interfere in what they perceive as cultural practices, and since police have limited financial resources that constrain their ability to intervene in active child protection cases and to carry out investigations. In addition, the Kenyan court system is heavily backlogged, so cases involving "traditional practices" tend to receive low priority and often do not go to trial.

In the case of early marriage, the existence of parallel systems of customary and religious personal law in Kenya has created further confusion. In addition to statutory marriage law (covered by the Marriage Ordinance and the African Christian Marriage and Divorce Ordinance), Kenya has legally recognized three other marriage regimes—Islamic, Hindu, and African customary marriage law. Though the Children's Act set the legal age of marriage at 18 for both men and women, the preexisting nonstatutory regimes took varying positions (Center for Reproductive Law and Policy 1997, 69–70). The Hindu Marriage and Divorce Ordinance set the minimum age of marriage at 18 for men but 16 for women who had the consent of a guardian. The Mohammedan Marriage, Divorce and Succession Ordinance did not specify a minimum age of marriage, nor did any of the customary law systems associated with Kenya's various ethnic groups. While statutory law legally supersedes customary law in the case of a conflict, this has often not been enforced. Indeed, because marriages under customary law in Kenya were not registered with the government, such marriages of girls and boys younger than age 18 could go unnoticed in the absence of a direct report to the authorities. But circumstances changed in 2014 with the introduction of a new Marriage Act, which brought all the marriage regimes under a single law (voiding the previous Marriage Ordinance and the African Christian, Hindu, and Mohammedan Marriage Ordinances). The Marriage Act reaffirms that the minimum age of marriage is 18 regardless of marriage regime, and also requires the registration of customary marriages.

10. A notable exception to this tendency is a 2010 case in which the circumciser and the father of a girl who bled to death after undergoing FGM were each sentenced to 10 years in prison (United Nations Population Fund 2013).

Beyond legal actions, the Kenyan government has pursued a number of policy measures and other actions to address FGM, though there have been few specific efforts to address early marriage. In 1999, the Ministry of Health coordinated with various other government ministries to initiate a National Plan of Action for the Elimination of Female Genital Mutilation in Kenya. The plan of action was designed to assist in the coordination and assessment of anti-FGM activities by governmental and nongovernmental organizations. Management of the plan was transferred to the Ministry of Gender, Children, and Social Development in 2005, and the plan was revised in 2008 to take a more rights-based approach and again in 2011 to take into account the Prohibition of FGM Act (United Nations Children's Fund 2010a, 36; United Nations Children's Fund 2013, 13). A National Secretariat for FGM/C was created within the Ministry of Gender in 2008, which enabled the creation of a National Committee on the Abandonment of FGM/C the following year that brought together both governmental and nongovernmental stakeholders (United Nations Population Fund and United Nations Children's Fund 2013c, 17–18). In 2010, Kenya's cabinet approved a National Policy on the Abandonment of Female Genital Mutilation, and Kenya acceded to the Maputo Protocol that same year. As provided for in the Prohibition of FGM Act, an Anti–Female Genital Mutilation Board was created in 2013 to manage government efforts and muster resources.

Much of the work to address FGM and early marriage in Kenya has, however, been performed by nongovernmental and international organizations. As described in chapter 1, the first major nongovernmental effort to tackle FGM came in the 1990s, under the leadership of Maendeleo Ya Wanawake (MYWO). The number of organizations addressing FGM in Kenya quickly grew from there, such that a National Focal Point for FGM, chaired by the NGO Northern Aid and funded by the United Nations Development Program (UNDP), was created in 1997 to coordinate anti-FGM activities (Chege, Askew, and Liku 2001, 3). In addition to the alternative rite of passage, which ultimately became a popular approach employed by a wide range of organizations to varying effect, other leading strategies have included intergenerational dialogue and approaches challenging religious justifications for circumcision (Evelia et al. 2007). The intergenerational dialogue approach was first implemented in Kenya by the former German state development company GTZ, and involved the facilitation of dialogue between younger and older women on normally sensitive issues. The religion-oriented approach has been employed by the NGO Womankind Kenya and others primarily in Muslim communities in northeastern Kenya, since many Muslims in this area view female circumcision as a requirement of Islam. The strategy has been to recruit Islamic scholars and religious leaders to speak out against FGM and to clearly articulate that the Koran does not require female circumcision. Many Christian churches and faith-based organizations have also advocated against FGM by drawing in part on biblical teachings.

Many other organizations have simply focused on raising awareness about the health and human rights consequences of FGM, using a variety of tactics including workshops, seminars, dramatic skits, radio programs, and the distribution of educational materials to get the message across. And in recent years, a few organizations have assisted in organizing the kind of public community declarations of FGM abandonment that have been associated with the Tostan program in West Africa. By 2008, the German-run Fulda-Mosocho Project had facilitated 52 public declarations among the Kisii ethnic group (United Nations Children's Fund 2010b, 37–39). Similar public declarations have also been made by the Njuri Ncheke Supreme Council of Ameru Elders (renewing their 1956 ban), the Pokot Council of Elders, and the Il Chamus Council of Elders (United Nations Children's Fund 2013, 13). All told, communities representing nearly 2.5 million people declared abandonment of FGM between 2009 and 2012 (United Nations Population Fund and United Nations Children's Fund 2012, 21).

Early-marriage activities have tended to focus on getting girls to stay in school. Organizations such as ChildFund (formerly Christian Children's Fund) have implemented programs to pay girls' families in exchange for sending the girls to school, as a substitute for the bridewealth that would attend the arrangement of an early marriage (International Center for Research on Women 2007, 39). In addition, a school-based HIV program run by the Ministry of Education in partnership with the Poverty Action Lab at MIT found that reducing school costs by paying for school uniforms reduced the incidence of teen marriage (Duflo et al. 2006). Other programs have engaged in general awareness-raising activities, often within the context of broader programs directed at girls and employing similar strategies as those used for FGM. World Vision, for example, has set up girls' advocacy clubs in schools that focus on the negative consequences of early marriage, as well as FGM (World Vision 2008, 13). One stand-alone program of note, run by the international NGO Population Council, raised awareness about early marriage in Nyanza Province by running local-language radio programs, organizing drama troupes, and recruiting local church leaders (Erulkar and Ayuka 2007, 4).

Beyond FGM and early-marriage prevention activities, many international and local NGOs have focused on advocacy, child protection, and professional trainings. The Federation of Women Lawyers (FIDA), the Kenya

Women Parliamentary Association, and the Children's Legal Action Network, all domestic Kenyan organizations, were instrumental in lobbying for passage and implementation of the Children's Act and the Prohibition of FGM Act, with UNFPA also taking a leading role in promoting the latter act (United Nations Population Fund and United Nations Children's Fund 2013c). Quite a few other organizations, including Tasaru Ntomonok Initiative (TNI) and the Forum for African Women Educationalists, have set up rescue centers to care for and educate girls who run away from home to escape FGM and early marriage (United Nations Children's Fund 2010a, 26). Finally, some civil society groups have developed and implemented curricula to train various relevant stakeholders and potential change agents, including healthcare workers, teachers, lawyers, paralegals, police, and journalists.

Much of the financial support for anti-FGM activities in Kenya comes from international aid agencies.[11] The leading multilateral donors are UNFPA, UNICEF, the UN High Council for Refugees, UNDP, and the WHO, while major bilateral contributions have come from Sweden, Italy, Norway, Germany, the Netherlands, and Austria (United Nations Population Fund and United Nations Children's Fund 2013c, 8). Other funding comes from large international NGOs such as CARE, World Vision, and Action Aid. In 2008, the UNFPA and UNICEF started a joint program that ultimately reached 15 African countries, including Kenya. The program followed a human rights-based approach of community sensitization and dialogue that also included active advocacy and lobbying at the national level, media campaigns, partnerships with NGOs and faith-based organizations, and capacity-building of relevant government agencies. Kenya was one of the largest recipients of aid from this program, with a budget of just over $2 million for the first five years (United Nations Population Fund and United Nations Children's Fund 2013b, 247).

On the domestic Kenyan side, a wide range of groups and organizations are addressing the issues of FGM and early marriage in some form. Some of these groups have been involved in the transnational campaign on violence against women from the beginning, and have played active roles on the international stage, including MYWO, FIDA, and the National Council of Women of Kenya. But such prominent organizations are just a small subset of the much broader set of civil society actors that are confronting

---

11. It is difficult to provide concrete details about financial support for early-marriage activities, since few organizations budget specifically for this issue, instead funding programs that address early marriage incidentally or as one element on a broader slate of issues.

FGM and early marriage in Kenya. Many Kenyan NGOs and community groups have taken up the mantle of these causes simply as part of their broader development work. Though the large-scale projects receive much of the international attention, there are hundreds of organizations dealing with these issues in some small-scale way and with varying degrees of commitment.

FGM and early marriage have also received a fair amount of media attention in Kenya (though a cross-country comparison suggests that the level of media coverage of FGM has been lower than in a number of other countries with moderate-to-high FGM prevalence rates) (United Nations Population Fund and United Nations Children's Fund 2012, 25). Between 2000 and 2013, "FGM" was mentioned in 234 articles in the *Nation*, one of Kenya's two leading newspapers.[12] Over that same period, 169 articles mentioned "early marriage." The Association of Media Women in Kenya has also taken a leading role in the campaign against FGM, seeking to promote and monitor media coverage of the issue across multiple platforms (Evelia et al. 2007, 16).

In the face of such attention from multiple fronts—international organizations, NGOs, churches and faith-based groups, government, and media—it appears there has been some meaningful change in the practices of FGM and early marriage in Kenya. In the 2008–2009 round of the DHS, 82 percent of all female respondents, and 68 percent of respondents who had undergone FGM, said they thought the practice should stop (Kenya National Bureau of Statistics and ICF Macro 2010, 268). In addition, the 2008–2009 DHS showed a five-percentage-point decline in FGM prevalence from the 2003 round of the survey and an 11-percentage-point decline from 1998 (Kenya Central Bureau of Statistics, Ministry of Health, and ORC Macro 2004, 251; Kenya National Bureau of Statistics and ICF Macro 2010, 265; Kenya National Council for Population and Development, Central Bureau of Statistics, and Macro International 1999, 168).[13] This decline over time is matched by sharply lower reported prevalence rates among younger girls and women—in the 2008–2009 survey, 44 percent of women aged 40 to 49 reported having been cut, compared with only 23 percent of women aged 20 to 29. Moreover, the decline across age cohorts is relatively steady,

12. Kenya's other major national newspaper, the *Standard*, does not provide an online archive.

13. North Eastern Province, a Somali-dominated region in which FGM is nearly universal, was not included in the 1998 DHS. Thus, the true nationwide prevalence of FGM in 1998 was almost certainly higher than 38 percent.

suggesting that FGM has been gradually decreasing in Kenya since the 1970s (United Nations Children's Fund 2013, 100). However, much of this decline appears to be concentrated in the Kalenjin, Kamba, Kikuyu, and Meru ethnic groups. There is also a somewhat uneven decline across age cohorts among the Embu, Maasai, and Taita/Taveta, while the Kisii and Somali have seen no meaningful change.

Early-marriage prevalence in Kenya also appears to have been declining somewhat over time. Although 36 percent of women aged 40 to 49 reported in the 2008–2009 DHS that they had been married by age 18, only 28 percent of women aged 20 to 29 reported having been married by that age. Yet the decline in early marriage across age cohorts has not been particularly smooth, an issue that is also captured by comparing early-marriage prevalence rates across survey rounds. The 2008–2009 early-marriage prevalence rates are the same as the 2003 rates, though they are three percentage points lower than the 1998 rate for marriage by age 15 and four percentage points lower than the 1998 rate for marriage by age 18.[14]

As noted in chapter 1, it is possible that some portion of the decline in FGM and early-marriage prevalence actually reflects reporting bias, particularly following the introduction of the Children's Act—women who participated in the 2003 and 2008–2009 rounds of the DHS might simply be disinclined to admit that they underwent an illegal practice. However, comparison of the three available survey rounds suggests that such misrepresentation cannot account for the overall declines. For example, if one restricts the survey data to only those age cohorts who were present in all three rounds—women aged 15 to 39 in 1998, aged 20 to 44 in 2003, and aged 25 to 49 in 2008—the decline in FGM prevalence becomes much smaller. Within these age groups, 36 percent of respondents in 1998 reported having been cut, compared with 35 percent in 2003 and 34 percent in 2008–2009. Thus, some underreporting may have occurred, but not at nearly a high enough rate to account for the 11-percentage-point drop in reported prevalence for the full sample between 1998 and 2008–2009. Instead, the larger decline is primarily accounted for by the entry of younger women into and the exit of older women out of successive rounds of the survey.

Despite these primary behavior changes, some people have responded to activist efforts in unintended or undesirable ways. With FGM, changes have been observed in a number of secondary behaviors. In particular,

14. As in the case of FGM, the exclusion of North Eastern Province from the 1998 DHS suggests that the actual nationwide prevalence of early marriage was higher than reported in that survey.

Kenya has exhibited a trend toward medicalization of the cut—as reported by their mothers, the percentage of circumcised girls on whom the procedure was performed by health personnel rose from 34 percent in 1998 to 41 percent in 2008–2009 (United Nations Children's Fund 2013, 110). This may be a response to the health-centered approach of some anti-FGM activism, which was particularly common in the early days of the campaign. Rather than give up the practice, some parents appear to have instead sought out medical practitioners to perform the cut in an attempt to reduce the likelihood of the health complications about which they had been informed. There is also evidence that girls are being cut at an earlier age, possibly as a strategy to limit their resistance to being cut. Indeed, in the 2008–2009 DHS, the proportion of circumcised respondents aged 45 to 49 who had been cut before the age of 10 was only 14 percent, but the proportion aged 15 to 19 who had been cut before age 10 was substantially higher, at 44 percent (United Nations Children's Fund 2013, 112).

In addition, there has been some direct backlash against activism targeting FGM and early marriage. Some have been critical of the health approach to FGM on the grounds that it does not fit with many women's lived experience of circumcision, particularly to the extent that activists have overstated the likelihood of serious health complications. Others have questioned the human-rights-centered approach, concerned that it can sometimes focus too heavily on individual rights while ignoring the importance of collective rights to local communities (Igras et al. 2004, 263). Still others have reacted negatively to intervention on these issues by outsiders (both foreigners and those from other ethnic groups), seeing an uninformed, paternalistic attempt to strip them of their culture. A particularly dramatic example of this reaction has been observed in the case of the outlawed Kikuyu religious sect and criminal organization Mungiki, which has taken a virulent procircumcision stance in an attempt to reclaim lost precolonial tradition, going so far as to forcibly circumcise adult Kikuyu women (United Nations Population Fund and United Nations Children's Fund 2013c, 8–9).

MAA-SPEAKING PEOPLES

Within Kenya, the Nilotic Maa language is spoken by a number of related groups, of which the Maasai and Samburu are the largest, jointly comprising between 2 and 3 percent of the Kenyan population (Kenya Central Bureau of Statistics 1989; Sommer and Vossen 1993, 32). Other Maa-speaking peoples (with dialectical variations) include the Il Chamus,

Arusha, and Okiek, as well as a number of smaller groups that in some cases have come to self-identify as Maasai over time (Spear 1993). The Maasai population is concentrated in the southern Rift Valley and straddles the Kenya–Tanzania border, while the Samburu are concentrated in the northern Rift Valley to the south and east of Lake Turkana.

Maasai and Samburu share very similar economic and cultural practices (though there are small variations both across and within these larger groupings), including a long tradition of female circumcision and early marriage. They are primarily pastoralists, herding cattle, sheep, and goats. However, agricultural production has become more common in recent decades, as has wage employment, business ownership, and homework to a lesser extent (Coast 2001, 49–50). Yet livestock ownership remains an important marker of wealth and status even for those who are not pastoralists as a primary or sole occupation.

Maasai and Samburu society follows a strict gerentocratic organization, and descent is patrilineal (P. Spencer 1965, 211). Men, but not women, are organized into a system of age sets that advance through a series of age grades. A new age set is formed approximately once every 15 years, when boys enter the age grade of *ilmurran* (warriors) upon their circumcision and initiation (P. Spencer 2003, 19). Traditionally, the members of the age set would not be able to marry until they became senior *ilmurran* or until they graduated into the second age grade and became junior elders (upon the creation of the next age set), although restrictions on marriage of *ilmurran* have weakened over time (Coast 2006, 401). The bond between age-mates within an individual age set is close and socially important, persisting throughout men's lives (Talle 1988, 99).

Women are connected to, but not part of, the age set with which they associated as girls (the age set that was in the warrior age grade at that time) (Talle 1988, 94). They provide almost all domestic labor, and married women derive prestige from the number and accomplishments of their children. Women do not own livestock but are instead granted "milking rights" to an allotted number of livestock by their husbands (Coast 2001, 36).

Prevalence and Characteristics of FGM and Early Marriage

Ethnographic research suggests that Maasai and Samburu girls are traditionally circumcised during puberty (around 12 to 15 years of age, but with some flexibility), prior to or after the onset of menstruation (Hodgson 2005, 55). Though boys are circumcised in public and sometimes in small groups, girls are generally circumcised individually and in private.

A traditional circumciser—generally an elderly local Maasai or Samburu woman—performs the operation, either clitoridectomy or excision, using a traditional knife (*olmurunya*) (Talle 1988, 105).

The procedure takes place inside or on the threshold of the girl's mother's home, shortly after dawn for the Maasai but sometimes in the evening for the Samburu (Hodgson 2005, 55; P. Spencer 1965, 237–38). Having been ritually washed and shaved, the girl is seated on a cowhide or a circumcision "couch" and supported by the women of her homestead. Two women hold her legs and one sits behind her and holds her back (Talle 1988, 105). Other women and perhaps small children will also be present to watch the cutting, while men and boys remain at a distance in the cattle corral. Following the operation, the wound is washed and may be smeared with butter to promote healing, and the girl is then able to lie down and rest and is given cow's blood to drink to regain her strength (Hodgson 2005, 28). At this time the celebration begins, with women singing songs, young people dancing, and men in particular consuming large quantities of meat and beer (making the celebration quite expensive) (Hodgson 2001, 247). A ritual tree (*elaitin*) is planted outside the girl's doorway as a symbol of fertility and of the growth of the community.

The girl remains at home for the next four or five days as she heals, and during this time a special head ornament (*olmarisian*) is prepared for her (Hodgson 2005, 56). She consumes meat, milk, and blood to aid in her recovery. At the conclusion of this period, she begins to move about and to visit family and friends, wearing black sheets that have been smeared with fat, black or dark blue beads, and the *olmarisian* to indicate her new status as *enkaibartani*—one who is transitioning between girlhood and womanhood (Talle 1988, 106–8). Mostly, however, she remains at home (P. Spencer 1988, 30). Though uncircumcised girls are frequently the sexual partners of *ilmurran*, these sexual relationships (which may or may not involve actual sexual intercourse) end upon the girl's circumcision (Hodgson 2005, 56). After a couple of months, the girl's head is shaved once again and she begins to dress in the clothing of an adult woman.

For the Maasai and Samburu, female circumcision serves as a rite of passage into adulthood, although unlike with boys, it does not function as a test of bravery (Hodgson 2005, 55; Talle 1988, 105–10). Girls are allowed to cry out or otherwise show their pain, but those who do endure it without crying are praised and may be given a small gift of livestock. Unlike with some other groups, circumcision is not related to preservation of virginity before marriage. In fact, it is looked upon as an embarrassment if Maasai and Samburu girls are virgins at the time of their marriage. Instead, female circumcision for the Maasai and Samburu signals readiness to marry and

the beginning of a woman's reproductive career, with the concomitant regulation (by men) of her fertility. According to Hodgson (2005, 56), "Once
[girls] were circumcised, their sexuality was linked to fertility and chan-
neled, through marriage, into procreation. Girls, in other words, became
not just women, but potential mothers."

Beyond the perceived value of female circumcision, Maasai and Samburu
also maintain beliefs about the consequences of a failure to circumcise. In
particular, there is a common belief than an uncircumcised woman will be
unable to conceive or that any child she does conceive will be born with
birth defects or suffer from blindness (Talle 1988, 110–11). As a result,
girls who become pregnant by their *ilmurran* boyfriends before their initiation are immediately circumcised. And among Tanzanian Maasai, many
believe that female circumcision protects against vaginal and urinary tract
infections (Winterbottom, Koomen, and Burford 2009, 59). There is also
the practical consequence of an uncircumcised girl being potentially unable
to find a husband, and uncircumcised girls may be ostracized (Skaine
2005, 153).

Traditionally, a girl would be married shortly after her circumcision
(Hodgson 2005, 56). According to Aud Talle (1988, 132), it is considered
"dangerous to delay the marriage of a mature girl because 'everybody's eyes
are upon her.'" She is unlikely to know her future husband well, if at all, in
advance of the marriage, despite the fact that the engagement, or "book-
ing" of the girl, generally takes place several years earlier (Skaine 2005,
165).[15] The bridegroom pays a bridewealth—consisting of livestock and
other goods or cash—to the bride's family in exchange for taking the girl
and her valuable domestic labor away from them under a patrilocal system.
The bridewealth is traditionally negotiated in multiple rounds and paid out
over many years, both before and after the wedding (including contributing sugar, a steer, and a heifer for the girl's circumcision celebration). The
bridegroom tends to be substantially older than the bride because he must
have the financial means to pay the bridewealth (P. Spencer 1965, 219).
Moreover, as described above, men were traditionally barred from marrying while they were still young *ilmurran*.

Polygyny is the preferred form of marriage, and is quite common for
men from wealthy families. The enforced age gap between husbands and

15. However, the engagement is not binding at this stage. Indeed, the marriage is
not certain until the girl has actually crossed through the gate of the bridegroom's
homestead (and even then may be dissolved under certain circumstances), although
the girl's family would be responsible for paying back any bridewealth they had already
received should the engagement be broken in favor of another suitor (Talle 1988, 134).

wives also facilitates this system by constraining the pool of men who are eligible to marry at any given time (P. Spencer 1965, 96). In turn, the institution of polygyny means that higher-order wives will often be significantly younger than their husbands (Coast 2001, 82). Thus, Talle (1988, 126) notes that "a Maasai girl regards herself as lucky if she is married to a young man, but she may become the third or fourth wife of a man older than her father." This sentiment is echoed by Paul Spencer (1965, 219) with respect to the Samburu, who states that "the prospect of being married to an elderly man is one which women admit terrified them before marriage." Yet even with the age differential, the preference for polygyny puts a premium on girls that pushes bridewealth payments up, such that fathers with limited means may be tempted to marry off even their young daughters or to pull daughters out of school so that they can marry (Talle 1988, 150).

The marriage ceremony itself lasts several days and involves the movement of the girl from her own family's homestead to that of her future husband, which may be quite far away because of clan exogamy (P. Spencer 1965, 220). To begin, the girl's father blesses her in her mother's house, and she is instructed on her responsibilities and behavior as a wife. The bridegroom also receives instructions on how to care for his new young wife (P. Spencer 1973, 103). The following morning, the bride's female relatives help her to dress in her bridal clothes, and both the clothes and her body are smeared with fat and ochre (P. Spencer 1988, 30). She then leaves her home, attended by the same relatives and by the bridegroom and his best man. However, her own family leaves her after a short distance. The girl cries and walks slowly, back bent, to demonstrate her sadness at leaving her natal home (Talle 1988, 128). As she approaches her future husband's homestead, her gait slows further until eventually she refuses to go on. At this time the bridegroom's female family members, including his wives if he is already married, leave the homestead and come toward the wedding procession, exhorting the girl to enter and offering her gifts (P. Spencer 1965). Once the bride enters through the gate of the homestead, the wedding feast begins. The feast is a large event for which animals are slaughtered and *moratina* (a kind of honey beer) is brewed. However, the bride herself sits inside for much of the celebration, holding a small child as a symbol of her future fertility. In the evening, she is blessed again by her husband and his age-mates (Talle 1988, 130). Following the wedding, the girl will generally live in her mother-in-law's home or in the home of a co-wife until she has built her own house within the homestead, which can take some time (P. Spencer 1973, 103).

For the Samburu, the circumcision and marriage ceremonies do exhibit some differences from their performance among the Maasai (P. Spencer

1988, 35–36). A Samburu girl is usually circumcised directly preceding her marriage, and thus is not generally able to travel immediately to her husband's homestead (Holtzman 2009, 76; P. Spencer 1973, 103). She will instead stay with her husband briefly in the homestead of one of her clansmen. Perhaps as a result of this, the celebration attending the wedding occurs at the homestead of the bride prior to her departure, rather than at the homestead of the bridegroom. In addition, the compression of the circumcision and marriage ceremonies eliminates the postcircumcision rituals described above. Still, the similarities between the groups with respect to these two practices outweigh the differences, particularly in terms of their social and cultural meaning. A number of individuals I interviewed noted that the Maasai and Samburu varied slightly in terms of dialect and accent, livelihood (extent of farming), degree of education, clan structures, age-set practices, and mode of dress, but that they share the same basic cultural practices.[16] One Samburu interviewee noted that the differences between the groups were not meaningful and that the Maasai are "our family," while a Maasai interviewee stated that the groups "speak the same language, they share the same cultural norms, they share the same cultural taboos."[17]

Among both groups, though, the practices of female circumcision and marriage have evolved somewhat over time in response to changing conditions and interests.[18] For instance, circumcisions are increasingly performed using a disposable razor blade rather than the traditional knife (Hodgson 2001, 246). The transition to razor blades is partly a matter of convenience—they work well, and so were embraced by circumcisers when they became widely available[19]—and partly a response to the HIV/AIDS epidemic, as activists warned that use of a single knife to cut multiple girls could contribute to the spread of the disease (Skaine 2005, 12–13).

Marriage practices have also shifted with the times. Rather than walking to her future husband's home as part of the marriage ceremony, it is

---

16. Author's interview with charitable trust director RL, June 6, 2011, Mukogodo; CBO worker JK, June 12, 2011, Mukogodo; CBO board member LL, June 13, 2011, Oldonyiro; community health worker AN, July 5, 2011, Mau; CBO director MS, July 5, 2011, Mau.

17. Author's interview with CBO worker JT, June 10, 2011, Mukogodo; councilor OL, June 13, 2011, Oldonyiro.

18. The discussion that follows is largely limited to indigenously generated changes in the practices of circumcision and marriage. An extended discussion of strategic changes to these practices in response to transnational activism and criminalization is presented in chapter 7.

19. Author's interview with traditional circumciser NL, November 13, 2008, Mukogodo.

increasingly common for a bride to travel there by car (Talle 1988, 128). The content of various bridewealth payments has changed as well. Instead of providing a girl's family with honey for beer making at the start of marriage negotiations, a prospective bridegroom may instead simply provide sugar or, in fact, commercial whiskey or beer (Talle 1988, 132). Cash payments, rather than actual livestock, are also an increasingly common part of the betrothal gifts, reflecting the general expansion of currency-based financial transactions (Talle 1988, 135). More generally, there has been a trend toward lump-sum bridewealth transactions at the time of marriage—in such a case the father is said to be "selling" his daughter to the highest bidder rather than building a lasting relationship between two families (Talle 1988, 135–37). In cases where the bride is "sold," she is likely to have a weaker position within her new husband's household, and she may be unable to leave the marriage if she is mistreated because her family may not be in a financial position to repay the bridewealth.[20] Even within more traditional marriage arrangements, there has been a decline in the payment of bridewealth in the years following the marriage ceremony, thus weakening the affinal ties among in-laws (Talle 1988, 145–46).

In addition, marriage patterns have changed as a result of increased school attendance among girls and a shortening of the amount of time men spend as *ilmurran*. Because schoolgoing girls marry later, their temporary absence from the marriage market reduces the supply of potential wives in the community (Talle 1988, 150). (The delay in marriage age for schoolgoing girls has also produced a breakdown in the temporal connection between circumcision and marriage, since circumcision generally continues to be performed at puberty.) At the same time, the earlier graduation of *ilmurran* to the status of junior elders increases the number of men on the marriage market (Talle 1988, 149). The decline in the number of marriageable women and the increase in the number of marriageable men have resulted in increases in the size of bridewealth payments, with corresponding consequences for men and women according to their means. Though sons of wealthy families are able to raise the necessary bridewealth and marry earlier than they would have been able to do in the past, sons of poorer families must delay marriage, potentially for a very long time (Talle 1988, 145). There is also some suggestion that the removal of schoolgoing girls from the marriage market and the increase in bridewealth

20. The only solution is for the father to find a new husband for his daughter (a man who is able to pay back the first husband), or to substitute another girl from his family (Talle 1988, 137). In general, though a woman may run away from her marriage, she will usually return if she has children, since they belong to her husband's lineage and must remain with him (P. Spencer 1988, 32).

have depressed the age of marriage (and as a result, of circumcision) for girls who do not attend school (Talle 1988, 150).

One thing that has remained relatively constant is that girls tend to have little control over their circumcision or their marriage (P. Spencer 1965; Talle 1988). With circumcision, a girl's mother makes the actual arrangements for the ceremony and is present throughout the process, and in that sense has decision-making power over most aspects of the event. However, though the father does not participate directly in the circumcision, he has significant control over its timing because it is a precursor to and requirement for marriage—the circumcision is scheduled once the marriage has been arranged. Fathers and other patrilineal male relatives also contribute meat and beer to the postcircumcision celebration. Moreover, as her guardian, a girl's father is responsible for ensuring that she is circumcised and may step in should the girl or her mother resist the cut (Talle 2007, 94). The father is also responsible for her marriage and has more or less complete authority in this arena. It is his right to select suitors, negotiate the bridewealth, and make the final marriage decision, though girls may protest these decisions, with varying degrees of success. Mothers may also play some role in marriage negotiations, particularly if they are widows.

The Kenya Demographic and Health Surveys provide detailed data about FGM and early marriage among the Maasai that support the ethnographic findings, although they do not provide equivalent information for the Samburu since it is a smaller group. In the 2008–2009 DHS, 81 percent of female Maasai respondents aged 20 to 49 reported having undergone FGM. Within this same group, however, 94 percent of those with no formal education reported being circumcised, compared to only 51 percent of those who attended secondary school.

By far the most common type of circumcision involved the removal of some flesh, corresponding to clitoridectomy or excision. Ninety-six percent of circumcised respondents aged 15 to 49 reported having some flesh removed, while 2 percent reported being sewn closed (corresponding to infibulation) and 2 percent reported being nicked but not having had any flesh removed (Kenya National Bureau of Statistics and ICF Macro 2010, 265). The median age at which respondents reported being circumcised was 14, with 46 percent of circumcised women aged 20 to 49 reporting that they were cut between the ages of 10 and 14, and 43 percent reporting that they were cut at age 15 or above. In fact nearly two-thirds (65 percent) of all circumcised girls were cut between the ages of 12 and 16. Only 5 percent were cut before age 10, while the remaining 6 percent did not know the age at which they were cut. A traditional circumciser performed the procedure in 82 percent of cases, while 1 percent of cases were performed by a traditional birth attendant, 13 percent were performed by a nurse or midwife, and 3 percent were performed by a doctor. The 1998 DHS also collected data about the site of the procedure and the instrument used for female respondents' eldest daughters. Among circumcised eldest daughters, 81 percent were cut in their own homes and 11 percent were cut in another home, with the remainder cut in an unspecified location. In terms of cutting instrument, 59 percent were cut with their own individual razor blade, 22 percent were cut with a shared razor blade, 7 percent were cut with a scalpel, and 7 percent were cut with another instrument.

In the 2008–2009 DHS, Maasai women aged 15 to 49 identified four benefits associated with female circumcision—13 percent said that circumcision led to social acceptance, 4 percent said that it improved women's cleanliness and hygiene, 2 percent said that it protected premarital virginity, and 1 percent said that it improved a girl's marriage prospects. Nonetheless, 83 percent said that there were no benefits associated with female circumcision. Furthermore, 79 percent said they thought female circumcision should be discontinued. This attitudinal resistance to circumcision has been accompanied by some degree of behavioral change. A comparison of the three DHS rounds shows a recent decline in FGM prevalence among the Maasai, with a prevalence rate of 73 percent for respondents aged 15 to 49 in 2008–2009, compared to 93 percent in 2003 and 89 percent in 1998 (Kenya Central Bureau of Statistics, Ministry of Health, and ORC Macro 2004, 251; Kenya National Bureau of Statistics and ICF Macro 2010, 265; Kenya National Council for Population and Development, Central Bureau of Statistics, and Macro International 1999, 168).

As noted above, the 2008–2009 DHS showed that 47 percent of 20- to 49-year-old female Maasai respondents had married by age 18, and 20 percent had married by age 15. The median age of marriage for female Maasai respondents aged 25 to 49 was 18. Maasai women with no formal education were particularly at risk of early marriage, with 73 percent of those aged 20 to 49 married by age 18. Comparatively, only 4 percent of those who had attended secondary school or above reported being married by age 18. Maasai women who married early were also more likely to be in polygynous unions and to be substantially younger than their husbands—34 percent of those who married before age 18 reported being in a polygynous marriage, compared to 25 percent of those who married after age 18, and women who married early were on average 9.8 years younger than their husbands, while those who married later were on average 6.2 years younger than their husbands. Women who married early also had less control over whom they married—while 73 percent of those who married after age 18 chose their own husband, only 37 percent of those who married before age 18 were able to do the same. However, early marriage of Maasai women does appear to have become somewhat less common over time, with 42 percent of women aged 20 to 29 reporting having been married by age 18, compared to 69 percent of women aged 40 to 49.[21]

Activism against FGM and Early Marriage

Though Maasai and Samburu were not drawn into the colonial-era female circumcision controversy in the same way that many Kikuyu were (mostly because few of the former had converted to Christianity), some educated Christian Maasai living at the African Inland Mission station at Siyiapei did become involved (Tignor 1976, 251–54). In 1930, the American missionaries at the station, in accordance with the general decision on the issue taken by the AIM in the colony, notified their members that they would have to renounce female circumcision or face suspension from the church. In response, all but two members left the mission, and the rebel members set up an alternative church nearby. However, the split between the missionaries and the Maasai Christians ultimately was not as total or defining as the split with the Kikuyu; the specific missionaries in question were themselves somewhat ambivalent about the new AIM policy, and also the Maasai lacked a political organization like the KCA that could turn the female circumcision issue into a test of loyalty and commitment to traditional practices. In these circumstances, the controversy remained localized and failed to register with wider Maasai society.[22] Indeed, the provincial commissioner of Masai Province, based at Ngong, and the Kajiado district commissioner both resisted even the implementation of a propaganda campaign against female circumcision, arguing that such a campaign would accomplish nothing and might interfere with other administrative actions.[23] The district commissioner of Marsabit similarly concluded that among the circumcising groups in his district, including the Samburu, "Practically nothing can be done in the way of discouraging them," and the provincial commissioner of Northern Frontier Province stated that the practice was not even harmful.[24]

21. Because of small sample sizes, the 95 percent confidence intervals around these figures slightly overlap, and thus one cannot rule out the possibility that there is no real decline across age cohorts.

22. Eventually, many of the breakaway church members came back to the mission.

23. 945/ADM.15/14 Provincial Commissioner, Masai Province, to Chief Native Commissioner, Nairobi, May 18, 1931; ADM. 15/27 District Commissioner Kajiado, to Provincial Commissioner, Masai Province, May 12, 1931.

24. ADM. 15/16/1 District Commissioner, Marsabit, to Provincial Commissioner, Northern Frontier Province, March 3, 1932; ADM. 15/16/1/287 Provincial

There also appears to have been no specific concern about or effort to regulate the age of marriage among the Maasai and Samburu during the colonial period. For example, in response to a survey circulated in 1930 by the office of the chief native commissioner on behalf of the secretary of state for the colonies, the district commissioner of Isiolo stated that Samburu girls generally married between the ages of 15 and 20, but concluded that this did not constitute child marriage and that such marriage practices were not harmful to girls, further asserting that the age of marriage did not need to be raised.[25]

In the postindependence era, however, the Maasai and Samburu were among the first to be targeted by activism against FGM and early marriage. In particular, Maasai and Samburu populations dominated two of the five program districts of MYWO's alternative-rite-of-passage program. MYWO sensitization activities began in Samburu District in 1993, and the first ARP was held in 2000, while in predominantly Maasai Narok District, MYWO started sensitization activities in 1994 and introduced the first rite of passage in 1998 (Chege, Askew, and Liku 2001). The alternative rite of passage approach has become generally popular as a strategy to address FGM among the Maasai, and has been implemented by a number of other organizations including World Vision and TNI. With respect to early marriage, a nonformal education program introduced in Samburu District in the 1990s helped to delay the age of marriage for girls, and a school in Maasailand compensated families in exchange for sending their daughters to the school (International Center for Research on Women 2007, 39; United Nations Children's Fund 2001, 13). Rescue centers to house and educate girls running away from FGM and early marriage are also quite common in Maasai and Samburu areas, including the high-profile TNI based in Narok, which has received international attention in part through its relationship with Eve Ensler's V-Day organization. TNI's founder, Agnes Pareiyo, was named the United Nations in Kenya Person of the Year in 2005. Other prominent organizations and agencies that have worked among the Maasai and Samburu to combat FGM and early marriage (often addressing both practices jointly) include the Coalition on Violence Against Women (COVAW), ChildFund, Samburu Aid in Africa, Action Aid, GTZ, Samburu

Commissioner, Northern Frontier Province, to Chief Native Commissioner, Nairobi, March 15, 1932.

25. NPH. 4/2/6 S. H. La Fontaine, representative for Chief Native Commissioner, Nairobi, to all Provincial Commissioners and District Commissioners, May 16, 1930; 21/3/9/30 District Commissioner, Isiolo, to Provincial Commissioner, Northern Frontier Province, November 20, 1930.

Girls Foundation, and the UNFPA-UNICEF Joint Programme on FGM/C (Evelia et al. 2007).

CASE STUDIES

Different Maa-speaking communities in Kenya have received different levels of attention on the issues of FGM and early marriage, and they have responded to this attention in different ways. Thus, the three case study communities discussed in this book represent significant variation in the extent of norm change. While the specifics of their responses to transnational activism are discussed in detail in the subsequent empirical chapters, each community is briefly introduced here. Figure 3.1 locates the three communities within Kenya, figures 3.2, 3.3, and 3.4 map the communities individually, and table 3.3 provides background characteristics drawn from data collected in the original survey.

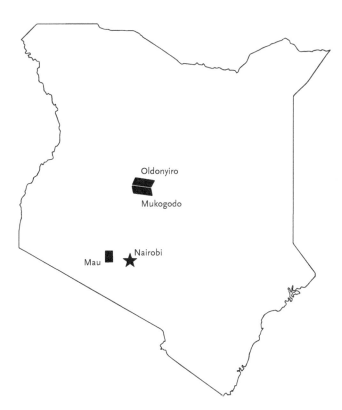

Figure 3.1: Case study areas

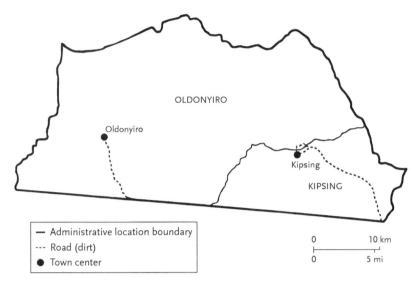

Figure 3.2: Oldonyiro

Oldonyiro

Oldonyiro is an administrative division sitting at the far western end of Isiolo District in Kenya's Eastern Province.[26] Within Oldonyiro Division there are two administrative locations—Oldonyiro Location and Kipsing Location—and four administrative sublocations. Oldonyiro Location, which contains Oldonyiro Centre, and Kipsing Location, which contains Kipsing Centre, are separated by a row of hills and are not connected to each other by any drivable roads. To reach Oldonyiro Location from Nairobi, one would first need to travel approximately four hours due north on paved roads to the town of Nanyuki, followed by an additional two and a half to three hours on mostly unpaved roads to Oldonyiro Centre. To reach Kipsing Location from Nairobi, one must travel for about five hours on paved roads to the town of Isiolo (one hour north of Nanyuki and the gateway to arid northern Kenya), followed by approximately three to four hours on unpaved roads to Kipsing Centre. However, the road between Isiolo and Kipsing is frequently impassable during the rainy season.

---

26. Under Kenya's 2010 constitution, Kenya's administrative units were reorganized, and districts were replaced by counties. However, because the research was conducted prior to this changeover, I will continue to describe the case study communities according to their classification under the previous system, which organized administrative units in descending order of province, district, division, location, and sublocation.

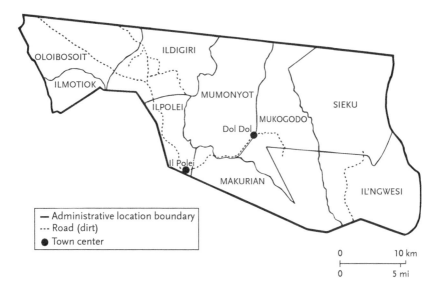

Figure 3.3: Mukogodo

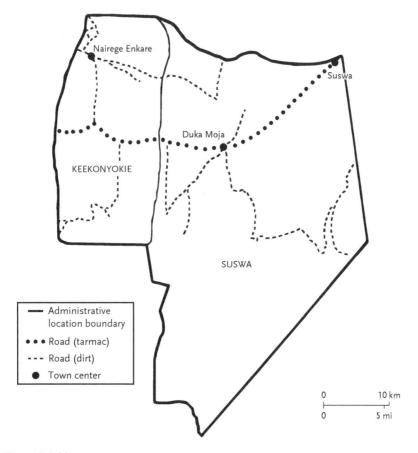

Figure 3.4: Mau

Table 3.3: CASE STUDY AREA BACKGROUND CHARACTERISTICS

Variable	Oldonyiro	Mukogodo	Mau	All areas	Observations
Education					598
No formal education	0.742	0.452	0.375	0.494	
	(0.03)	(0.04)	(0.04)	(0.02)	
Primary school	0.153	0.316	0.261	0.251	
	(0.03)	(0.04)	(0.03)	(0.02)	
Secondary school	0.073	0.182	0.235	0.176	
	(0.02)	(0.03)	(0.03)	(0.02)	
Higher education	0.032	0.050	0.129	0.078	
	(0.01)	(0.01)	(0.03)	(0.01)	
Wealth					
Radio ownership	0.311	0.518	0.811	0.585	593
	(0.04)	(0.04)	(0.03)	(0.02)	
Bicycle ownership	0.057	0.111	0.128	0.103	572
	(0.02)	(0.03)	(0.03)	(0.02)	
Automobile ownership	0.000	0.005	0.056	0.023	571
		(0.00)	(0.02)	(0.01)	
Occupation					580
Pastoralist	0.641	0.456	0.428	0.493	
	(0.04)	(0.04)	(0.04)	(0.02)	
Household work	0.138	0.197	0.136	0.157	
	(0.03)	(0.03)	(0.03)	(0.02)	
Student	0.065	0.113	0.176	0.127	
	(0.02)	(0.03)	(0.03)	(0.02)	
Businessperson	0.029	0.057	0.119	0.075	
	(0.01)	(0.02)	(0.02)	(0.01)	
Other occupation	0.023	0.093	0.116	0.084	
	(0.01)	(0.02)	(0.03)	(0.01)	
Unemployed	0.102	0.083	0.015	0.060	
	(0.02)	(0.02)	(0.01)	(0.01)	
Religion					594
Protestant	0.030	0.247	0.765	0.403	
	(0.01)	(0.03)	(0.04)	(0.02)	
Catholic	0.358	0.495	0.113	0.303	
	(0.04)	(0.04)	(0.03)	(0.02)	
Traditional religion	0.517	0.218	0.020	0.213	
	(0.04)	(0.03)	(0.01)	(0.02)	

Table 3.3: (CONTINUED)

Variable	Oldonyiro	Mukogodo	Mau	All areas	Observations
No religion	0.094	0.037	0.102	0.079	
	(0.02)	(0.02)	(0.03)	(0.01)	
Ethnicity					598
Samburu	0.993	0.032	0.000	0.266	
	(0.01)	(0.02)		(0.02)	
Maasai	0.000	0.275	0.991	0.502	
		(0.04)	(0.01)	(0.02)	
Yaaku	0.000	0.113	0.000	0.037	
		(0.03)		(0.01)	
Il'ngwesi	0.000	0.186	0.000	0.061	
		(0.03)		(0.01)	
Ildigiri	0.000	0.181	0.000	0.059	
		(0.03)		(0.01)	
Mumonyot	0.000	0.130	0.000	0.042	
		(0.03)		(0.01)	
Ewaso	0.000	0.078	0.000	0.025	
		(0.02)		(0.01)	

Note: Figures weighted by inverse sampling probabilities. Standard errors in parentheses.

As of the 1999 census, Oldonyiro Division had 9,669 residents, and approximately 20 percent of the population lived below the poverty line (Kenya Central Bureau of Statistics 2003). The Samburu community dominates the area, although there is a substantial Turkana minority—an ethnic group that is found mainly in the northwest part of Kenya. Oldonyiro had seven primary schools and no secondary schools in 2008, and the ratio of girls to boys enrolled in primary school at that time was 0.62. As of that same year, Oldonyiro had 14 registered CBOs. In 2014, 234 NGOs claimed to be working in the broader Isiolo District,[27] and 23 NGOs were actually headquartered in the district.

The survey data provide additional context about the area. Seventy-five percent of Oldonyiro respondents had received no formal education, with 15 percent attending primary school, 7 percent attending secondary school, and 3 percent attending college or university. While direct questions about income are problematic in a community in which few people receive a paycheck, it is possible to use respondents' ownership of a variety of goods as

27. This excludes 220 NGOs that claimed to be operating in every district of Kenya.

indicators of wealth. In Oldonyiro, 31 percent of respondents reported that they owned a radio, 6 percent reported that they owned a bicycle, and no respondents reported that they owned an automobile. Overall, 64 percent said that their primary occupation was pastoralist (including 87 percent of male respondents). A further 14 percent (all of whom were women) stated that they primarily engaged in household work, 7 percent said they were students, 3 percent said they were businesspeople, 2 percent reported some other occupation, and 10 percent said they were unemployed. With respect to religious adherence, 52 percent reported that they followed a traditional religion, 36 percent reported that they were Catholic, 3 percent reported that they were Protestant, and 9 percent reported that they followed no religion.

Mukogodo

Sitting just south of Oldonyiro and to the west of Mt. Kenya, Mukogodo is an administrative division that is completely coterminous with Laikipia North District of Rift Valley Province. Mukogodo was previously part of Laikipia District, but this larger district was divided into three smaller districts—Laikipia North, Laikipia East, and Laikipia West—in 2007. The division has nine administrative locations and 12 administrative sublocations, and covers an area of 483 square miles. To reach the main town center of Dol Dol from Nairobi, one must travel first to Nanyuki, and then an additional one and a half hours on mostly unpaved roads. The smaller trading center of Il Polei is situated on the road between Nanyuki and Dol Dol.

In 1999, the population of Mukogodo was 13,176, the share of the rural population living below the poverty line was 43 percent, and the share of the urban population living below the poverty line was 91 percent (Kenya Central Bureau of Statistics 2003). The population is divided among five subtribes, which are the Mukogodo or Yaaku, the Il'ngwesi, the Mumonyot, the Ildigiri, and the Ewaso. The Yaaku and Ewaso were hunter-gatherers and beekeepers who were historically settled in the Mukogodo area but who gradually adopted the language and practices of the Maasai during the later colonial period (Cronk 2004). Though subsisting as hunters during earlier periods, the Il'ngwesi and Ildigiri lived primarily as pastoralists from the late 19th century and adopted Maa as they migrated into Mukogodo during the early 20th century (Cronk 2004, 61–62). The Mumonyot were remnants of the Laikipiak Maasai, which were defeated by other Maasai groups in the 1870s (Cronk 2004, 61; Galaty 1993, 75). Despite pursuing pastoralism and adhering to Maasai cultural practices for many decades, all five groups are still sometimes referred to derogatorily as *il-torrobo* or Dorobo (essentially a class designation referring to poor hunter-gatherers) by "true" Maasai (Cronk 2004, 64–65). There are also some people from other tribes—mainly Kikuyu—living in Dol Dol. The Kikuyu hail from central Kenya and have long been an economically and politically dominant group. As of 2008 Mukogodo had 19 primary schools and two secondary schools—the public Dol Dol Secondary School, which is coeducational, and the private St. Francis Girls' Secondary School. The ratio of girls to boys enrolled in primary school in that year was 0.78. In 2011, there were approximately 17 CBOs working in Mukogodo, and in 2014, 256 registered NGOs claimed to be working in Laikipia District (including Laikipia North, East, and West), with 56 headquartered there.

The survey shows that 45 percent of Mukogodo respondents had received no formal education, while 32 percent had gone to primary school, 18 percent had gone to secondary school, and 5 percent had attended some form of higher education. Fifty-two percent reported that they owned a radio, 11 percent that they owned a bicycle, and 1 percent that they owned a car. Occupations varied, with 46 percent of all respondents and 72 percent of male respondents describing themselves as pastoralists, 20 percent (all women) reporting household work, 11 percent reporting that they were students, 6 percent reporting that they were businesspeople, 9 percent reporting another occupation, and 9 percent reporting unemployment. By religion, 50 percent said they were Catholic, 25 percent said they were Protestant, and 22 percent said they adhered to a traditional religion, with 4 percent saying they followed no religion.

Mau

Mau Division sits in southwestern Kenya and is part of Narok North District in Rift Valley Province. The division contains 11 administrative locations and is quite large, with a population of over 76,000 people in 1999, so to keep the three case study areas as comparable as possible I focus on only two of its locations, called Keekonyokie and Suswa. For ease of reference, I will refer to these two locations collectively as Mau throughout the book. Keekonyokie and Suswa contain four administrative sublocations between them and straddle the road connecting Nairobi with Narok town, covering an area of 196 square miles. To reach them takes approximately one and a half hours from Nairobi or one hour from Narok on paved roads. The largest town in the area is Nairege Enkare, found in Keekonyokie. Suswa also contains the two trading posts of Duka Moja and Suswa Centre.

The combined population of Keekonyokie and Suswa was 17,691 in 1999. Of the rural population, 43 percent lived below the poverty line in Keekonyokie, and 50 percent lived below the poverty line in Suswa at that time. In addition, 60 percent of the urban population lived below the poverty line (Kenya Central Bureau of Statistics 2003). Though the area is mostly Maasai from the Keekonyokie section, there is a substantial Kikuyu population as well as small minorities from several other Kenyan tribes. In 2008, the combined area contained 39 primary schools and two secondary schools—the public Olasiti Secondary School and the private St. Anthony's Secondary School, both of which are coeducational. The ratio of girls to boys enrolled in primary school in 2008 was 0.93, and the secondary school ratio was 0.50. There were 20 CBOs registered in Mau as of that year. In 2014, 314 registered NGOs claimed to be working in Narok District (including both Narok North and South), and 31 were headquartered in the district.

Additional details about the area are drawn from the survey. With respect to education, 38 percent of respondents in Mau stated that they had received no formal education, 26 percent stated that they had attended primary school, 24 percent stated that they had attended secondary school, and 13 percent stated that they had attended a college or university. On the subject of consumer goods, 81 percent of Mau respondents reported owning a radio, while 13 percent reported owning a bicycle and 6 percent reported owning a car. Forty-three percent of all respondents and 58 percent of male respondents said they were pastoralists, 14 percent (again, all women) said they performed household work, 18 percent said they were students, 12 percent said they were businesspeople, 12 percent said they were employed in some other occupation, and 2 percent said they were unemployed. Some 77 percent of respondents reported that they were Protestant, compared to 12 percent who reported that they were Catholic, 2 percent who reported that they followed a traditional religion, and 10 percent who reported that they followed no religion.

These three communities share many things in common, but they also have some important differences. Oldonyiro is the least accessible community in terms of travel time from the capital and road conditions, has no real urban centers, and provides few opportunities for interethnic interaction. Its residents also have the fewest opportunities to receive an education. These challenges are borne out by the survey data, which show that educational attainment is indeed limited and markers of wealth are few. Mukogodo falls in the middle, with some significant difficulties in terms of accessibility but also a fairly substantial network of schools and an ethnically heterogeneous town center. Accordingly, the survey shows higher educational achievement than in Oldonyiro and a substantially larger number of people who own goods such as radios and bicycles. Mau is the most cosmopolitan and networked of the three, with a substantial population living in towns, easy accessibility from major hubs, and plenty of schools, all of which bring together people from many different ethnic groups. Not surprisingly, Mau also displays the highest levels of secondary and tertiary education among survey respondents, as well as low unemployment and nonnegligible levels of ownership of expensive consumer goods like automobiles.

Prevalence and Characteristics of FGM and Early Marriage

My original survey provides details on the practice of FGM and early marriage across and within the case study communities, as described in tables 3.1 and 3.2 respectively.[28] Among female respondents aged 20 to 49, 95 percent reported having been circumcised. This included 99 percent of those with no formal education, compared to 83 percent of those who had attended secondary school or above. Across the three areas, circumcision prevalence was highest in Oldonyiro, at just over 98 percent, followed by Mukogodo at just under 98 percent, and Mau at 90 percent. The procedure itself was primarily carried out in adolescence, with 41 percent reporting that they were circumcised between the ages of 10 and 14, and 56 percent reporting that they were circumcised at or after age 15. A traditional circumciser performed the procedure in 95 percent of cases, while a doctor or other trained health worker performed the remainder of operations. Among those respondents who had at least one circumcised daughter, 11 percent of female respondents reported that they made the decision about when to circumcise the most recently cut daughter, and 29 percent reported that their husband decided. Among male respondents however, fully 47 percent stated that they themselves had made the decision, and only 5 percent of respondents attributed the decision to their wives. Across all respondents with a circumcised daughter, 43 percent reported that it was a joint decision of the husband and the wife, while 7 percent reported that their daughter had made the decision.

Beliefs about the value of female circumcision centered on its function as a rite of passage and its traditional significance: among all respondents, 68 percent stated that a benefit of circumcision was that it enabled graduation to adulthood, and 44 percent said that it gave the girl the respect of her community. Furthermore, 59 percent reported that a benefit of circumcision was that it enabled a girl to marry, and 32 percent reported that it enabled her to have children. Comparatively, only 6 percent believed that

28. Once again, it is important to acknowledge the possibility that these descriptive estimates may reflect some reporting bias, given the illegal status of both practices. However, the apparently limited reporting bias present in the Kenya-wide Demographic and Health Surveys, discussed above, should provide greater confidence in the localized survey results.

female circumcision improved hygiene, 2 percent believed it was a religious requirement, 1 percent believed it enhanced a man's sexual pleasure, and 1 percent believed it prevented premarital sex. Overall, though, 26 percent of all respondents stated that female circumcision had no benefits. Additionally, 40 percent of respondents reported that they thought female circumcision should be stopped, including 52 percent of women and 30 percent of men. Across study areas, 10 percent of Oldonyiro respondents, 43 percent of Mukogodo respondents, and 57 percent of Mau respondents thought female circumcision should stop. The practice of female circumcision was generally quite salient to respondents, with 89 percent of those who supported the continuation of circumcision, as well as 52 percent of all respondents, stating that the issue of female circumcision was very important to them.

On the issue of early marriage, 8 percent of female respondents aged 20 to 49 reported having been married by age 15, and 45 percent reported having been married by age 18. By case study area, 65 percent of female respondents in Oldonyiro, 43 percent of respondents in Mukogodo, and 36 percent of respondents in Mau reported being married by age 18. Women's educational attainment was closely associated with marriage age, as fully 70 percent of those who had received no formal education were married by age 18, compared to only 1 percent of those who had attended at least some secondary school. Among respondents with at least one married daughter, only 7 percent of women reported that they had decided when the most recently married daughter would marry, while 43 percent reported that their husband had decided. For the male respondents, 62 percent said they had decided and 3 percent said their wife had decided. Among both male and female respondents, 23 percent said that it had been a joint decision of the husband and the wife, while 18 percent said their daughter had decided for herself.

The purported benefits of marrying early were primarily financial and tied to women's roles as wives and mothers. Among all respondents, 27 percent said that early marriage improved girls' economic security, 24 percent said that it improved their marriage prospects, and 22 percent said that it improved their ability to have children. Other potential benefits were less popular, with 14 percent of respondents saying that early marriage prevented premarital sex and 3 percent saying that it protected girls against HIV/AIDS. Yet some 62 percent of respondents said there were no benefits associated with early marriage. The same proportion said they thought early marriages should be stopped, including 71 percent of women and 53 percent of men. By study area, 15 percent of Oldonyiro respondents, 62 percent of Mukogodo respondents, and 90 percent of Mau respondents stated that they wanted early marriage to be discontinued. Early marriage was not as locally salient as female circumcision, with 72 percent of respondents who supported the continuation of early marriage, and 37 percent of all respondents, stating that the issue was very important to them.

Activism against FGM and Early Marriage

The differences across the three communities extend to efforts to tackle FGM and early marriage. When asked to identify groups working to stop these practices in their area, only 6 percent of Oldonyiro respondents were able to name at least one group that was tackling female circumcision, and only 4 percent were able to name at least one group that was tackling early marriage. Groups listed by more than one person were Pastoralist Women for Health and Education, ILAMAIYO, Lifada, and church leaders. In Mukogodo, 66 percent could name a group addressing female circumcision and 64 percent could name a group addressing early marriage. Groups named at least twice were ILAMAIYO, Yaaku People's Association, World Vision, COVAW, Impact, Osiligi, Naretisho, and church leaders. Finally, in Mau, 70 percent could name a group working against female circumcision and 69 percent could name a group working against early marriage. Groups identified more than once were Tasaru Ntomonok Initiative, Maikoo Ate, World Vision, Olmarei Lang, Matonyak Ate, ChildFund, Women Fighting AIDS in Kenya, and the UN.

In terms of specific activities, many of these organizations have focused on awareness-raising and sensitization activities such as workshops and community meetings. A number of these groups also assist in the rescue of girls from both FGM and early marriage, mobilizing the police and government administration as needed (as of 2008, police records showed one successful prosecution for early marriage in Oldonyiro, and at least one arrest for early marriage in both Mukogodo and Mau). They may also facilitate placement of the girls in children's homes, or under appropriate circumstances, reconciliation of the girls with their families. TNI, World Vision, and Yaaku People's Association have also conducted ARPs, and, as discussed above, TNI operates a rescue center in Narok that cares for girls from Mau and other locations. Besides formal NGOs and CBOs, some church leaders (primarily from Protestant churches), teachers, and other individuals are engaged in the campaign against FGM and early marriage, speaking out about the practices in sermons and class discussions, as well as sometimes providing temporary safe havens for girls fleeing circumcision or marriage.

CONCLUSION

This chapter provided a tour of the practice of FGM and early marriage in Kenya, and of the efforts to stop that practice. FGM and early marriage are maintained for a variety of reasons in Kenya as a whole, but both appear to be on the decline. For the Maasai and Samburu, female circumcision serves primarily as a rite of passage to adulthood, signaling the ability to marry and have children, while early marriage enables the transfer of bridewealth and binds families together under a polygynous marriage system that places girls in high demand as potential wives. Nonetheless, as in the broader society, the evidence suggests that both practices are becoming less common, particularly in recent years. This is true of the three case study communities as well, though changes in attitudes and behavior there have been more modest, likely reflecting their rural location.

Activist efforts to combat FGM (and to a far lesser extent early marriage) in Kenya date back to the early colonial era. Such efforts by missionaries and colonial officials were, however, primarily focused on the Kikuyu, Meru, and Embu ethnic groups, leaving the Maasai and Samburu relatively untouched. In the modern period, the government demonstrated increasing levels of opposition to FGM in particular, beginning with presidential decrees prohibiting the practice in the 1980s, and culminating most recently in the passage of the Prohibition of FGM Act and the establishment of an anti-FGM board. The Kenyan government has also set the legal minimum age of marriage at 18. Government actions are complemented and, one could argue, exceeded by the activism of a wide range of civil society groups and international governmental and nongovernmental organizations. These organizations have employed diverse strategies to combat FGM and early marriage—ranging from awareness-raising activities and behavioral interventions to legal advocacy to child care and protection—countrywide, among Maa-speaking peoples generally, and in the case study areas specifically.

Thus, I have shown here both the varied history of activism to promote the international norms against FGM and early marriage in Kenya, and also the varied bases of support for the local norms defending these practices. The subsequent empirical chapters will show how these norms and their proponents interact on the ground—specifically, how the attributes of the norms themselves and of the communities in which the norm conflicts take place shape the speed and tenor of norm change. To begin, chapter 4 will investigate the determinants of exposure to the international norms against FGM and early marriage.

CHAPTER 4

Creating Local Awareness of International Norms

Having just described the context in which FGM and early marriage are performed in the three case study areas, I turn in the following chapters to empirically evaluating the theory within this context. Chapters 5, 6, and 7 address each of the three elements of norm change—attitude change, primary behavior change, and secondary behavior and rhetorical change—respectively. In this chapter, I investigate the factors that influence individuals' awareness about the international norms against FGM and early marriage, since it is awareness of these norms that creates the norm conflicts with which individuals and communities must contend. The path to achieving transnational activists' goal of eliminating FGM and early marriage is a long one, and the first step is to make sure people know that alternatives to their local norms exist.

But the awareness-raising efforts of transnational activists have not been uniform across issues and geographical settings. I argued in chapter 2 that three primary factors explain the degree of local-level exposure to a particular international normative message. An international norm's salience at the international level impacts the level of funding that is available to sustain activists' efforts, and thus the overall level of activism to promote the norm worldwide. At the same time, a local norm's salience in its particular local context impacts the willingness of local actors to take up the transnational campaign, since they must live among the people whose behavior they are trying to change. As a result, the local norm's salience also impacts the level of activism to promote the international norm. The respective saliences of the international and local norms work against one another, such that high salience for the international norm drives activism up, while high salience for the local norm drives activism down.

For the two cases discussed here, the twin forces function differently, but the net effect on the level of activism is comparable. The high salience of the international norm against FGM creates financial incentives for NGOs and similar organizations to take up the campaign, while the high salience of the local norm supporting female circumcision depresses the spread of the anti-FGM message by many local stakeholders. By contrast, the relatively low salience of the international norm against early marriage precludes significant financial support for campaign activities, but motivated activists can operate with minimal local resistance. With both FGM and early marriage, one should thus expect to see, on average, moderate levels of activism at the local level.

However, activism against either practice is contingent on the on-the-ground presence of NGOs and other civil society organizations that are able to take up the banner of these causes. Indeed, there is cross-national and temporal variation in NGO density, and importantly for this book's three case study areas, there is also significant subnational variation. Some of this subnational variation stems from convenience factors affecting the location decisions of larger NGOs, as well as from various practical constraints affecting the formation of local NGOs. In particular, large external organizations may be reluctant to work in remote, inaccessible rural areas, and rural areas that provide only limited educational opportunities may possess few people who are in a position to found, work for, and sustain homegrown organizations.

Thus, norm salience at both the international and local levels combines with the density of NGO activity in a given community to influence the level of local activism in favor of a particular international norm, and thus to influence individuals' awareness of the norm and its content. A number of observable implications can be drawn from this account. First, the level of local awareness about the international norms against FGM and early marriage should be similar across the two practices. Second, the sources of this awareness should vary. Groups and individuals who are dependent on international donors for their economic survival should be more likely than independent actors to engage in awareness-raising activities that align with donors' preferences. Conversely, independent local actors should be more likely to engage in awareness-raising activities that respond to issues that they perceive as local priorities. Accordingly, anti-FGM information should come more consistently from NGOs and other donor-dependent civil society organizations, while information about early marriage should come more consistently from economically self-sufficient sources such as churches, and to a lesser degree, government officials. Third, more accessible communities should exhibit higher levels of awareness about the international norms against both FGM and early marriage—there should be greater awareness in Mukogodo than in Oldonyiro, and greater awareness in Mau than in Mukogodo. And fourth, because NGOs and other civil society organizations tend to concentrate their activities in and around town centers, individuals who live closer to these centers and visit them regularly should exhibit higher levels of awareness than individuals who live in more remote parts of the community.

QUANTITATIVE EVIDENCE

Measuring Exposure to Transnational Activism

The survey included indicators of awareness about opposition to FGM and early marriage, as well as the hypothesized predictors of this awareness. Descriptive statistics are presented in table 4.1.[1] Among all respondents, 64 percent reported that they were *aware of groups in their community that were trying to stop female circumcision*. As expected, there is significant variation in awareness across the three case study areas. In Oldonyiro, only 12 percent of respondents were aware of anticircumcision groups, compared to 72 percent of respondents in Mukogodo and 89 percent of respondents in Mau. Awareness of opposition to early marriage followed a similar pattern. Across all areas, 60 percent of respondents were *aware of groups in their community that were trying to stop early marriage*. By study area, 9 percent of Oldonyiro respondents, 70 percent of Mukogodo respondents, and 85 percent of Mau respondents reported that they were aware of anti-early-marriage groups. The first observable implication—that awareness levels should be similar for FGM and early marriage—is borne out by these data. Awareness of anti-FGM groups is just slightly higher than awareness of groups opposing early marriage.

1. These descriptive statistics are for the full sample. However, because the survey also included an experimental element (discussed in chapter 7) to test respondents' willingness to misrepresent their behavior, I also calculate descriptive statistics for a restricted sample that includes only individuals in the control group. The methodological appendix presents the results for the restricted sample.

Table 4.1: DESCRIPTIVE STATISTICS

	Oldonyiro	Mukogodo	Mau	All areas	Observations
Accessibility					
Never visit town center	0.116 (0.02)	0.071 (0.02)	0.026 (0.01)	0.064 (0.01)	596
Protestant	0.030 (0.01)	0.247 (0.03)	0.765 (0.04)	0.403 (0.02)	594
Radio ownership	0.311 (0.04)	0.518 (0.04)	0.811 (0.03)	0.585 (0.02)	593
Awareness					
Aware of groups against female circumcision	0.123 (0.02)	0.724 (0.03)	0.888 (0.03)	0.636 (0.02)	598
Aware of groups against early marriage	0.086 (0.02)	0.701 (0.03)	0.850 (0.03)	0.603 (0.02)	598
Aware of circumcision health problems	0.190 (0.03)	0.242 (0.03)	0.418 (0.04)	0.301 (0.02)	597
Aware of early-marriage health problems	0.130 (0.02)	0.393 (0.04)	0.844 (0.03)	0.511 (0.02)	592

Note: Means weighted by inverse sampling probabilities. Standard errors in parentheses.

In addition, respondents were asked whether they were aware of any health consequences that might be associated with the two practices. Such awareness suggests knowledge of at least some of the content of the international norms. Among all respondents, 30 percent reported that *female circumcision could cause health problems*. In Oldonyiro, only 19 percent of respondents were aware of potential health problems, compared to 24 percent in Mukogodo and 42 percent in Mau. Awareness of the health consequences of early marriage was more extensive, and the differences between areas were more pronounced. Overall, 51 percent of respondents reported that *early marriage could cause health problems*, including 13 percent of respondents in Oldonyiro, 39 percent of respondents in Mukogodo, and 84 percent of respondents in Mau.

Finally, respondents were asked about factors indicating individual accessibility to international normative messages. First, the survey asked respondents whether they visited the main town center in their area—Oldonyiro Center in Oldonyiro, Dol Dol Center in Mukogodo, and Nairege Enkare Center in Mau—and 6 percent reported that they *never visit the town center*. By study area, 12 percent of Oldonyiro respondents never visited Oldonyiro Center, 7 percent of Mukogodo respondents never visited Dol Dol Center, and 3 percent of Mau respondents never visited Nairege Enkare Center. Second, the survey asked respondents about their religion to gauge their exposure to religious leaders, and Protestant pastors in particular, who might spread information about FGM and early marriage.[2] Overall, 40 percent of respondents reported that they were *Protestant*. By study area, 3 percent of Oldonyiro respondents, 25 percent of Mukogodo respondents, and 77 percent of Mau respondents were Protestants. Third, respondents were asked whether they *owned a radio*, since radio broadcasts and other media sometimes provide messages about FGM and early marriage, and radio is by far the most commonly accessed form of media in Kenya.[3] Across all areas, 59 percent of respondents reported radio ownership. In Oldonyiro, only 31 percent of respondents owned radios, compared to 52 percent of respondents in Mukogodo and 81 percent of respondents in Mau.

Evaluation

To evaluate the role of individual and community accessibility in explaining awareness of international norms, as well as the source of this awareness, I turn to multivariate analysis. Tables 4.2 through 4.5 present regression results for each of the four outcome variables—knowledge of groups that oppose female circumcision, knowledge of groups that oppose early marriage, knowledge of female circumcision's health consequences, and knowledge of early marriage's health consequences—using both linear and nonlinear models. The main right-hand-side variables are *town* (a dummy variable equal to one if the respondent reports that they never visit their community's town center and zero otherwise, *Protestant*

2. The qualitative interviews show that Protestant pastors are more likely than other religious leaders to provide information about FGM and early marriage.
3. Access to radio and other media can mitigate issues of physical remoteness, although the large number of spoken languages in Kenya means that few if any of these resources are available in local vernaculars. Educational attainment strongly predicts whether Kenyans speak one of the two national languages, since Kiswahili is the chief language of instruction in primary school, and English is the chief language of instruction in secondary school.

Table 4.2: AWARE OF GROUPS AGAINST FEMALE CIRCUMCISION

	(1)	(2)	(3)	(4)
	OLS		Logit[a]	
	Robust SE	Weighted/ clustered SE[b]	Robust SE	Weighted/ clustered SE[b]
Never visit town center	−0.233*** (0.06)	−0.233*** (0.04)	−0.415*** (0.09)	−0.392*** (0.08)
Mukogodo	0.525*** (0.04)	0.538*** (0.05)	0.528*** (0.04)	0.477*** (0.02)
Mau	0.625*** (0.06)	0.631*** (0.07)	0.614*** (0.05)	0.603*** (0.06)
Protestant	0.041 (0.05)	0.056 (0.06)	0.064 (0.09)	0.094 (0.10)
Radio owner	0.145*** (0.04)	0.152*** (0.03)	0.232*** (0.06)	0.232*** (0.06)
Female	0.068** (0.03)	0.060* (0.03)	0.117** (0.06)	0.099** (0.05)
Age	−0.001 (0.00)	−0.001 (0.00)	−0.002 (0.00)	−0.002 (0.00)
Treatment	0.077** (0.03)	0.058* (0.03)	0.138** (0.06)	0.097** (0.05)
Constant	0.091* (0.05)	0.091* (0.05)		
Observations	580	580	580	580

Notes: * $p<0.10$, ** $p<0.05$, *** $p<0.01$.
[a] Marginal effects coefficients.
[b] Standard errors clustered by sampling sublocation and weighted by probability of selection.

(a dummy variable equal to one if the respondent reports that they are Protestant and zero otherwise), and *radio* (a dummy variable equal to one if the respondent reports owning a radio and zero otherwise). I also include fixed effects for the three case study communities, since much of the variation in the level of NGO activity occurs at the community level. In addition, I include control variables for age and sex, and for whether the respondent received the experimental treatment discussed in chapter 7.

The results show fairly strong and robust support for the observable implications described above. First, while it has already been established

Table 4.3: AWARE OF GROUPS AGAINST EARLY MARRIAGE

	(1)	(2)	(3)	(4)
	OLS		Logit[a]	
	Robust SE	Weighted/clustered SE[b]	Robust SE	Weighted/clustered SE[b]
Never visit town center	-0.189***	-0.233**	-0.323***	-0.395***
	(0.06)	(0.08)	(0.10)	(0.13)
Mukogodo	0.518***	0.548***	0.587***	0.565***
	(0.04)	(0.05)	(0.05)	(0.03)
Mau	0.592***	0.614***	0.636***	0.647***
	(0.06)	(0.06)	(0.05)	(0.06)
Protestant	0.066	0.087	0.092	0.136
	(0.06)	(0.07)	(0.08)	(0.12)
Radio owner	0.144***	0.141***	0.235***	0.237***
	(0.04)	(0.04)	(0.06)	(0.07)
Female	0.107***	0.105**	0.187***	0.187**
	(0.03)	(0.04)	(0.06)	(0.08)
Age	0.000	-0.000	0.000	-0.000
	(0.00)	(0.00)	(0.00)	(0.00)
Treatment	0.053*	0.050	0.086	0.083*
	(0.03)	(0.03)	(0.06)	(0.05)
Constant	-0.008	0.004		
	(0.05)	(0.06)		
Observations	580	580	580	580

Notes: * $p<0.10$, ** $p<0.05$, *** $p<0.01$.
[a] Marginal effects coefficients.
[b] Standard errors clustered by sampling sublocation and weighted by probability of selection.

that average levels of awareness are similar for the international norms against FGM and early marriage, the source of individuals' awareness does seem to vary between the two norms. Being Protestant is positively associated with the probability that the respondent reported being aware that female circumcision could cause health problems, but this relationship is not consistently significant. By contrast, being Protestant is strongly and significantly associated with the probability that the respondent reported that early marriage could cause health problems, with a coefficient of at least .19. This suggests that while church leaders are spreading the message about early marriage, they are less likely

Table 4.4: AWARE THAT CIRCUMCISION CAN CAUSE HEALTH PROBLEMS

	(1)	(2)	(3)	(4)
	OLS		Logit[a]	
	Robust SE	Weighted/ clustered SE[b]	Robust SE	Weighted/ clustered SE[b]
Never visit town center	-0.126**	-0.145**	-0.167***	-0.180***
	(0.05)	(0.06)	(0.06)	(0.06)
Mukogodo	-0.031	-0.013	-0.033	-0.012
	(0.04)	(0.07)	(0.05)	(0.09)
Mau	0.063	0.068	0.059	0.072
	(0.07)	(0.10)	(0.07)	(0.12)
Protestant	0.171***	0.132	0.164***	0.125
	(0.06)	(0.09)	(0.06)	(0.10)
Radio owner	0.148***	0.104	0.158***	0.110
	(0.04)	(0.10)	(0.04)	(0.11)
Female	0.089**	0.083	0.098**	0.088
	(0.04)	(0.07)	(0.04)	(0.08)
Age	-0.004***	-0.004**	-0.005***	-0.004*
	(0.00)	(0.00)	(0.00)	(0.00)
Treatment	0.067*	0.063**	0.080**	0.072***
	(0.04)	(0.03)	(0.04)	(0.02)
Constant	0.219***	0.237**		
	(0.05)	(0.09)		
Observations	578	578	578	578

Notes: * $p<0.10$, ** $p<0.05$, *** $p<0.01$.
[a] Marginal effects coefficients.
[b] Standard errors clustered by sampling sublocation and weighted by probability of selection.

to speak out against FGM.[4] FGM norm awareness, therefore, is likely coming mainly from NGOs and other civil society organizations. This is consistent with the argument that local concerns are driving activism against early marriage, while international concerns are driving activism against FGM.

4. An alternative explanation is that Protestants have greater awareness about the health consequences of early marriage because they are simply more likely to encounter civil society organizations. However, being Protestant is not significantly associated with the probability that the respondent is aware of anti-early-marriage groups.

Table 4.5: AWARE THAT EARLY MARRIAGE CAN CAUSE HEALTH PROBLEMS

	(1)	(2)	(3)	(4)
	OLS		Logit[a]	
	Robust SE	Weighted/ clustered SE[b]	Robust SE	Weighted/ clustered SE[b]
Never visit town center	−0.131***	−0.072	−0.224***	−0.128
	(0.05)	(0.07)	(0.09)	(0.13)
Mukogodo	0.176***	0.179***	0.251***	0.265***
	(0.04)	(0.05)	(0.06)	(0.07)
Mau	0.424***	0.465***	0.516***	0.560***
	(0.06)	(0.07)	(0.06)	(0.06)
Protestant	0.185***	0.214***	0.219***	0.273***
	(0.05)	(0.06)	(0.07)	(0.06)
Radio owner	0.157***	0.148**	0.226***	0.229***
	(0.04)	(0.05)	(0.06)	(0.08)
Female	0.156***	0.150***	0.244***	0.249***
	(0.03)	(0.05)	(0.06)	(0.07)
Age	−0.003**	−0.002	−0.004**	−0.003
	(0.00)	(0.00)	(0.00)	(0.00)
Treatment	0.017	0.008	0.030	0.019
	(0.03)	(0.05)	(0.05)	(0.08)
Constant	0.127**	0.082		
	(0.05)	(0.05)		
Observations	575	575	575	575

Notes: * $p<0.10$, ** $p<0.05$, *** $p<0.01$.
[a] Marginal effects coefficients.
[b] Standard errors clustered by sampling sublocation and weighted by probability of selection.

Second, as expected, the other indicators for individual and community accessibility are strongly associated with awareness of opposition to both FGM and early marriage. Never visiting the community's main town center was negatively and significantly associated with the probability that the respondent was aware of groups in the community that wanted female circumcision to stop, and of groups that wanted early marriage to stop. These results are robust to multiple specifications, and the coefficients carry magnitudes that suggest the relationship is substantively meaningful. Never visiting town is associated with at least a 23-percentage-point decrease in the probability that the respondent reports an awareness of anti-FGM groups, and with at least a 19-percentage-point decrease in the probability that the respondent reports an awareness of anti-early-marriage groups. Along the same lines, never visiting the town center was negatively and significantly associated with the probability that the respondent was aware that female circumcision could cause health problems, with a coefficient of at least −.13. Never visiting the town center was also negatively associated with the probability that the respondent was aware that early marriage could cause health problems, although this finding was only significant in Models 1 and 3.

Radio ownership had a similar effect on awareness levels. Owning a radio was positively and significantly associated with the probability that the respondent was aware of groups in the community that wanted female circumcision to stop, and of groups that wanted early marriage to stop. In addition, owning a radio was positively and significantly associated (in Models 1 and 3) with the probability that the respondent was aware that female circumcision could cause health problems, and was positively and significantly associated with the probability that early marriage could cause health problems. In each case, the coefficients suggested that the relationship was substantively meaningful. Owning a radio was associated with at least a 14-percentage-point increase in the probability that the respondent reported an awareness of anti-FGM groups and anti-early-marriage groups, and with the probability that the respondent reported an awareness that female circumcision and early marriage can cause health problems.

Thus, at an individual level, people who have limited exposure to the outside world—whether because they don't have access to media or because they don't visit their communities' more urban centers—are missing out on the international normative messages against FGM and early marriage. The data confirm that the transnational campaign has not yet penetrated very remote areas, even in communities in which it is otherwise active.

Beyond individual-level factors, the community one lives in is also strongly associated with awareness levels. Relative to living in Oldonyiro, living in Mukogodo or Mau was positively and significantly associated with the probability that the respondent was aware of groups in the community that wanted female circumcision to stop, and of groups that wanted early marriage to stop. And as expected, the positive effect of living in Mau was even larger than the positive effect of living in Mukogodo—while living in Mukogodo was associated with at least a 47-percentage-point increase in the probability that the respondent reported an awareness of groups opposing FGM and of groups opposing early marriage, living in Mau was associated with at least a 59-percentage-point increase in the probability that the respondent was aware of such groups.

Study area was also positively and significantly associated with the probability that the respondent was aware that early marriage could cause health problems; living in Mukogodo was associated with at least an 18-percentage-point increase in the probability that the respondent knew of early marriage's health consequences, and living in Mau was associated with at least a 42-percentage-point increase in that probability. However, study area had no relationship with the probability that respondents were aware of female circumcision's health consequences. If study area fixed effects *do* predict awareness of anti-FGM groups, why don't they similarly predict basic awareness of the international norm's content? It appears that the presence of activist groups in and of itself is not a sufficient predictor of deeper levels of awareness in a community, particularly when it comes to a practice like FGM. Indeed, the correlation between knowing there are anti-FGM groups and knowing there may be health consequences associated with circumcision (.30) is substantially lower than the correlation between knowing there are groups opposed to early marriage and knowing there may be health consequences associated with early marriage (.48). This conforms with expectations, laid out in chapter 2 and supported empirically in chapter 5, that quantity doesn't always mean quality when it comes to anti-FGM activism. NGOs face incentives that limit their delivery of a high-quality normative message about FGM, even when conveying very basic information.[5]

In general, though, the region in which one lives does appear to play a significant role in explaining exposure to the international norms against FGM and early marriage. Some places, like Oldonyiro, are sufficiently remote that they do not attract or produce many civil society organizations, such that the level of activism against FGM and early marriage, and consequently the level of awareness about opposition to these practices, has remained at extremely low levels. By contrast, Mukogodo's relative accessibility and higher educational provision has set the stage for higher levels of activism and awareness, and Mau's situation has produced levels of activism and awareness that are higher still.

5. This interpretation is further supported by the fact that, while awareness of anti-FGM groups far outstrips awareness of health consequences in Mukogodo and Mau, awareness of groups and awareness of health consequences are fairly similar in Oldonyiro. Oldonyiro's remoteness means that although the overall level of anti-FGM activism is quite low, the activism that does take place is of a fairly high quality. While many of the groups working against FGM in Mukogodo and Mau are motivated to do so because they are aware of available funding from international donors, Oldonyiro is so inaccessible that the few civil society groups in the area aren't linked in to the international aid regime. Thus any organizations in Oldonyiro that are speaking out against FGM are likely doing so out of genuine commitment to the issue.

Overall, the survey data provide solid support for the theoretical account of how transnational activism produces awareness about FGM and early marriage. The empirical evidence suggests that while the centrality of the local norm in favor of female circumcision makes it difficult for many community leaders to spread the anti-FGM message, the issue's international salience offsets this effect by incentivizing activism among NGOs and other community-based organizations, bringing it up to par with efforts to eliminate early marriage. Of course, the level of activism against either practice in any given area depends on how developed local civil society is and how far its reach extends into the most isolated parts of the community. The less accessible the community, and the less accessible the individuals within that community, the lower the chance that anyone is aware of the international norms and their content.

QUALITATIVE EVIDENCE

These findings are further supported by evidence from my in-depth interviews with a wide range of community stakeholders in the three case study areas. First, the interviews showed general support for the idea that international and local norm salience influences various stakeholders' decisions about activism. One government worker, for example, argued that NGOs choose the issues they address based on what donors want.[6] When it comes to the government and other community leaders, however, they are more likely to speak out against a practice like early marriage than to speak out against a practice like FGM, because in the latter case they are afraid of how the community will respond.[7] Second, there is substantial variation across the study areas in levels of activism and awareness around both issues.

Oldonyiro

Most interviewees in Oldonyiro agreed that the community had very little awareness about FGM and early marriage,[8] although a few may have heard the message from workshops[9] or radio.[10] Not surprisingly, most also agreed

6. Author's interview with public health officer FM, September 22, 2008, Mau.
7. Author's interview with Pastor MS, October 2, 2008, Mau.
8. Author's interview with FN, May 6, 2008, Oldonyiro; location chief, May 6, 2008, Oldonyiro; nurse JK, May 6, 2008, Oldonyiro.
9. Author's interview with former church women's development coordinator LL, October 14, 2008, Oldonyiro.
10. Author's interview with FN, May 6, 2008, Oldonyiro.

that the level of activism was very low. When it came to activism against FGM and early marriage, the handful of civil society organizations in the area lacked funding to pursue awareness-raising activities. "The groups are there, but they have not been given the empowerment to do that full time."[11] Many were unable to identify a single organization that was campaigning against FGM or early marriage.[12] And while a few politicians have spoken out against early marriage,[13] the government and religious leaders have not shown much willingness to speak openly against FGM.[14] The local member of parliament never visits the area, and even the police are reluctant to act against the wishes of the community.[15]

Interviewees drew a strong connection between the low level of activism and the remoteness of the community. According to one chief, there are no groups working to stop FGM and early marriage in Oldonyiro because the area is too rural and too inaccessible to draw in the government and the NGOs.[16] The district officer agreed that the inhospitable terrain meant that it required a lot of resources for outside groups to come into the community.[17] Several interviewees reported that there were no NGOs of any kind working permanently in Oldonyiro, and nor were there any homegrown community organizations either.[18] A government official attributed this to the fact that the educated people leave the area and don't come back.[19] He further explained that few people from the community get educated in the first place, because there are not enough schools and there are no roads to bring children to the existing schools.[20]

As one local activist described it, "We are left behind by so many organizations because of the remoteness of the area."[21] She argued that the dearth of external organizations was compounded by the fact that there were also no local organizations. She said that any organizations that had

11. Author's interview with gender social development officer AG, July 22, 2008, Oldonyiro.

12. Author's interview with FN, May 6, 2008, Oldonyiro; NGO director JL, June 12, 2008, Oldonyiro.

13. Author's interview with location chief, May 6, 2008, Oldonyiro.

14. Author's interview with public health workers I and Y, July 25, 2008, Oldonyiro.

15. Author's interview with location chief, May 6, 2008, Oldonyiro.

16. Ibid.

17. Author's interview with district officer, July 21, 2008, Oldonyiro.

18. Author's interview with children's officer SJ, July 14, 2008, Oldonyiro; public health workers I and Y, July 25, 2008, Oldonyiro.

19. Author's interview with children's officer SJ, July 14, 2008, Oldonyiro.

20. While many secondary schools in Kenya are boarding schools, and thus children from Oldonyiro could theoretically attend schools in other areas, the costs associated with boarding a child at a distant school are frequently prohibitive.

21. Author's interview with former church women's development coordinator LL, October 14, 2008, Oldonyiro.

existed in the past had since withered away because they lacked access to funding. The civil society leaders simply didn't understand how the development system worked—at a basic level, they didn't know how to write grant proposals and submit them to donors. All of these obstacles meant that years would pass between visits by groups campaigning against FGM or early marriage.

Another activist put the situation in comparative perspective.[22] She concluded that because there were no secondary schools in all of Oldonyiro, people who wanted an education had to leave the area to get one, and once they left, they didn't return to start NGOs or community-based organizations. Oldonyiro is also too rural and far from a major town to draw in the government or large external NGOs. By contrast, although an area like Mukogodo is similarly too rural to bring in many external groups, it is slightly more accessible and has the advantage of possessing two secondary schools. Thus, she argued, Mukogodo had enough educated locals to produce its own homegrown organizations, and indeed many of the local NGO workers had attended Dol Dol Secondary School when it first opened in the 1990s. Upon graduation, these individuals realized that there were no jobs in the area for secondary school graduates, but that if they started an NGO they could create their own jobs by tapping into the foreign aid market. Although Mukogodo was in a better position than Oldonyiro, she further argued that both were at a disadvantage compared to a Maasai community like Narok, which, as a major town in Kenya, was able to attract local, national, and international NGOs.

Given the extremely low NGO density in Oldonyiro, interviewees agreed that the few people who were aware of opposition to FGM and early marriage were concentrated in the town centers.[23] One interviewee reported that government workers and NGOs would only come into the community for a few days at a time, so when they did visit, they tended to stay in town, such that people who lived in the interior—the areas farthest from town—were unlikely to receive the message.[24] Unfortunately, most people in the community fell into that category.

For Oldonyiro as a whole, then, the qualitative evidence points to a community that is far removed from the normative discourse that many other communities have experienced. The distance from Nairobi, the poor

22. Author's interview with nurse JK, May 6, 2008, Oldonyiro.
23. Author's interview with NGO director JL, June 12, 2008, Oldonyiro.
24. Author's interview with gender social development officer AG, July 22, 2008, Oldonyiro.

road conditions and difficult terrain, and the lack of access to education all mean that activism against FGM and early marriage, and thus awareness about the international norms around these two practices, remains at a very low level. Although NGOs have come to speak against FGM on rare occasions, and government officials will occasionally address early marriage, only the small number of residents who frequent the town center are able to benefit from this activism.

Mukogodo

In Mukogodo, by comparison, virtually all interviewees agreed that most people were aware of opposition to FGM and early marriage.[25] "Nobody has not heard that FGM is being fought against. They have all heard."[26] Even elders "know it's a world campaign."[27] One interviewee concluded that the only people who could have avoided the message against FGM and early marriage were those who didn't own a radio or TV, didn't send their children to school, and didn't go to church—a small share of the population.[28]

This awareness comes from a fairly sustained level of activism by NGOs and other community stakeholders,[29] although it could be more intensive.[30] According to one NGO worker, "We've broken the silence. It is now talked about. It used to be taboo."[31] Quite a few NGOs and community-based organizations have campaigned against FGM and early marriage, mainly since the late 1990s.[32] The community also receives information about FGM and early marriage from churches (particularly Protestant churches), government officials, and schools, although these efforts can be somewhat intermittent.[33] For example, because the Kenyan school curriculum doesn't

25. Author's interview with NGO board member F, June 17, 2008, Mukogodo; Pastor S, June 17, 2008, Mukogodo; deputy district commissioner MD, June 18, 2008, Mukogodo; district commissioner AM, June 18, 2008, Mukogodo; head teacher AR, July 1, 2008, Mukogodo; CBO director AM, July 5, 2008, Mukogodo; former CBO chairman JL, July 13, 2008, Mukogodo.
26. Author's interview with NGO worker AL, July 24, 2008, Mukogodo.
27. Author's interview with CBO board member MK, July 24, 2008, Mukogodo.
28. Author's interview with children's officer FW, June 4, 2008, Mukogodo.
29. Author's interview with Chief SK, June 18, 2008, Mukogodo; deputy district commissioner MD, June 18, 2008, Mukogodo; NGO worker AL, July 24, 2008, Mukogodo.
30. Author's interview with district commissioner AM, June 18, 2008, Mukogodo.
31. Author's interview with NGO worker AL, July 24, 2008, Mukogodo.
32. Author's interview with former CBO worker SK, June 18, 2008, Mukogodo; former CBO chairman JL, July 13, 2008, Mukogodo.
33. Author's interview with NGO board member F, June 17, 2008, Mukogodo; Pastor S, June 17, 2008, Mukogodo; district commissioner AM, June 18, 2008, Mukogodo.

include any direct lessons about FGM or early marriage, it falls to individual schools and teachers to incorporate this information as they see fit.[34]

Of course, many people are reluctant to speak out against these practices, and particularly about FGM. Elected officials like the member of parliament or local councilors shy away from the issue because it is sufficiently controversial that it would jeopardize their reelection efforts.[35] According to one chief, when it comes to the MPs, "If he's not getting elected from that area, he can speak about [FGM]," but nobody wants to talk about it in his own constituency.[36] Similarly, church leaders can be reluctant to bring up the topic for fear of driving away their congregation.[37] One NGO worker argued that there has not been enough activity on the part of churches because they still believe it is somebody else's work.[38] As the district commissioner described it, the Catholic Church is "pragmatic—we have not seen them be very firm in opposing FGM."[39] A teacher agreed, saying, "I belong to the Catholic Church and I've never heard them say anything. I think it's a topic everybody wants to avoid."[40] Even teachers can be hesitant to get involved: "Attention to early marriages is higher than to FGM, and the involvement in early marriages is higher than in FGM."[41]

So while anti-FGM activism has been dominated by NGOs, activism against early marriage has been more popular among other community stakeholders. A local activist reported that the government had started raising awareness about early marriage at least a decade before the first NGO took up the cause.[42] One NGO worker claimed he wasn't aware of any organizations in the community that were specifically addressing early marriage,[43] and a teacher said that NGOs were "not really talking about early marriage. When we talk about FGM, sometimes we forget about early marriage. It is just passed over."[44] With early marriage, churches

34. Author's interview with education officer EW, July 2, 2008, Mukogodo; head teacher LM, July 10, 2008, Mukogodo.
35. Author's interview with NGO board member F, June 17, 2008, Mukogodo; CBO board member MK, July 24, 2008, Mukogodo.
36. Author's interview with Chief P, June 18, 2008, Mukogodo.
37. Author's interview with medical officer CL, July 6, 2008, Mukogodo; former CBO chairman JL, July 13, 2008, Mukogodo.
38. Author's interview with NGO worker RL, June 23, 2008, Mukogodo.
39. Author's interview with district commissioner AM, June 18, 2008, Mukogodo.
40. Author's interview with head teacher AR, July 1, 2008, Mukogodo.
41. Author's interview with head teacher LM, July 10, 2008, Mukogodo.
42. Author's interview with former CBO worker SK, June 18, 2008, Mukogodo.
43. Author's interview with NGO board member F, June 17, 2008, Mukogodo.
44. Author's interview with head teacher AR, July 1, 2008, Mukogodo.

and the government appeared to be taking the lead,[45] while NGOs were more likely to talk about early marriage only in the context of their activism against FGM.[46]

Though the sources of activism differed somewhat, the moderate level of activism against both FGM and early marriage can be attributed in part to the density of NGOs in the area. Interviewees were able to identify a good number of homegrown NGOs, the first of which sprang up in the mid-1990s.[47] Still, Mukogodo is sufficiently far from Nairobi that it has received only sporadic attention from larger external NGOs and the media.[48] And accessibility is also an issue within the community. One government worker suggested that most of the activists were only working in the town centers, since that is where they themselves lived.[49] He and others agreed that most activists were not making the effort to go into the interior of the region to reach the girls who were most at risk.[50]

Overall, Mukogodo appears to have achieved fairly high levels of awareness about the campaign against FGM and early marriage. Interviewees agreed that this awareness was the product of relatively regular activism by various community stakeholders, though NGOs had focused more of their attention on FGM while other actors had focused more of their attention on early marriage. While the community's remoteness meant that most of this activism was homegrown, these various groups still managed to reach most of the local population with their message, although they were less successful at reaching the individuals who lived in the most rural parts of the area.

Mau

Of the three case study areas, residents of Mau exhibited the highest level of awareness about the international norms against FGM and early marriage, with interviewees agreeing that nearly all people in the area had

45. Author's interview with Pastor S, June 17, 2008, Mukogodo; Chief SK, June 18, 2008, Mukogodo.

46. Author's interview with former CBO chairman JL, July 13, 2008, Mukogodo.

47. Author's interview with CBO director JK, April 15, 2008, Mukogodo.

48. Author's interview with former CBO worker SK, June 18, 2008, Mukogodo; head teacher AR, July 1, 2008, Mukogodo.

49. Author's interview with community development officer MO, July 2, 2008, Mukogodo.

50. Author's interview with Chief P, June 18, 2008, Mukogodo; CBO board member MK, July 24, 2008, Mukogodo.

heard the message in some form.[51] As a teacher described it, "The message has gone to everybody—it is only that it has fallen on deaf ears."[52] A public health worker concurred that "nobody has not heard about it."[53] However, as in Mukogodo, the source of this information did vary somewhat. NGOs in general seemed more willing to speak out against FGM than did the government or churches,[54] although some of these latter groups were active in the campaign.[55] According to one local activist, "Most of the NGOs in Narok District deal with FGM,"[56] and a local chief pointed out that most of these organizations were funded by Western donors.[57] By contrast, a traditional age-set leader claimed that the government knew the practice was wrong, and if they really wanted to stop it they would take some kind of action, but instead they kept silent.[58] One government official that I spoke to was surprised to learn that the coordinating function for the government's anti-FGM activities had been transferred from the Ministry of Health to the Ministry of Gender, Children, and Social Development a couple years earlier, and stated that the changeover had not trickled down to the local level.[59] An activist reported that while a few Protestant churches had taken up the fight, other churches, like the Catholics, were remaining silent.[60] A pastor who was himself an activist lamented that "many other churches are not fighting FGM. They have compromised. They cannot speak loudly because maybe they fear [the community's response]. So we are standing alone."[61] At the same time, churches, government, and schools provided

51. Author's interview with NGO worker RK, September 8, 2008, Mau; CBO chairwoman EN, September 11, 2008, Mau; Chief SK, September 15, 2008, Mau; CBO director MS, September 15, 2008, Mau; CBO chairman PN, September 15, 2008, Mau; education officer MS, September 16, 2008, Mau; youth officer NS, September 22, 2008, Mau; public health officer SS, September 22, 2008, Mau; Pastor PN, September 25, 2008, Mau; head teacher PLT, September 25, 2008, Mau; self-help group chairwoman HK, September 26, 2008, Mau; public health officer EK, September 26, 2008, Mau; head teacher SK, September 29, 2008, Mau; CBO board member AK, September 30, 2008, Mau; age-set leader KK, October 2, 2008, Mau.

52. Author's interview with head teacher SKK, September 23, 2008, Mau.

53. Author's interview with public health officer FM, September 22, 2008, Mau.

54. Author's interview with Pastor J, September 15, 2008, Mau; CBO director MS, September 15, 2008, Mau; government worker RN, August 28, 2008, Mau; former circumciser MK, August 30, 2008, Mau; Chief SK, September 15, 2008, Mau; head teacher SS, September 19, 2008, Mau; youth officer NS, September 22, 2008, Mau.

55. Author's interview with traditional birth attendant MN, August 30, 2008, Mau; CBO chairman PN, September 15, 2008, Mau; head teacher VML, September 29, 2008, Mau.

56. Author's interview with CBO director MS, September 15, 2008, Mau.

57. Author's interview with Chief SK, September 15, 2008, Mau.

58. Author's interview with age-set leader KK, October 2, 2008, Mau.

59. Author's interview with gender social development officer CO, September 5, 2008, Mau.

60. Author's interview with CBO chairwoman EN, September 11, 2008, Mau.

61. Author's interview with Pastor PN, September 25, 2008, Mau.

more consistent information about early marriage[62] than did NGOs. One activist confirmed that her organization only addressed early marriage indirectly, as a byproduct of the campaign against FGM.[63]

The community's proximity to both Narok Town and Nairobi, along with its position straddling the major road between the two, made Mau an attractive destination for a number of international NGOs and big donors. And as a public health worker explained it, the number of organizations that are working in a place influences how quickly people change; Mau is at an advantage because it has so many groups.[64] The international NGO World Vision, for example, had been working consistently in the area since 2002,[65] and USAID's APHIA II project, Action Aid, and the Christian Children's Fund had been in the area for a few years.[66] This is combined with a fair number of homegrown organizations—particularly Tasaru Ntomonok Initiative—and with the efforts of the UN Population Fund. Moreover, in 2005 a group of pastors started a Maa-language radio station, Oltoilo Le Maa, that reaches most of the area and includes regular segments on FGM, early marriage, and girl child rights.[67]

Still, despite the solid presence of NGOs and other activists throughout the area, those living in the most remote parts of the community may still have slipped through the cracks.[68] One teacher reported that most of the campaigning is done in the more urban centers, such that those who live far into the interior of the area are likely to have only heard messages against FGM or early marriage once or twice.[69] Activists from one local group explained that lack of funding prevented their organization from reaching the farthest corners of the community, since transportation could be expensive.[70] And a pastor reported that the government also tended to stick to the more urban centers.[71] Moreover, those who lived farthest into the interior were not only

62. Author's interview with head teacher VML, September 29, 2008, Mau.

63. Author's interview with CBO chairwoman EN, September 11, 2008, Mau.

64. Author's interview with public health officer SS, September 22, 2008, Mau.

65. Author's interview with NGO worker RK, September 8, 2008, Mau.

66. Author's interview with head teacher VML, September 29, 2008, Mau; district officer SM, September 12, 2008, Mau.

67. Author's interview with Pastor PN, September 25, 2008, Mau. The national KBC radio station also does Maa-language broadcasts, but only for two hours per day.

68. Author's interview with head teacher ASM, September 19, 2008, Mau; CBO director MS, September 15, 2008, Mau; CBO chairman PN, September 15, 2008, Mau; age-set leader KK, October 2, 2008, Mau.

69. Author's interview with head teacher SS, September 19, 2008, Mau.

70. Author's interview with CBO chairwoman EN, September 11, 2008, Mau; CBO board member F, September 11, 2008, Mau.

71. Author's interview with Pastor PN, September 25, 2008, Mau.

missing out on workshops and meetings, but were also less likely to have access to radio[72] or churches.[73]

For Mau as a whole, the qualitative evidence suggests that the vast majority of the community has heard the international normative messages about FGM and early marriage, though a small number of the most rural individuals may have eluded them. This high awareness can be attributed to a sustained campaign by a variety of international and local actors (some of whom were clearly attracted to Mau's easy accessibility), including NGOs, the government, churches, and schools. While foreign organizations and the local groups they fund may devote more resources to FGM than to early marriage, various other community stakeholders are nonetheless involved in the campaign, and the reverse is true when it comes to early marriage.

CONCLUSION

Awareness of the international norms against FGM and early marriage is clearly a critical step in the broader process of norm change. Accordingly, it is important to understand what factors contribute most heavily to the extensiveness of activist programs overall and in specific communities. I have argued that high international norm salience drives up activism against a practice by reordering the priorities of activist organizations, while high local norm salience drives down activism as potential activists attempt to avoid alienating their community. In the cases of FGM and early marriage, these two effects tend to balance each other out to produce moderate levels of activism against both practices, although the sources of this activism are different. However, such activism depends on there being a sufficient density of activist organizations operating in the community in the first place. I find that the less accessible a community and its people are—whether because of distance from major cities or because of poor road conditions—the less likely it is that the community will receive or generate activists' attention. In the next chapter, I will consider whether simple awareness of the content of the international norms against FGM and early marriage translates into a shift in attitudes about these two practices, and whether one can expect that the sheer quantity of activism is a good proxy for the quality of activism.

72. Author's interview with social development committee chairwoman VK, September 30, 2008, Mau.
73. Author's interview with Pastor MS, October 2, 2008, Mau.

CHAPTER 5

Fostering Local Attitude Change

In the previous chapter I argued that awareness of the international norms against FGM and early marriage is most likely when communities, and individuals within communities, are in contact with a dense network of NGOs and other civil society groups. Moreover, overall levels of awareness are influenced by the relative salience of the competing international and local norms. This chapter addresses the translation of international norm awareness into attitude change. Particularly because we are considering the actions of individuals and communities, the ability of activists to actually persuade people of the validity of the international norms is critical. Since activists will generally lack the capacity to monitor individuals' behavior, they cannot use "naming and shaming" strategies to leverage strategic primary behavior change and must instead convince the targets of their activism that changing their behavior is simply the right thing to do.

Ultimately, the effectiveness of activists' persuasive efforts depends on both push and pull factors. On the push side, the quality of activism plays a crucial role in changing individuals' attitudes about FGM and early marriage. There are many specific choices that affect activism quality, but good activism exhibits some common characteristics. Organizations that are sufficiently dedicated and sufficiently knowledgeable about best practices in addressing a given issue will engage in long-term, intensive activities that are locally appropriate and effectively coordinated. But such high-quality activism is more rare than one might imagine, and the likelihood of observing it depends in part on the financial and social incentives faced by NGOs.

As described in chapter 2, NGOs are often highly dependent on international donors for their continued survival, and as a result may make strategic choices to curry those donors' favor, including working on donors' priority issues (even if those priority issues change over time). Unfortunately, the consequences of donor-driven issue selection and organizational mission creep are potentially significant—when NGOs work on many distinct issues and on issues that they are not independently motivated to address, their willingness and ability to provide a high-quality normative message are likely to be circumscribed. As a result, they may end up choosing less resource-intensive, time-consuming, and effective strategies.

Yet some NGOs and NGO programs are more likely to be afflicted by this problem than others. The salience of international and local norms comes into play here once again. Where international norm salience is high (as in the case of FGM), it drives up the overall level of activism on that issue, but many of the NGOs contributing to that heightened level of activism are simply following the money and lack much in the way of real commitment. The salience of the competing local norm at the local level may magnify the problem—to the extent that the local norm is highly salient, which is also true of FGM, NGOs that are ostensibly working on the issue may be particularly reluctant to take any kind of strong stand for fear of alienating their target audience. In comparison, where international norm salience is low (as in the case of early marriage) and donor attention limited, any NGOs that take up the cause anyway are likely doing so out of real interest in the issue and thus have a greater incentive to act effectively.

Yet activism quality is not the only factor affecting the likelihood of attitude change. On the pull side, one must recognize that susceptibility to even a high-quality normative message will vary across issues and individuals. Cognitive and motivated biases can contribute to belief perseverance insofar as individuals fail to seek out or internalize information that conflicts with their existing beliefs. Such biases are likely to be exacerbated by high local norm salience, as individuals display a higher degree of skepticism about evidence when it challenges their most closely held practices. Moreover, because attitude change is a continuum, a powerful local norm may prove resilient even if activists succeed in persuading people to embrace some portion of the content of the competing international norm.

Still, some types of people may be more open to international normative messages than others, though the susceptible groups are likely to vary according to the norm in question and perhaps also according to characteristics of the individual community. For FGM and early marriage, two groups in particular stand out. First, young people may be more receptive to activism against FGM and early marriage (United Nations Children's Fund 2013, 56–57). In general, the attitudes of the young about all types of issues are likely to be more malleable than those of their elders. And while older generations grew up and formed their beliefs about FGM and early marriage at a time when there was no internal debate about the merits of these practices, the introduction of transnational activism creates an opening for the younger generation to seriously consider alternatives to the status quo (Kuran 1995, 188).

In addition to young people, a second group that may be more open to attitude change is women. With practices like FGM and early marriage, women form a potential natural support base for the international norms because they can draw on their own experiences with circumcision and marriage. However, though activists have long painted FGM and early marriage as bastions of patriarchal control over women, one should not assume that women will necessarily rush to embrace the international norms.[1] In some contexts, women defend practices like female circumcision as granting them status and power (Ahmadu 2000). Moreover, there will be women who do not believe that they personally suffered any serious consequences as a result of undergoing these practices, and who will thus be more skeptical of reports of harm. Men are also generally more likely to be educated, to travel, and to have access to media, and thus to be exposed to alterative norms. Nonetheless, women should, on average and all else equal, be more open than men to changing their attitudes about FGM and early marriage.

I have thus identified a number of factors that influence individual attitude change in response to a norm conflict. On the one hand, the quality of the normative message goes a long way toward explaining the reception it earns, and there are financial incentives and structural constraints that explain some of the variation in message quality. On the other hand, in response to any given message, some people will be more receptive to that message than others. This suggests a number of observable implications. First, people who have received better information about the content of an international norm should be more likely to change their attitudes. Second, organizations that are heavily dependent on foreign aid and organizations that engage in many discrete tasks should produce a lower-quality normative message, as they overextend themselves and reorder their priorities away from issues to which they feel a strong commitment or for which they have some unique facility. Third, for any given level of activism, individuals should be less likely to change their attitudes about FGM than their attitudes about early marriage, since organizations are more likely to have reordered their

1. Indeed, DHS data suggest that men in some countries are actually more likely to oppose FGM than women (United Nations Children's Fund 2013, 62).

priorities toward the former than toward the latter in response to donor preferences, and thus to face an incentive to shirk in the delivery of the normative message. Finally, for a message of any quality, women and young people should be more open to attitude change than men or elders. As in chapter 4, I evaluate these implications using both interview and survey data.

QUANTITATIVE EVIDENCE

Measuring Attitudes and Message Quality

The survey included indicators of attitudes toward FGM and early marriage, as well as the hypothesized predictors of those attitudes. Descriptive statistics are presented in table 5.1. Among all respondents, 40 percent reported that they *believed female circumcision should be stopped*, though there was significant variation across the three study areas. In Oldonyiro, only 10 percent wanted female circumcision to stop, compared to 43 percent of respondents in Mukogodo and 57 percent of respondents in Mau. Opposition to early marriage

Table 5.1: DESCRIPTIVE STATISTICS

	Oldonyiro	Mukogodo	Mau	All areas	Observations
Message quality/individual openness					
Aware of circumcision health problems	0.190 (0.03)	0.242 (0.03)	0.418 (0.04)	0.301 (0.02)	597
Aware of early-marriage health problems	0.130 (0.02)	0.393 (0.04)	0.844 (0.03)	0.511 (0.02)	592
Female	0.465 (0.04)	0.457 (0.04)	0.481 (0.04)	0.469 (0.02)	600
Age	35.374 (1.28)	36.709 (1.50)	34.621 (1.27)	35.498 (0.79)	597
Attitudes					
Believe female circumcision should be stopped	0.097 (0.02)	0.429 (0.04)	0.571 (0.04)	0.402 (0.02)	592
Believe early marriage should be stopped	0.147 (0.03)	0.621 (0.04)	0.900 (0.02)	0.616 (0.02)	592

Note: Means weighted by inverse sampling probabilities. Standard errors in parentheses.

followed a similar pattern, but was higher on average. Across all areas, 62 percent of respondents *believed early marriage should be stopped*. By study area, 15 percent of Oldonyiro respondents, 62 percent of Mukogodo respondents, and 90 percent of Mau respondents wanted early marriage to stop. These data are consistent with the observable implication that opposition to early marriage should be higher than opposition to FGM, both because the anti-FGM message is of a lower quality and because people's beliefs about female circumcision are more resistant to updating.

Respondents were also asked about factors that indicate both the quality of the message they received and their susceptibility to that message. While it isn't possible to measure message quality directly, one *can* look at people's understanding of the content of the international norms as a proxy for message quality. We should expect that people who know more about the harms associated with FGM and early marriage have received a higher-quality message from activists, and thus will be more likely than their peers to embrace that message. As shown in chapter 4, among all respondents, 30 percent reported that *female circumcision could cause health problems*. In Oldonyiro, only 19 percent of respondents were aware of potential health problems, compared to 24 percent in Mukogodo and 42 percent in Mau. Awareness of the health consequences of early marriage was more extensive, and the differences between areas were more pronounced. Overall, 51 percent of respondents reported that *early marriage could cause health problems*, including 13 percent of respondents in Oldonyiro, 39 percent of respondents in Mukogodo, and 84 percent of respondents in Mau. This lends further support to the argument that anti-FGM activism tends to be less effective on average than activism against early marriage.

In terms of individual receptiveness to the normative messages against FGM and early marriage, two demographic characteristics are relevant. First, 47 percent of all respondents were *female*, a share that remained essentially consistent across study areas. Second, the average *age* of respondents was 35, and respondents ranged in age between 15 and 85.

Evaluation

To evaluate the role of message quality and individual characteristics in explaining attitudes toward female circumcision and early marriage, I turn again to multivariate analysis. Tables 5.2 and 5.3 show regression results for respondents' beliefs about whether female circumcision should

	(1)	(2)	(3)	(4)
	OLS		Logit[a]	
	Robust SE	Weighted/ clustered SE[b]	Robust SE	Weighted/ clustered SE[b]
Aware of circumcision health problems	0.401*** (0.04)	0.391*** (0.04)	0.513*** (0.06)	0.510*** (0.05)
Female	0.173*** (0.03)	0.181*** (0.05)	0.266*** (0.05)	0.277*** (0.05)
Age	−0.002* (0.00)	−0.003*** (0.00)	−0.003* (0.00)	−0.005*** (0.00)
Protestant	0.014 (0.05)	0.053 (0.06)	−0.004 (0.07)	0.054 (0.10)
Never visit town center	0.017 (0.05)	0.062 (0.06)	0.067 (0.09)	0.139 (0.09)
Radio owner	0.136*** (0.04)	0.137*** (0.03)	0.223*** (0.05)	0.224*** (0.04)
Treatment	−0.015 (0.03)	−0.006 (0.03)	−0.024 (0.05)	−0.015 (0.04)
Mukogodo	0.311*** (0.04)	0.277*** (0.05)	0.565*** (0.06)	0.565*** (0.07)
Mau	0.296*** (0.06)	0.289*** (0.03)	0.514*** (0.08)	0.526*** (0.06)
Constant	−0.022 (0.05)	0.004 (0.04)		
Observations	571	571	571	571

Notes: * $p<0.10$, ** $p<0.05$, *** $p<0.01$.
[a] Marginal effects coefficients.
[b] Standard errors clustered by sampling sublocation and weighted by probability of selection.

be stopped and whether early marriage should be stopped, which are the two primary outcome variables. The right-hand-side variables are *health* (a dummy variable equal to one if the respondent reports that he or she is aware the practice can cause health problems and zero otherwise), *female* (a dummy variable equal to one if the respondent is female and zero if the respondent is male), and *age*. The analysis also includes study area fixed effects, as well as controls for Protestantism, town visits, and radio

Table 5.3: BELIEVE EARLY MARRIAGE SHOULD BE STOPPED

	(1)	(2)	(3)	(4)
	OLS		Logit[a]	
	Robust SE	Weighted/ clustered SE[b]	Robust SE	Weighted/ clustered SE[b]
Aware of early-marriage health problems	0.195*** (0.05)	0.151*** (0.05)	0.260*** (0.06)	0.162** (0.08)
Female	0.115*** (0.03)	0.123** (0.05)	0.209*** (0.06)	0.213** (0.09)
Age	−0.002 (0.00)	−0.002** (0.00)	−0.003 (0.00)	−0.004** (0.00)
Protestant	0.123** (0.05)	0.143*** (0.03)	0.197** (0.08)	0.222*** (0.07)
Never visit town center	−0.023 (0.06)	−0.035 (0.04)	−0.010 (0.10)	−0.035 (0.07)
Radio owner	0.127*** (0.04)	0.102** (0.04)	0.224*** (0.06)	0.171*** (0.05)
Treatment	0.029 (0.03)	0.042 (0.03)	0.050 (0.06)	0.074 (0.05)
Mukogodo	0.397*** (0.05)	0.382*** (0.06)	0.438*** (0.06)	0.364*** (0.08)
Mau	0.458*** (0.07)	0.506*** (0.07)	0.511*** (0.07)	0.535*** (0.09)
Constant	0.068 (0.05)	0.096 (0.06)		
Observations	567	567	567	567

Notes: * $p<0.10$, ** $p<0.05$, *** $p<0.01$.
[a] Marginal effects coefficients.
[b] Standard errors clustered by sampling sublocation and weighted by probability of selection.

ownership (which were discussed in chapter 4 as predictors of norm aware-ness) and for receiving the experimental treatment.

The regression results are consistent with the observable implications described above. First, being aware that female circumcision can cause health problems is positively and significantly associated with the prob-ability that the respondent reports believing that female circumcision should be stopped. Similarly, being aware that early marriage can cause health problems is positively and significantly associated with the probability that the respondent reports believing that early marriage should be stopped. Moreover, the results are substantively significant in addition to being statistically significant. Being aware that circumcision can cause health problems is associated with at least a 39-percentage-point increase in the probability that the respondent reports opposition to circumcision, and being aware that early marriage can cause health problems is associated with at least a 15-percentage-point increase in the probability that the respondent reports opposition to early marriage. While awareness of international norm content isn't a perfect proxy for message quality, these findings are nonetheless in line with the theoretical story, in which receiving higher-quality information makes an individual more likely to oppose FGM and early marriage.

Second, as predicted, certain demographic characteristics are strongly associated with opposition to FGM and early marriage. Being a woman was positively and significantly associated with the probability that the respondent reported believing that female circumcision should be stopped, and was positively and significantly associated with the probability that the respondent reported believing that early marriage should be stopped. In both cases, the coefficient in all models suggested that the relationship was substantively meaningful; being a woman was associated with a 17-percentage-point increase in the probability that the respondent opposed circumcision and a 12-percentage-point increase in the probability that the respondent opposed early marriage. Respondents' age was also related to their attitudes about FGM and early marriage. Being one year older was associated with at least a 0.2-percentage-point decrease in the probability that the respondent wanted female circumcision to stop (significant in all models) and with the probability that the respondent wanted early marriage to stop (significant in Models 2 and 4).

On the whole, the empirical evidence is consistent with the theoretical account of the circumstances under which one might expect to see a shift in attitudes about FGM and early marriage. The data suggest that people are more likely to receive a high-quality normative message about early marriage than about FGM, and that message quality, as well as individual-level susceptibility to that message, are strong predictors of attitude change. Individuals who understand the content of the international norms, as well as women and young people, are less likely to support the local norms. Data from the qualitative interviews provide additional support for these conclusions and also provide insight into the factors that influence activism quality.

Oldonyiro

In Oldonyiro, awareness of the international norms against FGM and early marriage was sufficiently low that there were few opportunities for attitude change. However, even among those who had heard the message, "They don't take it gladly. They just see it as interfering with their culture."[2] Some interviewees attributed this to the fact that previous activist efforts had not been sustained.[3] NGOs would occasionally come into the area, but then leave after a short amount of time, such that the community did not take their efforts seriously.[4] In addition to being intermittent, the activism was less credible because it came mostly from foreigners or people from other ethnic groups.[5] "It is good if it comes from local people," because locals can show that it is possible to have a good life in the absence of these practices.[6] Interviewees suggested that for outsiders to overcome the natural suspicion locals would have of them, they ought to first contribute something positive to the community, like a school or hospital[7] or scholarships.[8]

Furthermore, while interviewees agreed that activists needed to target many different types of people in the community in order to be effective, the reality was that most previous efforts had focused only on young people.[9] According to one governmental official, even if the youth are empowered, it will not make a difference, because the youth do not have any real power in the community.[10] In contrast, men are "the custodians of the culture. They have the authority, more than women,"[11] and yet activists had not reached out to them. While activism tended to be poor on all fronts, activism against FGM particularly suffered because locals limited the message to groups they perceived as friendly, such as youth. For example, Catholic priests would speak against FGM in youth seminars, but they would ignore the topic in their regular sermons.[12] While

2. Author's interview with children's officer SJ, July 14, 2008, Oldonyiro.
3. Author's interview with district officer, July 21, 2008, Oldonyiro; CBO worker AD, July 22, 2008, Oldonyiro.
4. Author's interview with children's officer SJ, July 14, 2008, Oldonyiro.
5. Author's interview with public health workers I and Y, July 25, 2008, Oldonyiro.
6. Author's interview with former church women's development coordinator LL, October 14, 2008, Oldonyiro.
7. Author's interview with district officer, July 21, 2008, Oldonyiro.
8. Author's interview with children's officer SJ, July 14, 2008, Oldonyiro.
9. Author's interview with former church women's development coordinator LL, October 14, 2008, Oldonyiro.
10. Author's interview with youth officer EN, July 25, 2008, Oldonyiro.
11. Author's interview with NGO director JL, June 12, 2008, Oldonyiro.
12. Author's interview with location chief, May 6, 2008, Oldonyiro.

it seemed that youth were indeed more open to the normative message than their elders,[13] interviewees suggested that taking this path of least resistance was not helpful if the ultimate goal was community-wide attitude change.

For Oldonyiro as a whole, the generally low level of activism was compounded by the fact that the activism that did occur was either too irregular to be convincing or failed to reach actual decision-makers in the community. Thus, low levels of international norm awareness were matched by low levels of attitude change.

Mukogodo

In Mukogodo, the record on attitude change was more significant, though many still resisted the messages opposing FGM and early marriage.[14] According to one NGO worker, "The activists are having an effect, even if it is not as much as we desire. They listen to you for two hours, and at the end you have convinced a small percentage. Believing you is a difficult matter."[15] A second NGO worker was more optimistic, saying, "The idea of young girls marrying old men is becoming absurd. They want to adapt."[16] But a teacher suggested that, in fact, people were still not opposing FGM and early marriage.[17] An NGO director summed up the challenges by saying that "sometimes science does not provide the answers. It's not because there are no answers, but the answers don't satisfy the communities, who have their own beliefs."[18] A local chief agreed, saying, "On FGM, still we have a lot of work to do, as the leaders, as the NGOs, as the churches. The Maasai are very proud people. It is very hard to convince them. It is not easy to change them quickly. They believe in their culture strongly."[19]

While some organizations were spreading an effective normative message,[20] others appeared to be missing the mark.[21] One local activist pointed to an alternative rite of passage that had recently been held in the area,

13. Author's interview with NGO director JL, June 12, 2008, Oldonyiro; former church women's development coordinator LL, October 14, 2008, Oldonyiro.

14. Author's interview with district commissioner AM, June 18, 2008, Mukogodo.

15. Author's interview with NGO worker RL, June 23, 2008, Mukogodo.

16. Author's interview with NGO worker F, June 17, 2008, Mukogodo.

17. Author's interview with head teacher MK, July 1, 2008, Mukogodo.

18. Author's interview with NGO director JK, April 15, 2008, Mukogodo.

19. Author's interview with Chief P, June 18, 2008, Mukogodo.

20. Author's interview with head teacher LM, July 10, 2008, Mukogodo.

21. Author's interview with community development officer MO, July 2, 2008, Mukogodo.

in which the organizers had angered local elders by not consulting with them in advance. Instead of laying the groundwork for their undertaking, they had simply recruited girls from local schools without first educating their parents or the community.[22] Interviewees agreed that the message needed to be sustained and holistic, such that it addressed real concerns in the community and didn't just preach about FGM or early marriage.[23] Unfortunately, this was not always the approach taken. With external organizations, for example, their commitment to eradicating FGM and early marriage might have been genuine, but their effectiveness was somewhat limited. Locals could provide a sustained message—"I say it today, I say it tomorrow, I say it the day after"—but people know that outsiders aren't going to stick around.[24] Even in schools, the normative message may not be provided consistently, since it is generally left to the teachers' discretion whether to speak out about FGM and early marriage, and some teachers continue to support these practices. Of course, even people who receive these normative messages regularly may not be persuaded to change. "If there is a community that has gone to a lot of seminars, it is Dol Dol," but it is not because people are starting to care about FGM or early marriage.[25] Instead, people come to the meetings mainly to get a free lunch.

Sometimes the problem was with the people delivering the message, with outsiders facing particularly significant challenges because they don't understand the culture.[26] The district commissioner pointed out, "I don't come from this community, and so I can't go and say 'This is bad.'"[27] According to a health worker, "Whatever message they're getting is very minimal. I think if it were coming from people in the community they would get the message. But because we come from a different community—a community that doesn't practice FGM—they will not listen to us."[28] An NGO worker agreed that people were not likely to be persuaded when the message came from outside NGOs or from the government.[29] According to one teacher, the groups that had been most effective were the locally based ones, especially those that had engaged in more broad-based programs that benefited the community.[30]

22. Author's interview with former CBO chairman JL, July 13, 2008, Mukogodo.
23. Author's interview with Chief P, June 18, 2008, Mukogodo; former CBO chairman JL, July 13, 2008, Mukogodo.
24. Author's interview with head teacher AR, July 1, 2008, Mukogodo.
25. Ibid.
26. Author's interview with former CBO chairman JL, July 13, 2008, Mukogodo.
27. Author's interview with district commissioner AM, June 18, 2008, Mukogodo.
28. Author's interview with medical officer CL, July 6, 2008, Mukogodo.
29. Author's interview with NGO worker RL, June 23, 2008, Mukogodo.
30. Author's interview with head teacher LM, July 10, 2008, Mukogodo.

And sometimes the problem was which people the groups targeted. One teacher explained that activist organizations would sometimes come to her school, but the activists didn't talk to the right people. They would just focus on the girls, but ignore the boys, the parents, and the teachers. She questioned the wisdom of such an approach when girls don't actually get to decide whether to participate in these practices.[31] Another teacher agreed that "it is only in the school that the girls hear that circumcision is no good. But the parents have not heard the message about circumcision."[32] A health worker put the situation in comparative perspective, saying, "In Narok, there are so many people climbing mountains to fight FGM. Here in Mukogodo, and in Samburu, they just involve the women and the girls" in training. For a campaign to be successful, it has to involve men, since "according to the culture, a man is not supposed to marry a girl who has not been circumcised." If the men are not targeted, they will continue to insist on circumcised brides, and it will be difficult for the girls or their parents to refuse.[33] One local activist summed up the issue, concluding, "We need to do very many workshops for everybody. Not just women, not just men, but everybody."[34]

There was a certain level of skepticism about the goals and intentions of some of the local NGO leaders, though it's important to keep in mind that, to the extent local NGOs are in competition with one another, workers at some groups may have been inclined to give overly negative reports about others. One local activist said, "Most of the organizations that are here are working on FGM," but they are not having much of an effect. "People are doing it but they're not very committed. We are not seeing commitment to mobilization. I've not seen a commitment whereby people are going into the interior" to spread the anti-FGM message.[35] According to another interviewee, "We have some NGOs, but we are not seeing what they are doing so far. We have not seen them going out fully, or going out to the grassroots." These groups had thus far not made a concerted effort to eradicate FGM or early marriage.[36] Mission creep was also an issue, with the former chairman of one small CBO reporting that his organization worked not only on FGM, but also on income-generating activities for widows and orphans, preventive healthcare, land rights advocacy, paralegal training, and education promotion and provision.[37]

31. Author's interview with head teacher AR, July 1, 2008, Mukogodo.
32. Author's interview with head teacher MK, July 1, 2008, Mukogodo.
33. Author's interview with medical officer CL, July 6, 2008, Mukogodo.
34. Author's interview with CBO board member MK, July 24, 2008, Mukogodo.
35. Author's interview with CBO director AM, July 5, 2008, Mukogodo.
36. Author's interview with medical officer CL, July 6, 2008, Mukogodo.
37. Author's interview with former CBO chairman JL, July 13, 2008, Mukogodo.

A teacher suggested that some of the local activist organizations don't practice what they preach. She pointed to the director of one local organization who married an underage girl and pulled her out of school, and another who married his wife while she was still in secondary school. She concluded that they had only taken up this cause because of the availability of donor funding, and that they were having very little effect on the community because they were not actually committed to women's and children's rights. Of one organization's anti-FGM efforts, she said, "They do that because it has money. It is for raising funds" that they work on FGM. "They will write proposals very quickly." And with respect to a second local organization, "They also were doing it for money," as evidenced by the fact that one staff member got in trouble for domestic violence, and another for having sex with the daughter of a close relative. In general, NGOs go where the money is, and if money becomes available for a different issue, they will start working on that issue. In the wake of postelection violence in 2007, there was "a lot of money being poured into peace [activities], so right now they are talking about peace."[38]

The director of a third local organization acknowledged that the reason the organization was founded in the first place was to provide jobs for its members, who were previously unemployed (though the existence of instrumental interests does not necessarily mean that altruistic commitments are absent): "After we finished school, we were quite idle and we found that we were not doing anything. [Forming the organization] helps us, but indirectly it helps the community."[39] A local activist also indicated that some of the local NGOs claimed to be doing more to combat FGM than they actually were, because "seeing a *mzungu* [westerner], they start thinking about funding."[40]

Despite these shortcomings, some people appeared to be embracing the international normative message, particularly women.[41] "The women are more receptive, because women are the ones who usually experience the problems" with FGM.[42] By contrast, men don't care as much about the issue, so "when you discuss FGM with men, they'll tell you, 'It's not us who are performing this operation. It is the women.' "[43] The cultural inclinations are still very strong, so it is especially difficult to convince the elder men.[44] According to a local activist, "The *wazee* [elders] don't believe in what we say."[45]

---

38. Author's interview with head teacher AR, July 1, 2008, Mukogodo.
39. Author's interview with CBO director AM, July 5, 2008, Mukogodo.
40. Author's interview with former CBO chairman JL, July 13, 2008, Mukogodo.
41. Author's interview with district commissioner AM, June 18, 2008, Mukogodo.
42. Author's interview with CBO director AM, July 5, 2008, Mukogodo.
43. Author's interview with CBO board member MK, July 24, 2008, Mukogodo.
44. Author's interview with Pastor S, June 17, 2008, Mukogodo.
45. Author's interview with NGO worker RL, June 23, 2008, Mukogodo.

Overall, Mukogodo has experienced a fair amount of attitude change, but many people still remain unconvinced that the international norms against FGM and early marriage are superior to the local norms supporting these practices. While on the surface there is a great deal of activism against both practices, the reality is that the methods employed are frequently misguided, insubstantial, or otherwise ineffective. It also appears that some groups selected tasks (particularly FGM) with an eye primarily toward making money, which may explain why the message quality wasn't higher. For those groups genuinely committed to the cause, they were sometimes constrained by their outsider status or by the shortage of resources. Among those individuals who did receive the message, women and youths were more receptive to it than elder men.

Mau

Of the three areas, Mau appeared to have experienced the greatest degree of attitude change about FGM and early marriage.[46] Still, not everyone was convinced by the international normative message.[47] According to one teacher, "Most of them have heard it, but the problem is they have not taken it in a positive way. The reaction has been so slow. They fear the changes."[48] Another teacher agreed that "even the girl child herself is made to believe that circumcision is the way forward."[49] One pastor said that "many people look at us as enemies, because we are fighting FGM directly." The church has lost some parishioners because of this, but "with prayer, and trying to create awareness with our people, we have now those who have taken that stance" against FGM.[50] A cultural age-set leader explained the difficulty of embracing the international norms: "We are the people who are holding the culture in Maasailand, and our goal is to protect our culture. Some NGOs came and told us about FGM, that it was a bad practice, and so we are trying to find a solution. We did not view this as a problem until these groups came, and so we are still debating whether we can leave it."[51]

46. Author's interview with Pastor MS, October 2, 2008, Mau.
47. Author's interview with district officer SM, September 12, 2008, Mau; CBO chairman PN, September 15, 2008, Mau; education officer MS, September 16, 2008, Mau; youth officer NS, September 22, 2008, Mau; public health officer FM, September 22, 2008, Mau.
48. Author's interview with teacher RM, September 30, 2008, Mau.
49. Author's interview with head teacher SKK, September 23, 2008, Mau.
50. Author's interview with Pastor PN, September 25, 2008, Mau.
51. Author's interview with age-set leader KK, October 2, 2008, Mau.

While progress might be slow, several organizations were recognized as having made effective contributions to the cause.[52] One organization worked exclusively on FGM and early marriage and held alternative rites of passage twice a year that also involved training of the participating girls' parents and an agreement that the girls would not be circumcised later.[53] A second organization, active in the area for six years, had recruited extensively among the local population and had also been holding yearly alternative rites of passage with training for parents. In addition, the organization provided a girls' dormitory at one of the local secondary schools and had recently begun training boys as well as girls about FGM.[54] A third organization also emphasized the importance of training boys in addition to training girls and pointed out that they had both male and female trainers so that they could more effectively reach everyone in the community.[55] A pastor and presenter on the local Maa-language radio station said that he made an effort to reach parents in general and older men in particular, because otherwise, "When the girl refuses to be circumcised the parents become bitter."[56] Such organizations appeared to be internally motivated to tackle these issues and to therefore produce a higher-quality message.

Many people agreed that it was better if the normative message came from other Maasai.[57] People won't be as receptive if the activism comes from another ethnic group: "They'll say, 'He doesn't know the tradition or the culture.'"[58] The district officer, who was not Maasai, said, "If I talk a lot, they will say, 'He has brought his culture here,'" so it is better if the message comes from a local.[59] For an external organization to have an impact, it should provide something to the community to establish credibility.[60] As one teacher put it, "I think a person coming from far would only have

52. Author's interview with head teacher SKK, September 23, 2008, Mau; CBO board member AK, September 30, 2008, Mau.
53. Author's interview with NGO director AP, August 27, 2008, Mau.
54. Author's interview with NGO worker RK, September 8, 2008, Mau.
55. Author's interview with CBO worker EN, September 11, 2008, Mau.
56. Author's interview with Pastor PN, September 25, 2008, Mau.
57. Author's interview with district officer KA, September 1, 2008, Mau; CBO chairman PN, September 15, 2008, Mau; education officer MS, September 16, 2008, Mau; head teacher SS, September 19, 2008, Mau; Pastor PN, September 25, 2008, Mau; public health officer EK, September 26, 2008, Mau; head teacher SK, September 29, 2008, Mau; head teacher VML, September 29, 2008, Mau; teacher RM, September 30, 2008, Mau.
58. Author's interview with NGO worker RK, September 8, 2008, Mau.
59. Author's interview with district officer SM, September 12, 2008, Mau.
60. Author's interview with public health officer FM, September 22, 2008, Mau.

impact if he brings some rewards."[61] A local activist agreed that when it comes to people from another tribe, if they start with something useful, like how to get clean water, they can create an opening to then address FGM or early marriage. "You can start with a small project."[62] Fortunately, many of the organizations operating in Mau were locally based, or at the very least staffed by Maasai.

Still, not everybody was convinced that the NGOs were doing a good job. According to the district officer, "Nobody listens to NGOs. NGOs are seen as organizations that get money from donors and misuse it."[63] Another government official suggested that some of the NGO workers even secretly supported FGM and only opposed the practice publicly because they were being paid to do so.[64] An age-set leader said, "We see activists like businesspeople. They have business minds, so they come and try to seduce us, because when a person stands against FGM they will get funds from outside, from groups or NGOs, maybe in the US, so they treat this like a business."[65] And some organizations appeared to be overextended, with one local activist reporting that his organization, which employed no full-time staff, ostensibly tackled FGM, HIV/AIDS awareness, orphans and vulnerable children, clean water provision, poverty alleviation, education provision for adult learners, women's empowerment, a farmers' field school, youth group support, and healthcare provision.[66] According to one teacher, the problem was that people were speaking out against FGM and early marriage, but they weren't thoroughly explaining what the specific problems were, such as loss of sexual satisfaction, HIV, and childbirth complications.[67] And while some groups were reaching a wide swath of the community, others were missing the important decision-making groups of parents and elders.[68]

Ultimately, some people were more open to the normative message than others. One traditional circumciser said that while she had heard about the consequences of FGM—particularly that the practice could

61. Author's interview with head teacher ASM, September 19, 2008, Mau.

62. Author's interview with self-help group chairwoman HK, September 26, 2008, Mau.

63. Author's interview with district officer KA, September 1, 2008, Mau.

64. Author's interview with public health officer SS, September 22, 2008, Mau.

65. Author's interview with age-set leader KK, October 2, 2008, Mau.

66. Author's interview with CBO chairman PN, September 15, 2008, Mau.

67. Author's interview with head teacher SK, September 29, 2008, Mau.

68. Author's interview with head teacher SK, September 29, 2008, Mau; social development committee chairwoman VK, September 30, 2008, Mau; teacher RM, September 30, 2008, Mau.

spread HIV—she didn't really believe it.[69] Some other women were also skeptical about the international norms' content, especially if they didn't experience any health complications with their own circumcisions or the circumcisions of their daughters. Men, on the other hand, have no direct experience with the operation, and very little knowledge about women's bodies, so in some cases they are easier to convince.[70] But many other women appeared to be more easily persuaded,[71] and young people too were more open to change.[72]

Overall, the interviews suggest that Mau residents have made some significant strides in changing their attitudes about FGM and early marriage, although the process is far from complete and some people are more open to change than others. The success that has been achieved can be attributed to the sustained efforts of a number of committed organizations that have put in the effort to reach many types of people in the community, even if some other organizations have been less driven.

CONCLUSION

While awareness of the international norms against FGM and early marriage is clearly an important first step in producing norm change, the evidence presented in this chapter suggests that simple awareness cannot be assumed to translate directly into attitude change. Message quantity is not the same thing as message quality, and there are a number of reasons to believe that a high-quality normative message may in some instances be the exception rather than the rule. I argue that the incentives created by the international aid regime lead organizations of all stripes to attempt to tackle issues for which they are not well suited and to which they feel no particular commitment. And even those organizations that are dedicated to the cause face constraints such as human capital deficiencies and cultural communication barriers that limit their effectiveness. The result is that while some activism against FGM and early marriage is highly compelling, many other efforts are paltry and potentially misguided. I further contend that, beyond the variability in message quality, some individuals are likely to be more receptive to the international normative message

---

69. Author's interview with traditional circumciser JN, October 2, 2008, Mau.
70. Author's interview with NGO worker RK, September 8, 2008, Mau.
71. Author's interview with head teacher PLT, September 25, 2008, Mau.
72. Author's interview with Pastor JK, September 25, 2008, Mau; self-help group chairwoman HK, September 26, 2008, Mau; head teacher SK, September 29, 2008, Mau.

than others. In particular, women and young people will tend to be the first to embrace the international norms. However, in the next chapter I will show that simply agreeing with the content of the international norm is not necessarily sufficient to produce actual primary behavior change, since individuals rarely make decisions about norm compliance without considering the potential response such a decision might elicit from their communities.

CHAPTER 6

Facilitating Local Primary Behavior Change

Chapter 5 showed that individual attitude change in response to transnational activism against FGM and early marriage is most likely to occur when the international normative message people receive is not only frequent but also of high quality. Awareness of the international norm hinges on the level of activism, but attitude change depends also on the content of that activism. Accordingly, individuals with a strong grasp of the logic of the international norms are more likely to express opposition to the two practices. In this chapter I address the shift from attitude change to primary behavior change, recognizing that achieving the former does not automatically produce the latter. Because of the social component of norms, local expectations of norm compliance and the attendant social costs and benefits may trump individuals' own preferences over their behavior.

The extent to which individuals end up factoring in other people's preferences when making behavioral decisions depends on a number of factors, including the local salience of the local norm. The more strongly people in the reference group believe it is important to comply with the norm, the harder group members will work to defend it. Thus where local norm salience is high, the social barriers to defection from it are generally also high—groups are likely to impose significant penalties on those who fail to comply. In the case of FGM, uncircumcised girls face a range of potential negative outcomes, including social ostracism, ridicule, and an inability to marry within the group. In the case of early marriage, however, negative social sanctions for delaying marriage are generally more limited.

With highly salient local norms, the success of international norm entrepreneurs in eliciting primary behavior change hinges on their ability to reach individuals who can minimize their defection costs, especially through some sort of exit option from their original reference group, and on their ability to recruit influential norm leaders. For FGM, individuals who live among normative out-groups (especially those of equal or higher status) may, for example, be able to exit from the local norm by marrying into one of these out-groups. This calls into question Gerry Mackie's (1996) argument that FGM acts as a convention from which individuals cannot unilaterally defect—I argue that the option of exit through intermarriage means we are no longer dealing with a perfect convention. The presence of normative out-groups can also provide a demonstration effect, showing in-group members that daughters can lead good lives in the absence of female circumcision (and also in the absence of early marriage).

Once a few local norm defections have occurred, further defections then become easier. The first movers, or norm leaders, are striking out on their own with no social support, but the norm followers can draw on the example and assistance of the norm leaders. In the case of FGM, the daughters of norm followers can marry the sons of norm leaders, and neither the girls nor their families will face complete social ostracism. Over time, local social expectations may even shift to the degree that the path of least resistance is for parents *not* to circumcise their daughters.

Overall, then, individuals who have changed their attitudes about a particular norm must weigh their private preference for behavior change against the strength of their group's commitment to the status quo. Where the local norm is not particularly salient, as in the case of early marriage, individuals will generally be free to follow their own preferences with few other considerations. But the more salient the local norm and the higher the initial social barrier to defection, the greater the individual's dependence on some form of exit option or signal about changing local expectations. The degree to which any given community then experiences behavior change around a locally salient norm depends not only on the share of people who have changed their attitudes but also on the share of people who have access to such options and signals. Essentially, broader community behavior change requires individuals who are willing to be norm leaders (generally, people with strong attitudinal commitment to the international norm who also face lower-than-average social costs for local norm defection) and individuals who are willing to be norm followers (generally, people who can take advantage of the changing social expectations created by the norm leaders). The former are most likely to emerge where there is high-quality activism and good exit options, and the latter are most likely to emerge where there are many norm leaders and where those leaders are particularly influential individuals.

How well does reality mirror these theoretical expectations? Does primary behavior change lag behind attitude change for highly salient norms? If some individuals change their behavior anyway, does the presence of exit options and local influential norm leaders at least partially explain the patterns of change in these instances? It is possible to draw a number of observable implications from the theoretical framework. First, at the individual level, agreement with the international norm against FGM should be significantly more common than actual international norm compliance. Second, individual compliance with the international norm against early marriage should more closely track international norm agreement. Third, for both FGM and early marriage, exposure to normative out-groups, specifically in the form of ethnic heterogeneity, should be associated with individual abandonment of the local norms in communities that have experienced minimal norm change. Fourth, with respect to FGM, believing that influential locals—in this case traditional leaders and local political officials—oppose circumcision should be associated with individual abandonment of circumcision in all communities. Finally, at the community level, both ethnic heterogeneity and a widespread belief that local elites oppose circumcision should be associated with higher levels of abandonment of FGM and early marriage. I evaluate these implications by drawing once again on both survey and interview data.

QUANTITATIVE EVIDENCE

Measuring Behavior and Barriers to Defection

The survey included indicators of primary behavior and intentions with respect to FGM and early marriage, as well as the hypothesized predictors of those behaviors and intentions. Table 6.1 presents descriptive statistics. Among respondents with married daughters, 55 percent reported that their most recently married *daughter had been married before age 18*, for a mean marriage age of 17.5 years. But as with awareness and attitudes, respondents' reported behavior varied dramatically across the three study areas. In Oldonyiro, 75 percent of respondents with married daughters reported that the most recently married daughter had been married before age 18. This share dropped to 60 percent in Mukogodo and 38 percent in Mau.

In addition, among respondents with daughters, 75 percent stated that at least one *daughter had been circumcised or would be circumcised in the future*. By

	Oldonyiro	Mukogodo	Mau	All areas	Observations
Barriers to defection					
Meet other tribe once a week or more	0.519 (0.04)	0.682 (0.04)	0.960 (0.02)	0.756 (0.02)	584
Believe elders want circumcision to stop	0.024 (0.01)	0.039 (0.02)	0.149 (0.03)	0.081 (0.01)	597
Believe elders want early marriage to stop	0.031 (0.01)	0.148 (0.03)	0.566 (0.04)	0.292 (0.02)	597
Believe chiefs want circumcision to stop	0.292 (0.04)	0.900 (0.02)	0.846 (0.03)	0.722 (0.02)	585
Believe chiefs want early marriage to stop	0.306 (0.04)	0.964 (0.01)	0.921 (0.02)	0.775 (0.02)	581
Behavior and intentions					
Daughter is or will be circumcised	0.878 (0.03)	0.703 (0.05)	0.714 (0.05)	0.751 (0.03)	326
Plan to circumcise daughter in future	0.843 (0.04)	0.479 (0.06)	0.551 (0.06)	0.596 (0.03)	293
Daughter married before age 18	0.749 (0.09)	0.604 (0.10)	0.384 (0.10)	0.551 (0.06)	96[a]

Note: Means weighted by inverse sampling probabilities. Standard errors in parentheses.
[a] Number of observations reflects the small number of respondents who both had married daughters and could estimate the age at which their daughters were married.

study area, 88 percent of Oldonyiro respondents, 70 percent of Mukogodo respondents, and 71 percent of Mau respondents reported that at least one daughter had or would be circumcised. Combining past behavior and intended future behavior into a single indicator serves as a reasonable approximation of the current prevalence of FGM. Looking only at past behavior would be problematic because the set of parents who have not circumcised a daughter comprises two distinct groups: parents who have actually rejected female circumcision, and parents whose daughters will be circumcised once they are old enough. Thus, considering past behavior in isolation doesn't allow one to distinguish those who have truly defected from the local norm from those whose daughters aren't circumcised yet but will be when they come of age. Using the combined variable ensures that this latter group—local norm compliers—are not incorrectly categorized as local norm defectors.

Of course, it is also important to ensure that recent local norm defectors are not incorrectly categorized as compliers. As a consequence of transnational activism, some parents who circumcised their daughters in the past may nonetheless plan to leave their remaining daughters uncircumcised. Therefore, I also include a variable that tracks parents' future plans in isolation. Restricting the focus to only those individuals who still have the opportunity to decide whether to circumcise their daughters approximates the current incidence of the practice. When asked about their intentions, 60 percent of respondents with uncircumcised daughters stated that they intended to *circumcise their daughters in the future*. 84 percent of respondents in Oldonyiro reported that they intended to circumcise their daughters, as did 48 percent of respondents in Mukogodo and 55 percent of respondents in Mau.

The descriptive statistics from both measures clearly show that communities can abandon FGM incrementally, casting doubt on the real-world generalizability of Mackie's convention account. There is little evidence from the three communities that the early defectors coordinated their defection, and yet change has taken place. The convention account also predicts that, when change does occur, it will spread throughout the community very rapidly (Mackie 1996, 1015), and yet an examination of FGM prevalence by the age of female respondents doesn't bear this out. While individual abandonment of FGM began earliest in Mau, followed by Mukogodo and Oldonyiro, figure 6.1 shows that each of the three communities has experienced a continuous moderate decrease in prevalence for successively younger groups of women, with the decline occurring over a 20- to 40-year period.

To measure the influence of ethnic heterogeneity on behavior, the survey asked respondents whether they encountered people from other ethnic groups, and 76 percent reported that they *met somebody from another tribe once a week or more*. By study area, 52 percent of Oldonyiro respondents, 68 percent of Mukogodo respondents, and 96 percent of Mau respondents reported that they encountered somebody from another group once a week or more.

To gauge the perceived presence of influential local norm leaders, the survey also asked respondents whether they thought most elders and most chiefs wanted female circumcision and early marriage to continue or stop. Among Maasai and Samburu, elders are men in middle or old age who are respected locally as decision-makers. In Kenya, chiefs are

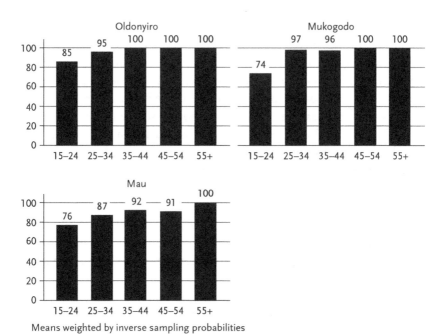

Means weighted by inverse sampling probabilities

Figure 6.1: Percentage of girls and women who have undergone FGM, by age cohort

local men who are appointed by the government as the primary author-ity at the location level. They generally hold office for many years, although they can be unseated in the face of significant community opposition. While they may not be the most powerful local elders by traditional standards (especially in recent years), they are certainly the most powerful by modern political standards. These traditional leaders and local political officials are often viewed as the custodians of the cul-ture, and they have the ability to make decisions that affect the entire community.

With respect to female circumcision, 8 percent of all respondents said they believed *elders want female circumcision to stop*. By region, 2 percent of respondents in Oldonyiro, 4 percent of respondents in Mukogodo, and 15 percent of respondents in Mau reported that elders wanted to stop female circumcision. When asked about chiefs, 72 percent of all respon-dents said they believed *chiefs want female circumcision to stop*, with 29 per-cent of Oldonyiro respondents, 90 percent of Mukogodo respondents, and 85 percent of Mau respondents reporting this belief. On the issue of early marriage, 29 percent of all respondents reported that they believed *elders want early marriage to stop*, and 78 percent reported that they believed *chiefs want early marriage to stop*.

Evaluation

To evaluate whether the observable implications described above are in fact observed, I turn to the survey data. First, it does appear that with FGM, primary behavior change is lagging considerably behind attitude change. Figure 6.2 compares male respondents' views about circumcision—since men are usually the decision-makers in the family—to the percentage of respondents who have circumcised their daughters or intend to circumcise them in the future. While only 52 percent of male respondents stated that they believed female circumcision should continue, fully 75 percent of respondents with daughters stated that they had circumcised their daughters or intended to circumcise them in the future. Moreover, the correlation between stating that circumcision should continue and reporting that one has a circumcised daughter or intends to circumcise their daughter in the future is only .45.

Second, although the evidence is not as straightforward, there is some reason to think that behavior with respect to early marriage more closely parallels attitudes. Figure 6.3 shows that only 34 percent of male respondents stated their support for early marriage, while 55 percent of respondents with married daughters reported that their daughter had been

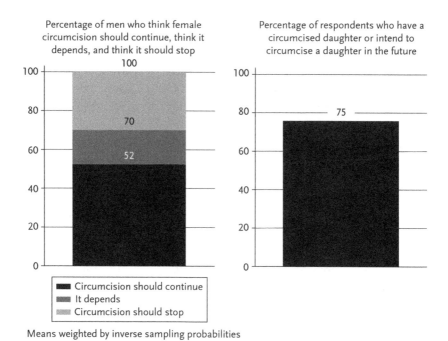

Means weighted by inverse sampling probabilities

Figure 6.2: FGM attitude change versus behavior change

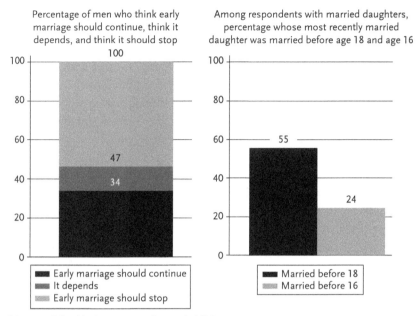

Figure 6.3: Early-marriage attitude change versus behavior change

married before the age of 18. However, in more than half of these cases, the daughter was married at age 16 or 17. While international treaties recognize 18 as the legal age of consent for marriage, many people do not think that marriage at age 16 or 17 qualifies as "early."[1] Returning to figure 6.3, one can see that only 24 percent of respondents with married daughters reported that their daughter had been married before the age of 16, and this level is actually slightly lower than the share of male respondents who openly support the practice. While the correlation between stating that early marriage should continue and daughters' marriage age is only .39, this is partially driven by the fact that 13 percent of respondents who support early marriage and have married daughters reported that their daughter was actually 18 or older at the time. This isn't surprising given that early marriages are not a specific cultural requirement among Maasai and Samburu. Accordingly, it is not a contradiction for parents to believe that early marriage is an acceptable practice and yet marry their daughters off when they are older. However, this outcome does mask the effect on behavior that agreeing with the international norm against the practice might have. If this group is dropped from the sample, the correlation between stating that

1. Author's interview with charitable trust director RL, June 7, 2011, Mukogodo.

early marriage should continue and daughters' marriage age rises to .6. The remaining divergence between reported attitudes and reported primary behavior may reflect both change in attitudes over time and nonnormative pressures in favor of early marriage. That is, daughters' marriage age takes into account past behavior, while believing early marriage should continue reflects only current attitudes. It is entirely possible that those families who subjected their daughters to early marriage in the past have genuinely changed their minds about the practice in subsequent years. In addition, families who in principle oppose early marriage may face unforeseen financial hardship and thus marry off a daughter earlier than planned.

Third, the descriptive statistics presented in table 6.1 show that community-wide ethnic heterogeneity and local elites' support for the international norms track community-wide primary behavior change. Oldonyiro, the community that has experienced the lowest level of behavior change, also has the lowest level of interethnic interaction and the fewest people who believe elders or chiefs want circumcision and early marriage to stop.

Furthermore, multivariate analysis can be used to evaluate the impact of ethnic heterogeneity and influential norm leaders on primary behavior and intentions at the individual level, as shown in tables 6.2, 6.3, and 6.4. The main right-hand-side variables are *elders* (a dummy variable equal to one if the respondent reports that most elders want the practice to stop and zero otherwise), *chiefs* (a dummy variable equal to one if the respondent reports that most chiefs want the practice to stop and zero otherwise), and *tribes* (a dummy variable equal to one if the respondent reports encountering other tribes once a week or more and zero otherwise). I also include fixed effects for the case study areas, as well as an interaction term for tribe and the area fixed effects. In addition, the model includes control variables for distance from town, age, sex, Protestantism, and receiving the experimental treatment.[2]

The regression results support the hypothesized relationships detailed above. As expected, the indicators for lowered barriers to defection are more important for the models related to FGM than for the model on early marriage. Believing that elders and chiefs opposed female circumcision was negatively and significantly associated with the probability that the respondent has a circumcised daughter or plans to circumcise a daughter in the future. An even larger negative relationship emerges when looking only at

2. I do not include a control for education because of a selection problem. Since neither secondary nor primary education is universal, certain types of people are more likely to achieve higher levels of education than others. However, the inclusion of an educational attainment variable does not affect the significance of other right-hand-side variables. Moreover, one should not expect that educated people are significantly more immune to community pressure than the uneducated.

Table 6.2: DAUGHTER IS CIRCUMCISED OR WILL BE CIRCUMCISED
IN THE FUTURE

	(1)	(2)	(3)	(4)
	OLS		Logit[a]	
	Robust SE	Weighted/ clustered SE[b]	Robust SE	Weighted/ clustered SE[b]
Meet other tribe once a week or more	−0.150* (0.08)	−0.120** (0.05)	−0.161** (0.08)	−0.116** (0.05)
Mukogodo	−0.192** (0.09)	−0.208** (0.09)	−0.281** (0.14)	−0.289* (0.15)
Mau	−0.175 (0.19)	−0.089 (0.09)	−0.231 (0.18)	−0.119 (0.11)
Meet other tribe *Mukogodo	0.154 (0.11)	0.122* (0.07)	0.167** (0.08)	0.134** (0.05)
Meet other tribe *Mau	0.222 (0.20)	0.104** (0.05)	0.222* (0.12)	0.130* (0.07)
Elders want circumcision to stop	−0.305*** (0.11)	−0.312*** (0.09)	−0.347** (0.14)	−0.352*** (0.12)
Chiefs want circumcision to stop	−0.125** (0.05)	−0.098 (0.07)	−0.143*** (0.05)	−0.122** (0.06)
Distance from town (km)	0.002 (0.00)	0.002 (0.00)	0.003 (0.00)	0.003 (0.00)
Treatment	−0.041 (0.05)	−0.047 (0.03)	−0.062 (0.05)	−0.065** (0.03)
Female	0.060 (0.05)	0.083* (0.05)	0.076 (0.05)	0.096** (0.04)
Age	0.012*** (0.00)	0.012*** (0.00)	0.015*** (0.00)	0.015*** (0.00)
Protestant	−0.041 (0.06)	−0.029 (0.06)	−0.039 (0.06)	−0.037 (0.04)
Constant	0.414*** (0.10)	0.382*** (0.11)		
Observations	304	304	304	304

Notes: * $p<0.10$, ** $p<0.05$, *** $p<0.01$.
[a] Marginal effects coefficients.
[b] Standard errors clustered by sampling sublocation and weighted by probability of selection.

Table 6.3: PLAN TO CIRCUMCISE DAUGHTER IN THE FUTURE

	(1)	(2)	(3)	(4)
	OLS		Logit[a]	
	Robust SE	Weighted/ clustered SE[b]	Robust SE	Weighted/ clustered SE[b]
Meet other tribe once a week or more	−0.193** (0.09)	−0.124** (0.05)	−0.281** (0.12)	−0.171** (0.07)
Mukogodo	−0.300*** (0.11)	−0.260** (0.11)	−0.439*** (0.14)	−0.371*** (0.12)
Mau	−0.321* (0.18)	−0.205 (0.20)	−0.443* (0.23)	−0.278 (0.25)
Meet other tribe *Mukogodo	0.163 (0.14)	0.108 (0.08)	0.254* (0.14)	0.165* (0.09)
Meet other tribe *Mau	0.385** (0.19)	0.210 (0.16)	0.441*** (0.17)	0.274 (0.17)
Elders want circumcision to stop	−0.355*** (0.10)	−0.396*** (0.11)	−0.422*** (0.12)	−0.467*** (0.13)
Chiefs want circumcision to stop	−0.168** (0.07)	−0.173** (0.07)	−0.214*** (0.07)	−0.235*** (0.08)
Distance from town (km)	0.001 (0.00)	0.001 (0.00)	0.001 (0.00)	0.001 (0.00)
Treatment	−0.129** (0.05)	−0.163* (0.08)	−0.155** (0.07)	−0.197* (0.10)
Female	−0.057 (0.06)	−0.054 (0.06)	−0.068 (0.07)	−0.066 (0.07)
Age	0.005** (0.00)	0.005** (0.00)	0.006** (0.00)	0.007** (0.00)
Protestant	−0.181** (0.08)	−0.175** (0.06)	−0.217** (0.10)	−0.221*** (0.09)
Constant	0.868*** (0.13)	0.845*** (0.14)		
Observations	271	271	271	271

Notes: * $p<0.10$, ** $p<0.05$, *** $p<0.01$.
[a] Marginal effects coefficients.
[b] Standard errors clustered by sampling sublocation and weighted by probability of selection.

intention to circumcise, a result that is consistent with expectations since parents who circumcised their daughters many years ago could not have been influenced by the current attitudes of elders and chiefs. Thus, believing that most elders oppose female circumcision is associated with at least a

Table 6.4: DAUGHTER WAS MARRIED BEFORE AGE 18

	(1)	(2)	(3)	(4)
	OLS		Logit[a]	
	Robust SE	Weighted/ clustered SE[b]	Robust SE	Weighted/ clustered SE[b]
Meet other tribe once a week or more	−0.298* (0.17)	−0.417*** (0.07)	−0.431** (0.18)	−0.544*** (0.09)
Mukogodo	−0.174 (0.21)	−0.212 (0.21)	−0.295 (0.26)	−0.325 (0.23)
Mau	−1.061*** (0.26)	−1.195*** (0.37)	−0.999*** (0.00)	−1.000*** (0.00)
Meet other tribe *Mukogodo	0.255 (0.26)	0.322 (0.22)	0.371* (0.21)	0.454** (0.18)
Meet other tribe *Mau	0.794*** (0.28)	1.016*** (0.21)	0.995*** (0.00)	1.000*** (0.00)
Elders want early marriage to stop	0.054 (0.15)	0.044 (0.12)	0.120 (0.17)	0.127 (0.17)
Chiefs want early marriage to stop	−0.095 (0.12)	0.016 (0.08)	−0.170 (0.16)	−0.040 (0.10)
Distance from town (km)	−0.005 (0.00)	−0.005 (0.00)	−0.008 (0.01)	−0.008 (0.00)
Treatment	−0.259** (0.11)	−0.357*** (0.09)	−0.374*** (0.13)	−0.482*** (0.11)
Female	−0.063 (0.11)	−0.055 (0.15)	−0.094 (0.15)	−0.078 (0.21)
Age	−0.007 (0.00)	−0.006 (0.00)	−0.013* (0.01)	−0.012 (0.01)
Protestant	0.077 (0.16)	0.057 (0.19)	0.048 (0.20)	0.012 (0.25)
Constant	1.563*** (0.26)	1.562*** (0.26)		
Observations	90	90	90	90

Notes: * $p<0.10$, ** $p<0.05$, *** $p<0.01$.
[a] Marginal effects coefficients.
[b] Standard errors clustered by sampling sublocation and weighted by probability of selection.

31-percentage-point decrease in the probability that the respondent reports having a daughter who is circumcised or will be circumcised, and with at least a 36-percentage-point decrease in the probability that the respondent reports planning to circumcise his or her daughters in the future. Along the same lines, believing that most chiefs oppose female circumcision is associated with at least a 10-percentage-point decrease in the probability that the respondent reports having a daughter who is circumcised or will be circumcised, and with at least a 17-percentage-point decrease in the probability that the respondent reports planning to circumcise his or her daughters in the future. These results are highly significant under multiple models.

With respect to early marriage, however, there is no significant relationship between the respondent's beliefs about whether elders and chiefs want early marriage to stop and the probability that he or she has a daughter who was married underage. Because the local norm supporting early marriage exhibits low local salience, the social barriers to defection are also low. Thus, individuals can make their own decisions about whether or not to subject their daughters to early marriage, without having to seriously consider the larger community's views. With female circumcision on the other hand, the local norm supporting it is highly salient, such that individuals will be inclined to look to local elites for a sign that the norm might be softening.

One might, however, be concerned about omitted variable bias with respect to the relationship between individuals' reported beliefs about local elites' attitudes and individuals' own behavior. First, individuals who are disposed to embrace the international norm against FGM might be more likely to interact with chiefs and elders who feel the same way. This could be a reflection of the fact that people in general tend to seek out like-minded others, or of the fact that the transnational campaign against the practice has simply had a simultaneous effect on both local elites and the general population in the communities where it is operational. The first case is unlikely because neither traditional elites nor ordinary citizens are particularly mobile—in these communities, people rarely move far from the area in which they were born—and because chiefs usually serve long terms at their posts. Thus, there is not much opportunity to alter the set of local elites with whom one interacts. The second case is more problematic, but I attempt to control for this possibility through the inclusion of community-level fixed effects. This shows that the relationship between chiefs' and elders' attitudes and individual behavior persists even when any general effect of activism on the community as a whole is taken into account.

A second potential area of concern is that individuals' beliefs about local elites' attitudes might not closely track with elites' actual attitudes. Chiefs and elders may be claiming an allegiance to the international norm against FGM that is not matched by their actual beliefs and behavior, and people in their community may be misled. However, even if such misrepresentation is occurring, it is not a problem for the theory. What matters for communal behavior change is *perceptions* of local elites' attitudes, not their true attitudes. For the purpose of explaining an individual's decision-making calculus, believing that chiefs and elders support norm change is equivalent to chiefs and elders actually supporting norm change.[3] So long as the formation of this belief occurs *prior* to individuals' decisions about behavior, the source and veracity of the belief is ultimately irrelevant to the story. It is also possible, however, that individuals who have defected from the local norm supporting female circumcision are attempting to justify their defection to themselves by exaggerating the extent to which the local norm has really weakened—essentially trying to convince themselves ex post that they haven't really violated local expectations about appropriate behavior. Yet while this sort of self-deceptive thinking may be taking place, it cannot explain away the entire relationship between local elites' attitudes and individual behavior. Specifically, the relationship persists, and is in fact stronger, when the outcome variable is restricted only to future intentions with respect to circumcision, a scenario in which ex post rationalization is not possible. Overall, then, while the empirical evidence cannot definitively show a causal relationship between the attitudes of chiefs and elders and individuals' own behavior, it is certainly consistent with this causal story. The theoretical account also seems to be the most plausible explanation for the empirical relationship.

Also consistent with expectations, frequent interaction with members of other ethnic groups is negatively and significantly associated with the probability that the respondent reports having a daughter who is or will be circumcised, but only in Oldonyiro. The same holds true for the probability that the respondent plans to circumcise his or her daughter in the future, and for the probability that the respondent reports that his or her daughter was married before age 18. Compared to living in Oldonyiro and meeting people from another ethnic group less frequently than once a week, living in Oldonyiro and meeting people from another ethnic group once a week or more is associated with at least a 12-percentage-point decrease in the probability that the respondent reports having circumcised or planning to circumcise a daughter, at least a 12-percentage-point decrease in

---

3. In any case, there is no way to independently verify chiefs' and elders' true attitudes, because if they are willing to misrepresent themselves to their own community, they are likely also willing to misrepresent themselves to external observers. Indeed, community members' reports about local elites' attitudes are almost certainly closer to the objective truth than elites' self-reported attitudes, since it is undoubtedly harder to hide one's true beliefs from friends and neighbors than to hide them from a foreign researcher. I will further discuss the various incentives for misrepresentation in chapter 7.

the probability that the respondent plans to circumcise a daughter in the future, and at least a 30-percentage-point decrease in the probability that the respondent has a daughter who was married underage. By contrast, there is no significant difference between those Mukogodo residents who interact with other ethnic groups frequently and those who interact with other ethnic groups infrequently. In Mau, there is almost no variation across individuals in the frequency of interaction with other ethnic groups, so it is difficult to conclude anything definitive about the effect of ethnic heterogeneity on behavior.

These results support the theoretical expectation that the exit option and the demonstration effect provided by normative out-groups are most relevant when a community has experienced minimal norm change, as is the case for respondents in Oldonyiro. For respondents in Mukogodo and Mau, enough people have already abandoned FGM that those who are considering following suit know that their daughters will have access to an in-group marriage market, even if that market is somewhat circumscribed. Similarly, those individuals considering abandoning female circumcision and early marriage will be less influenced by any out-group demonstration effect because they can already witness the effects of norm change within their own group.

Again, while the empirical evidence is consistent with the theoretical account, I cannot decisively show a causal relationship between ethnic heterogeneity and individual behavior change. It is possible that certain types of people are both more inclined to embrace the international norms against FGM and early marriage and more likely to interact with other ethnic groups. However, to mitigate the risk of omitted variable bias, I control for the most likely factors, specifically the distance that the respondent lives from town (town residents were both more open to change and more likely to meet members of other ethnic groups), the respondent's age (young people were more open to change and more likely to meet members of other ethnic groups), and community fixed effects (some regions have higher levels of activism and higher levels of ethnic heterogeneity than others).[4]

In sum, then, the survey data provide good support for the theoretical account of primary behavior change in response to the norm conflicts around FGM and early marriage. The empirical evidence suggests that it is neither easy nor impossible to abandon the local norm supporting FGM, and that the norm supporting early marriage is also vulnerable to change.

4. Women were more open to change than men but less likely to meet members of other ethnic groups, probably because they are less likely than men to travel from home on a regular basis.

It further shows that ethnic heterogeneity is a strong predictor of individual behavior change for a community in the early stages of a norm transition away from both FGM and early marriage, and that believing local elites oppose FGM is a strong predictor of individual behavior change for communities in both early and more advanced stages of transition. Finally, the evidence suggests that levels of ethnic heterogeneity and elite activism also predict the extent of behavior change at the community level.

QUALITATIVE EVIDENCE

The qualitative interviews provide more robust support for these findings. In each case study area, I find clear signals about the state of local norms and the impetus for behavior change.

Oldonyiro

Interviewees in Oldonyiro reported almost no change in behavior related to either female circumcision or early marriage. With respect to FGM, one local government official said that "every girl who is to be married off has to be circumcised,"[5] while a police officer reported that circumcision "is rampant and the Samburu community is still a big problem."[6] Most interviewees reported that there had been no decline in the practice and that all women still undergo it.[7] According to a government official, "If it has gone down, it might be by just 1 percent. It is very high."[8] A local activist confirmed that "as much as we are trying to tell [people here] that FGM is not an important [practice], FGM is still there. It is still very high, very high indeed. Right now it is still constant. They will even cut uncircumcised girls from [neighboring] Samburu District if they marry into this community."[9] Early marriages persist at a similarly high and constant rate.[10] One government official estimated that "almost 50 percent, or even higher, go and marry before the age of 18. If you don't take the girls to school, you can't

5. Author's interview with children's officer SJ, July 14, 2008, Oldonyiro.
6. Author's interview with police child and gender officer PL, July 21, 2008, Oldonyiro.
7. Author's interview with public health workers I and Y, July 25, 2008, Oldonyiro.
8. Author's interview with gender social development officer AG, July 22, 2008, Oldonyiro.
9. Author's interview with former church women's development coordinator LL, October 14, 2008, Oldonyiro.
10. Ibid.

expect [early marriage] to decline. The girls aren't liberated to say, 'I don't want to be married.'"[11]

In Oldonyiro, the local norm supporting female circumcision is still taken very seriously. The chief of Kipsing Administrative Location said that girls would never even consider resisting female circumcision, because it is tradition.[12] Others concurred that girls themselves want to be circumcised because "they fear not getting a husband,"[13] and because if they aren't cut they will be ostracized.[14] "The problem with the Samburu, once you don't [get circumcised], you're considered an outcast."[15] In contrast, the local norm supporting early marriage is less punitive; while female circumcision is required by the culture, early marriage is not.[16]

The few exceptions to the local norms' dominance prove the rule because of the response they elicited from the community. FN was 15 when she became pregnant, but she had not yet been circumcised.[17] At that point, her mother tried to have her circumcised, because a baby born to an uncircumcised woman is taboo and as a result may be given away or even killed through the forced ingestion of tobacco. However, FN refused to be cut. She said that she resisted because one of her primary school teachers had warned her class that the practice was dangerous and illegal, after another girl at the school experienced severe bleeding following her circumcision and had to be hospitalized.

The reaction to both FN's decision and her teacher's intervention was harsh. The teacher belonged to the Meru ethnic group, and after he spoke out against circumcision, the Samburu teachers at the school, who all supported the practice, reported him to the head teacher and he was transferred to a different school. In FN's case, she initially faced harassment from the other students at her school, and she said that peer pressure is an important factor in explaining why so many girls want to be circumcised. Still, she resisted, but when she became pregnant, some of the elder women in the community threatened to forcibly abort her pregnancy. This led FN to run away from home until after her son was born. As far as FN knew, she was the only girl in her community who had ever refused to be circumcised. She said that other girls were too afraid to resist the practice, because the *wazee* would put a curse on them so that they couldn't get married or have children.

11. Author's interview with children's officer SJ, July 14, 2008, Oldonyiro.
12. Author's interview with location chief, May 6, 2008, Oldonyiro.
13. Author's interview with NGO director JL, June 12, 2008, Oldonyiro.
14. Author's interview with public health workers I and Y, July 25, 2008, Oldonyiro.
15. Author's interview with children's officer SJ, July 14, 2008, Oldonyiro.
16. Ibid.
17. Author's interview with FN, May 6, 2008, Oldonyiro.

A case of interference in an early marriage met with a similarly harsh response. A local nurse, JK, discovered that an elderly man intended to marry off his 10-year-old daughter as repayment for a debt (*Saturday Standard* 2008). The intended husband was 55 years old and had three other wives. To prevent the marriage, JK took the girl to the district children's office. However, with the debt still outstanding, the girl's father then decided to offer another daughter in marriage. The second daughter, who was only six years old, was quickly circumcised and married the following day. When JK discovered this, she involved the police, who arrested the father and rescued the girl. Because of her actions, JK received death threats from members of the community, and was ultimately forced to leave the area and seek employment elsewhere.

The overall lack of norm change in Oldonyiro, and the punishment meted out to the rare defector, can be attributed partly to the low level of interaction with members of respected noncircumcising ethnic groups and to the reluctance of local elites to speak out against these practices. Many Samburu in Oldonyiro interact only with other Samburu or Maasai, so there aren't many opportunities for intermarriage. Moreover, Samburu view the only other ethnic group with a significant presence in the area—the Turkana—as being of a lower status, and there is some history of tension between the groups, so the demonstration effect is less prominent.[18] Indeed, in cases of intermarriage between Samburu and Turkana, it is more likely that a Turkana girl will be circumcised than that a Samburu girl will be able to escape circumcision.[19] Thus, perhaps the best chance for the diffusion of the international norms across ethnic groups is when the Samburu in Oldonyiro meet Maasai from neighboring Mukogodo who have already given up these practices.[20]

Interviewees also pointed to the importance of local elites in guiding others' behavior, while emphasizing those elites' extreme reluctance to join the ranks of norm leaders. Elders and chiefs in particular were singled out as having the respect of the local population and the greatest ability to lead others toward change, if only they were willing to take the first step.[21] But instead, these elites are "not involved [in the anti-FGM campaign], because they might lose credibility [with

18. Author's interview with student association member JP, June 19, 2011, Oldonyiro; charitable trust director ML, June 20, 2011, Oldonyiro; CBO board member LL, June 13, 2011, Oldonyiro.

19. Author's interview with CBO director FL, October 8, 2008, Oldonyiro.

20. Author's interview with police child and gender officer PL, July 21, 2008, Oldonyiro.

21. Author's interview with district officer, July 21, 2008, Oldonyiro.

the community]. Even they themselves may be practicing. Also, they fear criticism."[22] Even though some of these local leaders are younger or educated, they don't speak out against the practices because "they fear what the community will say. They assume it's hard to stop these things."[23] Overall, interviewees overwhelmingly agreed that chiefs and elders had not played an active role in promoting norm change, and that they didn't want female circumcision or early marriage to stop.[24] Indeed, only one interviewee, a local government official, suggested that chiefs were willing to intervene to prevent FGM and early marriage.[25]

Far from assisting in the transnational campaign, most people instead perceived local elders to be an impediment to norm change. "When the old people will die, we will change, because right now, it is the old people who are pushing" for the continuation of these practices.[26] Girls don't want female circumcision or early marriage, but their grandparents insist.[27] The *wazee* are the keepers of tradition, and so they perpetuate these practices.[28]

Overall, then, Oldonyiro is stuck in the status quo, with very high and constant levels of both FGM and early marriage. Most people in the community, both young and old, are committed to the local norms supporting these practices, and few question the value of maintaining them. For those rare individuals willing to deviate from the status quo, the communal response has been decisive and harsh. Ultimately, the combination of ethnic homogeneity and local elites' resistance to transnational activism suggests that meaningful primary behavior change in Oldonyiro will still be some time in coming.

Mukogodo

In Mukogodo, by comparison, the early stages of behavior change are already underway. One hint that norm change is a relatively recent

22. Author's interview with public health workers I and Y, July 25, 2008, Oldonyiro.
23. Author's interview with former church women's development coordinator LL, October 14, 2008, Oldonyiro.
24. Author's interview with police child and gender officer PL, July 21, 2008, Oldonyiro.
25. Author's interview with children's officer SJ, July 14, 2008, Oldonyiro.
26. Author's interview with former church women's development coordinator LL, October 14, 2008, Oldonyiro.
27. Ibid.
28. Author's interview with FN, May 6, 2008, Oldonyiro.

phenomenon is the lack of consensus among interviewees about whether FGM and early marriage were actually declining. Estimates for the prevalence of female circumcision ranged from less than 50 percent on the low end[29] to 99 percent on the high end.[30] A number of interviewees believed that no change had taken place,[31] noting that the "community is a stubborn one."[32] One interviewee said that "people still believe they should do this,"[33] while another remarked that even schoolgirls still want to be circumcised. "We are telling them, but it is hard to convince the girls not to do it."[34]

Yet many others thought that a slow decline in the incidence of female circumcision had begun,[35] particularly in response to the campaign against the practice.[36] According to one interviewee, "It's curving downwards, slowly by slowly. Towards the beginning they thought [the activists were] talking rubbish, but with time things are changing slowly by slowly."[37] Another interviewee noted, "At first they were not welcoming at all. They were resisting. Slowly it is changing. It's very difficult to go and tell people all of a sudden to leave this [practice]. It is a continuous process. Somehow it has [declined]. Not a lot, but slowly. Every year there is some change."[38] A third agreed that "it has declined, and I am expecting it to decline further."[39] A pastor observed that while people who were new to his congregation could sometimes be driven away by his preaching against FGM, many others who had heard the message for a long time were starting to change.[40] And according to one teacher, "Some girls refuse, and some parents don't allow their girls to undergo FGM."[41]

Signs of nascent change abound. One interviewee noted that, while it used to be taboo for a man to marry an uncircumcised girl, in recent years some local men had married uncircumcised women from other tribes, and nobody in the community really challenged these marriages.[42] Several interviewees volunteered that their own daughters had not been and would

29. Author's interview with CBO director AM, July 5, 2008, Mukogodo.
30. Author's interview with head teacher AR, July 1, 2008, Mukogodo.
31. Author's interview with medical officer CL, July 6, 2008, Mukogodo.
32. Author's interview with head teacher AR, July 1, 2008, Mukogodo.
33. Author's interview with Chief P, June 18, 2008, Mukogodo.
34. Author's interview with head teacher MK, July 1, 2008, Mukogodo.
35. Author's interview with community development officer MO, July 2, 2008, Mukogodo; Chief RS, July 10, 2008, Mukogodo.
36. Author's interview with children's services officer FW, June 4, 2008, Mukogodo.
37. Author's interview with education officer EW, July 2, 2008, Mukogodo.
38. Author's interview with CBO board member MK, July 24, 2008, Mukogodo.
39. Author's interview with former CBO chairman JL, July 13, 2008, Mukogodo.
40. Author's interview with Pastor S, June 17, 2008, Mukogodo.
41. Author's interview with head teacher LM, July 10, 2008, Mukogodo.
42. Author's interview with Pastor S, June 17, 2008, Mukogodo.

not be circumcised,[43] and a local government official even reported that he had formed a de facto anti-FGM club with his friends so that none of their daughters would be cut.[44] Another interviewee remarked that there were a number of activist men in the community who had publicly declared that they wouldn't circumcise their daughters.[45]

Early marriage also appears to have been on the decline for the past few years.[46] According to a chief, "It's starting slowly, slowly. Many years ago, our community married girls when they were very young. Now, the numbers are being reduced" by as much as 90 percent in the last decade.[47] Once again, though, there are those who believe that such change has not occurred[48] or has been overreported.[49] Part of this discrepancy appears to come from a sharp divide between girls who are enrolled in school and girls who are not; parents who see the value of education have been less likely to pull their daughters out of school to get married.[50] Several teachers confirmed that while the girls at their schools have faced declining rates of early marriage, nothing has changed for those living in the interior and not attending school.[51] Unfortunately, "the number of girls out of school here is very high."[52]

While efforts to eradicate early marriage haven't met with too much resistance, the challenges facing anti-FGM activists were substantial.[53] One interviewee argued that "the rigid customary practices of the communities, particularly the Maasai and the Samburu, prevent change."[54] While educated girls can resist early marriage, it is much more difficult to resist circumcision, since uncircumcised women are isolated and forced to marry outside the community.[55] Although girls are gaining awareness about their rights with respect to both practices, circumcision is simply too central to the Maasai tradition for that awareness

43. Author's interview with CBO board member MK, July 24, 2008, Mukogodo.
44. Author's interview with district commissioner AM, June 18, 2008, Mukogodo.
45. Author's interview with NGO worker AL, July 24, 2008, Mukogodo.
46. Author's interview with former CBO chairman JL, July 13, 2008, Mukogodo; NGO worker AL, July 24, 2008, Mukogodo.
47. Author's interview with Chief P, June 18, 2008, Mukogodo.
48. Author's interview with medical officer CL, July 6, 2008, Mukogodo.
49. Author's interview with community development officer MO, July 2, 2008, Mukogodo.
50. Author's interview with head teacher LM, July 10, 2008, Mukogodo.
51. Author's interview with head teacher AR, July 1, 2008, Mukogodo.
52. Author's interview with community development officer MO, July 2, 2008, Mukogodo.
53. Author's interview with Pastor S, June 17, 2008, Mukogodo.
54. Author's interview with children's services officer FW, June 4, 2008, Mukogodo.
55. Author's interview with Chief P, June 18, 2008, Mukogodo.

to translate easily into behavior change.[56] The district commissioner confirmed that "if you become pregnant and you have not been cut, culturally you are just supposed to be escorted to another community."[57] One teacher reported that there were still the "traditional beliefs that if the girl is not circumcised, no one will marry her" and she won't be treated as an adult.[58] Another teacher agreed: "When the FGM is done, that signifies that you are a grown-up, you are a woman," so girls themselves are reluctant to abandon the practice.[59] All of this pressure means that "even for those who are practicing it, they still know it is not good." Although they would rather not circumcise their daughters, they do it because it is required by the culture.[60]

This divergence between beliefs and behavior makes the activist's task that much more difficult. "You become a bad person in the community" when you are the only one speaking out against these practices.[61] Because of the culture, "You really have to make a lot of effort. You have to train them that these are the bad things [about FGM]. But you can't just go and tell them to stop it."[62] According to the director of one local organization that works on many topics related to women's rights and empowerment, "The reason why I find that FGM is far more challenging is because of peer pressure, and because of the rite of passage which is part of a community as a whole, a culture. All of the other projects related to women are going on well in terms of going and increasing respect for women. So these are bearing fruit. But when it comes to having direct influence and [successful] initiatives with regard to FGM, the [achievements] are normally a bit more sporadic."[63]

Still, ethnic heterogeneity and activism by some local elites helped to mitigate the influence of the local norms. A number of interviewees pointed to the impact of interacting with people from other tribes, particularly through intermarriages. According to the district commissioner, "The thing that is assisting [norm change] is the intermarriages," because people in other ethnic groups are "not very keen on FGM."[64] A chief agreed that, in the town centers especially, people change their views when they

---

56. Author's interview with Chief SK, June 18, 2008, Mukogodo.
57. Author's interview with district commissioner AM, June 18, 2008, Mukogodo.
58. Author's interview with head teacher MK, July 1, 2008, Mukogodo.
59. Author's interview with head teacher AR, July 1, 2008, Mukogodo.
60. Author's interview with CBO board member MK, July 24, 2008, Mukogodo.
61. Author's interview with head teacher AR, July 1, 2008, Mukogodo.
62. Author's interview with medical officer CL, July 6, 2008, Mukogodo.
63. Author's interview with CBO director JK, April 15, 2008, Mukogodo.
64. Author's interview with district commissioner AM, June 18, 2008, Mukogodo.

intermarry with other ethnic groups and "adapt to their [spouse's] culture."[65] The demonstration effect is also at work, as people become "civilized" through their interactions with other tribes like the Kikuyu and the Meru.[66] This effect is felt at all levels of the community, including when Maasai children interact with children from other groups at school and are exposed to their ideas.[67]

One interviewee broke down the ethnic heterogeneity effect further, arguing that which other tribe a group interacts with matters significantly. He said that the southern Maasai, including those living in Mau, were the most likely to abandon local norms supporting female circumcision and early marriage, because they meet and intermarry with many people from the Kikuyu community, which is a high-status group in Kenya that doesn't generally engage in these practices. In Mukogodo, it is the people who live near the main town center, Dol Dol, who have been most exposed to new ideas and other ethnic groups. Comparatively, the people who live in the Mumonyot area of Mukogodo, which is far from Dol Dol and also close to Oldonyiro, are more committed to the traditional practices because the main group they interact with is the Samburu, which shares the same cultural norms. He argued that the Samburu are the most traditional of all the Maa-speaking groups.[68]

In terms of local elites' stance on FGM and early marriage, the record is mixed, which is consistent with a community that has experienced relatively limited norm change. Many interviewees suggested that chiefs and other elders were reluctant to change their own behavior or to speak out openly against the practices, either because they themselves still genuinely supported the local norm or because they were afraid of how the community would respond. "The elders want to continue [with these practices], so they will tell their people not to change. They become a stumbling block. The elders, if you start talking about FGM, you will start to see some movements [toward the door]."[69] Many chiefs apparently feel the same way,[70] with one teacher reporting that the brother of an assistant chief married an underage girl and that chiefs in general would collude with other local elites to protect perpetrators of FGM and early marriage.[71]

65. Author's interview with Chief P, June 18, 2008, Mukogodo.
66. Ibid.
67. Author's interview with Chief RS, July 10, 2008, Mukogodo.
68. Author's interview with former CBO worker SK, June 18, 2008, Mukogodo.
69. Author's interview with deputy district commissioner MD, June 18, 2008, Mukogodo.
70. Author's interview with NGO workers JK and RL, June 23, 2008, Mukogodo; medical officer CL, July 6, 2008, Mukogodo.
71. Author's interview with head teacher AR, July 1, 2008, Mukogodo.

"We have a problem in that the chiefs and some local leaders are usually involved in these cases. They usually would not like these cases to be taken to court. They like their own kangaroo courts."[72] Another interviewee agreed that "most of the chiefs are not learned. Most of them are illiterate," so they don't fully grasp the anti-FGM message. Therefore, "Most of the cases [of FGM] are not reported. Sometimes, the chiefs might know. [They keep quiet] instead of stopping the issue, because they are the ones who are doing the same thing."[73] A third interviewee concurred: "The chiefs are silent on FGM because they themselves are practicing it. They don't get involved, for political reasons."[74] A fourth said, "The chiefs just go and relax. They don't do anything [to stop FGM]. The problem with our chiefs is that some are not learned. They are still deep in the culture."[75]

Interviewees also reported that chiefs were more strategic in their behavior than elders, speaking out against FGM only when more senior government officials were present.[76] "When the people who matter are there, [the chiefs] usually talk loudly. But once you depart, they usually go to their normal life. The culture binds these people together."[77] But local elites in general appear to have an easier time speaking out against early marriage.[78] One interviewee reported that chiefs don't want to speak against female circumcision because they don't want to lose power and status in the community. They leave the discussion of FGM to outsiders who don't have local status concerns, even though outsiders are less effective at persuading people. Yet when it comes to early marriage, chiefs speak out frequently.[79]

Still, a number of interviewees reported that certain local elites were at the vanguard of anti-FGM activism,[80] because "they are interacting with a wider society" and so have been exposed to different ideas and cultural practices. "A number of elites have picked up the message, despite the fact that this is a very sensitive issue. It can make you unpopular, so you have to tread carefully. It is a delicate issue."[81] One local activist reported that some chiefs had been very helpful and would talk openly against

72. Author's interview with education officer EW, July 2, 2008, Mukogodo.
73. Author's interview with community development officer MO, July 2, 2008, Mukogodo.
74. Author's interview with former CBO chairman JL, July 13, 2008, Mukogodo.
75. Author's interview with CBO director AM, July 5, 2008, Mukogodo.
76. Author's interview with head teacher AR, July 1, 2008, Mukogodo; NGO workers JK and RL, June 23, 2008, Mukogodo.
77. Author's interview with education officer EW, July 2, 2008, Mukogodo.
78. Author's interview with former CBO chairman JL, July 13, 2008, Mukogodo.
79. Author's interview with former CBO worker SK, June 18, 2008, Mukogodo.
80. Author's interview with deputy district commissioner MD, June 18, 2008, Mukogodo; head teacher LM, July 10, 2008, Mukogodo.
81. Author's interview with former CBO chairman JL, July 13, 2008, Mukogodo.

FGM, and that none of the chiefs had actively resisted anti-FGM activities in their area.[82] A second activist believed that some elders genuinely opposed FGM. "Some elders are educated. They are going out [to other communities] and they see that we are very behind. As Africans, we usually give respect to those people who have seen more of the world than most. They can compare the life other people live to the life we are living at the moment."[83]

Many interviewees agreed that chiefs and elders could play a significant role in wider communal norm change if they wanted to,[84] because people would really listen to these opinion leaders.[85] A local government official argued that "the area chief should be the person on the ground who should be used most" in the campaign, because the chiefs know every family in their area, and so they have a wide reach. This was evident in a past campaign to promote education; when the chiefs made education a priority, enrollment increased dramatically.[86] A second government worker agreed that "chiefs need to be involved a lot. The chief is the one who can actually stop FGM, and also the elders, because they are the ones who force the practices to continue. [The community] believes so much in the chiefs."[87] One local activist concluded that if somebody like the former Kenya National Assembly speaker Francis ole Kaparo (who is also a local Maasai) were to speak out strongly against FGM, it would create a big splash in the community. Although people wouldn't necessarily stop circumcising their daughters right away, it would give other elders pause and they'd start to reconsider the issue seriously.[88]

For Mukogodo as a whole, the qualitative evidence points to a community in the early stages of a norm transition. Among interviewees, there is still some confusion over whether FGM and early marriage are declining, although most seem to believe that both practices are on the wane, albeit slowly. While many people in the community are still resistant to change, especially with respect to female circumcision, those who have interacted frequently with members of other ethnic groups have been among the

82. Author's interview with CBO board member MK, July 24, 2008, Mukogodo.
83. Author's interview with CBO director AM, July 5, 2008, Mukogodo.
84. Author's interview with head teacher AR, July 1, 2008, Mukogodo.
85. Author's interview with Chief RS, July 10, 2008, Mukogodo; head teacher LM, July 10, 2008, Mukogodo.
86. Author's interview with medical officer CL, July 6, 2008, Mukogodo.
87. Author's interview with community development officer MO, July 2, 2008, Mukogodo.
88. Author's interview with former CBO worker SK, June 18, 2008, Mukogodo.

first to embrace norm change. In addition, the handful of local elites who belong to this core group of activists are beginning to speak out openly and will likely recruit others to their cause in the near future.

Mau

Of the three case study areas, the Maasai community in Mau has experienced the greatest degree of primary behavior change with respect to both FGM and early marriage, although the transition is far from complete. On the issue of FGM, virtually all interviewees agreed that the practice was declining, and disagreed only about the rate of decline.[89] Estimates of the decrease ranged from 5 percent[90] to 95 percent,[91] with many others falling somewhere in between.[92] According to the district officer, "These days, this generation, people are changing. There is a positive response" to the anti-FGM message. "Many are still undergoing [FGM], but it's in the process of declining."[93] One teacher agreed that "parents are no longer keen on forcing their girls to undergo the rite,"[94] while another believed that "the message is getting across to our people,"[95] and a government official reported that "the majority do agree [with the anti-FGM message], and they agree to change."[96] One chief claimed that "FGM is a cultural value which at the moment has outlived its usefulness in the

89. Author's interview with CBO chairwoman EN, September 11, 2008, Mau; youth officer NS, September 22, 2008, Mau; head teacher TM, September 16, 2008, Mau; NGO worker RK, September 8, 2008, Mau; Pastor MS, October 2, 2008, Mau; CBO director MS, September 15, 2008, Mau; age-set leader KK, October 2, 2008, Mau; Pastor PN, September 25, 2008, Mau; self-help group chairwoman HK, September 26, 2008, Mau; public health officer EK, September 26, 2008, Mau; head teacher SK, September 29, 2008, Mau; CBO board member AK, September 30, 2008, Mau; teacher RM, September 30, 2008, Mau.
90. Author's interview with NGO worker RK, September 8, 2008, Mau; traditional birth attendant MN, August 30, 2008, Mau.
91. Author's interview with Chief SK, September 15, 2008, Mau.
92. Author's interview with CBO director MS, September 15, 2008, Mau; CBO chairman PN, September 15, 2008, Mau; education officer MS, September 16, 2008, Mau; public health officer FM, September 22, 2008, Mau; Pastor PN, September 25, 2008, Mau; head teacher PLT, September 25, 2008, Mau; public health officer EK, September 26, 2008, Mau; head teacher SK, September 29, 2008, Mau; social development committee chairwoman VK, September 30, 2008, Mau; CBO board member AK, September 30, 2008, Mau.
93. Author's interview with district officer KA, September 1, 2008, Mau.
94. Author's interview with head teacher ASM, September 19, 2008, Mau.
95. Author's interview with head teacher SS, September 19, 2008, Mau.
96. Author's interview with district officer SM, September 12, 2008, Mau.

community. You know, things keep on changing gradually. Our campaign has made a lot of impact."[97]

There are many small signs that a shift in behavior has taken place. Several interviewees reported that the marriageability issue had become less of a concern because some Maasai men—particularly educated ones—now wanted to marry uncircumcised women.[98] One teacher said that many girls now attended alternative rites of passage in lieu of circumcision,[99] a second reported that mothers would assist him in protecting the girls at his school from FGM,[100] and a third said that when girls resisted circumcision, their parents generally respected their decision.[101] At least one traditional circumciser in the area has given up the practice, claiming that activists persuaded her that the cut was dangerous and resulted in the loss of sexual pleasure.[102] And a circumciser who was still active reported that fewer parents were having their daughters circumcised because of what they had learned from anti-FGM campaigners.[103]

Interviewees also agreed that early marriage had declined.[104] According to one government official, "In Keekonyokie and in Suswa, [early marriage] is very reduced. Here they have adopted modern ways of living."[105] A teacher agreed that the efforts of various activists had led to a significant decrease in early marriages, especially in urban areas,[106] and a government worker said, "Definitely, it is better now than in the past."[107] A local pastor and activist reported that, while early marriage was still an issue, girls understood their rights, and so many of them ran away if they were faced with an early marriage.[108] Several teachers also noted that girls' school enrollment

97. Author's interview with Chief SK, September 15, 2008, Mau.

98. Author's interview with traditional birth attendant MN, August 30, 2008, Mau; social development committee chairwoman VK, September 30, 2008, Mau.

99. Author's interview with head teacher SKK, September 23, 2008, Mau.

100. Author's interview with head teacher PLT, September 25, 2008, Mau.

101. Author's interview with head teacher VML, September 29, 2008, Mau.

102. Author's interview with former circumciser MK, August 30, 2008, Mau.

103. Author's interview with circumciser JN, October 2, 2008, Mau.

104. Author's interview with district officer KA, September 1, 2008, Mau; CBO chairwoman EN, September 11, 2008, Mau; head teacher TM, September 16, 2008, Mau; head teacher ASM, September 19, 2008, Mau; public health officer FM, September 22, 2008, Mau; head teacher PLT, September 25, 2008, Mau; self-help group chairwoman HK, September 26, 2008, Mau; head teacher VML, September 29, 2008, Mau; social development committee chairwoman VK, September 30, 2008, Mau; Pastor MS, October 2, 2008, Mau; age-set leader KK, October 2, 2008, Mau.

105. Author's interview with education officer MS, September 16, 2008, Mau.

106. Author's interview with head teacher SS, September 19, 2008, Mau.

107. Author's interview with youth officer NS, September 22, 2008, Mau.

108. Author's interview with Pastor PN, September 25, 2008, Mau.

had been increasing in recent years, and more importantly, dropouts had declined, a sure sign that early marriages were on the wane.[109]

Most interviewees reported that early marriage had declined at a faster rate than FGM, because the latter was more central to local tradition given its association with a rite of passage.[110] "Early marriage has gone down by a bigger percentage than FGM. FGM has some roots deeper in the community. It is deep-rooted in the veins of some of the community."[111] As one local activist put it, "FGM is not an easy thing. For you to come out and say 'Stop it,' you need to have deeply internalized the message. It needs courage."[112] For some, the cultural barrier is still too high, and there is a gap between those who have heard the anti-FGM message and those who have altered their behavior accordingly.[113] "The Maasai believe that girls must undergo FGM. They believe FGM must be done to girls. The government has come in and NGOs have come in to sensitize people about FGM, but all the same, it happens. Even the girl child herself is made to believe that this is the way forward."[114]

Although challenges clearly remain, the effect of ethnic heterogeneity and of local elite norm leaders has been substantial. A number of interviewees pointed to the initial importance of interaction with other ethnic groups, which is quite common in the area,[115] and particularly to the importance of intermarriage.[116] You have a "Maasai married to a Kikuyu, a Kikuyu married to a Luhya. So there are these intermarriages" that lead to adaptation.[117] One interviewee also identified something of a shaming effect. She said that Maasai owned many of the farms in the area, but they hired laborers from other ethnic groups. These laborers sent their children to school and didn't circumcise them, and some Maasai felt that it reflected badly on them if the laborers' children were educated but the Maasai farm owners' children were not.[118]

The demonstration effect provided by other ethnic groups was also relevant, because "nowadays people are intermingling" and sharing ideas.[119]

109. Author's interview with head teacher SKK, September 23, 2008, Mau; head teacher SK, September 29, 2008, Mau.

110. Author's interview with Pastor JK, September 25, 2008, Mau.

111. Author's interview with public health officer FM, September 22, 2008, Mau.

112. Author's interview with CBO chairwoman EN, September 11, 2008, Mau.

113. Author's interview with age-set leader KK, October 2, 2008, Mau.

114. Author's interview with head teacher SKK, September 23, 2008, Mau.

115. Author's interview with district officer KA, September 1, 2008, Mau; Pastor PN, September 25, 2008, Mau.

116. Author's interview with public health officer FO, September 4, 2008, Mau.

117. Author's interview with head teacher VML, September 29, 2008, Mau.

118. Author's interview with NGO worker RK, September 8, 2008, Mau.

119. Author's interview with public health officer FM, September 22, 2008, Mau.

People can see the example of education and development leading to success for people in other tribes, and even for some other Maasai, and so they begin to abandon their traditional ways because they want to emulate that success.[120] According to the district officer, "Keekonyokie is a bit better [with respect to FGM], because it is a bit cosmopolitan. There are people from other communities. It is easier for a cosmopolitan area to change, because they will copy from other tribes."[121] A local chief agreed that "this area is densely populated. We have Kenyans from all over the country. They reside together, doing business. There are groups that don't practice FGM, and their girls are better off," and so the Maasai emulate them—particularly Kikuyu and Luo—because they are successful.[122] A teacher concurred that FGM and early marriage were fading because of the influx of people from other areas, especially the Kikuyu from Central Province, since people view this group as more developed and they no longer practice FGM or early marriage. The groups mix through intermarriage and through their children, who go to school together. These other tribes "seem to be more advanced, and so their lifestyle is envied, not by the old, but by the young people."[123] Of course, at some point, the demonstration effect no longer needs to come from other ethnic groups. The process of abandoning FGM began sufficiently long ago in Mau that some uncircumcised Maasai girls are now adults and are successful in their own right, so they can serve as role models for their own community.[124]

Some local elites have also rejected FGM and early marriage. While this stance is far from universal, it appears to have made greater inroads in Mau than in either Oldonyiro or Mukogodo. A few interviewees still believed that local chiefs and elders remained committed to the local norms supporting these practices.[125] With chiefs, "Some of them shy off from talking about FGM, because they are very much attached to their own culture."[126] According to a local activist, it is rare for chiefs to talk about these practices, because they are circumcising their own daughters.[127] A teacher agreed: "When you go to barazas [community meetings], they do talk about FGM, but when you go to their homes, you realize that they are still doing

120. Author's interview with CBO chairwoman EN, September 11, 2008, Mau.
121. Author's interview with district officer SM, September 12, 2008, Mau.
122. Author's interview with Chief SK, September 15, 2008, Mau.
123. Author's interview with head teacher SK, September 29, 2008, Mau.
124. Author's interview with head teacher SS, September 19, 2008, Mau.
125. Author's interview with head teacher VML, September 29, 2008, Mau.
126. Author's interview with education officer MS, September 16, 2008, Mau.
127. Author's interview with social development committee chairwoman VK, September 30, 2008, Mau.

it."[128] Beyond their own beliefs, local elites may also be reluctant to take action against a popular practice[129] because they are still part of the culture and they fear the community response.[130] While "the chiefs can be compromised" when it comes to FGM, they are more willing to speak out against early marriage.[131]

By contrast, a handful of interviewees believed that elders' and chiefs' response to the transnational campaign was straightforwardly positive. Several people reported that the chiefs speak out against FGM and early marriage a lot, especially in the *barazas*,[132] and a public health worker believed that the decline in early marriage was the direct result of the unified actions of the local administration.[133] But most interviewees agreed that local chiefs' and elders' commitment to the international norms was more mixed.[134] Some elders have heard and embraced the campaign's message about FGM and early marriage, and some chiefs will get involved to protect girls from these practices.[135] However, "It is not uniform. The chiefs are also human beings, and they are from the community. The learned ones embrace change. But some of the chiefs would also want to please their community, because this is their community. You might find that the person who is marrying [an underage girl] is the brother of the chief. Then they will not take action."[136]

According to the district commissioner, chiefs do talk about FGM when they hold their semimonthly *barazas*, but when he visits the area himself to talk about FGM, he can tell by the attendees' reactions whether the different chiefs have spoken about the practice extensively. He said that some chiefs do a better job than others.[137] Several interviewees agreed that the Suswa chief in particular was especially supportive of anti-FGM and anti-early-marriage efforts,[138] but when it comes to other chiefs, "Not all of them are as positive."[139] In Keekonyokie, some believed the head chief was less than fully committed to the cause,[140] although others viewed his

128. Author's interview with teacher RM, September 30, 2008, Mau.
129. Author's interview with public health officer SM, September 22, 2008, Mau.
130. Author's interview with Pastor PN, October 2, 2008, Mau.
131. Author's interview with head teacher SK, September 29, 2008, Mau.
132. Author's interview with youth officer NS, September 22, 2008, Mau; public health officer EK, September 26, 2008, Mau; Pastor PN, September 25, 2008, Mau.
133. Author's interview with public health officer SS, September 22, 2008, Mau.
134. Author's interview with district officer KA, September 1, 2008, Mau.
135. Author's interview with head teacher TM, September 16, 2008, Mau.
136. Author's interview with district officer SM, September 12, 2008, Mau.
137. Author's interview with district commissioner AR, September 4, 2008, Mau.
138. Author's interview with NGO worker RK, September 8, 2008, Mau; head teacher SS, September 19, 2008, Mau; head teacher PLT, September 25, 2008, Mau.
139. Author's interview with CBO chairwoman EN, September 11, 2008, Mau.
140. Author's interview with NGO worker RK, September 8, 2008, Mau.

commitment as being more substantial.[141] Some concluded that it was simply difficult to know what chiefs believed with any certainty. According to a public health worker, while one local chief was "so instrumental" in the campaign, "being a Maasai, he might not enforce what is in the law." Although he opposes the practices in public, one cannot know what he does in private—it is possible that he is conspiring with the community to hide cases of FGM and early marriage.[142]

Overall, though, the evidence seemed to indicate substantial behavior change among at least some local elites, and many interviewees agreed that the effect on the wider community had been and would continue to be significant.[143] As the district officer described it, "The ones who people can listen to the most are elders and opinion leaders. These elderly people are the custodians of the Maasai law. If they decide to change, people will change."[144] One teacher believed that "the moment the local leaders see the sense of campaigning against early marriages, against FGM, the campaign will succeed."[145] When elder men finally decide to speak out against these practices, "It will be one day, game over," because they are the most important opinion leaders in the community.[146]

For Mau as a whole, the abandonment of local norms supporting female circumcision and early marriage appears to be at an intermediate stage, in which both practices are still common, but enough people have already defected that the repercussions for such defections are minor. While some Maasai still hold tightly to local tradition, the high level of interaction with other ethnic groups and the activist role played by some local elites has allowed others in the community to walk away from these practices.

CONCLUSION

The collision between international and local norms forces individuals to make difficult choices, especially when local norms are highly salient to group identity. Individuals must weigh their own beliefs against their community's expectations when deciding whether to change their primary

141. Author's interview with head teacher SKK, September 23, 2008, Mau.

142. Author's interview with public health officer SS, September 22, 2008, Mau.

143. Author's interview with CBO chairman PN, September 15, 2008, Mau; self-help group chairwoman HK, September 26, 2008, Mau; social development committee chairwoman VK, September 30, 2008, Mau.

144. Author's interview with district officer SM, September 12, 2008, Mau.

145. Author's interview with head teacher SS, September 19, 2008, Mau.

146. Author's interview with Pastor PN, September 25, 2008, Mau.

behavior and embrace an international norm. Certain community-level factors play a significant role in speeding the process of genuine behavior change. I have shown that, particularly when there are significant barriers to defection from local norms, as is the case with female circumcision, high levels of group heterogeneity and local elite activism can shift an individual's decision calculus enough that they are willing to abandon traditional practices, and also that early defections have an additive effect that make subsequent defections less costly. Thus, communities that meet these conditions may eventually find themselves experiencing a norm cascade that takes them toward eventual international norm compliance. In the next chapter, however, I will look at how incentives created by a norm conflict lead some individuals to choose to change their secondary behavior and rhetoric rather than (and occasionally in addition to) their primary behavior.

CHAPTER 7

Explaining Local Misrepresentation of Normative Commitments

In the previous chapter I argued that under certain conditions, individuals and communities are in the process of making genuine changes in their normative commitments in response to transnational activism. Specifically, where local norm salience is low, as with early marriage, individuals will generally be able to make their own independent choices about their behavior, such that change at the community level occurs somewhat idiosyncratically. Where local norm salience is high, however, as with female circumcision, individuals must factor in not only their own personal preferences but also the preferences of other group members. As a result, one should expect to observe behavior change first among individuals who have strong preferences to defect as well as access to good exit options from the local norm, and one should expect that communities with many such individuals will experience a greater degree of norm change.

But though some primary behavior change does appear to be occurring in the case study areas, the signal can become somewhat muddled to the extent that people choose to change other, secondary aspects of their behavior or to change their rhetorical stance on the competing international and local norms. In chapter 2 I drew on work in social psychology and argued that individuals' reputational and material concerns could lead them to project an image of norm compliance that diverged from their true normative commitments. In particular, individuals—especially local NGO and CBO workers—might rhetorically embrace international norms for strategic reasons insofar as they hope to please donors and thus to benefit financially from the international aid system. In addition, individuals might legitimately value the good opinion of transnational activists to the extent that they view them as having power and prestige, particularly if they wish they could comply with the international norm.

While such rhetorical change is likely to be most effective when attempting to hide local-norm-compliant behavior from external groups, individuals can also make changes to their secondary behavior in an attempt to conceal their primary behavior from local observers. For a practice like female circumcision, this could involve circumcising a daughter in private, cutting her at an earlier age, and using a less severe version of the cut so as not to attract the attention of local activists and authorities.

Beyond attempts to conceal local-norm-compliant behavior from proponents of the international norm, one may also observe attempts to conceal international-norm-compliant behavior from proponents of the local norm. Though the availability of such a strategy within a close-knit community may be limited, it is still potentially attractive for those who have embraced the international norm but wish to minimize negative social sanctions from their community.

Thus, in the face of a norm conflict, individuals may choose to attempt to conceal their true normative commitments from one side or the other, to the extent that misrepresentation or hiding is viable and to the extent that they anticipate some reputational or material advantage from doing so. A number of observable implications can be derived from this account. First, all else equal, individuals should be more likely to misrepresent their normative commitments to prestigious audiences than to low-status audiences. Second, individuals should be more likely to misrepresent themselves and hide their behavior when they anticipate material advantages from doing so. Third, the greater the material advantage associated with perceived support for the international norms—as is present for local NGO and CBO workers—the greater should be the probability of misrepresentation. Fourth, individuals should be more likely to attempt to misrepresent themselves and hide their behavior as the probability of success increases—they should be more likely to misrepresent themselves to international activists than to local activists, and to hide circumcisions from local activists than to hide early marriages from local activists. And fifth, individuals in communities that have had higher levels of exposure to activism against FGM and early marriage should be more likely to misrepresent themselves and to hide their behavior. I evaluate these implications by drawing on the survey experiment and the qualitative interviews.

EXPERIMENTAL EVIDENCE

Survey Design

The larger survey contained an experimental component to evaluate individuals' willingness to make claims that differed from their true normative commitments.[1] Survey respondents were randomly assigned to treatment and control groups. While all of the respondents were asked the same set of questions, those assigned to the treatment group received priming statements emphasizing an international audience interested in the outcome of the survey.

The first priming statement appeared at the beginning of the survey:

> This questionnaire was developed in consultation with American researchers from Yale University. These researchers will look at the responses you give and share them with organizations and policymakers in other countries, like the United States and England, and with international organizations like the United Nations. The results will also be shared with international newspapers, like the *New York Times*, that are read by millions of people around the world.

A second statement appeared directly before a series of personal opinion questions, to remind respondents that their opinions were of particular interest to an international audience:

> Now I would like to ask about your opinions on circumcision and marriage. The American researchers who have developed this survey are especially interested in the answers you provide to these next questions, as are the international organizations and foreign policymakers with whom the Americans are working. Because circumcision and early marriages are issues that the Americans and the United Nations care about very deeply, they will be looking at your answers to help them make decisions about future programs and policies.

The control group received a version of the questionnaire that included priming statements about the presence of a local audience, in order to ensure that any recorded treatment effect was not simply a response to the signal about the presence of an audience generally, as opposed to an

---

1. There is no evidence that Africans in general or Kenyans in particular are uniquely prone to making false commitments to international norms. Studies conducted in the United States have found evidence of a "social desirability" bias in survey response, on topics ranging from voting behavior and charitable giving (Parry and Crossley 1950) to racial prejudice (Phillips and Clancy 1972). A number of cross-national studies have also identified social desirability effects in a wide range of cultural contexts (see, e.g., Smith, Smith, and Seymour 1993; Williams, Satterwhite, and Saiz 1998).

international audience specifically. The two control group priming statements were worded similarly to those of the treatment group, and read as follows:

> This questionnaire was developed in consultation with some other people from this area. [ILAMAIYO / Pastoralist Women for Health and Education / Tasaru Ntomonok Initiative] will look at the responses you give and share them with the community. The results will also be shared with newspapers that are read by people in this area.

> Now I would like to ask about your opinions on circumcision and marriage. [ILAMAIYO / Pastoralist Women for Health and Education / Tasaru Ntomonok Initiative] is especially interested in the answers you provide to these next questions, as are other organizations from this area. Because circumcision and early marriages are issues that [ILAMAIYO / Pastoralist Women for Health and Education / Tasaru Ntomonok Initiative] and these other local organizations care about very deeply, they will be looking at your answers to help them make decisions about future programs and policies.

If respondents in the treatment group respond systematically differently to questions about their attitudes and behavior than respondents in the control group, this will be supporting evidence that at least some individuals faced with a norm conflict are willing to hide their true preferences and actions in the hope of gaining some type of benefit from the international community. The survey experiment thus provides the opportunity to quantify a proclivity for misrepresentation of normative commitments that has often been suspected but has rarely been directly tested.

Measuring Attitudes, Experiences, and Behavior

As discussed in previous chapters, the survey included a number of indicators of attitudes, experiences, and behavior associated with FGM and early marriage. Table 7.1 presents descriptive statistics. In expressing their attitudes, 40 percent of respondents reported that they thought *female circumcision should be stopped*, while 46 percent thought it should continue and 14 percent said their attitude depended on other circumstances. Thirty percent of respondents also reported that their *view on female circumcision had changed*, while 26 percent reported that there were *no benefits associated with female circumcision*. A further 53 percent reported that they would *prefer their son marry a circumcised woman*. With respect to early marriage,

Table 7.1: DESCRIPTIVE STATISTICS

	Oldonyiro	Mukogodo	Mau	All areas	Observations
Attitudes					
Believe circumcision should be stopped	0.097 (0.02)	0.428 (0.04)	0.571 (0.04)	0.402 (0.02)	592
Circumcision view has changed	0.089 (0.02)	0.417 (0.04)	0.336 (0.04)	0.298 (0.02)	588
Believe circumcision has no benefits	0.103 (0.02)	0.162 (0.03)	0.432 (0.04)	0.258 (0.02)	596
Prefer that son marry a circumcised woman	0.821 (0.03)	0.549 (0.04)	0.333 (0.04)	0.529 (0.02)	597
Believe early marriage should be stopped	0.147 (0.03)	0.621 (0.04)	0.900 (0.02)	0.616 (0.02)	592
Early-marriage view has changed	0.087 (0.02)	0.537 (0.04)	0.200 (0.03)	0.283 (0.02)	589
Believe early marriage has no benefits	0.235 (0.03)	0.578 (0.04)	0.898 (0.02)	0.620 (0.02)	584
Experiences					
Circumcised	0.941 (0.02)	0.900 (0.04)	0.855 (0.04)	0.891 (0.02)	302
Married before age 18	0.688 (0.08)	0.427 (0.10)	0.319 (0.07)	0.432 (0.05)	134
Behavior and intentions					
Daughter is circumcised	0.542 (0.05)	0.569 (0.05)	0.520 (0.05)	0.542 (0.03)	326
Plan to circumcise daughter in future	0.843 (0.04)	0.479 (0.06)	0.551 (0.06)	0.596 (0.03)	293
Daughter married before age 18	0.749 (0.09)	0.604 (0.10)	0.384 (0.10)	0.551 (0.06)	96

Note: Means weighted by inverse sampling probabilities. Standard errors in parentheses.

62 percent reported that they thought *early marriage should be stopped*, whereas 29 percent thought it should continue and 9 percent said their attitude depended on other circumstances. Twenty-eight percent said their *view on early marriage had changed*, and 62 percent reported that there were *no benefits associated with early marriage*.

Respondents were also asked about their own experiences. Among female respondents, 89 percent reported that they themselves were *circumcised*, while 43 percent reported that they had *married before the age of 18*, for a mean female marriage age of 18.5. Finally, respondents were asked about their past behavior and intended future behavior with respect to their daughters, since parents are the primary decision-makers over female circumcision and early marriage. Among respondents with daughters, 54 percent stated that at least one *daughter had been circumcised*, while among respondents with married daughters, 55 percent reported that the most recently married *daughter had been married before age 18*, for a mean marriage age of 17.5.[2] In terms of future behavior, 60 percent of respondents with uncircumcised daughters stated that they intended to *circumcise their daughters in the future*.

Evaluation

Before reporting treatment effects, it is important to establish that the treatment and control groups were indeed very similar in pretreatment covariates, since simple randomization will occasionally produce uneven results by chance. Table 7.2 presents the results of comparison-of-means tests for a series of demographic indicators. Among these only the difference in means for age is significant at the 10 percent level.

To investigate the presence of treatment effects in a regression framework, I once again employ both linear and nonlinear models to regress the array of outcome variables described above on *treatment* (a dummy variable equal to one if the respondent received the international audience prime and zero if the respondent received the control group prime). As a robustness check, I include two specifications—one in which I regress the various outcome variable indicators on the international audience treatment alone, and one in which I regress the outcome variables on the treatment and a series of controls (specifically, age, sex, Protestantism, exposure to other tribes, beliefs about elders' and chiefs' attitudes, and study area fixed effects).

Table 7.3 presents all specifications of both the linear and nonlinear analyses for each of the outcome variables. The results show a clear difference between the impact that receiving the treatment prime has on expressed attitudes and experiences, compared to the impact it has

---

2. The percentage reporting that at least one daughter had been circumcised is low because the question was asked of all respondents with daughters, even if those daughters were too young to be circumcised at the time.

Table 7.2: COMPARISON OF COVARIATE MEANS
BY TREATMENT (INTERNATIONAL AUDIENCE)

	Treatment	Control	Difference in means
Female	0.50	0.50	0.00
	(0.03)	(0.03)	(0.04)
Age	35.75	33.36	2.39*
	(0.89)	(0.89)	(1.26)
Level of education	1.36	1.31	0.05
	(0.10)	(0.10)	(0.14)
Married	0.68	0.63	0.04
	(0.03)	(0.03)	(0.04)
Pastoralist	0.51	0.45	0.06
	(0.03)	(0.03)	(0.04)
Protestant	0.33	0.37	−0.04
	(0.03)	(0.03)	(0.04)
Catholic	0.36	0.32	0.04
	(0.03)	(0.03)	(0.04)
Traditional religion	0.21	0.25	−0.04
	(0.02)	(0.02)	(0.03)
Radio ownership	0.58	0.51	0.07
	(0.03)	(0.03)	(0.04)

Note: p < 0.10

on expressed past behavior and intended future behavior. Among the behavior-related outcome variables, I find that receiving the treatment prime is negatively and significantly associated with the probability that the respondent plans to circumcise his or her daughter in the future, and with the probability that the respondent reports having a daughter who was subjected to early marriage.[3] These results are robust across all models,

---

3. With respect to the intention to circumcise, one could argue that this is not necessarily misrepresentation, since the action hasn't happened yet. It is possible that simply referencing an international audience in the context of the survey causes respondents to genuinely reevaluate their future plans. However, the priming statements do not specify what international actors believe, which means the prime is only meaningful if the respondent already has information about international audience preferences prior to participating in the survey. In that case, simply being reminded of the existence of an international audience is unlikely to cause a respondent to change his or her true plans on the spur of the moment—if that change were going to happen, it would almost certainly have occurred when the respondent first learned about the international audience's preferences, prior to the treatment intervention.

Table 7.3: IMPACT OF INTERNATIONAL AUDIENCE TREATMENT
ON RESPONDENTS' ATTITUDES, EXPERIENCES, AND BEHAVIOR

Outcome variable	(1)	(2)	(3)	(4)	(5)	(6)
	OLS (robust SE)		Logit (robust SE)		Logit (weighted, clustered SE)[a]	
	Treatment only	Full model	Treatment only	Full model	Treatment only	Full model
Believe female circumcision should be stopped	0.016 (0.04)	0.016 (0.04)	0.016 (0.04)	0.026 (0.05)	0.006 (0.03)	0.022 (0.04)
Believe early marriage should be stopped	0.047 (0.04)	0.049 (0.03)	0.047 (0.04)	0.083 (0.06)	0.043 (0.03)	0.087 (0.04)
Believe circumcision has no benefits	−0.010 (0.04)	0.001 (0.03)	−0.010 (0.04)	0.004 (0.04)	−0.034 (0.04)	−0.001 (0.04)
Believe early marriage has no benefits	−0.010 (0.04)	0.021 (0.03)	−0.010 (0.04)	0.025 (0.05)	−0.041 (0.05)	0.001 (0.06)
Prefer that son marry a circumcised woman	0.008 (0.04)	−0.012 (0.04)	0.008 (0.04)	−0.015 (0.05)	0.032 (0.03)	0.005 (0.06)
Circumcised	0.022 (0.03)	−0.010 (0.03)	0.022 (0.03)	−0.005 (0.01)	0.028 (0.04)	−0.006 (0.02)
Married before age 18	0.009 (0.09)	0.024 (0.09)	0.009 (0.09)	0.027 (0.10)	−0.081 (0.13)	−0.086 (0.15)
Daughter is circumcised	−0.010 (0.06)	−0.060 (0.05)	−0.018 (0.06)	−0.117 (0.08)	−0.013 (0.03)	−0.127*** (0.05)
Daughter married before age 18	−0.216** (0.10)	−0.235** (0.11)	−0.216** (0.10)	−0.285** (0.12)	−0.304*** (0.08)	−0.355*** (0.12)
Plan to circumcise daughter in future	−0.116** (0.06)	−0.126** (0.05)	−0.116** (0.06)	−0.154** (0.07)	−0.145** (0.07)	−0.193* (0.10)

Notes: * *p*<0.10, ** *p*<0.05, *** *p*<0.01.
[a] Standard errors clustered by sampling sublocation and weighted by probability of selection.
Each cell is the product of a separate regression. Models 3–6 show marginal effects coefficients.
"Treatment only" models show the coefficient on the international audience treatment variable in a regression of the outcome variable on treatment. "Full" models show the treatment coefficient in a regression of the outcome variable on treatment and other covariates with hypothesized relationships to the outcome variable. These covariates are age, sex, Protestantism, frequency of exposure to other tribes, beliefs about elders' and chiefs' attitudes, and study area fixed effects.

and the coefficients carry magnitudes that suggest the treatment effect is substantively meaningful. Receiving the treatment decreases the probability that a respondent will report plans to circumcise his or her daughter in the future by between 11 and 19 percentage points, and decreases the probability that a respondent will report having a daughter who was subjected to early marriage by between 21 and 35 percentage points.[4] In addition, I find that receiving the treatment prime is negatively associated with the probability that the respondent reports having a daughter who was subjected to female circumcision, but this finding is significant in Model 6 only.

While people in all three case study communities were more likely to report international-norm-compliant past behavior and intended future behavior if they happened to be in the treatment group, the extent of this tendency varied. Figures 7.1 and 7.2 show the treatment effect on respondents' reports that they plan to circumcise a daughter in the future and that their most recently married daughter was married underage, disaggregated by study area. The graphs show that respondents in Oldonyiro are substantially less likely to misrepresent themselves than respondents in Mukogodo or Mau. This finding fits well with expectations, since people who have a low level of awareness about an international norm ought to be less likely to perceive any advantage to deceiving international actors. Moreover, the graphs also show that in both the treatment and control groups, respondents from Oldonyiro were much more likely than respondents from Mukogodo or Mau to report that they had a daughter who was married underage or that they intended to circumcise a daughter in the future—the lower observed treatment effect in Oldonyiro is thus highly unlikely to be the product of greater compliance with the international norm.

Overall, then, when the outcome variables of interest relate to past behavior and intended future behavior, treatment effects are consistently large for the entire sample and vary across the study communities in predicable ways. However, as table 7.3 shows, there appears to be no meaningful treatment effect for any of the outcome variables related to attitudes

---

4. The larger treatment effect for the early-marriage variable may be a product of the fact that only parents who were actually able to estimate the age of a daughter at her marriage were included in the sample. Among Maasai and Samburu, ages are sometimes unknown and are more likely to be known among those in higher education brackets. More educated individuals are also more likely to be aware of international norms against FGM and early marriage, and thus to misrepresent themselves in response to the international audience treatment.

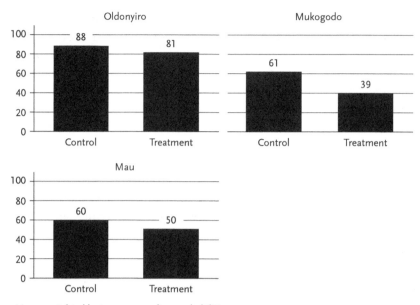

Means weighted by inverse sampling probabilities

Figure 7.1: Treatment effect by study area: Percentage of respondents who intend to circumcise a daughter in the future

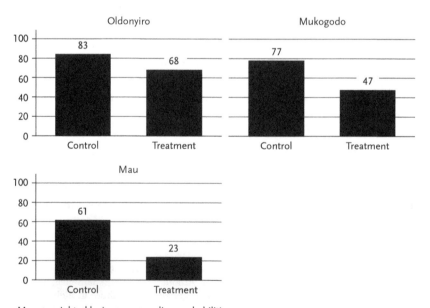

Means weighted by inverse sampling probabilities

Figure 7.2: Treatment effect by study area: Among respondents with married daughters, percentage whose most recently married daughter was married before age 18

and experiences.[5] Among the five indicators for attitudes toward female circumcision and early marriage and the two indicators for respondents' own experiences, the treatment coefficients are substantively small and none are statistically significant. In addition, while receiving the treatment has a consistently positive association with the probability that the respondent reports thinking female circumcision should stop and thinking early marriage should stop, the signs of the treatment coefficients for the remaining attitude and experience variables are not consistent across models.

Thus, there is a clear divergence between the treatment's impact on behavior-related variables and its impact on attitude- and experience-related variables. What might explain this? As discussed in chapters 2 and 6, the social expectation of compliance is a unique and important feature of norms. The local norms supporting female circumcision and early marriage can have a strong influence even on those individuals who would like to defect from them; agreeing with the international norm is not the same thing as actually complying with it. Indeed, survey respondents were consistently less supportive of female circumcision and early marriage when expressing their opinions than when expressing their past behavior and intended future behavior (see table 7.1). Many of the people who state opposition to FGM may genuinely mean it, and yet still plan to circumcise their daughters in the future. Similarly, parents may regret having subjected them to female circumcision or early marriage in the past. Especially since activism against FGM and early marriage is a relatively recent phenomenon in the case study communities, some of these parents may have adopted the international norm in the period after their daughters' circumcisions or early marriages.

These findings are largely in line with the psychology literature on self-presentation and deception, which argues that while straightforward material concerns may motivate some image management, many individuals primarily seek psychological rewards such as appearing consistent, modern, good, and so on. These motivations are likely to be magnified when the audience is perceived as having high status. The findings are also consistent with constructivist IR theory on the power of norms to create desirable personas. Within this framework, respondents who have been truly fully compliant with the international norm have no reason to misrepresent their attitudes and behavior in the presence of an international audience. Similarly, those who are truly fully compliant

5. Beyond the content of the response, there were also no significant differences between the treatment and control groups in the refusal rate for individual questions.

with the local norm—still a majority of the population—may have little interest in misrepresenting their attitudes and behavior. In the face of transnational activism, continued true believers in the local norm are least likely to view the international audience as having high status, and thus to seek a good reputation in the eyes of that audience. The individuals with inconsistent attitudes and behavior, on the other hand—the individuals who want to defect from the local norm, but are in the present or were in the past not quite confident enough to do so—have the incentive to impress an international audience but not the past behavior or intended future behavior to support it. I argue that these ambivalent individuals are most likely to misrepresent their behavior and intentions, so that they appear consistent with the international norm and with their own attitudes.[6]

An alternative explanation for the observed treatment effect, however, is that respondents misrepresent themselves to an international audience not because they hold that audience in high regard, but rather because they don't think it is possible to influence the way the international audience thinks about FGM or early marriage (whereas this might be possible if the audience were local), and so the most expedient strategy is to tell the international audience what it wants to hear and hope that leads the international audience to back off. Yet if this were the case, one would also expect to observe a treatment effect with respect to attitude-related survey questions.

Another alternative explanation is that respondents are actually honestly representing their behavior and intentions to the international audience, and misrepresenting their behavior and intentions to the local audience. That is, some respondents are actually complying with the international norms, but report that they are complying with the local norms. But while this alternative story is possible, it is not consistent with the bulk of the qualitative evidence presented below. Moreover, there is no obvious reason for respondents to misrepresent themselves in this way, since the local audience depicted in the control priming statements consists of local NGOs and press that are also publicly opposed to FGM and early marriage (which most respondents would know since the communities are small and local NGOs tend to play a highly visible role in those communities). Thus,

---

6. Under these conditions, one would not expect respondents to misrepresent their own experiences with female circumcision and early marriage, since as discussed in chapter 3, girls have little control over either event. Since their parents ultimately held the decision-making power, female respondents who reported being circumcised or married before they turned 18 would not necessarily see any inconsistency in admitting this while simultaneously voicing opposition to the two practices.

both the treatment and control groups are "exposed" to an audience that opposes these practices—the critical difference between the two audiences is that the international audience has the ability to provide psychological benefits because it is a high-status group.[7] In addition, even the treatment group was exposed to the local audience, if in a more limited way—as discussed in chapter 1, local NGOs served as the public face of the survey for all respondents, not just those in the control group. So if respondents were inclined to misrepresent themselves to a local audience, this would affect both the treatment and control groups, and thus could not account for the observed treatment effect. This is not, however, a claim that the control group point estimates are therefore necessarily "true"—as with any survey, the possibility of some kind of reporting bias remains, but any such bias ought to affect the treatment and control groups equally.

It is important to note that some kind of material motive might also be at work in these communities in addition to the psychological motive. However, the survey experiment was not designed to pick up material incentives for misrepresentation. The international audience prime presents that audience as remote—the international actors referenced in the priming statement are not described as being physically present in the community—and thus respondents could reasonably conclude that they were unlikely to receive any direct personal material benefits based on their answers.[8] Perhaps a more likely source of material reward would be the local NGOs referenced in the local audience priming statement (though, as discussed in chapter 2, most local NGOs are funded by international actors, and thus international actors would be the original source of any material rewards disbursed by local NGOs). It is possible that some control group respondents perceived this and chose accordingly to represent their behavior and intentions as conforming to international norms. But if that is indeed the case, then the observed treatment effect is actually an underestimation of the true treatment effect.

7. One could perhaps imagine a scenario in which respondents misrepresent themselves to a lower-status group like local NGOs precisely because those local NGOs are not viewed as important enough to require thoughtful, honest responses, but this reading of the evidence is inconsistent with the social psychology literature on self-presentation, which suggests that misrepresentation is most likely to occur when one confronts a powerful or otherwise high-status audience.

8. However, this is in no way to suggest that international actors cannot be a source of material reward in the real world. Indeed, the qualitative interviews demonstrate clearly that they can be, particularly when foreign NGOs and foreign NGO workers visit rural communities as part of their activism. The only claim being made here is that it would be implausible for respondents in the treatment group to think that they might receive any material rewards from the international audience as a direct result of participating in the survey.

Data from the qualitative interviews helps to more fully draw out the mechanisms underlying individuals' misrepresentation and concealment of their normative commitments. The results of these interviews produced several important findings: (1) Misrepresentation to international audiences is occurring; (2) reputational concerns motivate some misrepresentation to international audiences, particularly because foreigners are viewed as having high status; (3) material concerns motivate some misrepresentation to international audiences, especially among local civil society workers; (4) material concerns also motivate misrepresentation and secondary behavior changes directed at local civil society groups and local authorities; (5) both reputational and material concerns motivate (limited) misrepresentation and secondary behavior change directed at proponents of local norms; and (6) the extent of misrepresentation and secondary behavior change varies across the three case study communities.

First, interviewees pointed to the commonness of misrepresentation to international audiences—many community members were inclined to impress, please, or simply humor international activists who come to their area, but these efforts did not necessarily signal a change in underlying behavior. According to one teacher, "With the campaign, even those who have undergone the cut [female circumcision], they will say 'I have not undergone the rite [of passage].'"[9] If somebody in the community encounters a foreign activist, "They'll just hear [what the activist has to say], but they'll not take heed."[10]

Misrepresentation is made easier by the fact that foreign activists come into the area for only very brief visits, so there is no way for them to ascertain whether the people they meet are representing themselves honestly.[11] This conforms to the expectation, derived from the social psychology literature, that misrepresentation will increase with the probability of being believed. According to several interviewees, community members will listen to an outsider, but as soon as these people leave, they will go back to their culture.[12] In Oldonyiro there are no locally based NGOs, so when outside NGOs come in, people have an attitude that the local government children's officer described

9. Author's interview with head teacher ASM, September 19, 2008, Mau.
10. Author's interview with education officer MS, September 16, 2008, Mau.
11. Author's interview with head teacher AR, July 7, 2008, Mukogodo.
12. Author's interview with gender and social development officer AG, July 22, 2008, Oldonyiro; public health workers I and Y, July 25, 2008, Oldonyiro; former church women's development coordinator LL, October 14, 2008, Oldonyiro.

as "'OK, we'll sit, we'll listen,' but when it comes to practicing [female circumcision], they'll still do it."[13]

Second, reputational motives featured heavily in the explanations for misrepresentation to international audiences. Again conforming to expectations proposed in the literature on image management, many interviewees emphasized the high status that international actors wielded, especially among Maasai and Samburu populations.[14] As one pastor put it, "They like white people like you. Since the beginning, they like hearing from the white [people]. They view them like friends."[15] Indeed, interviewees attributed a host of positive attributes to foreigners. Some focused on their perceived intelligence and knowledge, while others noted such qualities as altruism and honesty.[16] One CBO board member said community members "just think that these people want to help them."[17] A public health officer said of local residents that "once they see a *mzungu*, they normally view a *mzungu* like a person who knows everything. They normally say a *mzungu* is trustworthy. A *mzungu* does not cheat."[18] And one local government official said that "when a *mzungu* comes, first they will admire him or her, because *wazungu* [westerners, plural] are rare. They are positive about the *wazungu*."[19]

Many perceived attributes of foreigners ultimately reflected unequal power relations, especially in terms of wealth, modernity, and worldliness. Community members "believe *wazungu* are always right. They believe a *mzungu* is advanced."[20] "They always say, 'A *mzungu* is correct. They've got all the facts.'"[21] Some people also "think that [foreigners] have gone

13. Author's interview with children's officer SJ, July 14, 2008, Oldonyiro.
14. This high regard for westerners was not universal, however. According to one NGO worker, "An outsider will not be listened to. They will just say, 'Who is this foreigner?'" (Author's interview with NGO worker AL, July 24, 2008, Mukogodo.) A CBO chairman concluded that because of cultural differences, foreigners "shouldn't go alone to speak directly to the people. People will say that they have just come with their cultural beliefs, so they will not respond to the message. People know that *wazungu* have never done FGM, so they don't know what it's like." (Author's interview with CBO chairman PN, September 15, 2008, Mau.) And a teacher appeared disenchanted with the supposed contributions of international actors. Local residents "will just say, 'This is another *mzungu* . . . We have seen so many who've come, and [then] they go, and everything remains the same.'" (Author's interview with head teacher VML, September 29, 2008, Mau.)
15. Author's interview with Pastor PN, September 25, 2008, Mau.
16. Author's interview with head teacher MK, July 1, 2008, Mukogodo.
17. Author's interview with CBO board member MK, July 24, 2008, Mukogodo.
18. Author's interview with public health worker FM, September 22, 2008, Mau.
19. Author's interview with district officer SM, September 12, 2008, Mau.
20. Author's interview with community development official MO, July 2, 2008, Mukogodo.
21. Author's interview with public health worker DL, October 8, 2008, Oldonyiro.

so many places."[22] One pastor placed these beliefs in historical perspective: "People know that *wazungu* brought education and Christianity [to Kenya], so now they think *wazungu* will bring change and modernization. People desire change because they see that other groups and people have better and more comfortable lives."[23] A traditional birth attendant went so far as to say that Maasai don't think very highly of themselves, so they want to emulate outsiders who are better respected or, at least by some measures, more successful.[24]

Of course, just because international actors enjoy a high-status reputation doesn't mean that local residents can easily change their actual behavior in order to conform to international norms. People might be impressed by outsiders, but they are unlikely to wholly reject female circumcision or early marriage, "even if you take . . . a *mzungu* there."[25] According to one CBO director, "A *mzungu* [can't] influence our community, even though [community members] think the *wazungu* are superior. The *wazungu* are more modern, and they want to change the world fast, but our community thinks we should be changing gradually. They'll listen, but most Africans don't share very much [with] *wazungu*."[26] In the face of significant local pressure to continue to conform to local norms, it makes sense that some people, when they encounter international actors, would choose to hide the fact that they are still practicing FGM and early marriage. The cross-pressures from international and local actors make misrepresentation an attractive option. If people hide their behavior, "It's because they want to belong to both sides. They want to look civilized, and at the same time they want to be looked upon by their kinsmen as ones who have maintained their culture."[27]

Over and above the basic reputational benefits of image management, one CBO chairwoman suggested that some people pretend to agree with foreigners who come to talk about FGM and early marriage out of a general sense of politeness. It is bad manners to walk out of a meeting, so "they will sit down and listen to you, but they will not take anything [to heart]."[28]

Third, while the survey experiment was not designed to capture material incentives for misrepresentation, quite a few of the qualitative interviewees stated that in addition to reputational concerns associated with status,

22. Author's interview with CBO worker AK, September 30, 2008, Mau.
23. Author's interview with Pastor MS, October 2, 2008, Mau.
24. Author's interview with traditional birth attendant MN, August 30, 2008, Mau.
25. Author's interview with head teacher MK, July 1, 2008, Mukogodo.
26. Author's interview with CBO director AM, July 5, 2008, Mukogodo.
27. Author's interview with deputy head teacher VML, September 29, 2008, Mau.
28. Author's interview with CBO chairwoman EN, September 11, 2008, Mau.

material interests also motivated many community members to misrepresent their attitudes and behavior to international activists. These material incentives are significant because many Maasai and Samburu live on subsistence incomes and are dependent on some form of outside assistance. Many seem to believe that expressing agreement with activists' priorities is a good idea since activists bring resources into the community.

According to one chief, "Most of the NGOs were started by people from outside Kenya. They are always welcome, because some have benefited a lot from [these] people."[29] Another chief reported that "they respect the NGOs because most of the NGOs fund the community."[30] Some interviewees discussed this relationship between activists and locals quite explicitly. According to one teacher, "A person coming from far [away] would only have an impact if he brings some rewards," such as sponsoring girls to go to secondary school,[31] starting a clean water project,[32] or building a school or hospital.[33] Another reported that "a *mzungu* is different from any other African. The rural [people] will be very keen to listen to you. They think that you will be bringing maybe some financial support. They will always see that maybe they will get something from you. They expect some advantage, some support from that *mzungu*."[34] A public health officer claimed that if you're a foreigner, "You are likely to be listened to so much. You will be given so much attention, because [locals] think that you always come with goodies."[35]

Although international activists may encounter misrepresentation from the general communities they are attempting to persuade, it is also sometimes the case that local NGO and CBO workers themselves misrepresent their true beliefs and behavior for material benefit, since they are essentially being paid to speak out against FGM and early marriage. According to one CBO director:

> After some time we felt that a lot of organizations are simply just using double-speak. They talk so passionately against these things when it comes to seeing white people like you, donors, other kinds of [foreigners], but when it comes to the reality on the ground, they don't have the confidence to say that exactly. Because of peer pressure, and because of the rite of passage which

29. Author's interview with Chief SK, September 15, 2008, Mau.
30. Author's interview with Assistant Chief FL, October 14, 2008, Oldonyiro.
31. Author's interview with head teacher ASM, September 19, 2008, Mau.
32. Author's interview with CBO chairwoman HK, September 26, 2008, Mau.
33. Author's interview with district officer, July 21, 2008, Oldonyiro.
34. Author's interview with head teacher SL, October 8, 2008, Oldonyiro.
35. Author's interview with public health officer SS, September 22, 2008, Mau.

is part of the community as a whole, the culture, it is very difficult to just [change]. Right now, those people spearheading this [campaign], all of their daughters, and also their sisters, are undergoing the operation without a voice.[36]

Another local activist reported that many grassroots NGO workers marry circumcised girls, so they've lost credibility in the community. The local NGOs are addressing FGM because they think they will get more money from donors, so they tell foreigners what they think they want to hear.[37] According to one elder, "We see [local] activists as businesspeople. They have business minds, so they come and try to seduce us [away from FGM], because when a person stands against FGM they will get funds from outside, from groups or NGOs, maybe in the US."[38]

Fourth, individuals also appeared to engage in misrepresentation, as well as in secondary behavior change, in order to reap material benefits from or evade negative material sanctions by local civil society groups and local authorities (actors that are ostensibly interested in promoting the international norms against FGM and early marriage). On the material benefit side, when NGOs and CBOs hold events and trainings against FGM and early marriage, they usually provide food or some kind of payment to attendees, and this incentive alone can bring in hundreds of people. For example, if parents let their daughters participate in an alternative rite of passage, the whole family is likely to receive a free lunch at the ceremony, or possibly a goat. Later, though, many of these same girls will undergo a low-profile circumcision.[39]

Even basic seminars and workshops can draw crowds. People come to these seminars regardless of the topic because they are hoping for a free lunch, yet by their presence they are at least tacitly signaling their opposition to these practices.[40] "People are fond of meetings, but they aren't really persuaded by them."[41] One teacher reported that "when people hear of NGOs, they attend that meeting expecting to be given [something]. People think that NGOs are there to give out."[42] According to a priest, "You have to pay [people] when they come to listen. They call it a sitting allowance. If you pay them, at the next meeting you will have so many people, not because

36. Author's interview with CBO director JK, April 15, 2008, Mukogodo.
37. Author's interview with children's home manager HG, June 25, 2008, Mukogodo.
38. Author's interview with age-set leader KK, October 2, 2008, Mau.
39. Author's interview with NGO worker JK, June 23, 2008, Mukogodo.
40. Author's interview with head teacher AR, July 1, 2008, Mukogodo.
41. Author's interview with Father J, October 31, 2008, Mukogodo.
42. Author's interview with head teacher SKK, September 23, 2008, Mau.

of the message, but because of the payment they are getting."[43] One NGO worker recalled that when the organization first started holding meetings, they only provided sodas and other small items. Many people came to the first meeting, thinking they would receive something more substantial. But after discovering that they were only getting soda, they didn't come to any of the future meetings.[44]

Activist efforts against FGM and early marriage have also produced secondary behavior changes. In some cases, these peripheral behavior changes could still be viewed as positive, such as the adoption of a less severe circumcision procedure[45] or the use of clean razor blades to prevent the transmission of HIV,[46] but in other cases the behavioral response appeared to undermine activists' efforts to elicit meaningful primary behavior change. In particular, many individuals chose to hide circumcisions and early marriages in an effort to avoid negative material sanctions by local authorities.

Interestingly, while almost nobody believed that the Children's Act banning FGM and early marriage had produced any real primary behavior change, the law and the police did seem to be the dominant force behind individuals' efforts to hide their behavior.[47] That is, while the threat of punishment didn't seem to dissuade anybody from actually engaging in FGM or early marriage, it did drive the practices underground.[48] "These things are illegal, so they are not done out there in the light. They are mostly done in the darkness."[49] Even though arrests were rarely made, and prosecutions were even less common, many people seemed to take a "better safe than sorry" stance when it came to the government. According to an NGO worker, "They are beginning to hide. They are afraid of the law enforcement agents. They know it is unlawful, and they don't want to be the first one to be arrested."[50] Another activist agreed,

43. Author's interview with Father AG, October 8, 2008, Oldonyiro.
44. Author's interview with NGO worker RK, September 8, 2008, Mau.
45. Author's interview with circumciser JN, October 2, 2008, Mau; charitable trust director RL, June 7, 2011, Mukogodo; head teacher AR, June 9, 2011, Mukogodo; CBO worker JM, June 9, 2011, Oldonyiro; community health worker AN, July 5, 2011.
46. Author's interview with councilor OL, June 13, 2011, Oldonyiro.
47. Author's interview with district officer SM, September 12, 2008, Mau; Chief SK, September 15, 2008, Mau.
48. Author's interview with CBO board member MK, July 24, 2008, Mukogodo; CBO director AM, July 5, 2008, Mukogodo; former circumciser MK, August 30, 2008, Mau; district officer KA, September 1, 2008, Mau; NGO worker RK, September 8, 2008, Mau; education officer MS, September 16, 2008, Mau; Pastor PN, September 25, 2008, Mau; public health officer EK, September 26, 2008, Mau; CBO board member AK, September 30, 2008, Mau; age-set leader KK, October 2, 2008, Mau.
49. Author's interview with youth officer NS, September 22, 2008, Mau; CBO board member LL, June 13, 2011, Oldonyiro.
50. Author's interview with NGO worker AL, July 24, 2008, Mukogodo.

saying, "They do circumcision secretly because they fear the law," even though "they know there's no police officer who's going to get them."[51]

For FGM, this generally meant holding a smaller celebration ceremony after the cut,[52] or forgoing a celebration altogether.[53] Parents might circumcise both a daughter and a son on the same day, and then claim that the celebration was only on behalf of the son,[54] or else send their daughters to family members in other regions with less vigilant activists and authorities. Circumcisions might take place at night and behind closed doors,[55] and girls might be cut over school holidays so that they didn't miss any school during recovery and thereby raise suspicion. Girls might also be cut at an earlier age, before they were old enough to resist,[56] though there were also reports about the age of marriage increasing among schoolgoing girls.[57] Additionally, parents might simply bribe a chief or the police to keep them quiet.[58] While it is more difficult to hide an early marriage, some people still attempted to conceal them.[59] "They do early marriages very secretly because they are very much aware the government is against it."[60] One teacher reported that when parents withdrew a daughter from school to get married, they would pretend that they were simply transferring her to a different school so as not to let the headmaster know that she was actually dropping out.[61] And as with circumcision, the family might attempt to bribe a chief who has learned about the marriage.[62]

Fifth, beyond efforts to conceal one's true normative commitments from proponents of the international norms, there is also limited

51. Author's interview with CBO director MS, September 15, 2008, Mau.
52. Author's interview with NGO workers JK and RL, June 23, 2008, Mukogodo; head teacher TM, September 16, 2008, Mau; Chief NN, July 12, 2011, Mau.
53. Author's interview with social development committee chairwoman VK, September 30, 2008, Mau; CBO worker JK, June 12, 2011, Mukogodo; community health worker AN, July 5, 2011, Mau.
54. Author's interview with head teacher AR, July 1, 2008, Mukogodo; teacher RM, September 30, 2008, Mau.
55. Author's interview with police officer GM, July 2, 2008, Mukogodo.
56. Author's interview with head teacher AR, June 9, 2011, Mukogodo; CBO worker JK, June 12, 2011, Mukogodo.
57. Author's interview with women's representative EMS, July 5, 2011, Mau.
58. Author's interview with former CBO chairman JL, July 13, 2008, Mukogodo.
59. Author's interview with NGO workers JK and RL, June 23, 2008, Mukogodo; CBO chairwoman EN, September 11, 2008, Mau.
60. Author's interview with police officer GM, July 2, 2008, Mukogodo.
61. Author's interview with head teacher SKK, September 23, 2008, Mau. A similar story, about a 16-year-old girl from Mukogodo, was reported in a document obtained from the Nanyuki Children's Home.
62. Author's interview with head teacher SS, September 19, 2008, Mau.

evidence of attempts to conceal international-norm-compliant behavior from proponents of the local norms. Being among the group of early defectors from a local norm can involve significant negative material and reputational sanctions, particularly if that norm is highly salient, as in the case of female circumcision, and so some who have chosen to defect may try to keep their choice private. In fact, one interviewee reported that some women who have been persuaded by the transnational campaign against FGM have chosen to fake their daughters' circumcisions in an effort to hide the truth from their own husbands.[63] Since men are not present at circumcision ceremonies, there is no easy way for them to know whether their daughters have actually been cut. In addition to this kind of intrafamilial subterfuge, another interviewee claimed that the former Kenya National Assembly Speaker Francis ole Kaparo had faked the circumcision of his two youngest daughters in order to save face with local elders.[64] Despite the fact that Kaparo's wife was an anti-FGM activist, when his daughters refused to be cut, he was afraid to openly admit it. Instead, he pretended that his daughters had been circumcised by holding a postcircumcision celebration for the community to attend.

Sixth, consistent with the survey results, regional differences appeared to play some role in explaining how community members interacted with international and local audiences. In particular, the relative infrequency of interactions with foreigners in Oldonyiro lent an air of novelty to these exchanges that was not quite matched in the other communities. Because of this, interviewees in Oldonyiro were less likely to report that community members' interactions with foreigners were purely material or to be jaded about the possible benefits international actors could provide. More generally, interviewees in Oldonyiro were less likely than interviewees in Mukogodo or Mau to have anything at all to say about locals' responses to international pressure, because they could not speak about events that had not happened. Similarly, while hiding FGM and early marriage from local activists and authorities appeared common in Mukogodo and Mau, the lower level of activism and general awareness in Oldonyiro meant that few people felt any pressure to hide their behavior. Since many people don't know that the practices are illegal, they aren't afraid of being arrested.[65] "They don't hide. They do it openly. They have

63. Author's interview with Pastor S, June 17, 2008, Mukogodo.
64. Author's interview with former CBO worker SK, June 18, 2008, Mukogodo.
65. Author's interview with public health workers I and Y, July 25, 2008, Oldonyiro; police officer PL, July 21, 2008, Oldonyiro.

never been threatened. Even the local chiefs have never threatened, so they don't fear at all."[66]

CONCLUSION

One can conclude from the combined analyses that individuals sometimes face incentives to conceal their true attitudes and behavior in response to transnational activism. In the face of a norm conflict, some people will represent themselves honestly at the risk of alienating or angering one side or the other, and some people will try to please everyone through ultimately dishonest means. Both the survey experiment analysis and qualitative interviews show a clear tendency toward deception and subterfuge when individuals have been exposed to conflicting normative positions and believe they have something to gain from playing both sides. The quantitative data support the idea that one can derive psychological benefits from misrepresenting oneself to high-status international actors, and the qualitative data support a material benefits story in addition to the psychological one, especially for local civil society workers who depend on international donors for their livelihood. The interviews further demonstrate that strategic (and sometimes aspirational) changes in rhetoric and secondary behavior can be directed at both international and local proponents of international norms, as well as at local proponents of local norms.

That some people choose to misrepresent or hide their behavior with respect to FGM and early marriage does not automatically signify the failure of activist efforts to produce real norm change. First, the fact that many people want to be perceived as compliant with the international norm could be regarded as a first step toward primary change. Moreover, although some rhetorical norm adopters may be motivated by purely material considerations, it is clear from both the qualitative and quantitative evidence that others genuinely subscribe to the logic of the international norm or at least seek the approbation of international actors; it is only that they have not (yet) been bold enough to take the step from attitude change to behavior change.

Second, the more that people are willing to profess compliance with the international norm, the more it sends a signal to others in the community that the local norm is softening. Fellow community members will likely guess that not all of these statements are genuine, but if the local norm

66. Author's interview with former church women's development coordinator LL, October 14, 2008, Oldonyiro.

were truly unassailable, then only the most materially minded would have an incentive to misrepresent their behavior. As a new generation grows up, it may be less likely to perceive anything disingenuous in these statements, and simply take them at face value. Although no single statement of international norm compliance is above reproach, the sum total of these statements sends a message that some people are abandoning FGM and early marriage, and this may lower the barriers for others to defect in reality.

CHAPTER 8

Conclusion

THEORY AND CENTRAL FINDINGS

This book has presented and evaluated a theoretical framework for thinking about individual decision-making processes and collective changes in response to a conflict between international and local norms. Local norms can certainly evolve on their own, but as ideas and people increasingly circulate in a globalizing world, there are more opportunities for external actors to attempt to generate norm change. As a result, individuals and communities that may once have been relatively isolated are now embedded in larger networks and must weigh competing demands on their loyalties and commitments. The local targets of transnational activism are being pulled in different directions—toward local expectations on the one hand, and toward international expectations on the other.

Looking at the practices of female genital mutilation and early marriage among Maa-speaking peoples in Kenya, I argue that individuals faced with a norm conflict must make choices about their attitudes, their behavior, and the public image they present, and that these choices both influence and are influenced by the choices of others in their communities, resulting in a dynamic process of norm change.

Exposure to the international normative message is naturally the first step in this process. The level of activism on the part of international norm entrepreneurs is heavily shaped by the salience of the international norm at the international level—higher salience drives activism up as resources are made available to tackle the issue—and of the local norm at the local level—higher salience drives activism down as potential local activists shy away from vocally challenging closely held local practices. Beyond the respective salience of the international and local norms, the existing density of NGOs on the ground in any particular community also affects the level of activism. Issues such as a community's accessibility and educational provision influence its ability to attract external activists and create local ones.

Given awareness of the international norm, individuals may or may not choose to change what they think, what they do, and what they say. The first element of norm change is attitude change, and it hinges on the quality of activism as well as on individual- and issue-specific responsiveness to that activism. Unfortunately, NGOs face a set of incentives that sometimes limit the quality of the normative message they project. Whether because they have reordered or expanded their priorities to suit international donors, or whether because they fail to coordinate or evaluate in order to further the goal of self-preservation, activists at all levels may not always do everything in their power to seek out and implement the best possible programs. This problem can be exacerbated in cases of high international and high local norm salience, since each can push NGOs to pursue activities that do not match their own preferences, leading to shirking. Moreover, highly salient local norms can make individual recipients resistant to even a high-quality international normative message, as can personal characteristics (though the particular characteristics are likely to vary across issues).

Primary behavior change is the second major element of norm change and does not necessarily follow automatically from attitude change. I argue that the more salient a local norm, the more difficult it is for an individual to unilaterally defect from that norm, regardless of her desire to do so. Facing community pressure to conform, meaningful behavior change is most likely when an individual is able to mitigate the social costs of defection or when she receives signals that the local norm may be weakening. In particular, interaction with normative out-groups can reduce costs for the norm leaders by providing an exit option and a demonstration effect, while the presence of influential locals within the group of norm leaders can send a signal about norm strength to norm followers. While it may be difficult to move first, each defection makes additional defections easier.

Finally, individuals can change secondary aspects of their behavior or their public stance on the competing international and local norms. The primary advantage of engaging in this third element of norm change is that it enables individuals to conceal their true normative commitments from proponents of the international norm, and in some cases, proponents of the local norm. Individuals who take this approach may be motivated by reputational concerns, perhaps wishing to be perceived as "modern" by respected outsiders or as "traditional" by respected insiders. Alternatively, they may be motivated by material concerns, misrepresenting themselves to proponents of the international norm in order to protect themselves from arrest or to gain access to resources these proponents may be able to provide, or misrepresenting themselves to proponents of the local norm in order to shield themselves from any negative social sanctions associated with local norm defection.

How, then, do international norms diffuse across individuals and through communities? The introduction of transnational activism has the potential to catalyze communal norm change, jolting people out of the status quo. The extent to which such norm change actually occurs then depends on the distribution of likely norm leaders and norm followers within the community. One should expect to see norm leaders in communities that have received high-quality activism (more people will privately oppose the local norm) and in which many people have access to an exit option (more people will be able to limit their exposure to any social costs of defection). Furthermore, one should expect to see norm followers in communities that have many and influential norm leaders. With sufficient numbers of potential norm leaders and followers, the community may then experience a norm cascade.

Applying the theory to the issues of FGM and early marriage, I argue that the highly salient international norm against FGM boosts local exposure to the normative message, although this message is often of low quality because many of the NGOs spreading the message are not pursuing effective programs. However, the high salience of the local norm supporting FGM simultaneously depresses the quantity and quality of activism, such that attitude change is slow to emerge. Moreover, the high barrier to defecting from the local norm means that attitude change outpaces behavior change. The communities that *do* exhibit some degree of behavior change will be those in which NGO presence is significant, in which exit options from the local norm—in particular, exit through intermarriage with noncircumcising ethnic groups—are relatively plentiful, and in which locally influential people are among the group of norm leaders. With respect to early marriage, I argue that the relatively low salience of the international norm reduces activism against the practice, though the similarly low salience of the local norm means that, at least where NGO density is fairly high, those activists who do take up the cause tend to be sincere and thus provide a fairly high-quality normative message. Conditional on exposure to the message, attitude change is relatively more easily achieved, and because the barrier to defecting from the local norm is low, behavior change closely tracks attitude change.

The empirical chapters evaluated the theory with respect to the three case study communities. I find that Oldonyiro has experienced the least degree of overall norm change away from the practices of FGM and early marriage. Given the area's extreme inaccessibility and low educational provision, awareness about the international norms against FGM and early marriage is very low, and concentrated among a handful of town dwellers. From this starting point, it is unsurprising that attitude change is also extremely uncommon, and primary behavior change rarer still. The community has had few opportunities to receive a high-quality normative message against either FGM or early marriage, and the few people who might have heard one are constrained by their lack of exit options. The Samburu of Oldonyiro interact mainly with the Turkana people—a group they perceive as being inferior—and few if any local elites have been willing to take a stand against these practices. Isolated cases of resistance to the local norms have met with a harsh response from the larger community, thereby deterring others from following suit. And because there is so little awareness of the international norms, the people of Oldonyiro also have had very little incentive to hide their behavior from either international or local audiences. While Oldonyiro may yet transition away from the local norms supporting female circumcision and early marriage and embrace the international norms against these practices, such a result is many years away.

Though Oldonyiro and Mukogodo are neighbors, Mukogodo has demonstrated a substantially higher degree of community norm change. Its residents have relatively high levels of awareness about the international norms against FGM and early marriage, attributable in large part to the community's population of homegrown activists. While the area is not particularly accessible to outside organizations, it provides sufficient educational opportunities to keep its more motivated young people in the community. Many people in the area have also changed their attitudes about FGM and early marriage, although naturally the conversion between awareness and attitude change is not one-to-one. While a handful of organizations are seemingly quite dedicated to eradicating these practices, others are providing a lower-quality message, particularly when it comes to FGM. Some of these groups have been drawn to the anti-FGM campaign through the lure of available funding rather than through strong personal commitment to eradicating the practice, and others are hampered by their outsider status. In terms of primary behavior, changes have been significant if not especially large. Thus far, those individuals who interact frequently with the local Kikuyu population have been the quickest to embrace change, while more isolated individuals have held back, especially when it comes to FGM. The fact that a handful of local elites have spoken out against FGM and early marriage has also had an effect on the larger community's behavioral decisions. Overall, the course of norm change has been slow but steady and will likely pick up speed in the not-too-distant future. At the moment, many in the community are in a state of uncertainty about how to react to this trend, which may explain why so many people attempt to hedge their bets by misrepresenting their normative commitments to international and local audiences.

Of the three communities, Mau has experienced the greatest degree of change toward the international norms against FGM and early marriage. It has amassed very high levels of international norm awareness through its substantial population of local activists and its easy accessibility to external organizations. The majority of its people are also opposed to FGM and especially to early marriage—the product of a long-term and consistent campaign by both internal and external groups, though some have been less committed than others. Behavior change is still lagging significantly behind attitude change, particularly when it comes to FGM, but the buildup of awareness and attitudinal opposition suggests that a large change in behavior may take place in the near future, particularly as the younger generations grow up and have children of their own. As it stands now, the high frequency of interaction with Kikuyu and other ethnic groups, and the vocal opposition to FGM and early marriage displayed by some local elites, have contributed to a marked decline in the prevalence of both practices. Still, universal primary behavior change is sufficiently far off that many people feel compelled to misrepresent their normative commitments to international and local actors.

Though they share a culture, these three communities exhibit markedly different experiences with norm change. Still, while girls in all three communities are at lower risk of being subjected to FGM and early marriage than ever before, none of the communities has transitioned to complete compliance with the international norms. Various structural constraints and incentives have shaped individuals' access to activism and the choices they have made in response to that activism, and international norm entrepreneurs have faced significant challenges in persuading people to abandon closely held local norms in favor of international ones.

APPLYING THE THEORY TO FGM AND EARLY MARRIAGE IN OTHER CONTEXTS

Although close attention to the three case study communities is valuable in order to enable a mixed-methodological approach and the careful tracing of causal mechanisms, it is also valuable to consider how well the theory explains the extent of norm change around FGM and early marriage in other places. Throughout the empirical chapters I identified many different observable implications of the theory, which can be compared to the empirical record in additional cases.

On the issue of exposure to and awareness of the international norms against FGM and early marriage, the theory predicts that NGOs and other donor-dependent groups should be more likely to engage in activism against FGM than against early marriage in places where both practices are prevalent, and that independent local groups should be more likely to engage in activism against early marriage than against FGM. On the first count, I've already shown in chapter 1 that there is more NGO-driven anti-FGM activism worldwide than activism against early marriage. On the second count, the prediction is harder to evaluate because activism by people like religious leaders and local government officials often does not occur within the context of a formal program, and thus is difficult to track. However, an evaluation of a USAID early marriage program in Ethiopia showed that at least some religious leaders in the program areas were quite willing to take a stand against the practice, and that churchgoing girls were less likely to marry early (Gage 2009). This is at least suggestive of a general freedom to speak out against early marriage in churches.

In addition, the theory predicts that people in places with higher general NGO density will exhibit higher levels of awareness. One indication of this comes from the 2008 Egyptian DHS, which asked women whether they had received information about female circumcision in the past year.[1] Egypt is a country with a large NGO sector (it has more than 20,000 NGOs for a population of 80 million people), and so it fits with expectations that a substantial share of respondents (72 percent) reported that they had received such information (Abdelrahman 2004, 6; El-Zanaty and Way 2009, 207). Moreover, noting that Egypt's NGOs are concentrated in urban rather than rural areas, the DHS shows that 76 percent of women in urban areas had received information about female circumcision, compared to only 69 percent of women in rural areas (despite the fact that 95 percent of rural women reported having been circumcised, compared to 85 percent of urban women) (El-Zanaty and Way 2009, 197, 207; LaTowsky 1997). Thus, it appears that information about female circumcision is being disseminated in areas where NGOs happen to be, rather than in areas that exhibit the greatest need. However, a necessary caveat is that this evidence

1. Unfortunately, the DHS and MICS have never asked about exposure to activism against early marriage.

is also consistent with some alternative hypotheses, including that urban women are getting more information about circumcision because of higher educational attainment or media exposure.

No direct questions about exposure were asked of DHS respondents in Kenya, but the survey did ask women whether they had heard of female circumcision. The gap between the percentage of women who have heard of circumcision and the percentage of women who report being circumcised can serve as a very rough proxy for exposure, on the logic that uncircumcised women are more likely to know about circumcision if the country has benefited from a high level of activism. Kenyan women's awareness of female circumcision is very high (96 percent) even though its FGM prevalence rate is moderate (27 percent), and Kenya also has a high density of NGOs—by 2013 there were more than 7,000 registered NGOs in a country of 43 million people, and one estimate suggests that there are over 220,000 registered CBOs (Kanyinga, as cited in Brass 2012, 388). Kenyan women who lived in rural areas were also slightly less likely (96 percent) than women in urban areas (98 percent) to report that they had heard of female circumcision, despite the fact that women in rural areas were almost twice as likely to report that they themselves were circumcised (Kenya National Bureau of Statistics and ICF Macro 2010, 265). Again, Kenyan NGOs are disproportionately concentrated in urban areas (Brass 2012, 394).

With respect to attitude change, the theory predicts that people who have received better information about FGM and early marriage should be more likely to change their attitudes. Outside of the case study areas, the available evidence is suggestive rather than conclusive. For example, an evaluation of the Tostan program in Senegal showed that being a program participant, and thus receiving concentrated information firsthand, had a greater impact on attitudes about FGM than simply living in one of the program villages and thus receiving program information secondhand (though both were more likely to change their attitudes than individuals in villages that had not received the program) (Diop et al. 2004, 20). With respect to early marriage, the ICRW conducted a metaanalysis of evaluations of early-marriage interventions, which suggested that programs employing in-depth multipronged strategies had somewhat greater success in changing attitudes (Malhotra et al. 2011, 21–22). As discussed in chapter 2, however, there appear to be many poorly designed programs addressing FGM, and to a lesser degree early marriage, which is consistent with theoretical expectations. The theory also predicts that attitudes about FGM should be more resistant to change than attitudes about early marriage, but it isn't possible to evaluate this proposition outside of the case study areas because of a lack of comparable data for FGM and early marriage.

On the issue of primary behavior change, the theory predicts that behavior change with respect to FGM should lag well behind attitude change. Usefully, the DHS and MICS track women's attitudes about circumcision as well as the circumcision status of their daughters. A comparison of data from 14 countries shows that among circumcised female respondents, between 12 and 58 percent of those who think FGM should stop nonetheless have at least one circumcised daughter (United Nations Children's Fund 2013, 79). The theory also predicts that primary behavior change with respect to early marriage should more closely track attitude change. Unfortunately, the DHS and MICS have not collected data on attitudes with respect to early marriage, and thus it is difficult to evaluate this prediction conclusively. However, the ICRW early-marriage meta-analysis suggests that attitude change is not outstripping behavior change in program areas (Malhotra et al. 2011, 23). An evaluation of the Tostan program also showed changes in attitudes toward early marriage going hand in hand with changes in behavior (United Nations Children's Fund 2008, 47).

The theory further predicts that countries in which FGM practitioners are mixed with normative out-groups should experience greater declines in FGM prevalence, and that, contrary to Mackie (1996), declines in FGM prevalence can be gradual within communities—if, as Mackie argues, coordination is necessary, then we should only ever observe declines in FGM prevalence that exhibit a tipping point effect of minimal change followed by rapid decline within communities. My theory's predictions are consistent with the cross-national data—among countries for which DHS and MICS data are available, the largest declines in FGM prevalence have been concentrated in countries with moderate to low baseline FGM prevalence (United Nations Children's Fund 2013, 114). These are countries where at least some circumcising groups are likely to live near or among noncircumcising groups. By contrast, a country like Somalia, which has a 98 percent FGM prevalence rate (meaning that circumcising groups have essentially no opportunity to interact with noncircumcising groups), has not experienced any decline in FGM prevalence across age cohorts (United Nations Children's Fund 2013, 102). This situation persists among Somalis living in Kenya, many of whom are geographically isolated from other Kenyans because they live in refugee camps or remote areas of North Eastern Province—98 percent of Somali respondents in Kenya reported in the 2008–2009 DHS that they were circumcised, even though Kenya as a whole marked a substantial reduction in FGM prevalence between the 1998 and

2008–2009 survey rounds (Kenya National Bureau of Statistics and ICF Macro 2010, 265).[2]

In addition, though there are variations in starting point and speed of decline, only a few countries exhibit any kind of marked discontinuity in FGM prevalence across age cohorts, even at the regional level (exceptions include regions of the Central African Republic and Liberia) (United Nations Children's Fund 2013, 102–6). Notably, an evaluation of the Tostan program in Senegal—the program that is most commonly associated with the public pledge coordination strategy—shows that while daughters of women in villages that went through the program are less likely to undergo circumcision, the villages in question are not exhibiting anything close to complete village-wide abandonment (Diop and Askew 2009, 313). And despite the fact that thousands of Senegalese villages have made such public pledges, Senegal as a whole has not experienced any meaningful decline in FGM prevalence or in attitudinal support for FGM (United Nations Children's Fund 2013, 95). Moreover, a multivariate analysis of DHS data from the Gambia shows that very little of the variation in the relationship between respondents' circumcision status and their attitudes toward the continuation of female circumcision can be explained by village-level variables, which one would not anticipate if communities were coordinating (Bellemare, Novak, and Steinmetz 2015).

Finally, with respect to the issue of rhetorical and secondary behavior change, the theory predicts that misrepresentation and hiding of local-norm-compliant behavior should be directed at high-status audiences and should be more common in situations in which there are material advantages to be gained or material disadvantages to be avoided. Misrepresentation and hiding should also be more frequent in places that have had greater exposure to activism. It does appear that underreporting of FGM is more common in countries that have been exposed to a high level of activism against the practice (e.g., Mali) or in which there are strong laws against the practice (e.g., Burkina Faso) (United Nations Children's Fund 2013, 88). A longitudinal study in Ghana also showed that some women who initially reported being circumcised later denied it following the introduction of a law and an increase in the level of activism against the practice (Jackson et al. 2003). Misrepresentation

---

2. My own experience in North Eastern Province suggests the potential difficulties of promoting primary behavior change among the Somali. In 2007 I spoke with two traditional Somali circumcisers near the town of Garissa, who believed that if the clitoris was not cut when a girl was young it would continue to grow until it touched the ground. Having never before met an uncircumcised woman, they had no way of knowing that their shared belief was false.

in the later period was particularly common among younger, educated women—that is, women whose peers were actually giving up the practice, perhaps in response to activism. To my knowledge, however, misrepresentation to international and high-status audiences with regard to FGM has not been previously studied, and I could find no studies providing hard evidence of misrepresentation or hiding of any kind with respect to early marriage (which is understandable given the greater difficulty of effectively hiding early marriage).

APPLYING THE THEORY TO GIRL-CHILD EDUCATION AND DOWRY

Beyond FGM and early marriage, the overarching theoretical framework has broader ramifications for how one might think about other transnational, and perhaps intranational, campaigns. The scope of the theory covers any norm conflict in which the behavior governed by the norms is undertaken by individuals or families and cannot be adequately changed by legal regulation alone. Potential applications include environmental campaigns such as those against cut-and-burn charcoal production, whaling, overfishing, and poaching of endangered and threatened species, as well as public health campaigns to promote condom use and vaccinations. Moreover, it has applications to a host of other international norms related to gender-based violence and women's rights more broadly, including campaigns against domestic violence, sexual violence, honor killings, force feeding, bride burning, veiling, widow inheritance, and purdah. Wherever local norms lag behind international expectations, it is worth considering how communities will respond to transnational activism.

Here I will briefly apply the theory to two additional issues in the area of women's rights: education of girls in developing countries and dowry in South Asia. The norm conflicts around these issues are of particular interest because they demonstrate the two combinations of international and local norm salience that the book has not discussed in detail. That is, while FGM exhibits high international and local norm salience, and early marriage exhibits low international and local norm salience, girl-child education exhibits high international and low local norm salience (the lower-right cell in figure 2.1) and dowry exhibits low international and high local norm salience (the upper-left cell in figure 2.1).

International attention to the issue of girls' education has grown dramatically over the past several decades. The broad consensus appears to be that educating girls will help cure a variety of ills in the developing world—beyond being good for the girls themselves and a basic human right, the belief is that it will contribute to improved health outcomes for girls and their families and to broader economic growth through increased labor force participation (Plan 2012). One indicator of international commitment is that girls' education has been explicitly prioritized within the UN's Millennium Development Goals (MDGs)—eliminating gender disparities in primary and secondary school enrollment is one of the specific targets set out by the MDGs. In addition, girls' right to education has been prioritized by the Global Partnership for Education and in the Beijing Declaration and Platform for Action and Dakar Education for All Platform for Action, and has been enshrined in the Convention on the Rights of the Child and CEDAW. Many states have also made a contribution by extending free primary and sometimes free secondary education, but few developing countries are in a position to actually enforce girls' school enrollment. Thus, the highly salient international norm in favor of educating girls does come into conflict in some places with local norms that either do not value girls' education or view it as potentially threatening. For example, going to school takes girls away from potentially extensive household responsibilities, and parents sometimes view such education as pointless if they expect their daughters to marry rather than work. Some may also fear that educated girls will challenge the patriarchal status quo. Nonetheless, the salience of these local norms is relatively limited in most places (exceptions include some conservative Muslim societies that enforce strict purdah, or separation of the sexes), such that parents who do choose to educate their daughters rarely face significant negative social sanctions.

Consistent with the theory's predictions, activism in favor of girl-child education has been significant and is promoted by a diverse set of organizations. Responding to the international norm's salience, NGOs have implemented a wide range of programs cross-nationally, with the most popular being the provision of scholarships to girls and general awareness-raising campaigns about the value of girls' education. Other programs involve building schools, training teachers to improve gender sensitivity, and distributing sanitary pads so that girls do not miss school (Plan 2012). Because girls' education is such a dominant global issue, however, some of these efforts have been superficial and uneven—some NGOs that are primarily interested in other issues nonetheless recognize that it is valuable to be seen promoting education of girls (Swainson et al. 1998). Still, speaking out in favor of girl's education has also become a common activity among many groups that are not responding specifically to donor incentives, such as private sector businesses and religious leaders ("Private Sector and Foundations" 2014; "Resources on Faith, Ethics, and Public Life" 2014).

Though systematic cross-national data on attitude change about girls' education are not available, anecdotal reports suggest that, as expected given such intense campaigning in the face of weak local norms, there has been a substantial change in parents' attitudes (Raymond 2014, 12). Perhaps more importantly, it is clear that meaningful primary behavior change has kept up with attitude change. Indeed, girls' enrollment in primary and secondary school in the developing world has expanded rapidly over the past couple of decades. Global gender parity in primary schools has been effectively achieved, with only small gaps remaining in sub-Saharan Africa and western Asia (United Nations 2013). While in 1997 there were only 91 girls in primary school in the developing world for every 100 boys, by 2010 that number had increased to 97. Significant progress has also been made on secondary enrollment, particularly in western and southern Asia, where the ratio of girls to boys in secondary school increased from 74 and 75 respectively in 1997 to 91 in 2010.

By contrast, activism and observable change around the issue of dowry look remarkably different. The payment of dowry at marriage is widespread in South Asia and some other regions. The function of dowry payments is ostensibly to provide for a woman's well-being in her marriage in societies where women generally do not receive inheritances, and to enable hypergamy (the marrying of daughters into higher-status families) (Caldwell, Reddy, and Caldwell 1983). At least in South Asia, the salience of local dowry norms is very high, and families that resist the dowry system face potentially significant negative social sanctions. Most importantly, a report from India suggested that it was nearly impossible for a woman to get married without dowry (Jagori 2009). In opposition to the local norms there is an existent international norm against the payment of dowry, which argues that the obligation to pay large dowries leads to son preference and that unmet demands of large dowry lead to abuse and even murder of women by their husbands and in-laws—what has come to be known as dowry violence and dowry death (United Nations Commission for Human Rights 1997). However, this norm has not been particularly salient at the international level, receiving only minimal attention by donors and minimal recognition in international treaties and consensus documents.

As a result, activism against dowry has been minimal, and what public opposition exists is being spearheaded by local reformers who are not necessarily engaging with the international community per se. Though there was an uptick in domestic activists' attention to dowry in the 1980s, that has largely subsided (Jagori 2009). In India, for example, one organization's call for a "boycott" of marriages involving dowry payments went almost entirely unheeded, even by other women's groups (Kishwar 2005).

In addition, police and courts have been ill equipped or reluctant to enforce laws prohibiting dowry or to protect women from dowry violence. Though (rare) antidowry activism appears to be generally sincere rather than instrumentally motivated, given the degree of social pressure to conform to dowry, there are reports that even some antidowry campaigners have allowed dowry to be given or received within their own families (Kishwar 2005). Overall, attitude change and primary behavior change have been minimal to nonexistent. There appears to be very little resistance to dowry as an institution, even among women. And though systematic data about the prevalence of dowry payments have not been collected, the available evidence suggests that dowry demands in India have not declined over time and may even have increased (Bhat and Halli 1999). Dowry demands have also become more common in Bangladesh (Amin and Cain 1997). On the issue of dowry deaths, one estimate suggests that in India they increased from approximately 400 per year in the mid-1980s to some 6,000 per year in the 1990s, and some unofficial estimates have been substantially higher (Jagori 2009).

Though I have only presented brief sketches of the norm conflicts around girls' education and dowry, the broad strokes of the evidence are consistent with the predictions of the theoretical framework laid out in this book. The fact that the theory applies beyond the specific geographic context of Kenya and beyond the specific issues of FGM and early marriage gives greater credence to the generalizability of the theory as a whole.

THEORETICAL AND EMPIRICAL CONTRIBUTIONS

Overall, the work presented in this book has applications to the international relations literature on norm promotion and to the African studies literature on the politics of culture, tradition, and modernity, as well as to the study of gender violence generally and FGM and early marriage specifically.

International Norm Promotion

Within the field of international relations, the book makes new contributions with respect to the scope of the research, the theoretical approach, and the methodological strategy. In terms of scope, it adds to the small but growing IR literature on norm diffusion and implementation at the subnational level and among nonstate actors. However, to date this literature has concentrated overwhelmingly on how international norms impact non-state organizations such as corporations, industry associations, and rebel groups. My theory is unique in its focus on the micro-level processes by which individuals negotiate competing demands placed on them by international and local norms. Understanding how private individuals respond to international norm promotion is important because, as suggested above, an increasing number of international norms apply to the behavior of individuals rather than states or firms.

In fact, the book provides strong evidence that international norms actually do trickle down to the local level—even to rural areas in developing countries—and influence individuals' attitudes, behavior, and rhetoric. It also illuminates some similarities and differences between how private individuals respond to international norm promotion and how states and nonstate organizations respond. In a number of respects, individuals act a lot like organizational targets of international norms, which makes sense given that much of the state-centric theory is making assumptions about states as unitary actors that depend on individual-level social-psychological arguments. First, the neighborhood effect frequently observed among states is relevant for individuals as well—international norms diffuse more rapidly and are more quickly adopted when those around the target, whether other countries or coethnics, have already taken up the international norm. Second, the role of power players in spreading international norms is important in both the national and local contexts. The local elite effect on primary behavior change identified in my analysis parallels the outsize impact, noted in the state-focused international norms literature, that powerful states and states with "moral stature" have on the uptake of international norms by less powerful states (see, e.g., Finnemore and Sikkink 1998, 901).

Third, the empirical results show that individuals can be strategic actors in the international arena. Just as states weigh the preferences of the international community against their own preferences and the preferences of their citizens when making decisions about norm compliance, so too do individuals take the wishes of transnational activists and their own communities into account. They are not passive recipients of activism, but instead react according to their interests, sometimes in ways that international norm promoters don't anticipate. This can involve secondary changes in the practice of local norms, or it can mean that individuals simply attempt to hide their behavior or otherwise deceive activists. Thus, just as some states sign international treaties because they anticipate financial or reputational benefits from doing so, some individuals profess allegiance to international norms for similarly calculated reasons. Even at the local level, individuals often recognize that there are benefits to projecting an international-norm-compliant image. They may wish to be perceived as "modern," and they know that many local activists and external actors consider practices like FGM and early marriage to be backward. And in areas of high poverty and substantial aid dependence, individuals may also wish to receive material assistance from these actors and believe that the appearance of compliance with favored international norms will help in that effort.

However, there are a couple of important ways in which individuals are different from states and nonstate organizations, suggesting that they deserve scholarly attention in their own right. In particular, states and other corporate bodies are sufficiently large and few that transnational activists can actively monitor them. Thus, activists can directly pressure such groups to make public rhetorical and legal commitments to international norms (such as treaty ratification) and then attempt to leverage such "cheap talk" into actual behavior change by drawing international attention to any perceived norm violations. Indeed in both the "boomerang" and "spiral" models of international norm accession, "naming and shaming" is a dominant strategy employed by activists (Keck and Sikkink 1998; Risse and Sikkink 1999). However, individuals generally aren't asked to make binding public commitments to international norms because their compliance with those commitments cannot be easily observed by norm entrepreneurs.[3] As a result, while eliciting public commitments to international norms is generally viewed as a necessary early stage in the longer process of norm change at the state level, the same cannot be said at the individual level. (False) rhetorical commitments may very well still occur at this lower level, but they cannot really be used to the direct advantage of transnational activists.[4]

Relatedly, the balance of international norm adopters who are instrumentally versus intrinsically motivated should on average be different for

3. As discussed in chapters 1 and 3, there have been instances of communal public declarations of abandonment of FGM and early marriage, particularly in West Africa. However, there is no evidence that the communities that have made these declarations are actively penalizing individuals who do not uphold the commitments made therein (United Nations Children's Fund 2008, 35).

4. This is not, however, to diminish the theoretical and practical value of understanding rhetorical commitments at the local level. False rhetorical commitments are still theoretically interesting insofar as they represent an unintended consequence of international norm promotion and interfere with attempts to assess the degree of actual primary behavior change. They are also substantively meaningful to the extent that they raise the strength of the international norm and signal the weakening of the competing local norm (Cortell and Davis 2000, 76; Price 1998, 636).

individuals than for states and other monitored organizations. Existing models of norm diffusion at the state level have argued that while norm leaders are usually truly committed to the international norm, the bulk of later norm adopters—the norm followers—are generally emulating the norm leaders for strategic reasons (Finnemore and Sikkink 1998, 895). However, at the community level there should be less variation in the motives of norm adopters over time—most people who come to comply with the international norm will do so because they genuinely want to, and one should expect that only the tail end of norm adopters are doing so for instrumental purposes. This is because in the absence of extensive monitoring capability among activists, leveraged behavior change is unlikely, and thus individuals will only change the primary behavior covered by the norm if the activists succeed in actually persuading them of its validity (or if a large majority of their community has already made the change and is now exerting pressure on stragglers to follow suit). Thus, what separates norm leaders from norm followers at the community level is not motive per se, but rather commitment and opportunity—relative to norm followers, norm leaders have stronger or earlier attachment to the international norm, face lower barriers to defection from any competing local norm, and have greater personal aversion to discordant attitudes and behavior.

Beyond looking at a new level of analysis, the book also makes several new theoretical contributions to the international norms literature. First, I contribute to scholarship on the domestic fit of international norms, which considers aspects of the "cultural match" between international and domestic norms and acknowledges the agency of norm "takers." However, while most of the literature concludes that poor cultural match largely precludes domestic adoption of international norms, I argue that it is important to consider not just the initial fit between international and local norms but also the salience of the norms to their respective adherents. Acharya (2011, 5) acknowledges half of the equation in recognizing variation in the salience of international norms (what he refers to as "prominence"), but because he does not meaningfully consider variation in the salience of the corresponding regional norms, he reasons that international norm proponents will nearly always fail in the face of international-regional norm contestation unless the international norms can be first adapted or "localized." However, I argue that, particularly under conditions of high international norm salience and low local norm salience, cultural mismatch can be offset and displacement of the local norm can occur. Moreover, the issue of local norm salience highlights the importance of conceptually distinguishing attitude change from primary behavior change, in line with the social psychology literature on norms. The broader transnational activism literature has generally assumed that when norm entrepreneurs successfully persuade the targets of their activism of the validity of the international norm, behavior change will swiftly follow (see, e.g., Finnemore and Sikkink 1998; Nadelmann 1990; Price 1998). Yet if a local norm is highly salient, even individuals who have changed their minds may actively choose not to change their corresponding behavior. Motivated norm entrepreneurs who want to facilitate individual and communal behavior change must then find ways to help people overcome social barriers to local norm defection.

In addition, I contribute further to the domestic fit literature by investigating cases of direct norm conflict. Many works have considered cases of norm contestation, in which international norms come into contact with domestic norms with which they are not fully or easily compatible (see, e.g., Acharya 2011; Betts and Orchard 2014). But direct norm conflict could best be described as a special, extreme case of norm contestation, in which two norms are not simply inconsistent with one another or initially incompatible, but are actually fundamentally opposed. Such a situation presents a particularly difficult challenge for international norm entrepreneurs, because the conflict largely eliminates the possibility that the international norm can simply be adapted to fit local conditions. There may be room for locally specific framing of the international norm, but ultimately for it to succeed it must displace the local norm—the competing norms cannot be reconciled.

More broadly, my theory is original in its merging of social psychological approaches with traditional constructivist and rationalist IR frameworks. Drawing on theoretical insights from social psychology about confirmation bias, belief perseverance, social pressure, obedience to authority, and image management, I argue that psychological pressures and cognitive biases shape the conditions under which the constructivist logic of appropriateness and the rationalist logic of consequences operate in the world of norms—I observe a good deal of variation in whether individuals are motivated by material, reputational, or ideational considerations when making decisions about norm compliance and about how they present themselves to international and local audiences. The advantage of the social psychological approach is that it doesn't force one to choose between moral and instrumental motivations for the various elements of norm change—it allows individuals to make decisions based on complex motives.

In terms of methodological strategy, my focus on the individual and community levels enabled me to employ mixed methods that allowed for fine-grained empirical analysis of the mechanisms of norm compliance. This is something that has been a perpetual challenge for norms scholars focused on the state level or on nonstate organizations, where it is generally difficult to gain direct access to elite decision-makers. Indeed, much of the qualitative evidence in the existing norms literature has been drawn from secondary sources, and large-*n* quantitative studies have mainly identified correlations between treaty ratification and behavior, without being able to establish relevant causal mechanisms. There is also a particular dearth of quantitative work on nonstate actors' norm compliance (Simmons 2013, 59). Yet to say that the book looks at local-level norm change is not to say that it has no relevance at higher levels of analysis. For international norms targeting the behavior of individuals, any meaningful norm change observed at the national, regional, and even international level is ultimately the aggregation of many discrete changes on the part of individuals and communities.

On a more general note, the survey experiment provides leverage on questions about the reliability of survey responses with respect to norm-governed behavior and otherwise sensitive or contested topics. The percentage difference between the treatment and control groups in their responses to various questions yields a sense of the magnitude of the misrepresentation problem in this particular case, but the findings also contribute to the broader literature on social desirability bias in survey response.

The Politics of Culture

Though the theory itself is not Africa-specific, the empirical content of the book focuses on an African case, and so it is important to acknowledge the specificity of context and consider the ways in which the book speaks to the broader field of scholarship on the continent. Perhaps the book's most significant point of contact with this literature is its attention to the issue of agency in cultural maintenance and adaptation. Mbembe (2001, 10–11), for example, argues that much of Western philosophy views African societies as "primitive, simple, or traditional in that, in them, the weight of the past predetermines individual behavior and limits the areas of choice—as it were, a priori. The formulation of norms in these latter societies has nothing to do with reasoned public deliberation, since the setting of norms by a process of argument is a specific invention of modern Europe." The notion that Africans are unthinking slaves to tradition is pervasive, and wrong. Instead, "local" cultures are always being reinterpreted and adapted—they do not exist outside of time and space (Gupta and Ferguson 1997). There is in addition a long history of resistance and reappropriation, rather than uncritical acceptance, of Western attempts to impose alternative cultural norms from outside (Comaroff and Comaroff 1993). Reflecting this position, my theory emphasizes, and the empirical evidence clearly demonstrates, that holders of local norms are active decision-makers capable of rational deliberation about their beliefs and actions, and this is true of both those who embrace international norms and those who continue to adhere to local norms and traditions. In fact, my research subjects are strategic players in the game of culture clash, responding thoughtfully to new information and new incentives.

The African studies literature on culture and modernity advances discourse in several additional ways that are relevant to the argument offered in this book. First, the literature recognizes that cultural change is inherently political, occurring in the context of highly unequal power relations between the West and Africa that have persisted from the colonial period to the present and involved a great deal of force (Ferguson 1999). Affirming this point, social, financial, and political power is an ever-present part of the story I tell, implicitly and sometimes explicitly shaping the choices of activists and community members alike. Second, cultural conflict is not new. Linkages between different cultures have always existed, and so it doesn't make sense to think of present-day cultural conflicts as occurring between one fixed, bounded culture (us, the metropole) and another (them, the periphery) (Gupta and Ferguson 1992). Though the book acknowledges this point, it shares the recognition that a globalizing world pushes different cultures into conflict with greater frequency. Third, the literature problematizes the way in which Africa's history with the West has frequently led Africans to internalize the notion that they are indeed "backward" and to embrace the idea that they should strive to become "modern" following a Western model (Ferguson 1999; Ekeh 1975). Such an obsession with modernity ran like a thread through my qualitative interviews. As described in chapter 7 in particular, many of those with whom I spoke were quite blunt in their assessment that westerners are more advanced and that backward Maasai and Samburu should aspire to similar heights; so blunt, in fact, as to make a Western audience steeped in political correctness feel uncomfortable. Finally, scholars engaging with the politics of law note the complex attitudes Africans hold toward the law and to the formal political and legal sphere more broadly. The central state (and the legal regimes it creates) often lacks legitimacy, perceived as a holdover from the colonial period (Ekeh 1975). In the present, African societies tend to exhibit multiple overlapping and partial sovereignties, where individuals live simultaneously under civil and customary law and where there is frequently a disjuncture between legal and moral regimes (Comaroff and

Comaroff 2006; Mamdani 1996). This perspective helps to frame the way in which the individuals and communities described in the book engaged with the government and the law—particularly the notion that evading the law is an acceptable, and perhaps even a laudable, act.

Gender Violence

The book also makes contributions to the literature on activism against gender violence (see, e.g., Johnson 2009; Merry 2006; Montoya 2013; Sundstrom 2005; Weldon 2002). Though existing research usefully considers the interplay between international, state, and domestic actors in the pursuit of women's rights, the attention has been either mainly or exclusively on activists' own actions and their ability to elicit policy changes and policy implementation from the state. Yet because violence against women is primarily carried out in private spaces, I have argued that one must also consider activists' ability to elicit change from individual gender violence perpetrators. As a result, the book explores and directly observes sources of variation in real attitude and behavior change at the local level.

In addition, the book contributes to the substantial interdisciplinary literature on FGM and to the much smaller literature on early marriage, which is substantively valuable given the worldwide scope of these two practices. Within the corpus of work on FGM, a number of scholars have attempted to identify the sources of observed behavior change, and to explain variations in its speed and scope. Some have focused on the effect of socioeconomic characteristics and temporal factors: El-Gibaly et al. (2002) argue that heightened public debate following the International Conference on Population and Development, held in Cairo in 1994, helps explain the modest recent decline in the incidence of FGM in Egypt, particularly among girls with educated mothers and living in urban areas. Yount (2002) similarly points to the impact of mothers' education in Egypt, while Orubuloye, Caldwell, and Caldwell (2000) note the importance of both education and urbanization in explaining the decline of FGM among the Yoruba of Nigeria. In addition to these efforts, other studies have evaluated the impact of various specific anti-FGM programs and activist strategies (see discussion in chapter 2). Collectively, these works contribute to our overall understanding of changes in the prevalence of FGM. But there continues to be significant debate about the actual mechanisms of this change—how change happens and not just whether and when it happens (see, e.g., El-Gibaly et al. 2002; Hayford 2005; Shell-Duncan and Hernlund 2006; Shell-Duncan et al. 2011; Yount 2002). Among these, Gerry Mackie's

(1996) social convention account has been particularly prominent, and I respond to it directly. I find that the empirical evidence does not support his contention that coordination is critical for norm change—many communities have experienced gradual change rather than tipping rapidly to a (nearly) no-FGM equilibrium—and I show that the empirical pattern is instead consistent with my argument that unilateral defection is possible, particularly through interaction with normative out-groups.[5]

The limited existing literature on early marriage has provided some insight into causes of decline in early-marriage prevalence. A number of observational studies have focused on the impact of demographic and societal changes in the developing world, such as urban in-migration, longer life spans, increased and higher levels of schooling for girls, and increased female labor force participation (Caldwell, Reddy, and Caldwell 1983; National Research Council 2005). The impact of girls' schooling has been particularly emphasized, although debates continue about the mechanism or mechanisms underlying the relationship between schooling and marriage age: schooling may directly delay marriage because girls generally do not get married while they remain in school; it may instill a preference in girls for delayed marriage and give them the autonomy and voice to negotiate in favor of that preference; and it may give girls the skills to financially support themselves via paid work rather than marriage (Ikamari 2005, 3–4; International Center for Research on Women 2007, 10; Jejeebhoy 1995, 60). Several other studies (including evaluations of some of the programs described in chapter 2) have shown that financial incentives for girls and their families in exchange for staying in school also lead to increases in marriage age, as do unconditional financial payouts and income-generating activities for girls (Arends-Kuenning and Amin 2000; Baird, McIntosh, and Özler 2011; Baird et al. 2010; Duflo et al. 2006; International Center for Research on Women 2007). However, relative to the literature on FGM, there has been substantially less theoretical attention to questions of how norm change actually occurs with respect to early marriage. I begin to address such questions in arguing that decreases in early-marriage prevalence are at least partly driven by changes in individuals' attitudes about the normative value of marrying early, and that because early-marriage norms often exhibit low local salience, concerted activism could actually

5. Moreover, though the apparent success of the Tostan program, with its accompanying public declarations of FGM abandonment, has frequently been linked to the logic of social convention theory, evaluations of the program have not established that the public coordination component is enabling change in and of itself. Instead, much of the impact of the program appears to stem from the sustained educational component (Berg and Denison 2013, 38).

have a significant impact on the practice even in the absence of coordination or other structural changes in society.

POLICY IMPLICATIONS

Because the subject matter of this book is of practical concern to many people, it is important to consider what policy implications can be derived from its findings. In particular, I identify implications for donors and for NGOs and other activist organizations that are actually operating on the ground. First, at a fundamental level, it is critical that donor organizations (including major multilateral and bilateral organizations, foundations, and large NGOs that subcontract work) recognize their power to set and reorder NGOs' agendas, and thus seriously consider whether they have their priorities straight. This is not to suggest that donors are prioritizing the wrong issues per se—indeed major donors like the UNFPA-UNICEF Joint Programme, the Donors Working Group on FGM/C, and the Department for International Development have made thoughtful and well-reasoned cases for their financial and programmatic commitment to FGM abandonment efforts—but rather that there can be a bandwagon effect among donors in which they all come to prioritize a narrow set of important issues at the expense of a much wider set of also-important issues. Thus, an issue like FGM becomes highly internationally salient while an issue like early marriage has historically garnered very little meaningful attention. Because there is a limited amount of available aid to NGOs, many will go where the money is, and this can end up crowding out work on serious (and potentially solvable) problems.

Second, donors should be particularly vigilant when selecting and monitoring grantees and contractors for programs that address internationally salient issues. As available donor funding for any given issue increases, the number of NGOs willing to address that issue will also increase, and many of the new organizations will have shifted to the issue because of the money and not because of a deeper commitment to the problem. Thus, programs directed at internationally salient issues will be somewhat worse on average, but donors can work against this to some degree by seeking out partner NGOs that can demonstrate a clear commitment to the particular issue over an extended period of time. Generally, good potential NGO partners will tend to have a relatively focused mission and programmatic track record—all but the very largest NGOs lack the capacity and human capital to work in multiple entirely discrete issue areas simultaneously. To be clear, this is not an injunction against organizations that pursue multipronged approaches to particular goals. Indeed, to address an issue like FGM, which may involve significant initial resistance from the community, an NGO can build local credibility by providing other needed or desirable public goods and programming. The red flag is, instead, when an organization with limited capacity adopts a schizophrenic programming strategy, jumping from, say, land rights to water projects to income-generating activities for widows to FGM, without building a significant ground presence.

Third, donor organizations shouldn't assume that local NGOs will be inherently better at spreading international norms than larger external groups. A popular stance in the aid community in recent years has been to champion "local ownership" of projects, on the assumption that local groups will have better knowledge of the local context. This may be true, but there is no guarantee that local NGOs will actually take advantage of their contextual knowledge in implementing projects. This can be observed with the alternative-rite-of-passage "bubble," in which a programming approach that is only appropriate in a limited number of cases has nonetheless been widely adopted through a vicious cycle: donors embraced the rite following its initial demonstration by MYWO and PATH, which led many NGOs on the ground to pick it up, which in turn led donors to conclude the approach was appropriate and indigenous and fund it further.

All NGOs, whether local, national, or international, face a survival imperative, but this imperative may be especially significant for local NGOs in developing countries, where NGO workers often have poor alternative employment prospects. The mere fact that NGOs have instrumental motives certainly does not preclude them from doing good work—it doesn't mean that they necessarily lack sincere altruistic motives—but it can make them susceptible to problems of donor-driven issue selection and mission creep. Such organizations may become overextended, lacking the time and commitment to pursue high-quality projects and adapt them to local conditions. To the extent that local ownership remains a priority, donors should choose carefully, adhering to the same criteria for selecting NGO partners described above.

The theory also provides guidance for activists working in-country. First, NGOs on the ground should recognize that while policy advocacy and lobbying have value, many problems will not be effectively solved solely through legal changes. For issues like FGM and early marriage, even motivated states often have limited ability to enforce laws that do not have widespread public support. Accordingly, NGOs should focus more of their efforts on direct activism within the relevant communities. Second, activism related to social norms will be most effective when it targets locally influential individuals (and not just the directly at-risk population if that population lacks decision-making power). Recruiting influential locals to one's cause will tend to have an outsize impact on the community as a whole, to the extent that many community members value their opinion and look to them for guidance. Yet because the influential individuals will vary across contexts and may also vary from issue to issue, activists will need to invest the time and energy to identify who these people are (see Valente and Pampuang 2007 for multiple identification methods).

Third, it is important for activists to recognize when they are challenging highly salient local norms and respond accordingly. In particular, their activities will need to be intensive and sustained over time if they hope to separate people from their most closely held practices. But beyond simply flooding a community with information, activists will need to be strategic in finding ways to help people move from changing their attitudes to changing their actual behavior. They can do this by drawing people's attention to any available exit options from the local norm and to success stories of those who've changed their behavior and been better off as a result. Fundamentally, they will need to do whatever they can to make defection from the local norm seem like a viable strategy.

Finally, activists should recognize the very real issues of misrepresentation and undesirable secondary behavior change. The greater the pressure to comply with international norms, the greater the incentives for people to falsely commit to those norms or hide their noncompliant behavior. Thus, activists should think carefully about whether they themselves are heightening such incentives through their actions and the content of their activism—for example, by providing "sitting allowances" and other material rewards or by creating an environment in which people believe they may be punished for subscribing to local norms. In addition, activists should be careful in interpreting self-reported behavior change as actual behavior change. Survey-based program evaluations have become a popular tool in recent years, but activists may need to dig deeper in their evaluation efforts before concluding that their programs have actually worked.

On the issues of FGM and early marriage, the overall record of transnational activism is mixed. Some donors have been careful and responsible, and some NGOs have been highly dedicated, but there are also many examples of flawed programs and strategies. Activism against FGM would benefit from being more sustained, intensive, and tailored to local contexts, while activism against early marriage would benefit from an injection of donor funding.

Though this study speaks to a number of theoretical and empirical questions and has significant practical implications, there are limits to its reach and questions that remain unanswered. Certainly much of the value of empirical scholarship depends on the design and execution of the research itself, and yet all design choices inevitably involve trade-offs. The decision to look at three communities in depth was based on the recognition that close study was necessary in order to tease out causal processes, particularly since the issues involved were complex and because the broader research question had not been investigated empirically in the past. But choosing depth means sacrificing breadth to some degree. Though in this chapter I have briefly considered the theory's ability to travel to different geographical locations and to different issues, and though I have made an effort throughout to consider the ways in which my cases might be unique, I cannot completely rule out the possibility that some of the observed empirical relationships described in this book may be particular to Kenya, to the Maasai and Samburu, or to FGM and early marriage. I hope that others will take up the baton and begin to test some or all of the theory against new cases.

There are also limits to the individual research methods employed.[6] Because surveys collect observational data, the persuasiveness of causal claims depends, among other things, on the ability of the analysis to rule out possible confounding factors and generally establish the independence of right-hand-side variables. The survey analysis presented in this book controlled for a range of socioeconomic and demographic characteristics that seemed likely to interfere with the causal relationships of interest, but it is possible that unobserved heterogeneity remains. By contrast, experimental work has the advantage of allowing for genuine causal inference, but can face external validity problems. My survey experiment, for example, was unable to test for the presence of material incentives for misrepresentation because the experimental conditions meant that the international audience presented to respondents was remote and thus unable to provide direct material rewards. Finally, qualitative interviews can illuminate causal mechanisms but are vulnerable to bias according to the nature of the relationship between interviewer and interviewees. In the context of my interviews, there was no way for me to evade my outsider status. My use of these various methods in combination does overcome many

6. Some specific issues with the implementation of the empirical strategy are described in the methodological appendix.

of the concerns with each method individually, but future research could further diversify the empirical approach. A field experiment, for instance, could employ random assignment of normative messaging by different types of community stakeholders to test directly for which types are most influential.

Last, by necessity there are limits to the scope of the theory and to the kinds of questions it can answer. My decision to focus on cases of direct norm conflict and active norm promotion means that the theory can't say much about processes of gradual, nondirected norm diffusion or processes of entirely indigenous norm change (though these processes are clearly important—indeed, chapter 3 revealed that FGM prevalence in Kenya began to decline in the 1970s, during a period in which there was relatively little concerted activism against the practice). It is, however, possible to speculate about extensions of the theory to contexts beyond those that initially motivated the research. For instance, my focus on persuasion as the dominant mechanism of norm change assumes that the targets of norm promotion will be reasonably open to the norm promoters ex ante—that they will at least be willing to listen to what activists have to say even if they prove reluctant to embrace the message. Yet this is not always a fair assumption (e.g., anti-Western sentiment is relatively common in the Middle East), and so an important lingering question is how norm promotion plays out when targets of activism are hostile to the norm promoters from the start.

To extend the theory to apply to such cases, it would be important to allow for the possibility that norm change could in fact reverse. I have assumed that when attitudes and primary behavior shift, they will shift in the direction of the international norm, such that the central questions relate to the size and speed of these shifts. But it is also possible for transnational activism to produce a backlash in which attachment to the local norm actually spreads. In that scenario, though, one might still expect the general conditions favoring norm change to continue to hold—norm salience, the public stance of influential locals, and the existence of exit options should all still matter. However, the geographic origins of activists and their ability to frame the normative message in local terms should prove more decisive. Further research could look at the reception to campaigns such as those against honor killings in Pakistan or violence toward the LGBT community in Russia.

A second possible extension relates to the scope of the norm conflict. Though this book has been framed as a contribution to the IR literature on international norm promotion, much of the theory should travel to cases of norm conflict in which *international* norms and actors are not directly implicated. Norm conflicts can certainly crop up among different groups within a single country—ethnic, religious, or urban–rural cleavages can bring norm differences into stark relief. National, or dominant culture, norms may also conflict with minority culture norms.

In thinking about extending the theory in this way, it is important to keep in mind the distinction between whether the norm in question is international in scope and whether the norm promoters are themselves from other countries. The theory as it has been presented in this book is clearly focused on cases of the former but somewhat more agnostic about the latter. That is, the theory already applies to instances in which many if not all of the individuals promoting the international norm on the ground are from the target society, only assuming that at least some of the support for these efforts comes from the international community. To talk about extending the theory, then, is to consider cases in which the norm being promoted has not engaged the international community in a meaningful way—either the norm itself has no international legitimacy or else the norm promotion efforts in a particular context occur entirely independently of any international support. In an increasingly globalized world, the set of such norms may be dwindling.

In any case, for the theory to be relevant to a truly intranational norm conflict, it is important that one of the parties to the conflict be engaged in overt norm promotion. That is, there are many latent norm conflicts in the world, but frequently the groups holding the competing norms are content to leave one another alone. A latent norm conflict becomes an explicit norm conflict when members of one group decide that they hold the moral high ground—or at least that their own way of acting is somehow superior and not just different (whether or not this is actually true is a separate question)—and that the group with the competing norm should change its ways. How commonly this occurs among latent intranational norm conflicts is an open question, but it is probably less common than among international–local norm conflicts; international activists from the global North are perhaps unusually confident that they know what other people should do. One might expect that, in an entirely intranational context, a similar feeling is most likely to arise among members of a dominant culture toward members of a minority culture, and less likely to arise among similarly situated subnational groups.

With this central constraint in mind, the theory should travel reasonably well. Regardless of whether the norm being promoted is international, the salience of the local norm to the target group should still affect attitude and primary behavior change in the predicted ways. Similarly, one would continue to expect that the presence of influential local norm leaders would hasten norm change at the community level, and that access to an exit option would lower barriers to defection from the local norm. There may also still be incentives for secondary behavioral and rhetorical change, depending on the perceived status and resources of the norm promoters and whether the external norm is also a legal norm.

However, two of the theory's assumptions require closer consideration. First, the theory assumes that a highly salient external norm will trigger the provision of funding to promote that norm. This assumption makes sense when the norm is international, since the international community writ large actually has the resources to make aid available and incentivize NGOs to take up the cause. But if the external norm in question is being promoted only by a national or subnational group, this is less certain—there is likely to be a lot of variability across such groups in how deep their pockets are, meaning that there will also be greater variability in the extent to which external norm salience affects the quantity and quality of activism. Second, the theory assumes some degree of "NGO-ization" of the target society—that NGOs will be a likely conduit for the normative message. This assumption is what makes NGO density and NGO incentive structures an important part of the story, but it is a more accurate assumption in the global South than the global North. As a result, intranational (and international) norm promotion efforts that take place in the global North may depend more on things like general media campaigns to spread their message, producing less geographic variability in messaging. Future research could begin to test the limits of the theory's applicability to norm conflicts in which the international community is not significantly involved, such as the norm conflict over vaccinations in the United States or the norm conflict over veiling in France.

I'll conclude by refocusing my attention on the questions that motivated this book, some empirical and some normative. As a scholar, I was deeply curious about the extent to which international norms might trickle down to the truly local level, and about the processes through which local-level norm change might occur. Through this study I found that individuals and communities faced with a norm conflict can react both sincerely and strategically to transnational activism, producing complex and interdependent changes in what they think, do, and say. As someone with a strong commitment to women's rights, I also wanted to know whether and how meaningful advances were being made in the protection of those rights. Practices like FGM and early marriage have real-world consequences for millions of women and girls around the world, and so understanding individual and community responses to activism against these practices is not simply an academic question. This book has demonstrated that real norm change is happening, but there is still a long way to go.

METHODOLOGICAL APPENDIX

SURVEY DESIGN AND IMPLEMENTATION

The original survey on FGM and early marriage was carried out in the three case study areas—Oldonyiro Division of Isiolo District, Mukogodo Division of Laikipia North District, and a subsection of Mau Division of Narok North District—in November 2008. Respondents were asked a series of questions that were designed to assess their knowledge, attitudes, and practices with respect to both FGM and early marriage. The survey also contained an experimental element, in which respondents were randomly assigned to receive a priming statement about international observers. An individual was eligible to participate in the survey if he or she was a Maa speaker, 15 years of age or older, and a resident of the selected household.

The survey questionnaire was largely original, although it included selected questions borrowed from Afrobarometer and the Measure DHS Demographic and Health Surveys. The Steadman Group, a survey research firm headquartered in Nairobi, was contracted to oversee the field administration of the survey and input the resulting data. A partner NGO or CBO in each division served as the public face of the survey—the Indigenous Laikipiak Maasai Integrated Youth Organization (ILAMAIYO) in Mukogodo Division, Pastoralist Women for Health and Education in Oldonyiro Division, and Tasaru Ntomonok Initiative in Mau Division. The survey questionnaire was translated into Kimaasai, and the interviews were conducted entirely in Kimaasai/Kisamburu.[1] Questionnaire enumerators were recruited from within each case study area.

---

1. Kimaasai and Kisamburu are very similar dialects of the larger Maa language family. Although the survey questionnaire was translated from English by Kimaasai speakers,

Sample Area

At the time of the survey, Kenyan administrative levels were organized in descending order of province, district, division, location, and sublocation. None of these levels are standardized in terms of size or population. There are nine locations and 12 sublocations in Mukogodo Division, and two locations and four sublocations in Oldonyiro Division. There are 11 locations in Mau Division, but because the division is much larger in terms of geography and population than the other two divisions (the 1999 census reports 76,303 people residing in Mau, compared to just 13,176 in Mukogodo and 9,669 in Oldonyiro), only two contiguous locations were selected to serve as the third case study area. These two locations—Keekonyokie and Suswa—contain four sublocations between them.

A multistage sampling design was employed, in which the primary sampling unit was the case study area (the division in the case of Mukogodo and Oldonyiro, and the two combined locations in the case of Mau), the secondary sampling unit was the sublocation,[2] the tertiary sampling unit was the household, and the final sampling unit was the individual.

Sample Size

Each case study area had a sample size of 200, for a total sample size of 600. Within each study area, the sample size was divided among the sublocations in proportion to the number of households in the sublocation (Kenya Central Bureau of Statistics 2002). This strategy was employed so that all households within a study area had an equal chance of being selected to participate in the survey. Ultimately, however, the survey administrators marginally oversampled some sublocations and undersampled others. The only major deviation from the original design occurred in Mau Division, in which the sample size was split evenly between Keekonyokie and Suswa Locations, despite very different population numbers. The ideal and actual samples are presented in table A.1. The survey data were weighted to compensate for the different probabilities of selection among Mukogodo, Oldonyiro, Keekonyokie, and Suswa.

the Kisamburu-speaking enumerators in Oldonyiro Division confirmed that the questionnaire as written was intelligible to Kisamburu speakers.

2. Because all 20 sublocations were included, this essentially bypassed the location level as a sampling unit.

Table A.1: SURVEY SAMPLE SIZE

Division	Location	Sublocation	Households	Intended sample size	Actual sample size
		Oldonyiro	1,128	107	103
		Lonkopito	495	47	45
	Oldonyiro		**1,623**	**154**	**148**
		Kipsing	189	18	25
		Lenguruma	288	28	28
	Kipsing		**477**	**46**	**53**
Oldonyiro			**2,100**	**200**	**201**
		Mumonyot	241	17	17
		Seek	237	16	16
	Mumonyot		**478**	**33**	**33**
		Sangaa	161	11	12
		Ngarendare	77	5	6
	Il'ngwesi		**2,383**	**16**	**18**
		Makurian	244	17	19
		Aljijo	214	15	13
	Makurian		**458**	**32**	**32**
		Kurikuri	458	31	27
	Mukogodo		**458**	**31**	**27**
		Tura	299	21	21
	Ildigiri		**299**	**21**	**21**
		Ewaso	391	27	26
	Oloibosoit		**391**	**27**	**26**
		Sieku	39	3	4
	Sieku		**39**	**3**	**4**
		Ilpolei	252	17	18
	Ilpolei		**252**	**17**	**18**
		Ilmotiok	285	20	20
	Ilmotiok		**285**	**20**	**20**
Mukogodo			**2,898**	**200**	**199**
		Keekonyokie	2,659	135	100
	Keekonyokie		**2,659**	**135**	**100**
		Suswa	659	34	60
		Olesharo	253	13	10
		Oloikarere	352	18	30
	Suswa		**1,264**	**65**	**100**
Mau			**3,923**	**200**	**200**

Sampling Methodology

Within each sublocation, respondents were selected at random in two stages. In the first stage, households were selected using the following method:[3]

1. Pairs of enumerators were randomly assigned to the different sublocations.
2. Enumerators traveled to the selected sublocation and identified a landmark, such as the local administration's camp, a church, a shopping center, a school, and so on.
3. Enumerators randomly selected the first household using the sum of the digits of the current date. For example, if the enumerators entered the sublocation on November 21, they would have added together the two digits of the number 21 (2 + 1 = 3) and selected the third household from the landmark to serve as the starting household.
4. After the starting household, subsequent households were selected by employing a random walk, combined with a specified household skip routine. The size of the skip was set at 8 in Oldonyiro, 10 in Mukogodo, and 15 in Mau. Following a left-hand rule, enumerators would skip over the first 8, 10, or 15 households they encountered after the previous selected household, selecting the 9th, 11th, or 16th household for participation in the survey. This ensured that respondents were spread out across the sublocation.
5. In the event a selected household contained no individuals who were eligible to participate in the survey or the household was empty, the

3. Some anthropologists and other field researchers have questioned the applicability of the "household" concept to survey research in rural Africa, suggesting that its use can distort findings because it is often defined in ways that privilege the notion of a male-headed, capitalist institution, despite a very different reality on the ground (see, e.g., Ekejiuba 1995). However, a household is defined here simply as a freestanding dwelling—no assumptions are made about the nature of household relations or production, or about gender roles. Moreover, concerns about flawed household definitions primarily relate to the use of the household as an actual unit of analysis (Beaman and Dillon 2012). In this study, by contrast, the household is merely a sampling unit—no data is being collected about any given household. Accordingly, one would expect the definition of household used here to introduce systematic error into the data only if it affected the probability that certain types of individuals would be sampled. This would be the case if there were individuals who did not live in any dwelling, individuals who for some reason would not be claimed as dwelling residents at any household (despite living in a dwelling), or individuals who would be claimed as dwelling residents at more than one household. However, actual homelessness does not appear to be especially common within the study communities, nor do I have any reason to believe that a particular group of people was systematically underidentified in the sampling process.

enumerators continued as usual but added a household to the end of the random walk.

6. In the event a selected residence was a compound or *manyatta*, rather than a single-family dwelling, the enumerators used a household selection grid to randomly select a household within the compound, such that each household had an equal probability of selection.

In the second stage, a respondent was selected from within the household using the following method:

1. Upon entering the household, the enumerators enlisted a member of the household to assist them in making a list of all eligible individuals in the household, from oldest to youngest.

2. The enumerators then used a respondent selection technique, commonly known as a Kish Grid, to randomly select a respondent from the list, such that each eligible member of the household had an equal probability of selection.

3. The enumerators traveled in mixed-sex pairs so that the female enumerator could administer the questionnaire if the Kish Grid selected a female respondent, and the male enumerator could administer the questionnaire if the Kish Grid selected a male respondent. This ensured that respondents would feel as comfortable as possible while discussing sensitive issues.

4. If the enumerator was unsuccessful in administering the questionnaire because the selected respondent was unavailable, the enumerator made up to three callbacks to the household in an attempt to find the selected respondent at home.

5. If the enumerator was unsuccessful in administering the questionnaire because the selected respondent was unavailable after three callbacks,

---

There *was* some risk that men in polygynous marriages would be overidentified: Among the Maasai and Samburu, what I have defined as a household corresponds to the smallest unit of residential organization, effectively a single house or hut made of wood, mud, and cow dung (*enkaji*) (Coast 2001, 26). Traditionally each married woman builds her own house, in which she dwells with her husband and children. This is roughly akin to what Ekejiuba (1995) has described as a hearthold; as recorded in the sampling process for the survey, households in the study communities ranged in size from 1 to 10 individuals who met the survey eligibility requirements, with a mean household size of 4. Thus, a man in a polygnous marriage would potentially have had an increased probability of being sampled, assuming each of his wives would have claimed him as a resident of her *enkaji* in the event that that *enkaji* was itself sampled. However, this concern ultimately proved overblown—298 men were sampled, compared to 302 women—perhaps because the traditional residential arrangement has declined in popularity in recent years, in favor of more permanent houses in the Western style that are "owned" by men (Talle 1988, 252; Coast 2001, 28).

refused to participate, or terminated the interview before completion, the respondent was replaced by a randomly selected respondent in another household.

Experiment Random Assignment Procedure

Respondents were randomly assigned to be in the treatment and control groups for the experimental element of the survey. Each pair of enumerators was given a list detailing a random order for administering the two versions of the questionnaire. Though the random order was different in each list, the lists conformed to the following general design:

Household 1	Questionnaire B
Household 2	Questionnaire A
Household 3	Questionnaire A
Household 4	Questionnaire B
Household 5	Questionnaire A
Household 6	Questionnaire B
Household 7	Questionnaire A
Household 8	Questionnaire A
Household 9	Questionnaire A
Household 10	Questionnaire B
Etc.	Etc.

Quality Control

The field supervisor accompanied the enumerators on 6.3 percent of all interviews, and back-checked 11.2 percent of all interviews with the respondents.

Field Procedure Implementation Problems

There were several instances in which field supervisors or enumerators deviated from the prescribed field procedures. First, the survey administrators failed to track nonresponse and ineligibility. Moreover, it appears that enumerators sometimes made fewer than three callbacks in an attempt to reach absent respondents. Since the characteristics of nonresponders are unknown, it is not possible to take the remedial, if imperfect, step of weighting the data to compensate for groups that were less likely to respond. However, my expectation from my own experience in the three case study areas suggests that nonresponse was likely to have been quite low. Most people can be found at home during the day and have time on their hands to talk. There is also a general culture of listening to what people have to say. This is consistent with US-based surveys that have found much lower rates of nonresponse in rural areas. Furthermore, it doesn't appear that any demographic group was systematically undersampled. At minimum, characteristics of actual respondents are fairly well distributed in terms of sex (49.7 percent male and 50.3 percent female) and age (mean = 35, median = 31, standard deviation = 15.4), although in the absence of census data available at the division level, no judgments can be made about the accuracy of the distribution of less straightforward demographic variables like education, occupation, and marital status.

Second, it appears that in some cases, the survey enumerators shortened the skip protocol in an effort to save time, but it also appears that this problem was not terribly pervasive, occurring only in the last one or two days of fieldwork and only among a few enumerators. Furthermore, enumerators in some areas appear to have started their random walk at the boundary of the sublocation—at the point closest to their previous location—rather than at the center. It is therefore not possible to know the precise extent to which a given sublocation was covered geographically, nor to speak with any certainty about households' probability of selection.

However, there is no reason to believe that there is a systematic component to the errors associated with the breakdown in field procedures. Since exposure to town centers is a variable of interest, it would be problematic if areas far from town were systematically undersampled. This does not appear to be the case, however, since each sublocation in a given division was reached. There are only one or two major town centers per division, so some sublocations are necessarily farther from these centers than others. There is also no reason to believe that there was anything systematic about the portions of sublocations that were not reached, or about the households that were selected once the skip protocol was shortened.

Helpfully, randomization procedures for selecting respondents from within households appear to have been maintained. This is important given that some of the variation in responses to survey questions is determined by variables for which the primary variation is within households. For example, two consistent control variables are sex and age, which vary substantially within households, but which are not likely to vary significantly in their distribution across geographic areas. Overall, it is quite likely that despite issues with household selection, the sample remains representative of the population.

Third, the randomization procedure for assigning respondents to the treatment and control version of the questionnaire appears to have broken down at some point in the process. This issue seems to have arisen from the fact that the enumerators did not have sufficient copies of each version of the questionnaire to allow them to follow their lists at all times. Specifically, enumerators were meant to complete approximately five to six interviews per day, but were only given perhaps three of each version of the questionnaire. Because the lists were fully randomized and did not simply alternate between treatment and control, it was possible that on any given day the list would instruct the enumerator to administer substantially more of one version of the questionnaire than the other—for example, five interviews using the treatment questionnaire and one using the control. In such a situation, the enumerator would end up having to administer a control questionnaire when he or she was instructed to administer a treatment questionnaire, simply because he or she was out of copies of the treatment questionnaire, and vice versa. Because these errors in the randomization process were themselves essentially randomly assigned—that is, outcomes of chance as opposed to conscious decisions on the part of the enumerators—there is no reason to believe that this could lead to systematic differences in the treatment and control groups. Indeed, comparison of pretreatment observables shows very little in the way of differences between the two groups. While strict adherence to the randomization lists would have produced exactly 300 treatment and 300 control questionnaires, the errors ultimately produced 292 completed treatment questionnaires and 308 completed control questionnaires.

ANALYSIS OF SURVEY DATA

Regression Equations

The regression analysis in chapters 4 through 7 employs both linear and nonlinear models.[4] The regression equations are presented here.

---

4. Angrist and Pischke (2009, 94) have argued that the linear probability model with binary dependent variables is often preferable to maximum likelihood estimators.

Chapter 4

The analysis evaluated the role of individual and community accessibility in explaining awareness of international norms. The linear model is represented as

$$\Pr(Y_i = 1) = \gamma \, town_i + \varphi \, radio_i + \xi \, Protestant_i + \alpha_i \, d_i + \mathbf{x}_i'\boldsymbol{\beta} + u_i,$$

where *town* is a dummy variable equal to one if the respondent reports that he or she never visits the community's town center and zero otherwise, *radio* is a dummy variable equal to one if the respondent reports owning a radio and zero otherwise, *Protestant* is a dummy variable equal to one if the respondent reports that he or she is Protestant and zero otherwise, and *d* represents fixed effects for the three case study communities. $\mathbf{x}_i$ is a vector of covariates: age, sex, and receiving the experimental treatment.

The logistic model is represented as

$$\Pr(Y_i = 1) = f\,(\gamma \, town_i + \varphi \, radio_i + \xi \, Protestant_i + \alpha_i \, d_i + \mathbf{x}_i'\boldsymbol{\beta}),$$

where f is the logistic function

$$f(z) = 1/(1 + e^{-z}) = \Lambda(z).$$

Chapter 5

The analysis evaluated the role of message quality and individual characteristics in explaining attitudes about female circumcision and early marriage. The linear model is represented as

$$\Pr(Y_i = 1) = \gamma \, health_i + \varphi \, female_i + \xi \, age_i + \mathbf{x}_i'\boldsymbol{\beta} + u_i,$$

where *health* is a dummy variable equal to one if the respondent reports that he or she is aware the practice can cause health problems and zero otherwise, *female* is a dummy variable equal to one if the respondent is female and zero if the respondent is male, and *age* is the respondent's self-reported age. $\mathbf{x}_i$ is a vector of covariates: Protestantism, town visits, radio ownership, receiving the experimental treatment, and fixed effects for the three case study communities.

The logistic model is represented as

$$\Pr(Y_i = 1) = f(\gamma \, health_i + \varphi \, female_i + \xi \, age_i + \mathbf{x}_i'\boldsymbol{\beta}).$$

The analysis evaluated the role of ethnic heterogeneity and beliefs about elites' attitudes in explaining primary behavior with respect to female circumcision and early marriage. The linear model is represented as

$$\Pr(Y_i = 1) = \gamma \, elders_i + \varphi \, chiefs_i + \xi \, tribes_i + \alpha_i \, d_i + \nu \, tribes^*d_i + \mathbf{x}_i'\boldsymbol{\beta} + u_i,$$

where *elders* is a dummy variable equal to one if the respondent reports that most elders want the practice to stop and zero otherwise, *chiefs* is a dummy variable equal to one if the respondent reports that most chiefs want the practice to stop and zero otherwise, *tribes* is a dummy variable equal to one if the respondent reports encountering other tribes once a week or more and zero otherwise, and *d* represents fixed effects for the three case study communities. *Tribes*d* is an interaction term. $\mathbf{x}_i$ is a vector of covariates: age, sex, Protestantism, distance from town, and receiving the experimental treatment.

The logistic model is represented as

$$\Pr(Y_i = 1) = f(\gamma \, elders_i + \varphi \, chiefs_i + \xi \, tribes_i + \alpha_i \, d_i + \nu \, tribes^*d_i + \mathbf{x}_i'\boldsymbol{\beta}).$$

Chapter 7

The analysis evaluated the presence of treatment effects in explaining respondents' attitudes, experiences, and behavior. The linear model is represented as

$$\Pr(Y_i = 1) = \gamma \, treatment_i + \mathbf{x}_i'\boldsymbol{\beta} + u_i,$$

where treatment is a dummy variable for receiving the international audience prime, and $\mathbf{x}_i$ is a vector of covariates. As a robustness check, I include two specifications—one in which the outcome variable indicators are regressed on the international audience treatment alone ($\mathbf{x}_i = 0$), and one in which the outcome variables are regressed on the treatment and a series of controls. The control variables are age, sex, Protestantism, exposure to other tribes, beliefs about elders' and chiefs' attitudes, and fixed effects for the three case study communities.

The logistic model is represented as

$$\Pr(Y_i = 1) = f(\gamma \, treatment_i + \mathbf{x}_i'\boldsymbol{\beta}).$$

Descriptive Statistics for Restricted Sample

Chapters 4 through 6 present relevant descriptive statistics from the survey data, drawing on the full sample. However, because the survey included the experimental treatment to test respondents' willingness to misrepresent their normative commitments, I also calculate descriptive statistics for a restricted sample that only includes individuals in the control group. These descriptive statistics are presented in tables A.2, A.3, and A.4.

SURVEY QUESTIONNAIRES

There were four total versions of the survey questionnaire: (1) a questionnaire for female respondents that included the treatment (international audience) priming statements; (2) a questionnaire for female respondents that included the control (local audience) priming statements; (3) a questionnaire for male respondents that included the treatment priming

Table A.2: DESCRIPTIVE STATISTICS (RESTRICTED SAMPLE), CHAPTER 4

	Oldonyiro	Mukogodo	Mau	All areas	Observations
Accessibility					
Never visit town center	0.101	0.106	0.012	0.064	307
	(0.03)	(0.03)	(0.01)	(0.01)	
Protestant	0.053	0.262	0.781	0.429	304
	(0.02)	(0.03)	(0.05)	(0.03)	
Radio ownership	0.297	0.465	0.772	0.548	302
	(0.05)	(0.05)	(0.05)	(0.03)	
Awareness					
Aware of groups against female circumcision	0.086	0.664	0.874	0.599	307
	(0.03)	(0.05)	(0.04)	(0.03)	
Aware of groups against early marriage	0.075	0.613	0.845	0.568	307
	(0.03)	(0.05)	(0.04)	(0.03)	
Aware of circumcision health problems	0.173	0.230	0.381	0.279	306
	(0.04)	(0.05)	(0.05)	(0.03)	
Aware of early-marriage health problems	0.175	0.332	0.859	0.514	302
	(0.04)	(0.05)	(0.04)	(0.03)	

Note: Means weighted by inverse sampling probabilities. Standard errors in parentheses.

Table A.3: DESCRIPTIVE STATISTICS (RESTRICTED SAMPLE), CHAPTER 5

	Oldonyiro	Mukogodo	Mau	All areas	Observations
Message quality / individual openness					
Aware of circumcision health problems	0.173 (0.04)	0.230 (0.05)	0.381 (0.05)	0.279 (0.03)	306
Aware of early-marriage health problems	0.175 (0.04)	0.332 (0.05)	0.859 (0.04)	0.514 (0.03)	302
Female	0.480 (0.05)	0.487 (0.06)	0.460 (0.06)	0.473 (0.03)	308
Age	34.074 (1.62)	34.550 (1.96)	32.617 (1.82)	33.584 (1.08)	307
Attitudes					
Believe female circumcision should be stopped	0.076 (0.03)	0.448 (0.05)	0.566 (0.06)	0.399 (0.03)	306
Believe early marriage should be stopped	0.115 (0.03)	0.610 (0.06)	0.881 (0.04)	0.594 (0.03)	303

Note: Means weighted by inverse sampling probabilities. Standard errors in parentheses.

statements; and (4) a questionnaire for male respondents that included the control priming statements. Figure A.1 provides the female treatment questionnaire.

QUALITATIVE INTERVIEW DESIGN AND IMPLEMENTATION

The qualitative interviews were semistructured. I asked the interviewees questions using a predesigned interview protocol as a guide, but I skipped questions when they were not appropriate for the interviewee, and I constructed follow-up questions on the spot in response to what the interviewees said. Some interviews were audio-recorded, while in others I relied on my own note taking during the interview. Interviews were conducted in offices or other places of work, private homes, and sometimes restaurants. Most interviews were one-on-one, but I occasionally spoke with two or three interviewees simultaneously.

I contacted potential interviewees via several methods. If an office phone number or mobile phone number was available (listed online or provided by another interviewee), I would generally attempt to arrange an in-person

Table A.4: DESCRIPTIVE STATISTICS (RESTRICTED SAMPLE), CHAPTER 6

	Oldonyiro	Mukogodo	Mau	All areas	Observations
Barriers to defection					
Meet other tribe once a week or more	0.540 (0.05)	0.725 (0.05)	0.941 (0.03)	0.769 (0.03)	300
Believe elders want circumcision to stop	0.022 (0.02)	0.050 (0.02)	0.150 (0.04)	0.086 (0.02)	307
Believe elders want early marriage to stop	0.035 (0.02)	0.144 (0.04)	0.581 (0.06)	0.304 (0.03)	308
Believe chiefs want circumcision to stop	0.236 (0.05)	0.891 (0.03)	0.828 (0.04)	0.692 (0.03)	300
Believe chiefs want early marriage to stop	0.281 (0.05)	0.963 (0.02)	0.915 (0.04)	0.758 (0.03)	306
Behavior and intentions					
Daughter is or will be circumcised	0.878 (0.05)	0.708 (0.07)	0.730 (0.06)	0.761 (0.04)	163
Plan to circumcise daughter in future	0.876 (0.05)	0.608 (0.08)	0.601 (0.08)	0.672 (0.05)	144
Daughter married before age 18	0.832 (0.10)	0.769 (0.12)	0.613 (0.14)	0.726 (0.07)	46

Note: Means weighted by inverse sampling probabilities. Standard errors in parentheses.

interview by phone. In many cases, however, this method was unavailable or unsuccessful, and so I would physically go to an NGO, CBO, or government office and simply ask to speak to someone. In order to speak to traditional circumcisers, traditional birth attendants, and traditional leaders, I generally depended on direct introductions by key informants, who traveled with me to meet the interviewee and were often present during the interview itself, serving as translators.

There were frequent logistical challenges in tracking down individual people and arranging to meet. Phone numbers were often out of service, and because of poor mobile phone network coverage at the time, people's phones were often switched off or out-of-network. Offices were sometimes unattended. Interviewees frequently missed appointments, which had to be rescheduled (sometimes multiple times). Nonetheless, the significant amount of time I spent in the field meant that I was eventually able to interview virtually everyone I attempted to meet.

PROJECT: DESTURI -FEMALE SURVEY B

Serial No: ☐☐☐☐

Interviewer name_____

Interviewer number:.......... ☐☐☐
DD   MM   YY

Date of Interview............. ☐☐ ☐☐ ☐☐☐☐

H H   M M   H H   M M
Interview Start time: ☐☐ : ☐☐   Interview end time : ☐☐ : ☐☐

Quality Checks

☐ Supervisor Backcheched

☐ Supervisor Accompanied

☐ Supervisor Edited

☐ Interviewer edited

Region

☐ Mukogodo   ☐ Oldonyiro   ☐ Keekokyokie   ☐ Suswa

Respondent name: ☐☐☐☐☐☐☐☐☐☐☐☐☐☐☐☐☐

Physical address :_____   Phone No: ☐☐☐☐☐☐☐☐☐

Permission Statement

Kaaji enkarna _____ naa kaasisho tee enkampuni naaji [ILAMAIYO/Pastoralist Women for Health and Education/Tasaru Ntomonok Initiative]. [ILAMAIYO/Pastoralist Women for Health and Education/Tasaru Ntomonok Initiative] naa enkampuni neme enesirkali natii [Laikipia North/Oldonyiro/Mau] naasita asiai naipirta emuratare oontoyie, enkima oontoyie. Ore pee kitumoki aipanga enasiai aitobiraki ekigira aikilikuanu mbaa naipirta nenatokitin pokira are tengeno ino aashu naikunari nena baa aashu tenidamu anaa enitodwa toonchet kumok esirkali. Ekiiyieu nekiyolou ajo kainyoo edamu iltunganak lele osho narpirta nenabaa naa ekirorie iltunganak kumok loo mpukunot naapaasha te kopikop enakop oo [Laikipia North/Ol Donyiro/Mau] pee kindim atayiolo enaadolita iltunganak inaishiakino anaa nemeshiakino.neaku kalo aikilikuanishore iyie makewon ormarel lino neisulaki mbaa anaa iniimayie te nkishon naipirta kuna baa are, amaa aningito eishu enindim atejo eishu ilarikok aanaa ilaiguanak orkasulani okulikae ake.

Ore imbaa pookin nilimu naa enormumai aashu keisudori. Ore erishata ino naa enkitainoto ekawon pi naa indim atolimu nena nikimparishoreki anaa ipal pii tosaai pooki, mekilaki tena siai enakisoma aashu mitum aitoki sidai, tenkarake enasiai naainguaa [ILAMAIYO /Pastoralist Women for Health and Education/Tasaru Ntomonok Initiative]. Kake ekiata osiligi aajo ore naapuku pooki ena kisoma naa keret murua i pooki elulunga. Tee niata enkikilikwanare naipirta ena kisuma ana enkias ino tena kisuma naa indim atooshoki kulo tungana [Francis Merinyi (0726129087) te ILAMAIYO/Ibrahim Jattani (0720177326) te Pastoralist Women for Health and Education/Agnes Pareiyo (0722844646) te Tasaru Ntomonok Initiative], olaigwenani lino, anaa ol DC le [Laikipia North/Isiolo/Narok].

Amaa anaa enitoningo to kuna baa, inyoora mekimparishoreki?

Ore ena kitamaaya neitobiraki tee retoto oo laisumak le Amerika oingua Sukuul naji Yale University. Ore kulo Aisumak keinguraa enijo neasishore oo nkulie ampunini , oo langeni lo kulie kwapi. Anaa Amerika , Nkirisa oo nkaapuni sapukin enkop anaa United Nations. Ore napuku neasishoreki oo Nkasetini oo nkuapi anaa New York Times naisom iltunganak kumo lee dunia.

"My name is _____. I am working with ILAMAIYO [Nomadic Girl Child Network/Tasaru Ntomonok Initiative]. ILAMAIYO [Nomadic Girl Child Network/Tasaru Ntomonok Initiative] is an NGO based here in Laikipia North District [Ol Donyiro Division/Narok Central Division] that is undertaking a project concerning female circumcision and girl-child marriage. To help us better plan this project, we are collecting some basic data about your knowledge and attitudes about these two practices, and about your attitudes and experiences with different parts of the government. We want to know what people in the community really think about these practices, and we are talking to many different people all over Laikipia North [Ol Donyiro/Narok Central] so that we are certain that we have a complete picture of how people feel, both positively and negatively. As a result, I would like to ask you some questions about yourself and your family - in particular about your own life experiences with these traditional practices, how you feel about these things, and the opinions that you hold about different government leaders such as chiefs, councilors, and so on.

All of the information that you provide will be kept confidential. Your participation is completely voluntary, and you can decline to answer any individual question or stop this discussion at any time. You will not be compensated for participating in this study, nor will participation lead you to receive any special consideration from ILAMAIYO [Nomadic Girl Child Network], but we hope that the overall results of this study will be useful for the whole community in the long run. If you have any questions about this research project or your participation in it, you can contact Francis Merinyi (0726129087) at ILAMAIYO [Juliette Letimalo (0720249788) at Nomadic Girl Child Network/Agnes Pareiyo (0722844646) at Tasaru Ntomonok Initiative], your Area Chief, or the Laikipia North [Isiolo/Narok] District Commissioner. After hearing this information, do you agree to participate?"

This questionnaire was developed in consultation with two American researchers from Yale University. These researchers will look at the responses you give and share them with organizations and policy makers in other countries, like the United States and England, and with international organizations like the United Nations. The results will also be shared with international newspapers, like the New York Times, that are read by millions of people around the world.

Figure A.1: Female treatment survey questionnaire

INTERVIEW RESPONDENT ACCORDING TO KISH GRID.

Firstly, I need to decide whom I should interview from this household. Can you give me the first names and ages of all the adults aged between 18 and above who are living here at the moment?

RECORD BELOW AND COMPLETE SELECTION PROCESS AS INSTRUCTED.

SELECTION OF RESPONDENT FOR INTERVIEWING

1. List all the adults aged 18 and above living in the household together with their ages whether or not they are in at present. Start with the oldest and work down to the youngest.
2. Take the last figure of the questionnaire number and find the same number in the top line of the Kish Grid below
3. Look along the row of the last person in the list. Where this meets the column of the last digit of the questionnaire number, is the number of the person on the list to be interviewed.
4. Refer back to the list of family members and ask to speak to the person whose number is the same as the one you have taken out of the Kish Grid.
5. If that person is not at home, YOU MUST arrange to call a second time and a third time to interview that individual. If he/she is not there on the third occasion, you should select another adult in the household by taking the number in the Kish Grid DIRECTLY ABOVE the number you took originally on even number dates or DIRECTLY BELOW on odd number dates.
6. If that person is also not available, go to another household.
7. Record call details on front of questionnaire. Last digit on questionnaire number

		Last digit on questionnaire number									
No. of Adults in Household.	AGE	1	2	3	4	5	6	7	8	9	0
1_____		1	1	1	1	1	1	1	1	1	1
2_____		2	1	2	1	2	1	2	1	2	2
3_____		1	2	3	1	2	3	1	2	3	1
4_____		1	2	3	4	1	2	3	4	1	2
5_____		4	5	1	2	3	4	5	1	2	3
6_____		4	5	6	1	2	3	4	5	6	1
7_____		3	4	5	6	7	1	2	3	4	5
8_____		3	4	5	6	7	8	1	2	3	4
9_____		2	3	4	5	6	7	8	9	1	2
10_____		1	2	3	4	5	6	7	8	9	1

Total number of adults household................ ☐☐☐

Maiteru aimaki mbaa naipirta iyie makewon./ *Let's begin by recording a few facts about yourself.*

Q1 Kaaja ilaarin liyate? PROBE: Mdimi atadamu larin linonok?/ *How old are you? PROBE: Can you guess your age?*

Ilaarin/ *Age:* ☐☐   Enkipimoto olarin/ *Age Estimate:* ☐☐   ☐ Mayiolo/ *Don't Know*   ☐ Etanya/ *Refused*

Q2. Kaji itabaikia tengisuma ino?/ *What is the highest level of education you have completed?*

☐ Mmeetai/ *None*
☐ Aidipa Primary/ *Primary Complete*
☐ Hidip Secondary/ *Secondary Complete*
☐ University/ *University*

☐ Eitu Aidip Primary/ *Primary Incomplete*
☐ Eitu Aidip Secondary/ *Secondary Incomplete*
☐ College/ *College*
☐ Mayiolo/ *Don't Know*   ☐ Etanya/ *Refused*

Figure A.1: Continued

Q3. Amaa tiatua kuna tukitik kakua iyaata makeeno?/ *Which of these things do you personally own?*

	Eee/ Yes	Aaa/ No	Mayiolo/ Don't know	Etanya/ Refused
Ebuku/ *A book*	☐	☐	☐	☐
Eredio/ *A radio*	☐	☐	☐	☐
Television/ *A television*	☐	☐	☐	☐
Ebasukili/ *A bicycle*	☐	☐	☐	☐
Entukutuk/ *A motorcycle*	☐	☐	☐	☐
Egari/Emutukaa/ *A motor vehicle/ Car*	☐	☐	☐	☐

Q4. Kebaa arisheta nibaiki [Dol Dol Centre/Oldonyiro Centre/Nairege Enkare Centre]? [Esoma toongelunot]
/How often do you visit Dol Dol [Ol Donyiro/Narok]? [Read out response options]

☐ Eitu Aikata/ *Never*   ☐ Enkata nabo to lari / *About once a year or less*
☐ Enkata nabo too laipaitin pookin/ *About once every several months*   ☐ Enkata nabo tolaspa/ *About once a month*
☐ Enkata nabo teioiki/ *About once a week*   ☐ Kamanya Ine/ *I live there*
☐ Mayiolo [Mesumaki]/ *Don't Know [Do Not Read]*   ☐ Etanya [Mesumaki]/ *Refused*

Q5. Kaji lukinuno tenchoto ekiama? [Esoma toongelunot]/ *What is your marital status? [Read out response options]*

☐ Imayaama/ *Single*   ☐ Kaayama/ *Married*   ☐ Enkolia/ *Widowed*
☐ Kitara enkaputi/ *Divorced*   ☐ Mayiolo [Mesumaki]/ *Don't Know [DNR]*
☐ Etanya [Mesumaki]/ *Refused*

[Tenaa keema, iida No. 013./If unmarried, skip to Question 009.]

Q6 [Amaa tenaa inyama] kebaa ilarin liyaata pee iyaam? PROBE: Idim atedamu ajo ibaa apa?
/ [If married] How old were you when you married? PROBE: Can you guess how old you were?

Ilarin/ *Age:* ☐☐   Enkipimoto olarin/ *Age Estimate:* ☐☐

☐ Mayiolo/ *Don't Know*   ☐ Madamu/ *Don't recall*   ☐ Etanya/ *Refused*

Q7. [Amaa tenaa inyama] Kebaa ilarin oota orpayian lino pee iyaam ninye? PROBE: Idim atedamu atajo kebaa apa ilarin aoya?
/[If married] How old was your husband when you married him? PROBE: Can you guess how old he was?

Ilarin/ *Age:* ☐☐   Enkipimoto olarin/ *Age Estimate:* ☐☐

☐ Mayiolo/ *Don't Know*   ☐ Madamu/ *Don't recall*   ☐ Etanya/ *Refused*

Q8 [Amaa tenaa inyama] Kolialo poror orpayian lino?/ *[If married] What is your husband's age set?*

Alo poror/ *Age set:* _____ ☐☐   ☐ Mayiolo/ *Don't Know*   ☐ Etanya/ *Refused*

Q9. Kaa siai ias? [Esoma toongelunot]/ *What is your main occupation? [Read out response options]*

☐ Orparakuoni looaashu/ *Pastoralist*   ☐ Orbiasharai/ *Businessperson*
☐ Enkerai Esukul/ *Student*   ☐ Iasisho Tiang /*Works in the Household*
☐ Maigero/ *Unemployed*   ☐ Kulie (Naalimuni)/ *Other (Specify):* _____ ☐☐☐
☐ Etanya [Mesumaki] /*Refused*

Figure A.1: Continued

Q10. Kaa dini ino, tenaa eyata? [Esoma toongelunot]/ *What is your religion, if any? [Read out response options]*

- [ ] Mmeetai/ *None*
- [ ] Irmusheni/ *Catholic*
- [ ] Inkulie Kanisani/ *Other Church*
- [ ] Muslim
- [ ] Traditional
- [ ] Orkuak liapa
- [ ] Kulie (Naalimuni)/ *Other (Specify):* _____ [ ][ ]
- [ ] Etanya [Mesumaki]/ *Refused*

Q11 Imurata?/ *Are you circumcised?*

- [ ] Eee/ *Yes*
- [ ] Aaa/ *No*
- [ ] Etanya/ *Refused*

Q12. Ilarin aja apa iyala peesayu ena? PROBE: Idim atedamu atajo ibaa apa ilarin aoya?
/[If circumcised] *How old were you when this occurred? PROBE: Can you guess how old you were?*

Ilarin/ *Age:* [ ]   Enkipimoto olarin/ *Age Estimate:* [ ]
- [ ] Kerai Kini/ *During infacy*
- [ ] Mayiolo/ *Don't Know*
- [ ] Madamu/ *Don't recall*
- [ ] Etanya/ *Refused*

Q13. Eingaye oshi nadung ormouo? [Esoma toongelunot]/ *[If circumcised] Who cut the genitals? [Read out options]*

- [ ] Enkolmoratani Eyape/ *Traditional Circumciser*
- [ ] Enkaitoyuoni/ *Traditional Birth Attendant*
- [ ] Oldakitari/ *Doctor*
- [ ] Endeketari naisume/ *Trained Nurse*
- [ ] Enkaitoyuoni nausume/ *Trained Midwife*
- [ ] Kulie (Naalimuni)/ *Other (Specify):* _____ [ ][ ]
- [ ] Mayiolo [Mesumaki]/ *Don't Know [DNR]*
- [ ] Madamu [Mesumaki]/ *Don't Recall [DNR]*
- [ ] Etanya [Mesumaki]/ *Refused*

Q14. Eyata ntoyie? / *Do you have any daughters?*

- [ ] Eee/ *Yes*
- [ ] Aaa/ *No*
- [ ] Etanya/ *Refused*

[Tenaa "Aaa," ida No. 024./ *If "No," skip to Question 024.]*

Q15. [Tenaa Eee] Eyate ntoyie naamurata?/ *[If yes] Are any of your daughters circumcised?*

- [ ] Eee/ *Yes*
- [ ] Aaa/ *No*
- [ ] Mayiolo/ *Don't Know*
- [ ] Etanya/ *Refused*

[Amaa tenaa "Eee" (015)] Kayieu naikulikuan ina tito natomorataki det. (Enkilikuanata 016 - 018)
[If response to 015 was "Yes"] I would now like to ask you about the daughter who was most recently circumcised. (Questions 016-018)
Q16. Ilarin aja apa eeta peesayu ena? PROBE: Idim atedamu atajo kebaa apa ilarin aoya? /*How old was she when this occurred?*
PROBE: Can you guess how old she was?

Ilarin/ *Age:* [ ]   Enkipimoto olarin/ *Age Estimate:* [ ]
- [ ] Kerai Kini/ *During Infancy*
- [ ] Mayiolo / *Don't Know*
- [ ] Madamu/ *Don't Recall*
- [ ] Etanya/ *Refused*

Q17. Eingaye oshi nadung ormouo? [Esoma toongelunot]/ *Who cut the genitals? [Read out response options]*

- [ ] Enkolmoratani Eyape/ *Traditional Circumciser*
- [ ] Enkaitoyuoni/ *Traditional Birth Attendant*
- [ ] Oldakitari/ *Doctor*
- [ ] Endeketari naisume/ *Trained Nurse*
- [ ] Enkaitoyuoni nausume/ *Trained Midwife*
- [ ] Kulie (Naalimuni)/ *Other (Specify):* _____ [ ][ ]
- [ ] Mayiolo [Mesumaki]/ *Don't Know [DNR]*
- [ ] Madamu [Mesumaki]/ *Don't Recall [DNR]*
- [ ] Etanya [Mesumaki] / *Refused*

The Steadman Group

Figure A.1: Continued

Q18. Engai natonyoyie ajo kanu emurati? [Esoma toongelunot]/ *Who decided when she would be cut? [Read out response options]*

☐ Iyie/ *You* ☐ Orpaiyan lino/ *Your Husband*

☐ Ntaye o orpaiyan lino tenebo/ *You and Your Husband Together* ☐ Entito ino/ *Your Daughter*

☐ Kulie (Naalimuni)/ *Other (Specify):* _____ ☐☐☐ ☐ Madamu [Mesumaki]/ *Don't Recall [DNR]*

☐ Etanya [Mesumaki] /*Refused*

Q19. [Tenaa entito] Iyiuo niata nabo tito ino namurata tooukolo'ngi naaponu?/ *[If daughters] Do you intend to have any of your daughters circumcised in the future?*

☐ Eee/ *Yes* ☐ Aaa/ *No* ☐ Keitegemea/ *Depends* ☐ Meishiakino/*Not Applicable*

☐ Mayiolo/ *Don't Know* ☐ Etanya/ *Refused*

Q20 [Tenaa entito] Keetae entito ino akatai nayamaki?/ *[If daughters] Have any of your daughters ever been married?*

☐ Eee / *Yes* ☐ Aaa/ *No* ☐ Mayiolo/ *Don't Know* ☐ Etanya/ *Refused*

[Tenaa ore orkilikua le 020 naa "Eee"] Kaayio naikiliuan kuhusu entito nayamaki deet. (Enkilikuanata 021 - 023)
[If response to 020 was "Yes"] I would now like to ask you about the daughter who was most recently married. (Questions 021-023)

Q21.Kaja larin oota pee eyaami? PROBE: Idim atedamu atajo kebaa apa ilarin aoya?
How old was she when she married? PROBE: Can you guess how old she was?

Ilarin/ *Age:* ☐☐ Enkipimoto olarin/ *Age Estimate:* ☐☐ ☐ Mayiolo/ *Don't Know*

☐ Madamu/ *Don't Recall* ☐ Etanya/ *Refused*

Q22. Kengai nalimu enkata nayaami? [Esoma toongelunot]/ *Who decided when she would marry? [Read out response options]*

☐ Iyie/ *You* ☐ Orpaiyan lino/ *Your Husband*

☐ Ntaye o orpaiyan lino tenebo/ *You and Your Husband Together* ☐ Entito ino/ *Your Daughter*

☐ Kulie (Naalimuni)/ *Other (Specify):* _____ ☐☐☐ ☐ Madamu [Mesumaki] /*Don't Recall [DNR]*

☐ Etanya [Mesumaki]/ *Refused*

Q23. Ilarin aja eeta orpayia lenye pee eyaam? PROBE: Idim atedamu atajo kebaa apa ilarin aoya?/ *How old was her husband when they married? PROBE: Can you guess how old he was?*

Ilarin/ *Age:* ☐☐ Enkipimoto olarin/ *Age Estimate:* ☐☐ ☐ Mayiolo/ *Don't Know*

☐ Madamu/ *Don't Recall* ☐ Etanya/ *Refused*

/Kaiyeu naikilikuan imbaa naiperata emuratere oo nkituak o kiama.
Now I would like to ask you some more general questions about female circumcision and marriage.

Q24. Amaa emuratare keidiumayu neyau enyamali ebiotisho?/ *Does circumcision ever cause health problems?*

☐ Eee/ *Yes* ☐ Aaa / *No* ☐ Mayiolo/ *Don't Know* ☐ Etanya/ *Refused*

Q25. Kijing'aki emuratere esipata oltungani?/ *Does circumcision violate human rights?*

☐ Eee/ *Yes* ☐ Aaa/ *No* ☐ Mayiolo/ *Don't Know* ☐ Etanya/ *Refused*

Q26. Amaa emuratare keishaa ana mishiaate sheria e Kenya?/ *Is circumcision legal or illegal in Kenya?*

☐ Keishaa/ *Legal* ☐ Meishiaa/ *Illegal* ☐ Mayiolo/ *Don't Know* ☐ Etanya/ *Refused*

Q27. Amaasa keetai mbaa natoningokinoteki too Nkuapi eboo aamit emuratare oo ntoyie?
/ Are there any international treaties or agreements that prohibit female circumcision?

☐ Eee/ *Yes* ☐ Aaa/ *No* ☐ Mayiolo / *Don't Know* ☐ Etanya/ *Refused*

Figure A.1: Continued

Q28. Amaa teyie kesaina Kenya leloningoritin?/ *Has Kenya signed any of these treaties or agreements?*

☐ Eee /Yes ☐ Aaal No ☐ Mayiolo/ Don't Know ☐ Etanya/ Refused

Q29. Keetai iltururi tele osho ongira aanyok aitasheire emuratare oo ntoyie?
/ Are there any groups or organizations in this community that are trying to stop female circumcision?

☐ Eee /Yes ☐ Aaal No ☐ Mayiolo/ Don't Know ☐ Etanya/ Refused

Q30. [Tenaa Eee] Ingero kulo tururi?/ *[If yes] Can you list any of these groups?*
Inkaran oltururi telulungata (Naalimuni)/ *Name(s) of Group(s) (Specify):* _____

☐☐
☐☐
☐☐

☐ Mmeetai Ilolimu/ *Cannot List Any* ☐ Etanya/ *Refused*

Q31. Kebaa irishat nitum rkiliku tiata kuna tokiting? [Esoma toongelunot]/ *How often do you get news from the following sources?*
[Read out response options]

	Eneaks Every Day	Inkutj reshat teok] A Few Times a Week	Inkuisj reshat tulapa A Few Times a Month	Eitu elahunye olapa Less Than Once a Month	Mmeetai Never	Mayiolo [Mesumaki] Don't Know [DNK]	Etanya [Mesumaki] Refused
a) Eredio/ Radio...............	☐	☐	☐	☐	☐	☐	☐
b) Television/ Television...	☐	☐	☐	☐	☐	☐	☐
c) Enkaseti/ Newspaper....	☐	☐	☐	☐	☐	☐	☐

Q32. Itonigo aikata orkiliku operata emuratere oontoyie teredio [Ida tenaa ore No. 031a "Mmeetai."]?
/ Have you heard any reports about female circumcision on the radio [Unless response to Q31a was "Never"]?

☐ Eee/ Yes ☐ Aaal No ☐ Mayiolo/Don't Know ☐ Etanya/ Refused

Q33. Itodua aikata orkiliku oaperate emuratere oontoyie te television [Ida tenaa ore No. 031b "Mmeetai."]?
/Have you seen any reports about female circumcision on television [Unless response to Q31b was "Never"]?

☐ Eee/ Yes ☐ Aaal No ☐ Mayiolo/Don't Know ☐ Etanya/ Refused

Q34. Itodua aikata lomon naitodolu emuratere oontoyie tenkaseti [Ida tenaa ore No. 031c "Mmeetai."]?/ *Have you seen any articles about female circumcision in the newspaper [Unless response to Q31c was "Never"]?*

☐ Eee/ Yes ☐ Aaal No ☐ Mayiolo/Don't Know ☐ Etanya/ Refused

Q35. Amaa kiama egorr ilarin tomon osiet keidiumayu neyau enyamali ebiotisho?
/Does marriage before age 18 ever cause health problems for girls?

☐ Eee/ Yes ☐ Aaal No ☐ Mayiolo/Don't Know ☐ Etanya/ Refused

Q36. Kijing'aki kiama egorr ilarin tomon osiet esipata oltungani?/ *Does marriage before age 18 violate human rights?*

☐ Eee/ Yes ☐ Aaal No ☐ Mayiolo/Don't Know ☐ Etanya/ Refused

Q37. Amaa kiama egorr ilarin tomon osiet keishaa ana mishiaate sheria e Kenya?/ *Is marriage before age 18 legal or illegal in Kenya?*

☐ Keishaa/ Legal ☐ Meishiaa/Illegal ☐ Mayiolo/ Don't Know ☐ Etanya/ Refused

Q38. Amaasa keetai mbaa natoningokinoteki too Nkuapi eboo aamit kiama egorr ilarin tomon osiet?/ *Are there any international treaties or agreements that prohibit marriage before age 18?*

☐ Eee/ Yes ☐ Aaal No ☐ Mayiolo/Don't Know ☐ Etanya/ Refused

Q39. Amaa teyie kesaina Kenya leloningoritin?/ *Has Kenya signed any of these treaties or agreements?*

☐ Eee/ Yes ☐ Aaal No ☐ Mayiolo/Don't Know ☐ Etanya/ Refused

Figure A.1: Continued

Q40. Keetai ittururi tele osho ongira aanyok aitasheire kiama egorr ilarin tomon osiet?/ *Are there any groups or organizations in this community that are trying to stop marriage before the age of 18?*

☐ Eee /*Yes*   ☐ Aaal */No*   ☐ Mayiolo/ *Don't Know*   ☐ Etanya/ *Refused*

Q41. [Tenaa Eee] Ingero kulo tururi?/ *[If yes] Can you list any of these groups?*
Inkaran oltururi telulungata (Naalimuni)/ *Name(s) of Group(s) (Specify):* _____

_____

_____

☐ Mmeeta Ilolimu/ *Cannot List Any*   ☐ Etanya/ *Refused*

Q42. Itonigo aikata orkiliku operata kiama egorr ilarin tomon osiet teredio [Ida tenaa ore No. 031a "Mmeetai."]?/ *Have you heard any reports about early marriage on the radio [Unless response to 031a was "Never"]?*

☐ Eee /*Yes*   ☐ Aaal */No*   ☐ Mayiolo/ *Don't Know*   ☐ Etanya/ *Refused*

Q43. Itodua aikata orkiliku oaperate kiama egorr ilarin tomon osiet te television [Ida tenaa ore No. 031b "Mmeetai."]?/ *Have you seen any reports about early marriage on television [Unless response to 031b was "Never"]?*

☐ Eee /*Yes*   ☐ Aaal */No*   ☐ Mayiolo/ *Don't Know*   ☐ Etanya/ *Refused*

Q44. Itodua aikata lomon naitodolu kiama egorr ilarin tomon osiet tenkaseti [Ida tenaa ore No. 031c "Mmeetai."]?/ *Have you seen any articles about early marriage in the newspaper [Unless response to 031c was "Never"]?*

☐ Eee /*Yes*   ☐ Aaal */No*   ☐ Mayiolo/ *Don't Know*   ☐ Etanya/ *Refused*

Kayieu tata naikilikuan makewon imbaa naipirta emuraratare oo nkiama. Ore lelo aisumak lee Amerika oitibiritua enaa kitamaaya kenyor oleng enilimu pee retoo enkipara nasuju oo nkaapuni sapukin oo langeni ooasisho oolamerikani.   Amu iyiolo emuratare oo ntoyie oo nkiama nasiokini naa imbaa sapukin naingurita tenguton Lamerikani oo nkaampunini sapukin, keinguraa ilomon lilimu peeretoo tengeno eramat olarin oopuonu.

Now I would like to ask about your opinions on circumcision and marriage. The American researchers who have developed this survey are especially interested in the answers you provide to these next questions, as are the international organizations and foreign policymakers with whom the Americans are working. Because circumcision and early marriages are issues that the Americans and the United Nations care about very deeply, they will be looking at your answers to help them make decisions about future programs and policies.

Q45. Kaa faida etum ntoyie tenemurati? [Esoma toongelunot] PROBE: Keetai ai faida? [Ingila mpaka nelimu uni asho nejo imeukure eltai.] NG'ERO NBAA UNI NATEJO. [Tenaa kengiro uni tiaki pee ngelo uni sidana.]
/What benefits do girls themselves get if they undergo female circumcision? [Read out response options] PROBE: Any other benefits? [Repeat until the respondent has listed three or says they can think of no others.] RECORD ALL MENTIONED, UP TO THREE.[If more than three are listed, ask respondent to choose top three.]

☐ Ailep Akut Oltungani Sapuk/ *Graduation to Adulthood*   ☐ Esidanu oo Afya/ *Cleanliness/Hygiene*

☐ Asuj Orkuak le Kanisa/ *Religious Approval*   ☐ Enganyit Naigua Olosho/ *Respect from the Community*

☐ Enkidimata Kiama/ *Ability to Marry*   ☐ Enkidimata pee Iyaata Nkera/ *Ability to Have Children*

☐ Emeloni "Sex" Toorpayian/ *More Sexual Pleasure for the Man*   ☐ Ebooyo Eloloito/ *Preserve Virginity/Prevent Premarital Sex*

☐ Kulie (Naalimuni):/ *Other (Specify):* _____

_____

☐ Mmeeta Faida/ *No Benefits*   ☐ Mayiolo [Mesumaki]/ *Don't Know [DNR]*   ☐ Etanya [Mesumaki]/ *Refused*

Figure A.1: Continued

Q46. Kaa faida etum intoyie tenememuratl? [Esoma toongelunot] PROBE: Keetai ai faida? [Ingila mpaka nelimu uni asho nejo imeukure eltai.] NG'ERO NBAA UNI NATEJO. [Tenaa kengiro uni tiaki pee ngelo uni sidana.] /What benefits do girls themselves get if they do not undergo female circumcision? [Read out response options] PROBE: Any other benefits? [Repeat until the respondent has listed three or says they can think of no others.] RECORD ALL MENTIONED, UP TO THREE. [If more than three are listed, ask respondent to choose top three.]

☐ Nyamalalitin Kuti Embare/ Fewer Medical Problems   ☐ Aibooyo Emion/ Avoiding Pain

☐ Aisuj Orkuak le Kanisa/ Follows Religion   ☐ Isidano "Sex" Toorpayiani/ More Sexual Pleasure for the Man

☐ Isidano "Sex" Toonkituak/ More Sexual Pleasure for the Women

☐ Kulie (Naalimuni)/ Other (Specify): _____

_____ ☐☐☐ ☐☐☐

☐ Mmeeta Faida /No Benefits   ☐ Mayiolo [Mesumaki]/ Don't Know [DNR]   ☐ Etanya [Mesumaki]/ Refused

---

Q47. Inyorra meyama oloyiani lino enito namurata ana enememurata, ashu mmeeta tofauti? / Hypothetically, would you prefer that your son marry a circumcised woman or an uncircumcised woman, or does it make no difference?

☐ Namurata/ Circumcised   ☐ Nememurata/ Uncircumcised   ☐ Keitegemea/ Depends

☐ Mmeeta Tofauti/ No Difference   ☐ Etanya/ Refused

Q48. Idoolta emuratare oo ntoyie endelea, anaa keitashe?/ Do you think that this practice should be continued, or should it be stopped?

☐ Kaendelea / Continued   ☐ Keitosha/ Stopped   ☐ Keitegemea/ Depends

☐ Mayiolo / Don't Know   ☐ Etanya/ Refused

Q49. Amaa inji itu anaake ana kibelekenye nduat inono temuratere?/ Have you always felt this way, or have your views on female circumcision changed?

☐ Anaake/ Always   ☐ Kibelekenya/ Changed   ☐ Etanya/ Refused

---

Q50. Amaa keata tipat emuratare oo ntoyie teyie? [Esoma toongelunot] / How important is the issue of female circumcision to you? [Read out response options]

☐ 1. Keata Tipat Oleng / Very Important   ☐ 2. Keidimayu Peno / Somewhat Important

☐ 3. Mmeeta Tipat Oleng/ Not Very Important   ☐ 4. Mmeeta Tipat Katukul/ Not At All Important

☐ 5. Etanya [Mesumaki]/ Refused

Q51. Idolda enaa kitasheiyeki emuratare oo ntoyie teleosho ana keendelea pireki kata?/ Do you think that female circumcision can be stopped in this community, or will it continue no matter what?

☐ Kitasheiki/ Can Be Stopped   ☐ Keendelea/ Will Continue   ☐ Keitegemea/ Depends

☐ Mayiolo/ Don't Know   ☐ Etanya/ Refused

Q52. Engai aashu oinyoo naji oleng nekinko indamunot too mbaa naipirta emuratare oo ntoyie? [Esoma toongelunot]/ Who or what is most influential in determining your views on female circumcision? [Read out response options]

☐ Indamunot inonok/ Your Own Experience   ☐ Kanisa / Church   ☐ Isiasani/ Politicians

☐ Ngutunji/ Your Mother   ☐ Papalino / Your Father   ☐ Orpaiyan lino/ Your Husband

☐ Ilchoreta/ Your Friends   ☐ Olosho/ The Entire Community   ☐ Sukul/ School

☐ Sheria/ The Law   ☐ Kulie (Naalimuni)/ Other (Specify): _____ ☐☐☐

☐ Mmeetai/Mme Oltungani [Naa Orkuak Olosho] [Mesumaki]/ Nothing/Nobody (It is Tradition) [DNR]

☐ Mayiolo [Mesumaki]/ Don't Know [DNR]   ☐ Etanya [Mesumaki]/ Refused

The Steadman Group

Figure A.1: Continued

Q53. Kaalo aliki Nkabilaritin oltunganak, ore aaliki enkama oltunur oje, kayiu nekiliki tenaa idamu ajo ore iltunganak kumok leilonturrur naa keyie emuratare oo ntoyie neendelea aashu epali./ I'm going to list some groups of people for you. As I tell you the name of each group, I want you to tell me whether you think most people in the group want female circumcision to continue or be stopped.

	Keyiau Neendelea Continue	Keyie Nepali Stop	Keitegemea Depends	Mayiolo Don't Know	Etanya Refused
Nkituak Lele Osho/ Women in this community:	☐	☐	☐	☐	☐
Ilewa Lele Osho/ Men in this community:	☐	☐	☐	☐	☐
Irpayiani Kituak/ Elders in this community:	☐	☐	☐	☐	☐
Chiefs Lele Osho/ Chiefs in this community:	☐	☐	☐	☐	☐
Nkamponini Neme Nesirkali Naitengenisho Lele Osho /Civil society leaders in this community:	☐	☐	☐	☐	☐
Ilarikok Le Kanisa Lele Osho/ Church leaders in this community:	☐	☐	☐	☐	☐
Irpilisi Lele Osho/ Police in this community:	☐	☐	☐	☐	☐
Orbungei Lele Osho/ Your MP:	☐	☐	☐	☐	☐
Sirkali oo Enkuapi Eboo/ Western governments:	☐	☐	☐	☐	☐
Nkamponini loo Nkuapi Eboo/ International organizations:	☐	☐	☐	☐	☐

Q54. Kaa faida etum ntoyie kiama egorr ilarin tomon osiet? [Esoma toongelunot] PROBE: Keetai ai faida? [Ingila mpaka nelimu uni asho nejo imeukure eltai.] NG'ERO NBAA UNI NATEJO. [Tenaa kengiro uni tiaki pee ngelo uni sidana.] /What benefits do girls themselves get if they marry before age 18? [Read out response options] PROBE: Any other benefits? [Repeat until the respondent has listed three or says they can think of no others.] RECORD ALL MENTIONED, UP TO THREE. [If more than three are listed, ask respondent to choose top three.]

☐ Dupoto Oomali/ Economic Security   ☐ Erisharoto ee Biitia/ Protection from HIV/AIDS

☐ Enkiama na Dupa/ Better Marriage Prospects   ☐ Enkidimata pee Iyaata Nkera/ Ability to Have Children

☐ Ebooyo Eloloito / Preserve Virginity/Prevent Premarital Sex

☐ Kulie (Naalimuni)/ Other (Specify): _____ ☐☐☐
_____ ☐☐☐

☐ Mmeeta Faida/ No Benefits   ☐ Mayiolo [Mesumaki]/ Don't Know [DNR]   ☐ Etanya [Mesumaki]/ Refused

Q55. Kaa faida etum intoyie kiama egorr ilarin tomon osiet? [Esoma toongelunot] PROBE: Keetai ai faida? [Ingila mpaka nelimu uni asho nejo imeukure eltai.] NG'ERO NBAA UNI NATEJO. [Tenaa kengiro uni tiaki pee ngelo uni sidana.] /What benefits do girls themselves get if they wait to marry until after age 18? [Read out response options] PROBE: Any other benefits? [Repeat until the respondent has listed three or says they can think of no others.] RECORD ALL MENTIONED, UP TO THREE.[If more than three are listed, ask respondent to choose top three.]

☐ Nyamalalitin Kuti Embare/ Fewer Medical Problems   ☐ Enkisoma Sapuk/ More Education

☐ Erisharoto ee Biitia/ Protection from HIV/AIDS   ☐ Enkiama na Dupa/ Better Marriage Prospects

☐ Enkiama Naishia/ Better Understanding of Marriage Responsibilities

☐ Kulie (Naalimuni)/ Other (Specify): _____ ☐☐☐
_____ ☐☐☐

☐ Mmeeta Faida/ No Benefits   ☐ Mayiolo [Mesumaki]/ Don't Know [DNR]
☐ Etanya [Mesumaki]/ Refused

Q56. Idoolta kiama egorr ilarin tomon osiet endelea, anaa keitashe? / Do you think that this practice should be continued, or should it be stopped?

☐ Kaendelea/ Continued   ☐ Keitosha/ Stopped   ☐ Keitegemea/ Depends

☐ Mayiolo/ Don't Know   ☐ Etanya/ Refused

The Steadman Group

Figure A.1: Continued

Q57. Amaa inji itu anaake ana kibelekenye nduat inono kiama egorr ilarin tomon osiet?/ *Have you always felt this way, or have your views on early marriage changed?*

- [ ] Anaake/ *Always*
- [ ] Kibelekenya/ *Changed*
- [ ] Etanya/ *Refused*

Q58. Amaa keata tipat kiama egorr ilarin tomon osiet teyie? [Esoma toongelunot]/ *How important is the issue of early marriage to you?* *[Read out response options]*

- [ ] Keata Tipat Oleng/ *Very Important*
- [ ] Keidimayu Peno / *Somewhat Important*
- [ ] Mmeeta Tipat Oleng/ *Not Very Important*
- [ ] Mmeeta Tipat Katukul/ *Not At All Important*
- [ ] Etanya [Mesumaki]/ *Refused*

Q59. Idolda enaa kitasheiyeki kiama egorr ilarin tomon osiet teleosho ana keendelea pireki kata? /*Do you think that marriage before age 18 can be stopped in this community, or will it continue no matter what?*

- [ ] Kitasheiki/ *Can Be Stopped*
- [ ] Keendelea / *Will Continue*
- [ ] Keitegemea/ *Depends*
- [ ] Mayiolo/ *Don't Know*
- [ ] Etanya / *Refused*

Q60. Engai aashu oinyoo naji oleng nekinko indamunot too mbaa naipirta kiama egorr ilarin tomon osiet? [Esoma toongelunot]/ *Who or what is most influential in determining your views on marriage before 18? [Read out response options]*

- [ ] Indamunot inonok/ *Your Own Experience*
- [ ] Kanisa / *Church*
- [ ] Isiasani/ *Politicians*
- [ ] Ngutunji/ *Your Mother*
- [ ] Papalino / *Your Father*
- [ ] Orpaiyan lino/ *Your Husband*
- [ ] Ilchoreta/ *Your Friends*
- [ ] Olosho/ *The Entire Community*
- [ ] Sukul/ *School*
- [ ] Sheria/ *The Law*
- [ ] Kulie (Naalimuni)/ *Other (Specify):* _____ [ ][ ][ ]
- [ ] Mmeetai/Mme Oltungani [Naa Orkuak Olosho] [Mesumaki]/ *Nothing/Nobody (It is Tradition) [DNR]*
- [ ] Mayiolo [Mesumaki]/ *Don't Know [DNR]*
- [ ] Etanya [Mesumaki]/ *Refused*

Q61. Kaalo aliki Nkabilaritin oltunganak, ore aaliki enkama oltunur oje, kayiu nekiliki tenaa idamu ajo ore iltunganak kumok leilonturrur naa keyie kiama egorr ilarin tomon osiet neendelea aashu epali./ *I'm going to list some groups of people for you. As I tell you the name of each group, I want you to tell me whether you think most people in the group want marriage before age 18 to continue or be stopped?*

	Kayiou Neendelea / Continue	Keyie Napali / Stop	Keitegemea / Depends	Mayiolo / Don't Know	Etanya / Refused
Nkituak Lele Osho/ *Women in this community:*	[ ]	[ ]	[ ]	[ ]	[ ]
Ilewa Lele Osho/ *Men in this community:*	[ ]	[ ]	[ ]	[ ]	[ ]
Irpayiani Kituak/ *Elders in this community:*	[ ]	[ ]	[ ]	[ ]	[ ]
Chiefs Lele Osho/ *Chiefs in this community:*	[ ]	[ ]	[ ]	[ ]	[ ]
Nkamponini Neme Nesirkali Naitengenisho Lele Osho /*Civil society leaders in this community:*	[ ]	[ ]	[ ]	[ ]	[ ]
Ilarikok Le Kanisa Lele Osho/ *Church leaders in this community:*	[ ]	[ ]	[ ]	[ ]	[ ]
Irpilisi Lele Osho/ *Police in this community:*	[ ]	[ ]	[ ]	[ ]	[ ]
Orbungei Lele Osho/ *Your MP:*	[ ]	[ ]	[ ]	[ ]	[ ]
Sirkali oo Enkuapi Eboo/ *Western governments:*	[ ]	[ ]	[ ]	[ ]	[ ]
Nkamponini loo Nkuapi Eboo/ *International organizations:*	[ ]	[ ]	[ ]	[ ]	[ ]

Matorinyioto siadi aimaki mbaa emaoe./ *Let's go back to talking about you.*

Q62. Ira oliaio orere? PROBE: Iyiolo olerere lino?/ *What is your tribe? PROBE: You know, your ethnic or cultural group.*

- [ ] Maasai
- [ ] Yaaku (Mukogodo)
- [ ] Il'ngwesi
- [ ] Mumonyot
- [ ] Ewaso
- [ ] Ildigiri
- [ ] Samburu
- [ ] Kulie (Naalimunie)/ *Other (Specify):* _____ [ ][ ][ ]
- [ ] Imaata/Enkabila Kara Olekenya/ *No Tribe/Kenyan Only*
- [ ] Mayiolo/ *Don't Know*
- [ ] Etanya/ *Refused*

The Steadman Group

Figure A.1: Continued

Q63. Amaa te pooki , idol anaa ore sheria ekenya naa keinguraa olrng enasiai anaa enkabila? [Arashu kejo erishata No. 062 "Enkabila Kara Olekenya"]/ *In general, do you believe that the Laws of Kenya promote the best interests of _____ (RESPONDENT'S TRIBE)? Unless response to 062 was "Kenyan Only"]*

☐ Eee/ *Yes*　　　☐ Aaa/ *No*　　　☐ Mayiolo/ *Don't Know*　　　☐ Etanya/ *Refused*

Q64. Amaa tenaa igelu pee ira orkenyai aashu enkabila eno _____, kakua turruni aare idil anaa inyikaui oleng? [Arashu kejo erishata No. 062 "Enkabila Kara Olekenya"]/ *If you had to choose between being a Kenyan and being a _____ (RESPONDENT'S TRIBE), which of these two groups do you feel most strongly attached to? [Unless response to 062 was "Kenyan Only"]*

☐ Ormkenyal/ *National Identity*　　☐ Enkabila /*Tribal Identity*　　☐ Nabo Pooki/ *Neither*

☐ Mayiolo/ *Don't Know*　　☐ Etanya/ *Refused*

Q65. Kebaa duo oshi inkolongi nitum oltungani le ai abila? [Esoma toongelunot]/ *How often do you encounter somebody from a different tribe? [Read out response options]*

☐ Eito aikataa too haapa/ *Never*　　　☐ Enkata nabo tolari/ *About once a year or less*

☐ Enkata nabo tolapaitini/ *About once every several months*　　☐ Enkata nabo tolapa/ *About once a month*

☐ Enkata nabo te wiki/ *About once a week*　　☐ Mgologi kumok tewoki/ *More than once a week*

☐ Ingolongi pooki/ *Every day*　　☐ Mayiolo [Mesumaki]/ *Don't Know [DNR]*

☐ Etanya [Mesumaki]/ *Refused*

Q66. Kainyo enkaabila niitum aanake? [Arashu kejo erishata No. 065 "Eito aikataa too happa"] / *What other tribe do you encounter most frequently? [Unless response to 065 was "Never"]*

☐ Irkokoyok/ *Kikuyu*　　☐ Ilsambuk/ *Samburu*　　☐ Turkana　　☐ Somali

☐ Ilborana/ *Borana*　　☐ Irendile / *Rendille*　　☐ Ilmaasai/ *Maasai*　　☐ Iljaluo/ *Luo*

☐ Ilbaluhyia/ *Luhya*　　☐ Ilkamba/ *Kamba*　　☐ Ilmeru/ *Meru*　　☐ Ilkisii / *Kisii*

☐ Ilkalenjin/ *Kalenjin*　　☐ Iltaita/ *Taita*　　☐ Ilkuria/ *Kuria*　　☐ Ilembu/ *Embu*

☐ Ilpokot/ *Pokot*　　☐ Mayiolo / *Don't Know*

☐ Kulie (Naalimunie)/ *Other (Specify):* _____ ☐☐☐ ☐ Etanya/ *Refused*

Q67. Amaa teneponge sheria ekenya onokuak lootungani kainyoeldim itungani atusij?/ *When laws of Kenya conflict with local customs, which should people follow?*

☐ Inkitanapat Ekenya/ *Laws of Kenya*　　☐ Irkuaki/ *Local Customs*　　☐ Nemetii/ *Neither*

☐ Keitegemea ana Enatiu/ *Depends on Situation*　　☐ Mayiolo/ *Don't Know*　　☐ Etanya/ *Refused*

Q68. Amaa tekuna baa kea nanyikita enduata ino? Tengelu A anaa ingelu B./ *Which of the following statements is closest to your view? Choose Statement A or Statement B.*
　　A: Ore tenkop ang, naa kishakino neta inkituak haki neramatisi anaa ilewa./ *In our country, women should have equal rights and receive the same treatment as men do.*
　　B: Ore inkistuak naa kesul orkuak liapa na kishaikino pee entoni nejia./ *Women have always been subject to traditional laws and customs, and should remain so.* [Wait for response] *PROBE:*
　　[Toanyu, mekitoliki] PROBE: Inyorao ake ashu inyioraa oleng?/ *Do you just agree, or agree very strongly?*

☐ Inyoraa Oleng ina A/ *Agree Very Strongly with A*　　☐ Inyoraa A/ *Agree with A*

☐ Inyoraa B/ *Agree with B*　　☐ Inyoraa Oleng ina B / *Agree Very Strongly with B*

☐ Inyoraa Nabo/ *Agree with Neither*　　☐ Mayiolo/ *Don't Know*　　☐ Etanya/ *Refused*

The Steadman Group

Figure A.1: Continued

Kaanyieo naikilikuan imbaa naipereta siasi/ *Now I would like to ask you some questions about politics.*

Q69. Kaabila olarikok oitai imbaa naipereta emuratare oo ntoyie? [Esoma toongelunot] PROBE: Keetai kulekai? [Ingila mpaka nelimu uni asho nejo imeukure eltai.] NG'ERO NBAA UNI NATEJO. [Tenaa kengiro uni tiaki pee ngelo uni sidana.]
/*What types of officials should make rules regarding female circumcision? [Read out response options] PROBE: Are there any others? [Repeat until the respondent has listed three or says they can think of no others.] RECORD ALL MENTIONED, UP TO THREE[If more than three are listed, ask the respondent to choose top three.]*

☐ Ilpaiyani Kituaki/ *Council of Elders*   ☐ Chief le booki/ *Chiefs*   ☐ Larikok Loloshol *Clan Leaders*

☐ Irkusaluni/ *Local Councilors*   ☐ National Assembly/ *National Assembly*

☐ Nkamponini Neme Nesirkali/*Civil Society Leaders*   ☐ Iltururi loo nkuapi le bool *International Organizations*

☐ Elaseremak loloshol *Religious Leaders*

☐ Kulle (Naalimunie)/ *Other (Specify):* _____   ☐☐☐

_____ ☐☐☐   ☐ Mayiolo [Mesumaki]/ *Don't Know [DNR]*

☐ Etanya [Mesumaki]/*Refused*

Q70. Edem aikata aitiaki olkitok oltunganiani oinyiliata enaa oluogil enkitoria emuratare oo ntoyie?/ *Would you ever tell a leader or official about someone breaking a rule about female circumcision?*

☐ Eee / *Yes*   ☐ Aaa/ *No*   ☐ Keitegemea/ *Depends on Situation*   ☐ Mayiolo/ *Don't Know*   ☐ Etanya/ *Refused*

Q71. Indim atonyorrai pee igelu olarikoni orrep emuratare oo ntoyie, ana koloony emuratare oo ntoyie, enaa emeeta enkibelekempate? /*Would you prefer to vote for a politician who supports female circumcision or a politician who opposes female circumcision, or does it make no difference?*

☐ Kerrepl *Supports*   ☐ Merrep/ *Opposes*   ☐ Mmeeta Enkibelekenyata/ *No Difference*

☐ Mayiolo/ *Don't Know*   ☐ Etanya/ *Refused*

Q72. Kaabila olarikok oidim aitayu sheria naipirtoa enkiama amareita? [Esoma toongelunot] PROBE: Keetai kulekai? [Ingila mpaka nelimu uni asho nejo imeukure eltai.] NG'ERO NBAA UNI NATEJO. [Tenaa kengiro uni tiaki pee ngelo uni sidana.]
/*What types of officials should make rules regarding marriage and families? [Read out response options] PROBE: Are there any others? [Repeat until the respondent has listed three or says they can think of no others.] RECORD ALL MENTIONED, UP TO THREE] If more than three are listed, ask the respondent to choose top three.]*

☐ Ilpaiyani Kituaki/ *Council of Elders*   ☐ Chief le booki/ *Chiefs*   ☐ Larikok Loloshol *Clan Leaders*

☐ Irkusaluni/ *Local Councilors*   ☐ National Assembly/ *National Assembly*

☐ Nkamponini Neme Nesirkali/*Civil Society Leaders*   ☐ Iltururi loo nkuapi le bool *International Organizations*

☐ Elaseremak loloshol *Religious Leaders*

☐ Kulie (Naalimunie)/ *Other (Specify):* _____   ☐☐☐

_____ ☐☐☐   ☐ Mayiolo [Mesumaki]/ *Don't Know [DNR]*

☐ Etanya [Mesumaki]/*Refused*

Q73. Edem aikata aitiaki olkitok oltunganiani oinyiliata enaa oluogil enkitoria enkiama?/ *Would you ever tell a leader or official about someone breaking a rule about marriage?*

☐ Eeel *Yes*   ☐ Aaal *No*   ☐ Keitegemea/ *Depends on Situation*

☐ Mayiolo/ *Don't Know*   ☐ Etanya/ *Refused*

Q74. Indim atonyorrai pee igelu olarikoni orrep kiama egorr ilarin tomon osiet, ana koloony kiama egorr ilarin tomon osiet, enaa emeeta enkibelekempate?/ *Would you prefer to vote for a politician who supports some marriages before the age of 18 or a politician who opposes all marriages before the age of 18, or does it make no difference?*

☐ Kerrepl *Supports*   ☐ Merrep/ *Opposes*   ☐ Mmeeta Enkibelekenyata/ *No Difference*

☐ Mayiolo/ *Don't Know*   ☐ Etanya/ *Refused*

Figure A.1: Continued

Q75. Amaa naji olnyor naaji mbaa napirta enkishon olosho? [Esoma toongelunot]
/ How interested would you say you are in public affairs? [Read out response options]

☐ Kanyor Oleng/ Very Interested ☐ Kanyor Penyo/ Somewhat Interested

☐ Manyor sii Oleng/ Not Very Interested ☐ Manyor Pi/ Not At All Interested ☐ Etanya [Mesumaki]/ Refused

Q76. Iningito entaanikinoto orkioma pooki?/ Do you feel close to any particular political party?

☐ Eee/ Yes ☐ Aaa/ No ☐ Mayiolo/ Don't Know ☐ Etanya/ Refused

Q77. (Tenaa Eee) Kalo kioma le siasa?/ [If yes]/ Which party is that?

☐ PNU ☐ ODM ☐ ODM-K ☐ NARC ☐ NARC-K

☐ KANU ☐ Ford-K ☐ Ford People

☐ Kulie (Naalimunie)/ Other (Specify): _____ ☐☐☐ ☐ Etanya/ Refused

THANK THE RESPONDENT AND CLOSE

Figure A.1: Continued

QUALITATIVE INTERVIEW PROTOCOL

1. First, can you tell me a little bit about the work your organization is doing? What year did you first start working on FGM and/or early marriage? What prompted you to begin working on these issues?
2. How many of the women in this community have undergone FGM? Has the number of women who undergo FGM changed over time, or has it stayed the same? If changed, why do you think this is?
3. Who normally decides whether/when a girl will be cut?
4. Are girls ever cut against their will? Has the number of girls who resist FGM changed over time, or has it stayed the same? If changed, why do you think this is?
5. What is the normal age at which most girls/women get married in this area? Has the normal age at which girls get married changed over time, or has it stayed the same? If changed, why do you think this is?
6. Who normally decides when and whom a girl will marry? (Do girls ever decide for themselves when and whom to marry?) Has the number of girls who decide for themselves changed over time, or has it stayed the same? If changed, why do you think this is?
7. Are girls ever forced to marry against their will? Has the number of girls who resist early marriage changed over time, or has it stayed the same? If changed, why do you think this is?
8. Have some people in this area changed their views on FGM? If changed, why do you think this is? Are some people more receptive to the anti-FGM message than others? If so, why? Are there any factors at the level of the community that you think are contributing to overall receptivity (resistance) to the anti-FGM message?
9. Have some people in this area changed their views on early marriage? If changed, why do you think this is? Are some people more receptive to the anti-early-marriage message than others? If so, why? Are there any factors at the level of the community that you think are contributing to overall receptivity (resistance) to the anti-early-marriage message?
10. Who are people most willing to listen to about whether or not to continue FGM and early marriage? Why are they so influential? Are people ever willing to listen to somebody from a different ethnic group? Would they ever listen to somebody from another country, like me?
11. Has there been much media coverage of FGM in this area? Has there been much media coverage of early marriage? If yes, has this attention affected the community? If no, why do you think that FGM and/or early marriage doesn't receive media attention?

12. Are there any (other) groups or organizations in this community that are trying to stop FGM? Have any of these efforts (including the efforts of your organization) had a measurable impact? How is that impact measured? Do you think the current campaign is sufficient? Why do you think there is so much (little) activity in this community?

13. Are there any (other) groups or organizations in this community that are trying to stop early marriage? Have any of these efforts (including the efforts of your organization) had a measurable impact? How is that impact measured? Do you think the current campaign is sufficient? Why do you think there is so much (little) activity in this community?

14. How have the police dealt with FGM in this community? Have there been any arrests? Has anybody gone to trial? How have the police dealt with early marriage?

15. What stance has the provincial administration—chiefs, district commissioner, district officer—taken on FGM? What about the area member of parliament and local councilors? What stance have local elders taken? What about religious leaders? Why do you think they've taken this stance?

16. What stance has the provincial administration taken on early marriage? What about the area MP and local councilors? What stance have local elders taken? What about religious leaders? Why do you think they've taken this stance?

17. How many people in this community would you say are aware of opposition to FGM? How many are aware of opposition to early marriage? Among those who are aware of (outside) opposition, what is the typical reaction? Do people ever try to hide FGM or early marriage? If yes, what is their motivation? Whom do they try to hide it from?

18. Do you think FGM can be stopped in this area, or will it continue no matter what? Do you think early marriage can be stopped? If yes, what will it take for eradication to occur? If no, why do you think the problem is so intractable?

ADDITIONAL MATERIALS

The background and contextual data introduced in chapter 3 are drawn from diverse sources. Quantitative data on FGM and early marriage for Kenya as a whole and for the Maasai come from the Kenya Demographic and Health Surveys, while comparable data for the case study communities come from my own original survey. In addition to the descriptive statistics, I also draw on ethnographies of the Maasai and Samburu to provide richer detail about the cultural meaning and significance of female circumcision and marriage within these groups. Qualitative evidence about the history of activist and government intervention in the issues of FGM and early marriage comes from a combination of primary and secondary sources, including histories of the colonial period as well as correspondence among colonial officials that I retrieved from the Kenya National Archives. Much of the evidence about modern activism is drawn from NGO and international organization reports and from my own observations in the case study areas. Finally, additional background information about the study areas comes from census data and from data I collected in person from national, district, and local offices of the Kenya Ministry of Education; the Ministry of Gender, Children, and Social Development; the Children's Department within the Ministry of Home Affairs; the Non-Governmental Organizations Coordination Board; and the Kenya Police.

BIBLIOGRAPHY

Abdelrahman, Maha M. 2004. *Civil Society Exposed: The Politics of NGOs in Egypt.*
    London: Tauris.
Abusharaf, Rogaia Mustafa. 1998. "Unmasking Tradition." *Sciences* 38 (2): 22–27.
Acharya, Amitav. 2011. *Whose Ideas Matter? Agency and Power in Asian Regionalism.*
    Ithaca, NY: Cornell University Press.
Ahmadu, Fuambai. 2000. "Rites and Wrongs: An Insider/Outsider Reflects on Power
    and Excision." In *Female "Circumcision" in Africa: Culture, Controversy, and
    Change*, edited by Bettina Shell-Duncan and Ylva Hernlund, 283–312. Boulder,
    CO: Lynne Rienner.
Amin, Sajeda, and Mead Cain. 1997. "The Rise of Dowry in Bangladesh." In *The
    Continuing Demographic Transition*, edited by Gavin W. Jones, Robert M. Douglas,
    John C. Caldwell, and Rennie M. D'Souza, 290–306. Oxford: Clarendon Press;
    New York: Oxford University Press.
Angrist, Joshua David, and Jörn-Steffen Pischke. 2009. *Mostly Harmless Econometrics:
    An Empiricist's Companion.* Princeton, NJ: Princeton University Press.
Appiah, Anthony. 2006. *Cosmopolitanism: Ethics in a World of Strangers.* New York:
    Norton.
Arends-Kuenning, Mary, and Sajeda Amin. 2000. "The Effects of Schooling Incentive
    Programs on Household Resource Allocation in Bangladesh." Policy Research
    Division Working Paper No. 133. Population Council. http://www.popcouncil.
    org/uploads/pdfs/wp/133.pdf.
Asch, Solomon E. 1963. "Effects of Group Pressure upon the Modification and Distortion
    of Judgments." In *Groups, Leadership and Men: Research in Human Relations*, edited by
    Harold Steere Guetzkow, 177–90. New York: Russell & Russell.
Baer, Madeline, and Alison Brysk. 2009. "New Rights for Private Wrongs: Female
    Genital Mutilation and Global Framing Dialogues." In *The International Struggle
    for New Human Rights*, edited by Clifford Bob, 93–107. Philadelphia: University
    of Pennsylvania Press.
Baird, Sarah, Ephraim Chirwa, Craig McIntosh, and Berk Özler. 2010. "The Short-Term
    Impacts of a Schooling Conditional Cash Transfer Program on the Sexual
    Behavior of Young Women." *Health Economics* 19 (September): 55–68.
Baird, Sarah, Craig McIntosh, and Berk Özler. 2011. "Cash or Condition? Evidence from
    a Cash Transfer Experiment." *Quarterly Journal of Economics* 126 (4): 1709–53.
Banerjee, Abhijit V. 2007. *Making Aid Work.* Cambridge, MA: MIT Press.
Barr, Abigail, Marcel Fafchamps, and Trudy Owens. 2005. "The Governance of
    Non-governmental Organizations in Uganda." *World Development* 33 (4): 657–79.

Beaman, Lori, and Andrew Dillon. 2012. "Do Household Definitions Matter in Survey Design? Results from a Randomized Survey Experiment in Mali." *Journal of Development Economics* 98 (1): 124–35.

Bebbington, Anthony. 2005. "Donor–NGO Relations and Representations of Livelihood in Nongovernmental Aid Chains." *World Development* 33 (6): 937–50.

Bellemare, Marc F., Lindsey Novak, and Tara L. Steinmetz. 2015. "All in the Family: Explaining the Persistence of Female Genital Cutting in West Africa." *Journal of Development Economics* 116: 252–65.

Berg, Rigmor C., and Eva Denison. 2013. *Interventions to Reduce the Prevalence of Female Genital Mutilation/Cutting in African Countries.* Systematic Review 009. Washington, DC: International Initiative for Impact Evaluation. http://www.3ieimpact.org/media/filer/2013/02/06/sr009_fgm_bergdenison.pdf.

Betts, Alexander. 2013. *Survival Migration: Failed Governance and the Crisis of Displacement.* Ithaca, NY: Cornell University Press.

Betts, Alexander, and Phil Orchard, eds. 2014a. *Implementation and World Politics: How International Norms Change Practice.* Oxford: Oxford University Press.

Betts, Alexander, and Phil Orchard. 2014b. "Introduction: The Normative Institutionalization–Implementation Gap." In *Implementation and World Politics: How International Norms Change Practice*, edited by Alexander Betts and Phil Orchard, 1–26. Oxford: Oxford University Press.

Bhat, P. N. Mari, and Shiva S. Halli. 1999. "Demography of Brideprice and Dowry: Causes and Consequences of the Indian Marriage Squeeze." *Population Studies* 53 (2): 129–48.

Birdsall, Nancy. 2004. "Seven Deadly Sins: Reflections on Donor Failings." Working Paper No. 50. Center for Global Development. http://dx.doi.org/10.2139/ssrn.997404.

Bob, Clifford. 2005. *The Marketing of Rebellion: Insurgents, Media, and International Activism.* New York: Cambridge University Press.

Boddy, Janice. 1982. "Womb as Oasis: The Symbolic Context of Pharaonic Circumcision in Rural Northern Sudan." *American Ethnologist* 9 (4): 682–98.

Boddy, Janice. 1991. "Body Politics: Continuing the Anticircumcision Crusade." *Medical Anthropology Quarterly* 5 (1): 15–17.

Börzel, Tanja A. 2002. "Non-state Actors and the Provision of Common Goods: Compliance with International Institutions." In *Common Goods: Reinventing European and International Governance*, edited by Adrienne Héritier, 159–82. Lanham, MD: Rowman & Littlefield.

Börzel, Tanja A., Adrienne Héritier, Nicole Kranz, and Christian Thauer. 2011. "Racing to the Top? Regulatory Competition among Firms in Areas of Limited Statehood." In *Governance without a State? Policies and Politics in Areas of Limited Statehood*, edited by Thomas Risse, 144–70. New York: Columbia University Press.

Börzel, Tanja A., Tobias Hofmann, Diana Panke, and Carina Sprungk. 2010. "Obstinate and Inefficient: Why Member States Do Not Comply with European Law." *Comparative Political Studies* 43 (11): 1363–90.

Börzel, Tanja A., and Thomas Risse. 2013. "Human Rights in Areas of Limited Statehood: The New Agenda." In *The Persistent Power of Human Rights: From Commitment to Compliance*, edited by Thomas Risse, Stephen C. Ropp, and Kathryn Sikkink, 63–84. Cambridge: Cambridge University Press.

Boyle, Elizabeth Heger. 2002. *Female Genital Cutting: Cultural Conflict in the Global Community.* Baltimore: Johns Hopkins University Press.

Boyle, Elizabeth Heger, and Kristin Carbone-Lopez. 2006. "Movement Frames and African Women's Explanations for Opposing Female Genital Cutting." *International Journal of Comparative Sociology* 47 (6): 435–65.

Boyle, Elizabeth Heger, and Amelia Cotton Corl. 2010. "Law and Culture in a Global Context: Interventions to Eradicate Female Genital Cutting." *Annual Review of Law and Social Science* 6: 195–215.

Boyle, Elizabeth Heger, and Sharon E. Preves. 2000. "National Politics as International Process: The Case of Anti-Female-Genital-Cutting Laws." *Law and Society Review* 34 (3): 703–37.

Brass, Jennifer N. 2012. "Why Do NGOs Go Where They Go? Evidence from Kenya." *World Development* 40 (2): 387–401.

Bratton, Michael. 1989. "The Politics of Government–NGO Relations in Africa." *World Development* 17 (4): 569–87.

Bruce, Judith. 2007. "Child Marriage in the Context of the HIV Epidemic: Promoting Healthy, Safe, and Productive Transitions to Adulthood." Population Council Brief No. 11. New York: Population Council. http://www.popcouncil.org/pdfs/TABriefs/PGY_Brief11_ChildMarriageHIV.pdf.

Bruce, Judith, and Shelley Clark. 2004. "The Implications of Early Marriage for HIV/AIDS Policy." Population Council Brief. New York: Population Council. http://www.popcouncil.org/uploads/pdfs/EMBfinalENG.pdf.

Brysk, Alison. 2005. *Human Rights and Private Wrongs: Constructing Global Civil Society.* New York: Routledge.

Brysk, Alison. 2013. "Changing Hearts and Minds: Sexual Politics and Human Rights." In *The Persistent Power of Human Rights: From Commitment to Compliance*, edited by Thomas Risse, Stephen C. Ropp, and Kathryn Sikkink, 259–74. Cambridge: Cambridge University Press.

Buss, Arnold H., and Stephen R. Briggs. 1984. "Drama and the Self in Social Interaction." *Journal of Personality & Social Psychology* 47 (6): 1310–24.

Caldwell, J. C., P. H. Reddy, and Pat Caldwell. 1983. "The Causes of Marriage Change in South India." *Population Studies* 37 (3): 343–61.

Cammett, Melani. 2013. "Using Proxy Interviewing to Address Sensitive Topics." In *Interview Research in Political Science*, edited by Layna Mosley, 125–43. Ithaca, NY: Cornell University Press.

Carpenter, R. Charli. 2007. "Studying Issue (Non)-Adoption in Transnational Advocacy Networks." *International Organization* 61 (3): 643–67.

Center for Reproductive Law and Policy. 1997. *Women of the World: Laws and Policies Affecting Their Reproductive Lives—Anglophone Africa.* New York: Center for Reproductive Law and Policy. http://reproductiverights.org/en/document/women-of-the-world-laws-and-policies-affecting-their-reproductive-lives-anglophone-africa.

Chayes, Abram, and Antonia Handler Chayes. 1993. "On Compliance." *International Organization* 47 (2): 175–205.

Chayes, Abram, and Antonia Handler Chayes. 1995. *The New Sovereignty: Compliance with International Regulatory Agreements.* Cambridge, MA: Harvard University Press.

Checkel, Jeffrey T. 1999. "Norms, Institutions, and National Identity in Contemporary Europe." *International Studies Quarterly* 43 (1): 83–114.

Checkel, Jeffrey T. 2005. "International Institutions and Socialization in Europe: Introduction and Framework." *International Organization* 59 (4): 801–26.

Chege, Jane Njeri, Ian Askew, and Jennifer Liku. 2001. *An Assessment of the Alternative Rites Approach for Encouraging Abandonment of Female Genital Mutilation in Kenya.* Nairobi, Kenya: Population Council. http://preventgbvafrica.org/wp-content/uploads/2013/10/FGC.Eval_.Kenya_.2001.pdf.

Cialdini, Robert B., Raymond R. Reno, and Carl A. Kallgren. 1990. "A Focus Theory of Normative Conduct: Recycling the Concept of Norms to Reduce Littering in Public Places." *Journal of Personality and Social Psychology* 58 (6): 1015–26.

Clark, Ann Marie, Elisabeth J. Friedman, and Kathryn Hochstetler. 1998. "The Sovereign Limits of Global Civil Society: A Comparison of NGO Participation in UN World Conferences on the Environment, Human Rights, and Women." *World Politics* 51 (1): 1–35.

Clark, Shelley. 2004. "Early Marriage and HIV Risks in Sub-Saharan Africa." *Studies in Family Planning* 35 (3): 149–60.

Clark, Shelley, Judith Bruce, and Annie Dude. 2006. "Protecting Young Women from HIV/AIDS: The Case against Child and Adolescent Marriage." *International Family Planning Perspectives* 32 (2): 79–88.

Clough, Marshall S. 1990. *Fighting Two Sides: Kenyan Chiefs and Politicians, 1918–1940.* Niwot: University Press of Colorado.

Cloward, Karisa. 2014. "False Commitments: Local Misrepresentation and the International Norms against Female Genital Mutilation and Early Marriage." *International Organization* 68 (3): 495–526.

Cloward, Karisa. 2015. "Elites, Exit Options, and Social Barriers to Norm Change: The Complex Case of Female Genital Mutilation." *Studies in Comparative International Development* 50 (3): 378–407.

Coast, Ernestina. 2001. "Maasai Demography." Ph.D. diss., University of London. http://personal.lse.ac.uk/coast/.

Coast, Ernestina. 2006. "Maasai Marriage: A Comparative Study of Kenya and Tanzania." *Journal of Comparative Family Studies* 37 (3): 399–419.

Comaroff, Jean, and John L. Comaroff. 1993. "Introduction." In *Modernity and Its Malcontents: Ritual and Power in Postcolonial Africa,* edited by Jean Comaroff and John L. Comaroff, xi–xxxvii. Chicago: University of Chicago Press.

Comaroff, Jean, and John L. Comaroff. 2006. "Law and Disorder in the Postcolony: An Introduction." In *Law and Disorder in the Postcolony,* edited by Jean Comaroff and John L. Comaroff, 1–56. Chicago: University of Chicago Press.

Cooley, Alexander, and James Ron. 2002. "The NGO Scramble: Organizational Insecurity and the Political Economy of Transnational Action." *International Security* 27 (1): 5–39.

Cortell, Andrew P., and James W. Davis Jr. 2000. "Understanding the Domestic Impact of International Norms: A Research Agenda." *International Studies Review* 2 (1): 65–87.

Cronk, Lee. 2004. *From Mukogodo to Maasai: Ethnicity and Cultural Change in Kenya.* Boulder, CO: Westview Press.

Dagne, Haile Gabriel. 2009. "Ethiopia: Social Dynamics of Abandonment of Harmful Practices—Experiences in Four Locations." Innocenti Working Paper No. 2009-07. Special Series on Social Norms and Harmful Practices. UNICEF Innocenti Research Centre. http://www.unicef-irc.org/publications/558.

Dahlerup, Drude. 2006. "Introduction." In *Women, Quotas and Politics,* edited by Drude Dahlerup, 3–31. New York: Routledge.

Daly, Mary. 1978. *Gyn/Ecology: The Metaethics of Radical Feminism.* Boston: Beacon Press.

Davison, Jean. 1989. *Voices from Mutira: Lives of Rural Gikuyu Women.* Boulder, CO: Lynne Rienner.

Davis, R. E., M. P. Couper, N. K. Janz, C. H. Caldwell, and K. Resnicow. 2010. "Interviewer Effects in Public Health Surveys." *Health Education Research* 25 (1): 14–26.

Deitelhoff, Nicole, and Klaus Dieter Wolf. 2013. "Business and Human Rights: How Corporate Norm Violators Become Norm Entrepreneurs." In *The Persistent Power of Human Rights: From Commitment to Compliance*, edited by Thomas Risse, Stephen C. Ropp, and Kathryn Sikkink, 222–38. Cambridge: Cambridge University Press.

DePaulo, Bella M., Deborah A. Kashy, Susan E. Kirkendol, Melissa M. Wyer, and Jennifer A. Epstein. 1996. "Lying in Everyday Life." *Journal of Personality and Social Psychology* 70 (5): 979–95.

DeSombre, Elizabeth R. 2006. *Flagging Standards: Globalization and Environmental, Safety, and Labor Regulations at Sea*. Cambridge, MA: MIT Press.

Diop, Nafissatou J., and Ian Askew. 2009. "The Effectiveness of a Community-Based Education Program on Abandoning Female Genital Mutilation/Cutting in Senegal." *Studies in Family Planning* 40 (4): 307–18.

Diop, Nafissatou J., Edmond Badge, Djingri Ouoba, and Molly Melching. 2003. *Replication of the TOSTAN Programme in Burkina Faso: How 23 Villages Participated in a Human Rights-Based Education Programme and Abandoned the Practice of Female Genital Cutting in Burkina Faso*. Washington, DC: Population Council.

Diop, Nafissatou J., Modou Mbacke Faye, Amadou Moreau, Jacqueline Cabral, Hélène Benga, Fatou Cissé, Babacar Mané, Inge Baumgarten, and Molly Melching. 2004. "The TOSTAN Program: Evaluation of a Community Based Education Program in Senegal." Population Council. http://www.popcouncil.org/pdfs/frontiers/ FR_FinalReports/Senegal_Tostan%20FGC.pdf.

Donnelly, Jack. 1989. *Universal Human Rights in Theory and Practice*. Ithaca, NY: Cornell University Press.

Dorkenoo, Efua. 1994. *Cutting the Rose: Female Genital Mutilation—The Practice and Its Prevention*. London: Minority Rights Group.

Duflo, Esther, Pascaline Dupas, Michael Kremer, and Samuel Sinei. 2006. "Education and HIV/AIDS Prevention: Evidence from a Randomized Evaluation in Western Kenya." Policy Research Working Paper No. 4024. World Bank. http://dx.doi. org/10.1596/1813-9450-4024.

Edwards, Michael, and David Hulme. 1996. "Introduction: NGO Performance and Accountability." In *Beyond the Magic Bullet: NGO Performance and Accountability in the Post–Cold War World*, edited by Michael Edwards and David Hulme, 1–20. West Hartford, CT: Kumarian Press.

Ekeh, Peter P. 1975. "Colonialism and the Two Publics in Africa: A Theoretical Statement." *Comparative Studies in Society and History* 17 (1): 91–112.

Ekejiuba, Felicia. 1995. "Down to Fundamentals: Women-Centred Heartholds in Rural West Africa." *Development: Journal of the Society for International Development* 1: 72–76.

El-Gibaly, Omaima, Barbara Ibrahim, Barbara S. Mensch, and Wesley H. Clark. 2002. "The Decline of Female Circumcision in Egypt: Evidence and Interpretation." *Social Science & Medicine* 54 (2): 205–20.

El Saadawi, Nawal. 1980. *The Hidden Face of Eve: Women in the Arab World*. London: Zed Press.

El-Zanaty, Fatma, and Ann Way. 2009. "Egypt Demographic and Health Survey 2008." Cairo, Egypt: Ministry of Health, El-Zanaty and Associates, and Macro International.

Equality Now. 2014. *Protecting the Girl Child: Using the Law to End Child, Early and Forced Marriage and Related Human Rights Violations*. New York: Equality Now. http://www.girlsnotbrides.org/reports-and-publications/protecting-girl-child-u sing-law-end-child-early-forced-marriage-related-human-rights-violations/.

Erulkar, Annabel, and Francis Ayuka. 2007. "Addressing Early Marriage in Areas of High HIV Prevalence: A Program to Delay Marriage and Support Married Girls in Rural Nyanza, Kenya." Brief No. 19. Promoting Healthy, Safe, and Productive Transitions to Adulthood. New York: Population Council. http://www.popline.org/node/187141.

Erulkar, Annabel S., and Eunice Muthengi. 2009. "Evaluation of Berhane Hewan: A Program to Delay Child Marriage in Rural Ethiopia." *International Perspectives on Sexual and Reproductive Health* 35 (1): 6–14.

Evelia, Humphres, Maryam Sheikh, Carolyne Njue, and Ian Askew. 2007. "Contributing towards Efforts to Abandon Female Genital Mutilation/Cutting in Kenya: A Situation Analysis." Nairobi, Kenya: Population Council.

Feldman-Jacobs, Charlotte, and Sarah Ryniak. 2006. *Abandoning Female Genital Mutilation/ Cutting: An In-Depth Look at Promising Practices*. Washington, DC: Population Reference Bureau. http://www.prb.org/pdf07/fgm-c_report.pdf.

Ferguson, James. 1999. *Expectations of Modernity: Myths and Meanings of Urban Life on the Zambian Copperbelt*. Berkeley: University of California Press.

Festinger, Leon. 1957. *A Theory of Cognitive Dissonance*. Evanston, IL: Row, Peterson.

Fihlani, Pumza. 2009. "Stolen Youth of SA's Child Brides." *BBC*, October 14, sec. Africa.

Finnemore, Martha. 1993. "International Organizations as Teachers of Norms: The United Nations Educational, Scientific, and Cultural Organization and Science Policy." *International Organization* 47 (4): 565–97.

Finnemore, Martha, and Kathryn Sikkink. 1998. "International Norm Dynamics and Political Change." *International Organization* 52 (4): 887–917.

Fishbein, Martin, and Icek Ajzen. 2010. *Predicting and Changing Behavior: The Reasoned Action Approach*. New York: Taylor & Francis.

Fisher, Robert J. 1993. "Social Desirability Bias and the Validity of Indirect Questioning." *Journal of Consumer Research* 20 (2): 303–15.

Flohr, Annegret, Lothar Rieth, Sandra Schwindenhammer, and Klaus Dieter Wolf. 2010. *The Role of Business in Global Governance: Corporations as Norm-Entrepreneurs*. New York: Palgrave Macmillan.

Flores-Macias, Francisco, and Chappell Lawson. 2008. "Effects of Interviewer Gender on Survey Responses: Findings from a Household Survey in Mexico." *International Journal of Public Opinion Research* 20 (1): 100–110.

Florini, Ann M., ed. 2000. *The Third Force: The Rise of Transnational Civil Society*. Tokyo: Japan Center for International Exchange; Washington, DC: Carnegie Endowment for International Peace.

Fowler, Alan. 1997. *Striking a Balance: A Guide to Enhancing the Effectiveness of Non-governmental Organisations in International Development*. London: Earthscan.

Fruttero, Anna, and Varun Gauri. 2005. "The Strategic Choices of NGOs: Location Decisions in Rural Bangladesh." *Journal of Development Studies* 41 (5): 759–87.

Fyvie, Claire, and Alastair Ager. 1999. "NGOs and Innovation: Organizational Characteristics and Constraints in Development Assistance Work in the Gambia." *World Development* 27 (8): 1383–95.

Gage, Anastasia J. 2009. *Coverage and Effects of Child Marriage Prevention Activities in Amhara Region, Ethiopia: Findings from a 2007 Study*. Washington, DC: US Agency for International Development. http://www.cpc.unc.edu/measure/publications/tr-09-70.

Galaty, John G. 1993. "Maasai Expansion and the New East African Pastoralism." In *Being Maasai: Ethnicity and Identity in East Africa*, edited by Thomas Spear and Richard Waller, 61–86. Athens: Ohio University Press.

Goffman, Erving. 1973. *The Presentation of Self in Everyday Life*. Woodstock, NY: Overlook Press.

Goodman, Ryan, and Derek Jinks. 2013. "Social Mechanisms to Promote International Human Rights: Complementary or Contradictory?" In *The Persistent Power of Human Rights: From Commitment to Compliance*, edited by Thomas Risse, Stephen C. Ropp, and Kathryn Sikkink, 103–21. Cambridge: Cambridge University Press.

Gordon, Daniel. 1991. "Female Circumcision and Genital Operations in Egypt and the Sudan: A Dilemma for Medical Anthropology." *Medical Anthropology Quarterly*, New Series, 5 (1): 3–14.

Granovetter, Mark, and Roland Soong. 1983. "Threshold Models of Diffusion and Collective Behavior." *Journal of Mathematical Sociology* 9 (3): 165–79.

Greenhill, Brian, Layna Mosley, and Aseem Prakash. 2009. "Trade-Based Diffusion of Labor Rights: A Panel Study, 1986–2002." *American Political Science Review* 103 (4): 669–90.

Gruenbaum, Ellen. 2001. *The Female Circumcision Controversy: An Anthropological Perspective*. Philadelphia: University of Pennsylvania Press.

Gunning, Isabelle R. 1991. "Arrogant Perception, World-Travelling and Multicultural Feminism: The Case of Female Genital Surgeries." *Columbia Human Rights Law Review* 23: 189–247.

Gupta, Akhil, and James Ferguson. 1992. "Beyond 'Culture': Space, Identity, and the Politics of Difference." *Cultural Anthropology* 7 (1): 6–23.

Gupta, Akhil, and James Ferguson. 1997. "Culture, Power, Place: Ethnography at the End of an Era." In *Culture, Power, Place: Explorations in Critical Anthropology*, edited by Akhil Gupta and James Ferguson, 1–29. Durham, NC: Duke University Press.

Hafner-Burton, Emilie M., and Kiyoteru Tsutsui. 2005. "Human Rights in a Globalizing World: The Paradox of Empty Promises." *American Journal of Sociology* 110 (5): 1373–1411.

Hart, William, Dolores Albarracín, Alice H. Eagly, Inge Brechan, Matthew J. Lindberg, and Lisa Merrill. 2009. "Feeling Validated versus Being Correct: A Meta-analysis of Selective Exposure to Information." *Psychological Bulletin* 135 (4): 555–88.

Hastie, Reid, and Bernadette Park. 1986. "The Relationship between Memory and Judgment Depends on Whether the Judgment Task Is Memory-Based or On-Line." *Psychological Review* 93 (3): 258–68.

Hathaway, Oona A. 2002. "Do Human Rights Treaties Make a Difference?" *Yale Law Journal* 111 (8): 1935–2042.

Hathaway, Oona A. 2003. "The Cost of Commitment." *Stanford Law Review* 55 (5): 1821–62.

Hathaway, Oona A. 2007. "Why Do Countries Commit to Human Rights Treaties?" *Journal of Conflict Resolution* 51 (4): 588–621.

Hayford, Sarah R. 2005. "Conformity and Change: Community Effects on Female Genital Cutting in Kenya." *Journal of Health and Social Behavior* 46 (2): 121–40.

Henderson, Sarah L. 2002. "Selling Civil Society: Western Aid and the Nongovernmental Organization Sector in Russia." *Comparative Political Studies* 35 (2): 139–67.

Herbst, Jeffrey Ira. 2000. *States and Power in Africa: Comparative Lessons in Authority and Control*. Princeton, NJ: Princeton University Press.

Hernlund, Ylva. 2000. "Cutting without Ritual and Ritual without Cutting: Female 'Circumcision' and the Re-ritualization of Initiation in the Gambia." In *Female "Circumcision" in Africa: Culture, Controversy, and Change*, edited by Bettina Shell-Duncan and Ylva Hernlund, 235–52. Boulder, CO: Lynne Rienner.

Hernlund, Ylva, and Bettina Shell-Duncan. 2007a. "Contingency, Context, and Change: Negotiating Female Genital Cutting in the Gambia and Senegal." *Africa Today* 53 (4): 43–57.

Hernlund, Ylva, and Bettina Shell-Duncan. 2007b. "Transcultural Positions: Negotiating Rights and Culture." In *Transcultural Bodies: Female Genital Cutting in Global Context*, edited by Ylva Hernlund and Bettina Shell-Duncan, 1–45. New Brunswick, NJ: Rutgers University Press.

Hervish, Alexandra, and Charlotte Feldman-Jacobs. 2011. "Who Speaks for Me? Ending Child Marriage." Policy Brief. Population Reference Bureau. http://www.prb.org/Publications/Reports/2011/ending-child-marriage.aspx.

Hetherington, Penelope. 2001. "Generational Changes in Marriage Patterns in the Central Province of Kenya, 1930–1990." *Journal of Asian & African Studies* 36 (2): 157–80.

Hodgson, Dorothy Louise. 2001. *Once Intrepid Warriors: Gender, Ethnicity, and the Cultural Politics of Maasai Development*. Bloomington: Indiana University Press.

Hodgson, Dorothy Louise. 2005. *The Church of Women: Gendered Encounters between Maasai and Missionaries*. Bloomington: Indiana University Press.

Holloway, Richard. 2001. "Corruption and Civil Society Organisations in Indonesia." Paper presented at the 10th International Anti-Corruption Conference. Prague. http://www.10iacc.org/download/workshops/cs30a.pdf.

Holtzman, Jon. 2009. *Uncertain Tastes: Memory, Ambivalence, and the Politics of Eating in Samburu, Northern Kenya*. Berkeley: University of California Press.

Hosken, Fran P. 1982. *The Hosken Report: Genital and Sexual Mutilation of Females*. 3rd ed. Lexington, MA: Women's International Network News.

Hulme, David, and Michael Edwards. 1997. "NGOs, States and Donors: An Overview." In *NGOs, States and Donors: Too Close for Comfort?*, edited by David Hulme and Michael Edwards, 3–22. New York: St. Martin's Press; Save the Children.

Hyde, Susan D. 2011. *The Pseudo-democrat's Dilemma: Why Election Observation Became an International Norm*. Ithaca, NY: Cornell University Press.

Igras, Susan, Jacinta Muteshi, Asmelash WoldeMariam, and Saida Ali. 2004. "Integrating Rights-Based Approaches into Community-Based Health Projects: Experiences from the Prevention of Female Genital Cutting Project in East Africa." *Health and Human Rights* 7 (2): 251–71.

Ikamari, Lawrence D. E. 2005. "The Effect of Education on the Timing of Marriage in Kenya." *Demographic Research* 12: 1–28.

International Center for Research on Women (ICRW). 2006. "Too Young to Wed: Advocacy Toolkit—Education and Change toward Ending Child Marriage." Washington, DC: ICRW. http://www.icrw.org/files/publications/Child-Marriage-Toolkit.pdf.

International Center for Research on Women (ICRW). 2007. "New Insights on Preventing Child Marriage: A Global Analysis of Factors and Programs." Washington, DC: ICRW. http://www.icrw.org/files/publications/New-Insights-on-Preventing-Child-Marriage.pdf.

International Planned Parenthood Federation (IPPF), and Forum on Marriage and the Rights of Women and Girls. 2006. "Ending Child Marriage: A Guide for Global Policy Action." London: IPPF. http://www.ippf.org/resource/Ending-Child-Marriage.

International Planned Parenthood Federation (IPPF), and International Women's Rights Action Watch (IWRAW). 2000. "Reproductive Rights 2000." London: IPPF; IWRAW.

Jackson, Elizabeth F., Patricia Akweongo, Evelyn Sakeah, Abraham Hodgson, Rofina Asuru, and James F. Phillips. 2003. "Inconsistent Reporting of Female Genital Cutting Status in Northern Ghana: Explanatory Factors and Analytical Consequences." *Studies in Family Planning* 34 (3): 200–210.

Jackson, Robert H., and Carl G. Rosberg. 1982. "Why Africa's Weak States Persist: The Empirical and the Juridical in Statehood." *World Politics* 35 (1): 1–24.

Jagori. 2009. "Marching Together: Resisting Dowry in India." New Delhi: Jagori. http://jagori.org/wp-content/uploads/2009/07/dowry_infopack.pdf.

Jejeebhoy, Shireen J. 1995. *Women's Education, Autonomy, and Reproductive Behaviour: Experience from Developing Countries*. Oxford: Clarendon Press.

Jensen, Robert, and Rebecca Thornton. 2003. "Early Female Marriage in the Developing World." *Gender and Development* 11 (2): 9–19.

Jetschke, Anja. 2011. *Human Rights and State Security: Indonesia and the Philippines*. Philadelphia: University of Pennsylvania Press.

Jetschke, Anja, and Andrea Liese. 2013. "The Power of Human Rights a Decade After: From Euphoria to Contestation?" In *The Persistent Power of Human Rights: From Commitment to Compliance*, edited by Thomas Risse, Stephen C. Ropp, and Kathryn Sikkink, 26–42. Cambridge: Cambridge University Press.

Jo, Hyeran, and Katherine Bryant. 2013. "Taming of the Warlords: Commitment and Compliance by Armed Opposition Groups in Civil Wars." In *The Persistent Power of Human Rights: From Commitment to Compliance*, edited by Thomas Risse, Stephen C. Ropp, and Kathryn Sikkink, 239–58. Cambridge: Cambridge University Press.

Jo, Hyeran, and Catarina P. Thomson. 2014. "Legitimacy and Compliance with International Law: Access to Detainees in Civil Conflicts, 1991–2006." *British Journal of Political Science* 44 (2): 323–55.

Johnson, Janet Elise. 2009. *Gender Violence in Russia: The Politics of Feminist Intervention*. Bloomington: Indiana University Press.

Johnson, Michelle C. 2000. "Becoming a Muslim, Becoming a Person: Female 'Circumcision,' Religious Identity, and Personhood in Guinea-Bissau." In *Female "Circumcision" in Africa: Culture, Controversy, and Change*, edited by Bettina Shell-Duncan and Ylva Hernlund, 215–33. Boulder, CO: Lynne Rienner.

Jones, Edward E. 1990. *Interpersonal Perception*. New York: W.H. Freeman.

Keck, Margaret E., and Kathryn Sikkink. 1998. *Activists beyond Borders: Advocacy Networks in International Politics*. Ithaca, NY: Cornell University Press.

Kenya Central Bureau of Statistics. 1989. "1989 Population and Housing Census."

Kenya Central Bureau of Statistics. 2002. "Kenya 1999 Population and Housing Census."

Kenya Central Bureau of Statistics. 2003. "Geographic Dimensions of Well-Being in Kenya: Where Are the Poor? From Districts to Locations." Volume 1. http://econ.worldbank.org/external/default/main?theSitePK=477894&contentMDK=2038 2755&menuPK=545573&pagePK=64168182&piPK=64168060.

Kenya Central Bureau of Statistics (CBS), Ministry of Health (MOH), and ORC Macro. 2004. "Kenya Demographic and Health Survey 2003." Calverton, MD: Kenya CBS, MOH, and ORC Macro.

Kenya National Bureau of Statistics (KNBS), and ICF Macro. 2010. "Kenya Demographic and Health Survey 2008–09." Calverton, MD: KNBS and ICF Macro.

Kenya National Council for Population and Development (NCPD), Central Bureau of Statistics (CBS), and Macro International. 1999. "Kenya Demographic and Health Survey 1998." Calverton, MD: Kenya NCPD, CBS, and Macro International.

Kenyatta, Jomo. 1965 [1938]. *Facing Mount Kenya: The Tribal Life of the Gikuyu*. New York: Vintage Books.

Keohane, Robert O. 1984. *After Hegemony: Cooperation and Discord in the World Political Economy*. Princeton, NJ: Princeton University Press.

Khagram, Sanjeev. 2004. *Dams and Development: Transnational Struggles for Water and Power*. Ithaca, NY: Cornell University Press.

Kishwar, Madhu Purnima. 2005. "Strategies for Combating the Culture of Dowry and Domestic Violence in India." Paper presented at the "Violence against Women: Good Practices in Combating and Eliminating Violence against Women"

Expert Group Meeting. Vienna. http://www.un.org/womenwatch/daw/egm/vaw-gp-2005/docs/experts/kishwar.dowry.pdf.

Klotz, Audie. 1995. *Norms in International Relations: The Struggle against Apartheid.* Ithaca, NY: Cornell University Press.

Konner, Melvin. 1990. "Mutilated in the Name of Tradition." *New York Times Book Review*, April 15, sec. Books.

Koso-Thomas, Olayinka. 1987. *Circumcision of Women: A Strategy for Eradication.* London: Zed Books.

Krasner, Stephen D., ed. 1985. *International Regimes.* Ithaca, NY: Cornell University Press.

Krook, Mona Lena. 2006. "Reforming Representation: The Diffusion of Candidate Gender Quotas Worldwide." *Politics & Gender* 2 (3): 303–27.

Kuran, Timur. 1991. "Now Out of Never: The Element of Surprise in the East European Revolution of 1989." *World Politics* 44 (1): 7–48.

Kuran, Timur. 1995. *Private Truths, Public Lies: The Social Consequences of Preference Falsification.* Cambridge, MA: Harvard University Press.

LaTowsky, Robert J. 1997. "Egypt's NGO Sector: A Briefing Paper." Occasional Papers Series No. 1(4). Reading, England: Education for Development. http://eric.ed.gov/?id=ED412412.

Leader-Williams, N., and S. D. Albon. 1988. "Allocation of Resources for Conservation." *Nature* 336 (6199): 533–35.

Leakey, Louis S. B. 1931. "The Kikuyu Problem of the Initiation of Girls." *Journal of the Royal Anthropological Institute of Great Britain and Ireland* 61 (January): 277–85.

Leary, Mark R., and Robin M. Kowalski. 1990. "Impression Management: A Literature Review and Two-Component Model." *Psychological Bulletin* 107 (1): 34–47.

Legro, Jeffrey W. 1997. "Which Norms Matter? Revisiting the 'Failure' of Internationalism." *International Organization* 51 (1): 31–63.

Lightfoot-Klein, Hanny. 1989. *Prisoners of Ritual: An Odyssey into Female Genital Circumcision in Africa.* New York: Harrington Park Press.

Lord, Charles G., Lee Ross, and Mark R. Lepper. 1979. "Biased Assimilation and Attitude Polarization: The Effects of Prior Theories on Subsequently Considered Evidence." *Journal of Personality and Social Psychology* 37 (11): 2098–2109.

Lutz, Ellen L., and Kathryn Sikkink. 2000. "International Human Rights Law and Practice in Latin America." *International Organization* 54 (3): 633–59.

Mackie, Gerry. 1996. "Ending Footbinding and Infibulation: A Convention Account." *American Sociological Review* 61 (6): 999–1017.

Mackie, Gerry. 2000. "Female Genital Cutting: The Beginning of the End." In *Female "Circumcision" in Africa: Culture, Controversy, and Change*, edited by Bettina Shell-Duncan and Ylva Hernlund, 253–80. Boulder, CO: Lynne Rienner.

Mackie, Gerry. 2012. "Effective Rule of Law Requires Construction of a Social Norm of Legal Obedience." Working paper. http://www.sas.upenn.edu/ppe/Events/uniconf_2013/documents/Mackie.G_EffectiveRuleofLawRequiresConstructionofASocialNormofLegalObedience.pdf.

Mackie, Gerry, and John LeJeune. 2009. "Social Dynamics of Abandonment of Harmful Practices: A New Look at the Theory." Innocenti Working Paper No. 2009-06. Special Series on Social Norms and Harmful Practices. Florence: UNICEF Innocenti Research Centre. http://www.unicef-irc.org/publications/558.

Mackie, Gerry, Francesca Moneti, Elaine Denny, and Holly Shakya. 2014. "What Are Social Norms? How Are They Measured?" Working paper. UNICEF/UCSD Center on Global Justice Project Cooperation Agreement. http://dmeforpeace.org/sites/default/files/4%2009%2030%20Whole%20What%20are%20Social%20Norms.pdf.

Maertens, Annemie. 2013. "Social Norms and Aspirations: Age of Marriage and Education in Rural India." *World Development* 47 (July): 1–15.

Malhotra, Anju, Ann Warner, Allison McGonagle, and Susan Lee-Rife. 2011. *Solutions to End Child Marriage: What the Evidence Shows*. Washington, DC: International Center for Research on Women. http://www.icrw.org/files/publications/Solutions-to-End-Child-Marriage.pdf.

Mamdani, Mahmood. 1996. *Citizen and Subject: Contemporary Africa and the Legacy of Late Colonialism*. Princeton, NJ: Princeton University Press.

March, James G., and Johan P. Olsen. 1998. "The Institutional Dynamics of International Political Orders." *International Organization* 52 (4): 943–69.

Mathur, Sanyukta, Margaret Greene, and Anju Malhotra. 2003. *Too Young to Wed: The Lives, Rights, and Health of Young Married Girls*. Washington, DC: International Center for Research on Women. http://www.icrw.org/files/publications/Too-Young-to-Wed-the-Lives-Rights-and-Health-of-Young-Married-Girls.pdf.

Mathur, Sanyukta, Manisha Mehta, and Anju Malhotra. 2004. *Youth Reproductive Health in Nepal: Is Participation the Answer?* Washington, DC: International Center for Research on Women; EngenderHealth. http://www.icrw.org/files/publications/Youth-Reproductive-Health-in-Nepal-Is-Participation-the-Answer.pdf.

Mbembe, Achille. 2001. *On the Postcolony*. Berkeley: University of California Press.

Measure DHS. 2014. "Demographic and Health Surveys STATcompiler." http://www.statcompiler.com/.

Mendelson, Sarah E., and John K. Glenn. 2002. "Introduction: Transnational Networks and NGOs in Postcommunist Societies." In *The Power and Limits of NGOs: A Critical Look at Building Democracy in Eastern Europe and Eurasia*, edited by Sarah E. Mendelson and John K. Glenn, 1–28. New York: Columbia University Press.

Merriam, Sharan B., Juanita Johnson-Bailey, Ming-Yeh Lee, Youngwha Kee, Gabo Ntseane, and Mazanah Muhamad. 2001. "Power and Positionality: Negotiating Insider/Outsider Status within and across Cultures." *International Journal of Lifelong Education* 20 (5): 405–16.

Merry, Sally Engle. 2006. *Human Rights and Gender Violence: Translating International Law into Local Justice*. Chicago: University of Chicago Press.

Migdal, Joel S. 1988. *Strong Societies and Weak States: State–Society Relations and State Capabilities in the Third World*. Princeton, NJ: Princeton University Press.

Milgram, Stanley. 1974. *Obedience to Authority: An Experimental View*. New York: Harper & Row.

Miron, Jeffrey A., and Jeffrey Zwiebel. 1991. "Alcohol Consumption during Prohibition." *American Economic Review* 81 (2): 242–47.

Mohamud, Asha, Samson Radeny, and Karin Ringheim. 2006. "Community-Based Efforts to End Female Genital Mutilation in Kenya: Raising Awareness and Organizing Alternative Rites of Passage." In *Female Circumcision: Multicultural Perspectives*, edited by Rogaia Mustafa Abusharaf, 75–103. Philadelphia: University of Pennsylvania Press.

Mohanty, Chandra Talpade. 1988. "Under Western Eyes: Feminist Scholarship and Colonial Discourses." *Feminist Review* 30: 61–88.

Montoya, Celeste. 2013. *From Global to Grassroots: The European Union, Transnational Advocacy, and Combating Violence against Women*. Oxford: Oxford University Press.

Morfit, N. Simon. 2011. "'AIDS Is Money': How Donor Preferences Reconfigure Local Realities." *World Development* 39 (1): 64–76.

Morrow, James D. 2007. "When Do States Follow the Laws of War?" *American Political Science Review* 101 (3): 559–72.

Morsy, Soheir A. 1991. "Safeguarding Women's Bodies: The White Man's Burden Medicalized." *Medical Anthropology Quarterly*, New Series, 5 (1): 19–23.

Murray, Jocelyn. 1976. "The Church Missionary Society and the 'Female Circumcision' Issue in Kenya, 1929–1932." *Journal of Religion in Africa* 8 (2): 92–104.

Mwangi, Wagaki, Lothar Rieth, and Hans Peter Schmitz. 2013. "Encouraging Greater Compliance: Local Networks and the United Nations Global Compact." In *The Persistent Power of Human Rights: From Commitment to Compliance*, edited by Thomas Risse, Stephen C. Ropp, and Kathryn Sikkink, 203–21. Cambridge: Cambridge University Press.

Nadelmann, Ethan A. 1990. "Global Prohibition Regimes: The Evolution of Norms in International Society." *International Organization* 44 (4): 479–526.

Nair, Janaki. 1995. "Prohibited Marriage: State Protection and Child Wife." *Contributions to Indian Sociology* 29 (1-2): 157–86.

Nairobi Times. 1982. "President Moi Bans Female Circumcision in Kenya." September 6.

National Research Council. 2005. *Growing Up Global: The Changing Transitions to Adulthood in Developing Countries*. Washington, DC: National Academies Press. http://www.nap.edu/catalog.php?record_id=11174.

National Stakeholders Forum on Female Genital Mutilation. 2007. "Meeting Report."

Nickerson, Raymond S. 1998. "Confirmation Bias: A Ubiquitous Phenomenon in Many Guises." *Review of General Psychology* 2 (2): 175–220.

Nisbett, Richard E., and Lee Ross. 1980. *Human Inference: Strategies and Shortcomings of Social Judgment*. Englewood Cliffs, NJ: Prentice-Hall.

Nowak, Andrzej, Jacek Szamrej, and Bibb Latané. 1990. "From Private Attitude to Public Opinion: A Dynamic Theory of Social Impact." *Psychological Review* 97 (3): 362–76.

Obiora, L. Amede. 1996. "Bridges and Barricades: Rethinking Polemics and Intransigence in the Campaign against Female Circumcision." *Case Western Reserve Law Review* 47: 275–378.

Okin, Susan Moller. 1997. "Is Multiculturalism Bad for Women?" *Boston Review* 22 (5): 25–28.

Organization for Economic Cooperation and Development. 2013. "StatExtracts: Creditor Reporting System." http://stats.oecd.org/.

Ottaway, Marina, and Thomas Carothers. 2000. "Toward Civil Society Realism." In *Funding Virtue: Civil Society Aid and Democracy Promotion*, edited by Marina Ottaway and Thomas Carothers, 293–310. Washington, DC: Carnegie Endowment for International Peace.

Pande, Rohini, Kathleen Kurz, Sunayana Walia, Kerry MacQuarrie, and Saranga Jain. 2006. *Improving the Reproductive Health of Married and Unmarried Youth in India: Evidence of Effectiveness and Costs from Community-Based Interventions*. Washington, DC: International Center for Research on Women. http://www.icrw.org/files/publi-cations/Improving-the-Reproductive-Health-of-Married-and-Unmarried-Youth-in-India.pdf.

Parry, Hugh J., and Helen M. Crossley. 1950. "Validity of Responses to Survey Questions." *Public Opinion Quarterly* 14 (1): 61–80.

Pascale, Richard, Jerry Sternin, and Monique Sternin. 2013. *The Power of Positive Deviance: How Unlikely Innovators Solve the World's Toughest Problems*. Boston: Harvard Business Press.

Payne, Rodger A. 2001. "Persuasion, Frames and Norm Construction." *European Journal of International Relations* 7 (1): 37–61.

Pedersen, Susan. 1991. "National Bodies, Unspeakable Acts: The Sexual Politics of Colonial Policy-Making." *Journal of Modern History* 63 (4): 647–80.

Phillips, Derek L., and Kevin J. Clancy. 1972. "Some Effects of 'Social Desirability' in Survey Studies." *American Journal of Sociology* 77 (5): 921–40.

Plan. 2012. *Because I Am a Girl: The State of the World's Girls 2012—Learning for Life*. Surrey, UK: Plan. http://becauseiamagirl.ca/reports/learning-for-life.

Prakash, Aseem, and Mary Kay Gugerty. 2010. "Advocacy Organizations and Collective Action: An Introduction." In *Advocacy Organizations and Collective Action*, edited by Aseem Prakash and Mary Kay Gugerty, 1–28. New York: Cambridge University Press.

Prakash, Aseem, and Matthew Potoski. 2007. "Investing Up: FDI and the Cross-Country Diffusion of ISO 14001 Management Systems." *International Studies Quarterly* 51 (3): 723–44.

Prazak, Miroslava. 2007. "Introducing Alternative Rites of Passage." *Africa Today* 53 (4): 19–40.

Price, Richard. 1998. "Reversing the Gun Sights: Transnational Civil Society Targets Land Mines." *International Organization* 52 (3): 613–44.

"Private Sector and Foundations." 2014. Global Partnership for Education. https://www.globalpartnership.org/private-sector-and-foundations.

Rahman, Anika, and Nahid Toubia. 2000. *Female Genital Mutilation: A Guide to Laws and Policies Worldwide*. London: Zed Books.

Rajadurai, Henrietta, and Susan Igras. 2005. *At the Intersection of Health, Social Well-Being and Human Rights: CARE's Experiences Working with Communities toward Abandonment of Female Genital Cutting (FGC)*. Atlanta: CARE. http://www.popcouncil.org/uploads/pdfs/frontiers/reports/CARE_FGC.pdf.

Raymond, Adella. 2014. *Girls' Education in Pastoral Communities: An Ethnographic Study of Monduli District, Tanzania*. Reading, England: CfBT Education Trust. http://cdn.cfbt.com/~/media/cfbtcorporate/files/research/2014/r-girls-education-in-pastoral-communities-2014.pdf.

Renteln, Alison Dundes. 1988. "Relativism and the Search for Human Rights." *American Anthropologist*, New Series, 90 (1): 56–72.

"Resources on Faith, Ethics, and Public Life." 2014. Berkley Center for Religion, Peace, and World Affairs, Georgetown University. http://berkleycenter.georgetown.edu/resources/topics/religion-and-development-database/subtopics/girls-education.

Risse, Thomas, ed. 2011. *Governance without a State? Policies and Politics in Areas of Limited Statehood*. New York: Columbia University Press.

Risse, Thomas, and Stephen C. Ropp. 2013. "Introduction and Overview." In *The Persistent Power of Human Rights: From Commitment to Compliance*, edited by Thomas Risse, Stephen C. Ropp, and Kathryn Sikkink, 3–25. New York: Cambridge University Press.

Risse, Thomas, Stephen C. Ropp, and Kathryn Sikkink, eds. 1999. *The Power of Human Rights: International Norms and Domestic Change*. Cambridge: Cambridge University Press.

Risse, Thomas, Stephen C. Ropp, and Kathryn Sikkink, eds. 2013. *The Persistent Power of Human Rights: From Commitment to Compliance*. New York: Cambridge University Press.

Risse, Thomas, and Kathryn Sikkink. 1999. "The Socialization of International Human Rights Norms into Domestic Practices: Introduction." In *The Power of Human Rights: International Norms and Domestic Change*, edited by Thomas Risse, Stephen C. Ropp, and Kathryn Sikkink, 1–38. Cambridge: Cambridge University Press.

Risse-Kappen, Thomas. 1995. "Bringing Transnational Relations Back In: Introduction." In *Bringing Transnational Relations Back In: Non-state Actors, Domestic Structures, and International Institutions*, edited by Thomas Risse-Kappen, 3–33. Cambridge: Cambridge University Press.

Robertson, Claire. 1996. "Grassroots in Kenya: Women, Genital Mutilation, and Collective Action, 1920–1990." *Signs* 21 (3): 615–42.

Ropp, Stephen C., and Kathryn Sikkink. 1999. "International Norms and Domestic Politics in Chile and Guatemala." In *The Power of Human Rights: International Norms and Domestic Change*, edited by Thomas Risse, Stephen C. Ropp, and Kathryn Sikkink, 172–204. Cambridge: Cambridge University Press.

Rosberg, Carl G., and John Nottingham. 1966. *The Myth of "Mau Mau": Nationalism in Kenya*. New York: Praeger.

Ross, Lee, Mark R. Lepper, and Michael Hubbard. 1975. "Perseverance in Self-Perception and Social Perception: Biased Attributional Processes in the Debriefing Paradigm." *Journal of Personality and Social Psychology* 32 (5): 880–92.

Rowcliffe, J. Marcus, Emmanuel de Merode, and Guy Cowlishaw. 2004. "Do Wildlife Laws Work? Species Protection and the Application of a Prey Choice Model to Poaching Decisions." *Proceedings of the Royal Society of London. Series B: Biological Sciences* 271 (1557): 2631–36.

Saturday Standard (Kenya). 2008. "Man Arrested for Marrying off Six-Year-Old Daughter." May 24.

Schlenker, Barry R., and Michael F. Weigold. 1989. "Goals and the Self-Identification Process: Constructing Desired Identities." In *Goal Concepts in Personality and Social Psychology*, edited by Lawrence A. Pervin, 243–90. Hillsdale, NJ: Lawrence Erlbaum Associates.

Schlenker, Barry R., and Michael F. Weigold. 1992. "Interpersonal Processes Involving Impression Regulation and Management." *Annual Review of Psychology* 43 (1): 133–68.

Schmitz, Hans Peter. 2001. "When Networks Blind: Human Rights and Politics in Kenya." In *Intervention and Transnationalism in Africa: Global–Local Networks of Power*, edited by Thomas M. Callaghy, Ronald Kassimir, and Robert Latham, 149–72. Cambridge: Cambridge University Press.

Schwedler, Jillian. 2006. "The Third Gender: Western Female Researchers in the Middle East." *PS: Political Science and Politics* 39 (3): 425–28.

Shadle, Brett L. 2006. *"Girl Cases": Marriage and Colonialism in Gusiiland, Kenya, 1890–1970*. Portsmouth, NH: Heinemann.

Shell-Duncan, Bettina. 2008. "From Health to Human Rights: Female Genital Cutting and the Politics of Intervention." *American Anthropologist* 110 (2): 225–36.

Shell-Duncan, Bettina, and Ylva Hernlund. 2000. "Female 'Circumcision' in Africa: Dimensions of the Practice and Debates." In *Female "Circumcision" in Africa: Culture, Controversy, and Change*, edited by Bettina Shell-Duncan and Ylva Hernlund, 1–40. Boulder, CO: Lynne Rienner.

Shell-Duncan, Bettina, and Ylva Hernlund. 2006. "Are There 'Stages of Change' in the Practice of Female Genital Cutting? Qualitative Research Findings from Senegal and the Gambia." *African Journal of Reproductive Health* 10 (2): 57–71.

Shell-Duncan, Bettina, Walter Obungu Obiero, and Leunita Auko Muruli. 2000. "Women without Choices: The Debate over Medicalization of Female Genital Cutting and Its Impact on a Northern Kenyan Community." In *Female "Circumcision" in Africa: Culture, Controversy, and Change*, edited by Bettina Shell-Duncan and Ylva Hernlund, 109–28. Boulder, CO: Lynne Rienner.

Shell-Duncan, Bettina, and Owuor Olungah. 2009. "Between Crime, Faith and Culture: Contesting Female Genital Cutting and the 'Best Interest' of the Child."

Paper presented at the 108th Annual Meeting of the American Anthropological Association. Philadelphia.

Shell-Duncan, Bettina, Katherine Wander, Ylva Hernlund, and Amadou Moreau. 2011. "Dynamics of Change in the Practice of Female Genital Cutting in Senegambia: Testing Predictions of Social Convention Theory." *Social Science & Medicine* 73 (8): 1275–83.

Shryock, Henry S., and Jacob S. Siegel. 1976. *The Methods and Materials of Demography.* London: Academic Press.

Sikkink, Kathryn. 1993. "Human Rights, Principled Issue-Networks, and Sovereignty in Latin America." *International Organization* 47 (3): 411–41.

Simmons, Beth. 2009. *Mobilizing for Human Rights: International Law in Domestic Politics.* New York: Cambridge University Press.

Simmons, Beth. 2010. "Treaty Compliance and Violation." *Annual Review of Political Science* 13 (1): 273–96.

Skaine, Rosemarie. 2005. *Female Genital Mutilation: Legal, Cultural, and Medical Issues.* Jefferson, NC: McFarland.

Slack, Alison T. 1988. "Female Circumcision: A Critical Appraisal." *Human Rights Quarterly* 10 (4): 437–86.

Slowiaczek, Louisa M., Joshua Klayman, Steven J. Sherman, and Richard B. Skov. 1992. "Information Selection and Use in Hypothesis Testing: What Is a Good Question, and What Is a Good Answer?" *Memory & Cognition* 20 (4): 392–405.

Smillie, Ian. 1995. "Painting Canadian Roses Red." In *Non-governmental Organisations: Performance and Accountability—Beyond the Magic Bullet*, edited by Michael Edwards and David Hulme, 157–66. London: Earthscan.

Smith, Jackie, Charles Chatfield, and Ron Pagnucco, eds. 1997. *Transnational Social Movements and Global Politics: Solidarity beyond the State.* Syracuse, NY: Syracuse University Press.

Smith, Seyda Türk, Kyle D. Smith, and Kristen J. Seymour. 1993. "Social Desirability of Personality Items as a Predictor of Endorsement: A Cross-Cultural Analysis." *Journal of Social Psychology* 133 (1): 43–52.

Somerset, Carron. 2000. *Early Marriage: Whose Right to Choose?* Forum on Marriage and the Rights of Women and Girls. https://www.crin.org/en/library/publications/early-marriage-whose-right-choose.

Sommer, Gabriele, and Rainer Vossen. 1993. "Dialects, Sectiolects, or Simply Lects? The Maa Language in Time Perspective." In *Being Maasai: Ethnicity and Identity in East Africa*, edited by Thomas Spear and Richard Waller, 25–37. Athens: Ohio University Press.

Spear, Thomas. 1993. "Introduction." In *Being Maasai: Ethnicity and Identity in East Africa*, edited by Thomas Spear and Richard Waller, 1–18. Athens: Ohio University Press.

Spencer, John. 1985. *The Kenya African Union.* London: KPI.

Spencer, Paul. 1965. *The Samburu: A Study of Gerontocracy in a Nomadic Tribe.* Berkeley: University of California Press.

Spencer, Paul. 1973. *Nomads in Alliance: Symbiosis and Growth among the Rendille and Samburu of Kenya.* London: Oxford University Press.

Spencer, Paul. 1988. *The Maasai of Matapato: A Study of Rituals of Rebellion.* Bloomington: Indiana University Press.

Spencer, Paul. 2003. *Time, Space, and the Unknown: Maasai Configurations of Power and Providence.* London: Routledge.

Sundstrom, Lisa McIntosh. 2005. "Foreign Assistance, International Norms, and NGO Development: Lessons from the Russian Campaign." *International Organization* 59 (2): 419–49.

Sundstrom, Lisa McIntosh. 2006. *Funding Civil Society: Foreign Assistance and NGO Development in Russia*. Stanford, CA: Stanford University Press.

Swainson, Nicola, Stella Bendera, Rosemary Gordon, and Esme Kadzamira. 1998. *Promoting Girls' Education in Africa: The Design and Implementation of Policy Interventions*. Education Research Serial No. 25. London: Department for International Development. http://eric.ed.gov/?id=ED437336.

Talle, Aud. 1988. *Women at a Loss: Changes in Maasai Pastoralism and Their Effects on Gender Relations*. Stockholm: Department of Social Anthropology, University of Stockholm.

Talle, Aud. 2007. "Female Circumcision in Africa and Beyond: The Anthropology of a Difficult Issue." In *Transcultural Bodies: Female Genital Cutting in Global Context*, edited by Ylva Hernlund and Bettina Shell-Duncan, 91–106. New Brunswick, NJ: Rutgers University Press.

Tarrow, Sidney G. 2005. *The New Transnational Activism*. New York: Cambridge University Press.

Taylor, Shelley E., and Jennifer Crocker. 1981. "Schematic Bases of Social Information Processing." In *Social Cognition: The Ontario Symposium*, volume 1, edited by E. Tory Higgins, C. Peter Herman, and Mark P. Zanna, 89–134. Hillsdale, NJ: Lawrence Erlbaum Associates.

Tetlock, Philip E., and A. S. R. Manstead. 1985. "Impression Management versus Intrapsychic Explanations in Social Psychology: A Useful Dichotomy?" *Psychological Review* 92 (1): 59–77.

Thomas, Daniel C. 2001. *The Helsinki Effect: International Norms, Human Rights, and the Demise of Communism*. Princeton, NJ: Princeton University Press.

Thomas, Lynn. 2000. "'Ngaitana (I Will Circumcise Myself)': Lessons from Colonial Campaigns to Ban Excision in Meru, Kenya." In *Female "Circumcision" in Africa: Culture, Controversy, and Change*, edited by Bettina Shell-Duncan and Ylva Hernlund, 129–50. Boulder, CO: Lynne Rienner.

Thörn, Håkan. 2011. "AID(S) Politics and Power: A Critique of Global Governance." In *Power and Transnational Activism*, edited by Thomas Olesen, 232–51. Lodon: Routledge.

Tignor, Robert L. 1976. *The Colonial Transformation of Kenya: The Kamba, Kikuyu, and Maasai from 1900 to 1939*. Princeton, NJ: Princeton University Press.

Toubia, N. F., and E. H. Sharief. 2003. "Female Genital Mutilation: Have We Made Progress?" *International Journal of Gynecology & Obstetrics* 82 (3): 251–61.

Tripp, Aili Mari. 2006. "Challenges in Transnational Feminist Mobilization." In *Global Feminism: Transnational Women's Activism, Organizing, and Human Rights*, edited by Myra Marx Ferree and Aili Mari Tripp, 296–312. New York: New York University Press.

United Nations. 1990. "CEDAW General Recommendation No. 14, Female Circumcision." http://www.un.org/womenwatch/daw/cedaw/recommendations/recomm.htm.

United Nations. 2013. "We Can End Poverty: Millennium Development Goals and Beyond 2015 Fact Sheet." New York: United Nations. http://www.un.org/millenniumgoals/pdf/Goal_3_fs.pdf.

United Nations Children's Fund (UNICEF). 2001. "Early Marriage: Child Spouses." Innocenti Digest 7. Florence: UNICEF Innocenti Research Centre. http://www.unicef-irc.org/publications/pdf/digest7e.pdf.

United Nations Children's Fund (UNICEF). 2005a. "Changing a Harmful Social Convention: Female Genital Mutilation/Cutting." Innocenti Digest 12. Florence: UNICEF Innocenti Research Centre. http://www.unicef-irc.org/publications/396.

United Nations Children's Fund (UNICEF). 2005b. *Early Marriage: A Harmful Traditional Practice—a Statistical Exploration 2005*. New York: UNICEF. http://www.child-info.org/publications_smsbytheme.html.

United Nations Children's Fund (UNICEF). 2006. *The State of the World's Children 2007: Women and Children—the Double Dividend of Gender Equality*. New York: UNICEF. http://www.unicef.org/sowc07/.

United Nations Children's Fund (UNICEF). 2008a. "Coordinated Strategy to Abandon Female Genital Mutilation/Cutting in One Generation: A Human Rights-Based Approach to Programming." Technical note. New York: UNICEF. http://www.childinfo.org/files/fgmc_Coordinated_Strategy_to_Abandon_FGMC__in_One_Generation_eng.pdf.

United Nations Children's Fund (UNICEF). 2008b. "Long-Term Evaluation of the Tostan Program in Senegal: Kolda, Thiès and Fatick Regions." Working paper. New York: UNICEF. http://www.unicef.org/evaldatabase/files/fgmc_tostan_eng_SENEGAL.pdf.

United Nations Children's Fund (UNICEF). 2009. *Progress for Children: A Report Card on Child Protection*. No. 8. New York: UNICEF. http://www.unicef.org/protection/Progress_for_Children-No.8_EN_081309(5).pdf.

United Nations Children's Fund (UNICEF). 2010a. "Child Protection: Child Marriage." http://www.devinfo.info/pfc/protection/2_child_protection_cm.html.

United Nations Children's Fund (UNICEF). 2010b. "Legislative Reform to Support the Abandonment of Female Genital Mutilation/Cutting." New York: UNICEF. http://www.unicef.org/policyanalysis/files/UNICEF_-_LRI_Legislative_Reform_to_support_the_Abandonment_of_FGMC_August_2010.pdf.

United Nations Children's Fund (UNICEF). 2010c. *The Dynamics of Social Change: Towards the Abandonment of Female Genital Mutilation/Cutting in Five African Countries*. Innocenti Insight. Florence: UNICEF Innocenti Research Centre. http://www.unicef-irc.org/publications/618.

United Nations Children's Fund (UNICEF). 2013a. *Female Genital Mutilation/Cutting: A Statistical Overview and Exploration of the Dynamics of Change*. New York: UNICEF. http://www.unicef.org/publications/index_69875.html.

United Nations Children's Fund (UNICEF). 2013b. "Multiple Indicator Cluster Surveys." http://www.childinfo.org/mics_available.html.

United Nations Commission for Human Rights. 1997. "Fact Sheet No. 23: Harmful Traditional Practices Affecting the Health of Women and Girls." http://www.ohchr.org/Documents/Publications/FactSheet23en.pdf.

United Nations Commission on the Status of Women. 2009. "United Nations Secretary-General's Report on Ending Female Genital Mutilation." E/CN.6/2010/6. http://www.un.org/womenwatch/daw/beijing15/documentation.html.

United Nations Commission on the Status of Women. 2011. "United Nations Secretary-General's Report on Ending Female Genital Mutilation." E/CN.6/2012/8. http://www.un.org/womenwatch/daw/csw/csw56/documentation.htm.

United Nations General Assembly, Resolution 67/146. 2012. "Intensifying Global Efforts for the Elimination of Female Genital Mutilations." http://www.un.org/en/ga/search/view_doc.asp?symbol=A/RES/67/146.

United Nations, Department of Economic and Social Affairs (UN DESA), Population Division. 2011. "Population Facts No. 2011/1." New York: UN DESA. http://www.un.org/en/development/desa/population/publications/pdf/popfacts/PopFacts_2011-1.pdf.

United Nations Population Fund (UNFPA). 2012. *Marrying Too Young: End Child Marriage*. New York: UNFPA. http://www.unfpa.org/sites/default/files/pub-pdf/MarryingTooYoung.pdf.

United Nations Population Fund (UNFPA). 2013. "Legislative Reform in Kenya to Speed Up Abandonment of FGM/C: Strong Government Policy to Support New Law." New York: UNFPA. http://www.unfpa.org/gender/docs/fgmc_kit/Kenya-1.pdf.

United Nations Population Fund (UNFPA), and United Nations Children's Fund (UNICEF). 2012. *UNFPA-UNICEF Joint Programme on Female Genital Mutilation/Cutting: Accelerating Change, Annual Report 2012*. New York: UNFPA; UNICEF. http://www.unfpa.org/public/home/publications/pid/14643.

United Nations Population Fund (UNFPA), and United Nations Children's Fund (UNICEF). 2013a. *Joint Evaluation of the UNFPA-UNICEF Joint Programme on Female Genital Mutilation/Cutting: Accelerating Change*. Volume 1. New York: UNFPA; UNICEF. http://www.unicef.org/evaluation/files/FGM-report_11_14_2013_Vol-I.pdf.

United Nations Population Fund (UNFPA), and United Nations Children's Fund (UNICEF). 2013b. *Joint Evaluation of the UNFPA-UNICEF Joint Programme on Female Genital Mutilation/Cutting: Accelerating Change*. Volume 2. New York: UNFPA; UNICEF. http://www.unicef.org/evaluation/files/FGM-report_11_14_2013_Vol-I.pdf.

United Nations Population Fund (UNFPA), and United Nations Children's Fund (UNICEF). 2013c. *UNFPA-UNICEF Joint Programme on Female Genital Mutilation/Cutting: Accelerating Change 2008–2012, Country Case Study: Kenya*. New York: UNFPA; UNICEF. http://www.unfpa.org/public/home/about/Evaluation/EBIER/TE/pid/10103.

United Nations Population Fund (UNFPA), and United Nations Children's Fund (UNICEF). 2014. "UNFPA-UNICEF Joint Programme on the Abandonment of Female Genital Mutilation/Cutting: Accelerating Change, Funding Proposal for a Phase II." UNFPA. http://www.unfpa.org/files/live/sites/unfpa/files/Documents/FGM/Funding%20Proposal%20for%20Phase%20II%20of%20the%20UNFPA-UNICEF%20Joint%20Programme.PDF.

Valente, Thomas W., and Patchareeya Pumpuang. 2007. "Identifying Opinion Leaders to Promote Behavior Change." *Health Education & Behavior* 34 (6): 881–96.

VanDeveer, Stacy D., and Geoffrey D. Dabelko. 2001. "It's Capacity, Stupid: International Assistance and National Implementation." *Global Environmental Politics* 1 (2): 18–29.

Vreeland, James Raymond. 2008. "Political Institutions and Human Rights: Why Dictatorships Enter into the United Nations Convention against Torture." *International Organization* 62 (1): 65–101.

Wagner, Natascha. 2015. "Female Genital Cutting and Long-Term Health Consequences: Nationally Representative Estimates across 13 Countries." *Journal of Development Studies* 51 (3): 1–21.

Wallace, Tina, Lisa Bornstein, and Jennifer Chapman. 2007. *The Aid Chain: Coercion and Commitment in Development NGOs*. Bourton on Dunsmore, UK: Intermediate Technology Publications.

Watkins, Susan Cotts, Ann Swidler, and Thomas Hannan. 2012. "Outsourcing Social Transformation: Development NGOs as Organizations." *Annual Review of Sociology* 38 (1): 285–315.

Weaver, Catherine. 2008. *Hypocrisy Trap: The World Bank and the Poverty of Reform*. Princeton, NJ: Princeton University Press.

Weldon, S. Laurel. 2002. *Protest, Policy, and the Problem of Violence against Women: A Cross-National Comparison*. Pittsburgh, PA: University of Pittsburgh Press.

Wiener, Antje. 2009. "Enacting Meaning-in-Use: Qualitative Research on Norms and International Relations." *Review of International Studies* 35 (1): 175–93.

Wilkie, David S., and Julia F. Carpenter. 1999. "Bushmeat Hunting in the Congo Basin: An Assessment of Impacts and Options for Mitigation." *Biodiversity & Conservation* 8 (7): 927–55.

Williams, John E., Robert C. Satterwhite, and José L. Saiz. 1998. *The Importance of Psychological Traits: A Cross-Cultural Study*. New York: Plenum Press.

Winterbottom, Anna, Jonneke Koomen, and Gemma Burford. 2009. "Female Genital Cutting: Cultural Rights and Rites of Defiance in Northern Tanzania." *African Studies Review* 52 (1): 47–71.

World Health Organization (WHO). 1979. *Traditional Practices Affecting the Health of Women and Children: Female Circumcision, Childhood Marriage, Nutritional Taboos, Etc*. WHO/EMRO Technical Publication No. 2. Alexandria: WHO Research Office for the Eastern Mediterranean. http://whqlibdoc.who.int/emro/tp/EMRO_TP_2.pdf.

World Health Organization (WHO). 2008a. *Eliminating Female Genital Mutilation: An Interagency Statement—OHCHR, UNAIDS, UNDP, UNECA, UNESCO, UNFPA, UNHCR, UNICEF, UNIFEM, WHO*. Geneva: WHO Press. http://www.who.int/reproductivehealth/publications/fgm/9789241596442/en/index.html.

World Health Organization (WHO). 2008b. "Fact Sheet No. 241: Female Genital Mutilation." http://www.who.int/mediacentre/factsheets/fs241/en/.

World Vision. 2008. *Before She's Ready: 15 Places Girls Marry by 15*. Federal Way, WA: World Vision. http://www.worldvision.org/resources.nsf/main/early-marriage.pdf/$file/early-marriage.pdf.

Young, H. Peyton. 2008. "Social Norms." In *The New Palgrave Dictionary of Economics*, edited by Steven N. Durlauf and Lawrence E. Blume, 2nd ed., 647–51. Basingstoke: Nature Publishing Group.

Yount, Kathryn M. 2002. "Like Mother, Like Daughter? Female Genital Cutting in Minia, Egypt." *Journal of Health and Social Behavior* 43 (3): 336–58.

INDEX

Page numbers in *italics* indicate figures and tables.

Cameroon, 26
CARE, 35, 109
Catholicism: and FGM, 38n27, 97, 150, 152, 163; in Kenyan population, *126*, 128, 129, 130
CEDAW. *See* Convention on the Elimination of All Forms of Discrimination Against Women (CEDAW)
Central African Republic, *26*, 27, 39, 40, 236
Chad, *26*, 27
chiefs: defined, 177–78; in Mau, 202–3; in Mukogodo, 195–97; in Oldonyiro, 190–91; role in primary behavior change, 181–86. *See also* norm leaders
ChildFund, 108, 122, 133. *See also* Christian Children's Fund
Children's Act, 105–6, 109, 111, 223
Christian Children's Fund, 108, 153. *See also* ChildFund
Church Missionary Society, 103, 104
Church of Scotland Mission, 101–2
clitoridectomy, 23, 24n19, 27, 56, 100, 114, 119. *See also* female genital mutilation (FGM)
Coalition on Violence Against Women (COVAW), 122, 133
community-based organizations (CBOs): differentiated from NGOs, 42n30; in Kenya, 127, 129, 130, 149, 234; material support provided by, 222–24; misrepresentation of international norm compliance by, 205–6, 221–22; as research participants, 43, 48. *See also* nongovernmental organizations (NGOs)
confirmation bias, 72, 73, 74, 244
constructivism, 5, 215, 244
Convention on the Elimination of All Forms of Discrimination Against Women (CEDAW), 1, 13n10, 39, 105, 238
Convention on the Rights of the Child, 1, 39, 105, 238
Coomaraswamy, Radhika, 2
Coptic Evangelical Organization for Social Services, 65
cultural relativism, 37–38
culture, 9, 37–38, 245–47

Daly, Mary, 36
Demographic and Health Surveys (DHS): attitudes regarding FGM, 110, 120, 157n1, 235, 236; awareness regarding FGM, 233, 234; and early-marriage practice, 27, 29, 40, *99*, 100–101, 111, 120; and FGM practice, 26, 30, 31, 40, 97, *98*, 99–100, 110, 112, 119–20, 235, 236; and reporting bias 111, 131n28
Djibouti, 26, 27, 78
domestic fit literature, 8–10, 243–44
Donors Working Group on Female Genital Mutilation/Cutting (FGM/C), 2, 35, 249
dowry, 31, *58*, 237, 239–40

early marriage: activism against, 1–2, 35, 36, 38–39, 54, 60, 64–65, 71, 107, 108–10, 112, 122–23, 133, 136, 139n2, 141–42, 144–45, 222–23, 230, 231, 232, 233, 234; attitudes about, 132–33, 156–59, 161–62, 208–10, 231, 232, 234; behavior regarding, 175, *176*, *209*, 210; beliefs about, 55, 73–74, *176*, 177–78; characteristics of, 29, *99*, 101, 120, 132; in colonial period, 38n27, 103–4, 122; correlates of, 27, 29, 35, *99*, 101, 120, 132; decline in, 40, 41, 111, 120–21, 248–49; defined, 24; and elite activism, 181, *184*, 185; and ethnic heterogeneity, 181, *184*, 186–88; and FGM practices, 53–54; in Kenya, 41, *99*, 100–101, 103–4, 105–6, 107, 108–10, 111, 112; international norm against, 3, 32, 34–35, 58–59, 136, 137–38, 141–46, 230; legal and legislative efforts against, 1–2, 39, 105–6, 223–24; local norms on, 3, 31–32, 59–60, 76, 93, 136, 173–74, 230; among Maasai people, 41, *99*, 115–19, 120, 122–23; misrepresentation with respect to, *212*, 213–17, 232; prevalence of, 2–3, 27, *28*, 40, *99*, 100–101, 111, 120, 132; primary behavior change in Mau, 41, 198–203, 232; primary behavior change in Mukogodo, 41, 192–93, 195–98, 231; primary behavior

Mukogodo: activism in, 133, 145, 149–51; attitude change in, 41, 164–168, 231; attitudes and opinions on early marriage in, 132–33, 137, 138, 144, *158*, 159, 208, *209*, 210; attitudes and opinions on FGM in, 131–32, 137, 138, 144, 145, 158, 159, *209*; behavior and experiences on early marriage in, *99*, 175, *176*, *209*, 210, 225; behavior and experiences on FGM in, *98*, 175–77, *178*, *209*, 225; description of, *126–27*, 128–29, 130; elite activism in, 194–98, 231; ethnic heterogeneity in, 177, 186, 194–95; international norm awareness in, 139, 164–65, 167–68, 231; misrepresentation of international norm compliance in, 213, *214*, 232; NGOs in, 129, 149, 150–51, 164, 165, 166; primary behavior change in, 41, 186, 191–98, 231

Multiple Indicator Cluster Surveys (MICS): and early marriage, 27, 29, 40, 233n1, 235; and FGM, 26, 30, 40, 235

Mungiki, 112

Muslims. *See* Islam

MYWO. *See* Maendeleo Ya Wanawake (MYWO)

Native Christian Marriage Ordinance of 1904, 103

Nepal, 27, 36, 65

NGO density, 148, 151; and activism, 21, 95, 136, 229, 230; factors affecting, 60–62; and norm awareness, 60, 136, 233. *See also* nongovernmental organizations (NGOs)

Niger, 26, 27, 29

Nigeria, *26*, 27, 29, 40, 73, 247

Njuri Ncheke Council of Meru, 103, 108

nongovernmental organizations (NGOs): activism against early marriage by, 107, 108–10, 122, 133; activism against FGM by, 104, 107–10, 122, 133, 230, 233–34; and activism quality, 64–65, 69–71; differentiated from community-based organizations (CBOs), 42n30; and donor-driven issue selection, 66–69, 83, 146, 156, 249–50; funding of, 60, 61–62, 66,

69–71, 136; and girl-child education, 38; material support provided by, 222–24; in Mau, 130, 152, 153, 154, 170; misrepresentation of international norm compliance by, 83–84, 205–6, 216, 221–22; in Mukogodo, 129, 149, 150–51, 164, 165, 166; and norm salience, 57, 60, 69, 71, 94–95, 229; in Oldonyiro, 127, 147, 148, 149, 163, 218; as research participants, 43, 48. *See also* mission creep; NGO density

nonstate actors: as activists, 6, 57, 60; as international norm violators, 10, 11–15, 240–43, 245

norm, 5, 8, 9. *See also* international norm; local norm; norm change; norm diffusion

norm cascade: conditions for, 22, 89n22, 90n23, 91–93, 96, 204, 230; defined, 8, 89

norm change: defined, 16; elements of, 15–19; sources of, 19–21. *See also* attitude change; primary behavior change; secondary behavior and rhetorical change

norm compliance, 5–6, 12, 172, 205, 244. *See also* primary behavior change

norm diffusion, 8–10, 11n9, 21, 86–94, 95, 230, 240–41, 243. *See also* norm change

norm entrepreneurs, 6, 8, 10, 17, 22, 23, 174, 228, 232, 242, 244

norm followers: defined, 8, 22, 174; and norm diffusion, 88, 89, 92, 94, 96; relation to norm leaders, 174–75, 229, 230, 243

norm leaders: chiefs and elders as, 177–78; defined, 22; emergence of, 22, 91–94, 95, 174–75, 230; and local norm defection, 78–79; and norm diffusion, 8, 86–90; and norm entrepreneurs, 8, 22, 174; and primary behavior change, 181–86, 187–88; relation to norm followers, 174–75, 229, 230, 243

norm salience, 19–20. *See also* international norm salience; local norm salience

normative out-groups: demonstration effect of, 79, 174, 187, 229; ethnic heterogeneity and, 175; and exit options, 21, 77, 174, 187, 229; and local norm defection, 49, 77–79, 89–90, 92, 235, 248. *See also* ethnic heterogeneity

normative reference groups. *See* reference groups

Oldonyiro: activism in, 133, 145, 146–49, 163–64; attitude change in, 41, 163–64, 231; attitudes and opinions on early marriage in, 132–33, 137, 138, *158*, 159, 208, *209*, 210; attitudes and opinions on FGM in, 131–32, 137, 138, 158, 159, *209*; behavior and experiences on early marriage in, *99*, 175, *176*, *209*, 210, 225–26, 231; behavior and experiences on FGM in, *98*, 175–77, *178*, *209*, 225–26, 231; description of, 124–25, 126–28, 130; elite activism in, 190–91; ethnic heterogeneity in, 177, 181, 186, 190; international norm awareness in, 139, 149, 163–64, 231; misrepresentation of international norm compliance in, 213, *214*; NGOs in, 127, 147, 148, 149, 163, 218; norm leaders in, *176*, 177–78, 181; primary behavior change in, 41, 181, 186–87, 188–91, 231

out-groups. *See* normative out-groups

Pareiyo, Agnes, 122

Pastoralist Women for Health and Education, 48, 133, 208, 257

PATH. *See* Program for Appropriate Technologies in Health (PATH)

persuasion, 15, 23, 64, 155, 243, 253

Pokot Council of Elders, 108

political threshold, 80, 86–87, 88n1, 89, 91, 92–93

polygyny, 29, 35, 101, 115–16, 120, 134

Population Council, 65, 108

primary behavior change: and attitude change, 18, 20, 63, 74, 80, 93, 95, 174, 179–81, 194, 229, 230, 235, 239; defined, 16–17; and elite activism, 92, 93, 174, 181–86, 188, 190–91, 195–97, 198, 201–3,

229, 230, 231–32, 241; and ethnic heterogeneity, 181, *182–84*, 186–88, 190, 191, 194–95, 197, 200–201, 203, 231, 232, 235; and exit options, 21, 76–78, 79, 88–89, 93, 95, 174, 187, 229, 230; in Mau, 41, 198–203, 232; in Mukogodo, 41, 192–98, 231; and norm diffusion, 21, 86, 177; and norm salience, 20, 21, 80, 93, 174, 200, 230, 254; in Oldonyiro, 41, 188–91, 231; and secondary behavior and rhetorical change, 18, 81, 205–6, 223, 226, 232, 242n4. *See also* local norm defection

Program for Appropriate Technologies in Health (PATH), 3, 250

Prohibition of Female Genital Mutilation (FGM) Act, 105, 107, 109, 134

Protestantism: and colonial-era missions, 101–2; and early marriage, 133, 139n2, 141–42, *143*, 149, *160*, *184*; and FGM, 97, 133, 139n2, *140*, 141–42, 149, 152, *160*, *182*, *183*; in Kenyan population, *126*, 128, 129, 130, *138*, 139

Protocol to the African Charter on Human and People's Rights on the Rights of Women in Africa. *See* Maputo Protocol

qualitative interviews: design and implementation of, 42–43, 44, 45–47, 49, 252; findings of, 50, 51, 54, 73, 117, 139n2, 146–54, 163–71, 180, 188–203, 217n8, 218–26, 246

rationalist approach, 5, 244

reference groups: alternative, 16, 18, 21, 92; defined, 5, 15n12; and norm change, 63, 76, 86, 91–94; and social costs, 22, 85, 88, 89, 90, 173–74. *See also* normative out-groups

research design: case selection, 40–42; limitations, 252–53; methodological contributions and field challenges, 45–49; methods, 42–45. *See also* qualitative interviews; survey; survey experiment

rhetorical change. *See* misrepresentation